Advanced

Apple

Debugging

& Reverse Engineering

By Walter Tyree

Based on material by Derek Selander

Advanced Apple Debugging & Reverse Engineering

Walter Tyree

Copyright ©2023 Kodeco Inc.

Notice of Rights

Notice of Liability

Trademarks

ISBN: 978-1-950325-63-4

Table of Contents

Before You Begin... 13

What You Need 15

Book Source Code & Forums 17
    About the Author 20
    About the Editors 20

Acknowledgments 21

Introduction 23
    Who This Book Is For 24
    Custom LLDB Scripts Repo 24

Section I: Beginning LLDB Commands 25

Chapter 1: Getting Started 27
    Getting around System Integrity Protection (SIP).................. 28
    Attaching LLDB to the Notes App 31
    Key Points.. 45
    Where to Go From Here? 45

Chapter 2: Overview & Getting Help 47
    Building LLDB via Xcode................................. 48
    The apropos Command 55
    Other Helpful Resources 57

Chapter 3: Attaching With LLDB 59
    Creating a Debuggee Program........................... 60
    Attaching to an Existing Process........................ 61
    Attaching to a Future Process 62
    Launching a Process Using LLDB 63
    Options While Launching................................ 64
    Environment Variables 66

stdin, stderr and stout 68

The curses Interface 70

Key Points 71

Where to Go From Here? 71

Chapter 4: Stopping in Code 73

Signals 74

lldb Breakpoint Syntax 78

Finally... Creating Breakpoints 84

Key Points 93

Where to Go From Here? 93

Chapter 5: Expression 95

Formatting With p and po 96

Swift vs Objective-C Debugging Contexts 102

User Defined Variables 103

Key Points 112

Where to Go From Here? 112

Chapter 6: Thread, Frame & Stepping Around 113

Stack 101 114

Examining the Stack's Frames 115

Stepping 119

Examining Data in the Stack 124

Key Points 126

Where to Go From Here? 126

Chapter 7: Image 127

Listing Modules 128

Swift Symbol Naming 133

Dyld Shared Cache 137

Key Points 142

Where to Go From Here? 142

Need Another Challenge? 143

Chapter 8: Watchpoints 145

Watchpoint Best Practices 146
Finding a Property's Offset 147
The Xcode GUI Watchpoint Equivalent 151
Key Points 155
Where to Go From Here? 155

Chapter 9: Persisting & Customizing Commands 157

Persisting... How? 158
Creating the .lldbinit File 158
Command Aliases With Arguments 160
Key Points 163
Where to Go From Here? 163

Chapter 10: Regex Commands 165

command regex 166
Executing Complex Logic 168
Chaining Regex Inputs 171
Key Points 174
Where to Go From Here? 174

Section II: Understanding Assembly 175

Chapter 11: Assembly Register Calling Convention 177

Assembly 101 178
arm64 Register Calling Convention 180
Objective-C and Registers 182
Putting Theory to Practice 183
Swift and Registers 188
The Return Register 192
Changing Around Values in Registers 193
Key Points 196
Where to Go From Here? 196

Chapter 12: Assembly & Memory 197

Reviewing Reading Assembly 198
The Program Counter Register..................................... 201
Registers and Breaking Up the Bits 204
Breaking Down the Memory 206
Endianness... This Stuff Is Reversed?........................... 209
Key Points 211
Where to Go From Here?... 211

Chapter 13: Assembly & the Stack 213

The Stack, Revisited 214
Stack Pointer, Frame Pointer and Link Register 215
Stack Related Opcodes... 216
Observing Registers in Action.................................... 218
The Stack and Extra Parameters 224
The Stack and Debugging Info..................................... 227
Key Points 230

Section III: Low Level 231

Chapter 14: System Calls & Ptrace 233

ptrace... 235
Creating Attachment Issues....................................... 237
Getting Around PT_DENY_ATTACH 238
Other Anti-Debugging Techniques................................. 241
Key Points 242
Where to Go From Here?... 242

Chapter 15: Shared Libraries........................... 243

Shared Libraries 101 244
Linking Tricks 249
Static Libraries 254
Modules and Module Maps 260
dyld Shared Cache... 264

Key Points 268
Where to Go From Here?.. 268

Chapter 16: Hooking & Executing Code With dlopen & dlsym 269

The Objective-C Runtime vs. Swift & C 270
Setting Up Your Project 270
Easy Mode: Hooking C Functions 271
Hard Mode: Hooking Swift Methods............................... 281
Key Points 289
Where to Go From Here?... 289

Chapter 17: Hello, Mach-O................................... 291

Terminology 292
The Mach-O Header.. 294
The Load Commands 302
Segments 304
Programmatically Finding Segments and Sections................. 306
Key Points 313
Where to Go From Here?... 313

Chapter 18: Mach-O Fun 315

Mach-O Refresher 316
The Mach-O Sections 316
Finding HTTP Strings.. 320
Sections in the __DATA Segment 324
Cheating Freemium Games 326
Key Points 331
Where to Go From Here?... 331

Chapter 19: Code Signing 333

Setting Up 334
Terminology 334
Public/Private Keys 334

Entitlements... 338

Provisioning Profiles 339

Exploring the WordPress App................................. 341

Resigning the WordPress App................................ 344

Key Points 354

Where to Go From Here?...................................... 354

Section IV: Custom LLDB Commands............. 355

Chapter 20: Hello, Script Bridging......................... 357

Credit Where Credit's Due..................................... 358

Python 101.. 358

Creating Your First LLDB Python Script 363

Setting Up Commands Efficiently 365

Key Points 367

Where to Go From Here?...................................... 367

Chapter 21: Debugging Script Bridging 369

Debugging Your Debugging Scripts With pdb.............. 370

pdb's Post-Mortem Debugging............................... 372

How to Handle Problems...................................... 379

Key Points 381

Where to Go From Here?...................................... 381

Chapter 22: Script Bridging Classes & Hierarchy 383

The Essential Classes.. 384

Learning & Finding Documentation on Script Bridging Classes..... 389

Creating the BreakAfterRegex Command 392

Key Points 403

Where to Go From Here?...................................... 403

Chapter 23: Script Bridging With Options & Arguments... 405

Setting Up 406

The optparse Python Module 408

Adding Options Without Params. 409
Adding Options With Params 416
Key Points 421
Where to Go From Here?. 421

Chapter 24: Script Bridging With SBValue & Memory 423

A Detour Down Memory Layout Lane 425
SBValue. 438
lldb.value 447
Key Points 448
Where to Go From Here?. 449

Chapter 25: SB Examples, Improved Lookup. 451

Automating Script Creation 452
lldbinit Directory Structure Suggestions 454
Implementing the Lookup Command 456
Adding Options to Lookup 465
Key Points 468
Where to Go From Here?. 468

Chapter 26: SB Examples, Resymbolicating a Stripped ObjC Binary 469

So How Are You Doing This, Exactly? 471
50 Shades of Ray 472
The "Stripped" 50 Shades of Ray 480
Building sbt.py. 482
Implementing the Code 482
Key Points 485
Where to Go From Here?. 485

Chapter 27: SB Examples, Malloc Logging 487

Setting Up the Scripts 488
MallocStackLogging Explained 489
Hunting for a Starting Point 493

Testing the Functions 497
Turning Numbers Into Stack Frames 502
Stack Trace From a Swift Object 505
DRY Python Code 506
Key Points 511
Where to Go From Here? 511

Section V: DTrace 513

Chapter 28: Hello, DTrace 515
The Bad News 516
Jumping Right In 516
DTrace Terminology 521
Learning While Listing Probes 524
A Script That Makes DTrace Scripts 526
Key Points 535
Where to Go From Here? 535

Chapter 29: Intermediate DTrace 537
Getting Started 538
DTrace & Swift in Theory 538
DTrace Variables & Control Flow 542
Inspecting Process Memory 546
Playing With Open Syscalls 548
DTrace & Destructive Actions 551
Key Points 554
Where to Go From Here? 555

Conclusion 557

Appendices 559

Appendix A: LLDB Cheat Sheet 561
Getting Help 561
Finding Code 562

Breakpoints 562
Expressions. 564
Stepping 565
GDB Formatting. 565
Memory 566
Registers and Assembly 566
Modules 568

Appendix B: Python Environment Setup 569
Getting Python 569
Python Text Editors 571
Working With the LLDB Python Module. 573

Appendix C: Helpful Code Snippets 575

Before You Begin

This section tells you a few things you need to know before you get started, such as what you'll need for hardware and software, where to find the project files for this book, and more.

What You Need

To follow along with the tutorials in this book, you'll need the following:

- A Mac running **macOS Ventura** (13.3) or later. Earlier versions might work, but they're untested.

- **Xcode 14.3 or later.** Packaged with Xcode is the latest and greatest version of **LLDB**, the debugger you'll use extensively throughout this book. At the time of this writing, the version of LLDB packaged with Xcode is **lldb-1403.0.17.64**.

- **Python 3**. LLDB uses Python 3.9.6 to run its Python scripts. Unfortunately, Python no longer automatically ships with macOS. To **Get Python**, please see **Appendix B: Getting Python** for download instructions. You can verify you have the correct version installed by typing `python --version` in `Terminal`.

- **A 64 bit iOS device running iOS 16 or later, and a paid membership to the iOS development program [optional].** For most chapters in the book, you can run any iOS programs in the Simulator. However, you'll get more out of this book by using a 64-bit iOS device to test out certain ideas or suggestions littered throughout the book.

Once you have these items in place, you'll be able to follow along with almost every chapter in this book. For certain sections, you'll need to disable the **Rootless** security feature in order to use some of the tools (i.e. **DTrace**). This is discussed in Chapter 1.

Book Source Code & Forums

Where to Download the Materials for This Book

The materials for this book can be cloned or downloaded from the GitHub book materials repository:

- https://github.com/kodecocodes/dbg-materials/tree/editions/4.0

Forums

We've also set up an official forum for the book at https://forums.kodeco.com/c/books/advanced-apple-debugging. This is a great place to ask questions about the book or to submit any errors you may find.

"To Nina, Carter, Icarus, Kitty, and Mattie who believed I could do this even when I didn't."

— *Walter Tyree*

About the Author

Walter Tyree started debugging when typing code by hand from paper magazines was a thing. When he's not working on this book, he runs the tiniest of technology consulting companies. He writes software and also gives talks and writes articles for others to learn how to write software. After hours, he likes to knit, bake bread, play with his dog, and dance with his wife. You can find him at his company website https://www.tyreeapps.com

About the Editors

Emily Wydeven is an avid scavenger of typos and grammatical errors. She has worked extensively in the tech industry and has also edited such varied projects as city recreation guides, college-level study material, and corporate acquisition proposals. She is a nerd for technology, cats, medical history, and comic books (among many other things). While her favorite comic book characters are Deadpool and Squirrel Girl, the character with whom Emily most closely identifies is Nancy Whitehead.

Matt Galloway is a software engineer with a passion for excellence. He stumbled into iOS programming when it first was a thing, and has never looked back. When not coding, he likes to brew his own beer.

Darren Ferguson is the final pass editor of this book. He is a Software Developer, with a passion for mobile development, for a leading systems integration provider based out of Northern Virginia in the D.C. metro area. When he's not coding, you can find him enjoying life with his wife and daughter trying to travel as much as possible.

Acknowledgments

We would like to thank many people for their assistance in making this possible:

- **Derek Selander:** For his extensive work on the previous editions of this book.

- **Our families:** For bearing with us in this crazy time as we worked all hours of the night to get this book ready for publication!

- **Everyone at Apple:** For developing an amazing platform, for constantly inspiring us to improve our games and skill sets and for making it possible for many developers to make a living doing what they love!

- **And most importantly, the readers of kodeco.com — especially you!** Thank you so much for reading our site and this book. Your continued readership and support is what makes all of this possible!

Introduction

Debugging has a rather bad reputation. I mean, if the developer had a complete understanding of the program, there wouldn't be any bugs and they wouldn't be debugging in the first place, right?

Don't think like that.

There are always going to be bugs in your software — or any software, for that matter. No amount of test coverage imposed by your product manager is going to fix that. In fact, viewing debugging as *just* a process of fixing something that's broken is actually a poisonous way of thinking that will mentally hinder your analytical abilities.

Instead, you should view debugging as simply **a process to better understand a program**. It's a subtle difference, but if you truly believe it, any previous drudgery of debugging simply disappears.

The same negative connotation can also be applied to reverse engineering software. Images of masked hackers stealing bank accounts and credit cards may come to mind, but for this book, reverse engineering really is just debugging without source code — which in turn helps you gain a better understanding of a program or system.

There's nothing wrong with reverse engineering in itself. In fact if debugging was a game, then reverse engineering is simply debugging on the "difficult" setting — which is quite a fun setting if you've been playing the game for a while. :]

In this book, you'll come to realize debugging is an enjoyable process to help you better understand software. Not only will you learn to find bugs faster, but you'll also learn how other developers have solved problems similar to yours. You'll also learn how to create custom, powerful debugging scripts that will help you quickly find answers to any item that piques your interest, whether it's in your code — or someone else's.

Who This Book Is For

The art of debugging code should really be studied by every developer. However, there will be some of you that will get more out of this book. This book is written for:

- Developers who want to become better at debugging with LLDB

- Developers who want to build complex debugging commands with LLDB

- Developers who want to take a deeper dive into internals of Swift and Objective-C

- Developers who are interested in understanding what they can do to their program through reverse engineering

- Developers who are interested in modern, proactive reverse engineering strategies

- Developers who want to be confident in finding answers to questions they have about their computer or software

This book is for intermediate to advanced developers who want to take their debugging and code exploration game to the next level.

Custom LLDB Scripts Repo

Finally, you can find a repo of interesting LLDB Python scripts here:

https://github.com/DerekSelander/LLDB

These scripts will help aid in your debugging/reverse engineering sessions and provide novel ideas for your own LLDB scripts.

Section I: Beginning LLDB Commands

This section will cover the basics of using LLDB, Apple's software debugger. You'll explore an application named **Signals**, an Objective-C/Swift application that illustrates how Unix signals can be processed within an application. You'll learn some strategies to find and create Swift syntax-style breakpoints as well as Objective-C style breakpoints. By the end of this section, you'll be able to wield the debugger to perform most of the basic tasks needed for debugging, as well as create your own simple custom commands.

Chapter 1: Getting Started

In this chapter, you're going to get acquainted with LLDB and investigate the process of introspecting and debugging a program. You'll start off by introspecting a program you didn't even write!

You'll take a whirlwind tour of a debugging session using LLDB and discover the amazing changes you can make to a program you've absolutely zero source code for. This first chapter heavily favors doing over learning, so a lot of the concepts and deep dives into certain LLDB functionality will be re-introduced, with explanation, in later chapters.

Let's get started.

Getting around System Integrity Protection (SIP)

Before you can start working with LLDB, you need to learn about a feature introduced by Apple to thwart malware. Unfortunately, this feature *also* thwarts your attempts to introspect and debug using LLDB and other tools like DTrace. Never fear though, because Apple included a way to turn this feature off — for those who know what they're doing. And you're going to become one of these people who knows what they're doing!

The feature blocking your introspection and debugging attempts is **System Integrity Protection (SIP)**, also known as **rootless**. This system restricts what programs can do — even if they have root access — to stop malware from planting itself deep inside your system.

Although SIP is a substantial leap forward in security, it introduces some annoyances as it makes programs harder to debug. Specifically, it prevents other processes from attaching a debugger to programs Apple signs.

Since this book involves debugging not only your own applications, but any application you're curious about, it's important you remove this feature while you learn about debugging so you can inspect any application of your choosing.

If you currently have SIP enabled, you'll be unable to attach to the majority of the programs on your computer.

For example, try attaching LLDB to the `Finder` application.

Open up a Terminal window and look for the Finder process, like so:

```
lldb -n Finder
```

You'll notice the following error:

```
error: attach failed: attach failed (Not allowed to attach to
process.  Look in the console messages (Console.app), near the
debugserver entries, when the attach failed.  The subsystem that
denied the attach permission will likely have logged an
informative message about why it was denied.)
```

> **Note**: There are many ways to attach to a process, as well as specific configurations when LLDB attaches successfully. You'll learn all about attaching to a process, in Chapter 3, "Attaching With LLDB".

Disabling System Integrity Protection

> **Note**: A safer way to follow along with this book would be to create a dedicated virtual machine using **VMWare** or **VirtualBox** and disable SIP on that VM following the steps detailed below. Downloading and setting up a macOS VM can take about an hour depending on your computer's hardware (and internet speed!). Get the latest installation virtual machine instructions from Google since the macOS version and VM software will have different installation steps.

At WWDC 2022, Apple, updated their own virtualization technologies to support macOS VMs. If you are running a computer with Apple Silicon, check out Session 10002 "Create macOS or Linux virtual machines" (https://developer.apple.com/videos/play/wwdc2022/10002/) that explains the technology and even offers a demo project that creates a VM you can use with this book. If you do use Apple's demo code, can start your VM in Recovery Mode by setting the .startUpFromMacOSRecovery option to true and adding that to the virtualMachine.start command in the **AppDelegate**. Your changes to their demo code would look something like:

```
let options = VZMacOSVirtualMachineStartOptions()
options.startUpFromMacOSRecovery = true
virtualMachine.start(options: options, completionHandler:
```

If you choose to disable SIP on your computer without a VM, it would be ideal to re-enable SIP once you're done with that particular chapter. Fortunately, there's only a handful of chapters in this book that require SIP to be disabled!

To disable SIP, perform the following steps:

1. Restart your macOS machine.

2. When the screen turns blank, press and hold down **Command-R** until the Apple boot logo appears for x86 Macs, or hold the power button until the Apple boot logo appears for Apple Silicon Macs. This puts your computer into **Recovery Mode**.

3. Now, find the **Utilities** menu from the top and then select **Terminal**.

4. With the Terminal window open, type:

```
csrutil disable && reboot
```

5. Provided the `csrutil disable` command succeeded, your computer will restart with SIP disabled.

> **Note**: Apple provides documentation (https://support.apple.com/guide/mac-help/intro-to-macos-recovery-mchl46d531d6/mac) for how to get into Recovery Mode on different Mac models. If you can't get into Recovery Mode following the instructions above, check the documentation.

You can verify if you've successfully disabled SIP by querying its status in Terminal once your computer starts up by typing:

```
csrutil status
```

You should see the following:

```
System Integrity Protection status: disabled.
```

Now that SIP is disabled, perform the same "Attach to Finder" LLDB command you tried earlier.

```
lldb -n Finder
```

Your computer will ask for your password and then LLDB should attach itself to the current Finder process. The output of a successful attach should look like this:

```
virtualadministrator@Virtuals-Virtual-Machine ~ % lldb -n Finder
(lldb) process attach --name "Finder"
Process 399 stopped
* thread #1, queue = 'com.apple.main-thread', stop reason = signal SIGSTOP
    frame #0: 0x00000001a4512050 libsystem_kernel.dylib`mach_msg2_trap + 8
libsystem_kernel.dylib`mach_msg2_trap:
->  0x1a4512050 <+8>: ret

libsystem_kernel.dylib`macx_swapon:
    0x1a4512054 <+0>: mov    x16, #-0x30
    0x1a4512058 <+4>: svc    #0x80
    0x1a451205c <+8>: ret
Target 0: (Finder) stopped.
Executable module set to "/System/Library/CoreServices/Finder.app/Contents/MacOS
/Finder".
Architecture set to: arm64e-apple-macosx-.
(lldb)
```

After verifying a successful attach, detach LLDB by either closing the Terminal window, or typing quit and confirming in the LLDB console.

Attaching LLDB to the Notes App

Now that you've disabled SIP, you can attach LLDB to any process on your macOS machine (some hurdles may apply, such as with ptrace system call, but we'll get to that later). You're first going to look into an application that's guaranteed to be installed on your computer – Notes!

Open a new Terminal window. Next, edit the Terminal tab's title by pressing **Command-Shift-I** to display the Inspector popup. Edit the **Tab Title** to be **LLDB**.

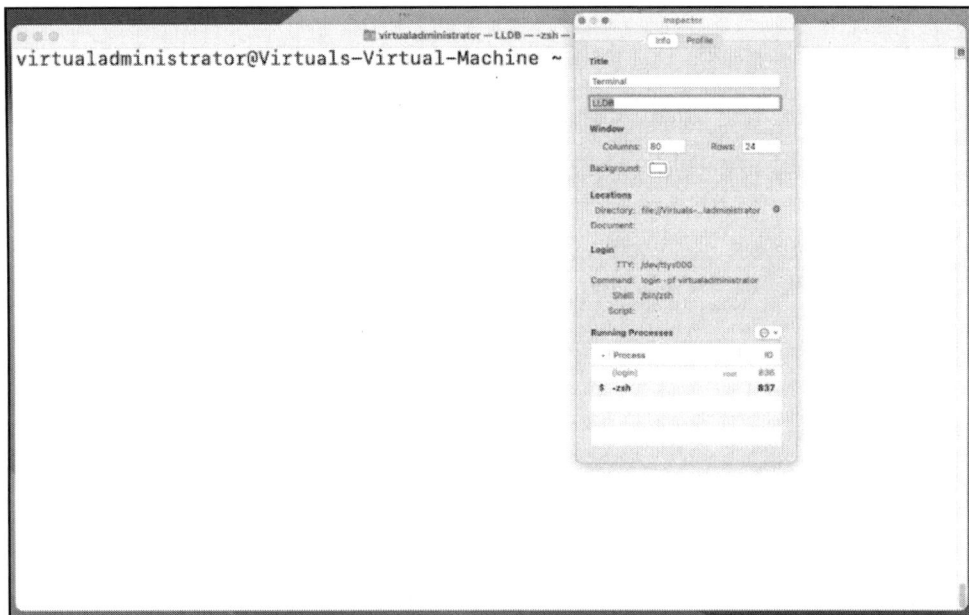

Next, close Notes on your Mac if it's running. You wouldn't want to have multiple instances of Notes running, it would get confusing.

In Terminal, type the following:

```
$ lldb
```

This launches LLDB! Create a new Terminal tab by pressing **Command-T**. Edit the new tab's title using **Command-Shift-I** and name the tab **stderr** or something interesting. This tab is going to contain all of the output that Notes.app normally sends to the system logs when it's running. It'll also contain any output you print from the debugging session.

Make sure you're still in the new Terminal tab and type the command to get it's address:

```
$ tty
```

Terminal should respond with the address to the tab. It should look simiar to below:

```
/dev/ttys001
```

Don't worry if yours is different; it's the address of this, specific terminal instance.

To illustrate what you'll be doing with the **stderr** tab, create *yet another* tab and type this command into it:

```
$ echo "hello debugger" 1>/dev/ttys001
```

Be sure to use the address you obtained from the tty command if it's different from the one in the example. Now switch back to the **stderr** tab. The words hello debugger should have appeared. You'll use this same trick to pipe the output of Notes' stderr to this tab.

Finally, close the unnamed, third tab and go back to the LLDB tab.

To summarize, you should now have two Terminal tabs open:

- a tab named "LLDB", which contains an instance of LLDB running

- a tab named "stderr", which contains the tty command you just performed

From there, enter the following into the LLDB Terminal tab:

```
(lldb) file /System/Applications/Notes.app
```

This will set the executable target to Notes.

Now launch the Notes process from LLDB, replacing /dev/ttys027 with your Notes stderr tab's tty address again:

```
(lldb) process launch -e /dev/ttys027 --
```

The launch argument e specifies the location of stderr. Common logging functionality, such as Objective-C's NSLog or Swift's print function, outputs to stderr — yes, not stdout! You'll print your own logging to stderr later.

Notes will launch after a moment. Switch over to Notes and make sure that you're looking at a new, clean note. You're going to be making changes with the debugger and it would be a shame if you ruined that great chocolate chip cookie recipe note or some other important note.

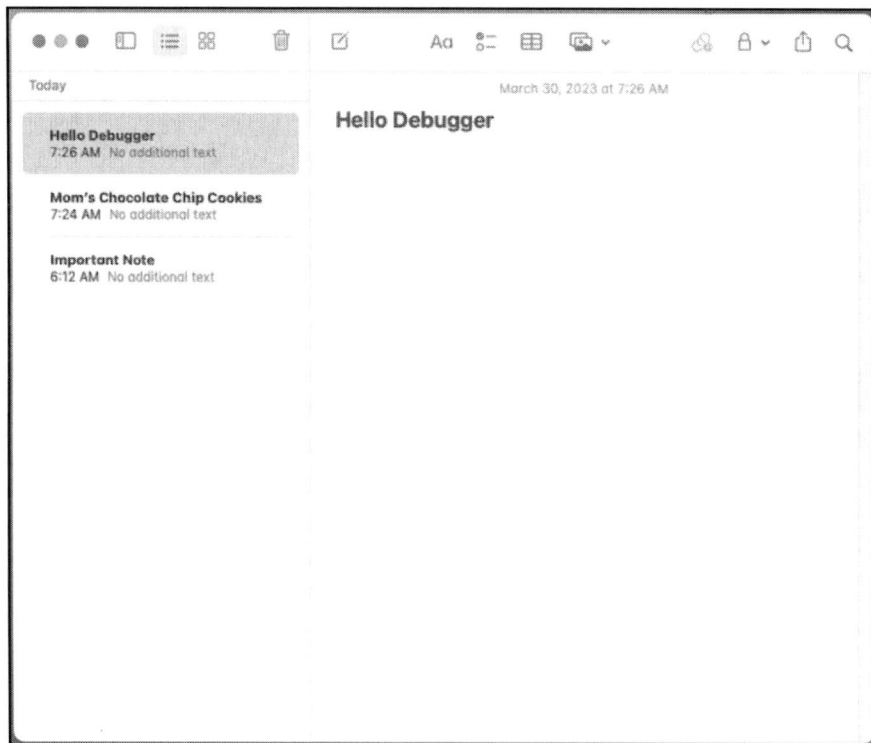

You now have a new note. Arrange the windows so you can see both Terminal and Notes.

> **Note**: You might notice some output on the stderr Terminal window – ok lots of output :]. This is due to content logged by the authors of Notes via NSLog or another stderr console printing function.

A "Swiftly" Changing Landscape

Apple has been cautious in its adoption of Swift in its own software. However Apple has been ramping up the usage of Swift ever since the language was born. Adoption is still cautious, and understandably so given that the language is still evolving and needs further battle testing.

The adoption of Swift in Apple's own applications range from the iOS Simulator and even Xcode to the Notes app!

Notes has a few hundred Swift functions and references thirty or so Swift libraries.

> **Note**: How can you verify this information yourself? This info was obtained using a combination of nm and otool and the helper LLDB scripts found in Appendix C "Helpful Python Scripts" which are free to all. Installation instructions are in the README of the repo. I'll refer to this repo throughout the book when there's a situation that's significantly easier through these LLDB scripts.

The scary command to obtain this information is the following. You'll need to install the repo mentioned in the note above if you wish to execute this command.

```
(lldb) sys echo "$(dclass -t swift)" | grep -v _ | grep "\." |
cut -d. -f1 | uniq | wc -l
```

Breaking this command down, the **dclass -t swift** command is a custom LLDB command that dumps all classes known to the process that are Swift classes. The **sys** command will allow you to execute commands like you were in Terminal, but anything in the $() will get evaluated first via LLDB. From there, it's a matter of manipulating the output of all the Swift classes given by the dclass command.

Swift class naming will typically have the form ModuleName.ClassName where the module is the framework that the class is implemented in. The rest of the command does the following:

- grep -v _: Exclude any Swift names that include an underscore, which is a typical trait of the class names in the Swift standard library.

- grep "\.": Filter by Swift classes that contain a period in the class name.

- cut -d. -f1: Isolate the module name before the period.

- uniq: Then grab all unique values of the modules.

- wc -l: and get the count of it.

These custom LLDB commands (dclass, sys) were built using Python along with LLDB's Python module (confusingly also called lldb). You'll get very accustomed to working with this Python module in Section IV of this book as you learn to build custom, advanced LLDB scripts.

Finding a Class With a Click

Now that Notes is running and your Terminal debugging windows are correctly created and positioned, it's time to start exploring using the help of the debugger.

While debugging, knowledge of the Cocoa SDK can be extremely helpful. For example, **-[NSView hitTest:]** is a useful Objective-C method that returns the class responsible for the handled click or gesture for an event in the run loop. This method will first be triggered on the containing NSView and recursively drill into the furthest subview that handles this touch.

You can use this knowledge of the Cocoa SDK to help determine the class of the view you've clicked on.

In your LLDB tab, press **Control-C** to pause the debugger. From there, type:

```
(lldb) b -[NSView hitTest:]
```

LLDB will respond with information about the new breakpoint, its name and where it's been set. This is your first breakpoint of many to come. You'll learn the details of how to create, modify, and delete breakpoints in Chapter 4, "Stopping in Code", but for now simply know you've created a breakpoint on -[NSView hitTest:].

Notes is now paused thanks to the debugger. Resume the program by typing the continue command in LLDB:

```
(lldb) continue
```

Click anywhere in the Notes window, or in some cases even moving your cursor over Notes will do the same; Notes will instantly pause and LLDB will indicate a breakpoint has been hit.

```
Target 0: (Notes) stopped.
(lldb) b -[NSView hitTest:]
Breakpoint 1: where = AppKit`-[NSView hitTest:], a
ddress = 0x00000001a7a11170
(lldb) continue
Process 1009 resuming
Process 1009 stopped
* thread #1, queue = 'com.apple.main-thread', stop
 reason = breakpoint 1.1
    frame #0: 0x00000001a7a11170 AppKit`-[NSView h
itTest:]
AppKit`-[NSView hitTest:]:
->  0x1a7a11170 <+0>:  pacibsp
    0x1a7a11174 <+4>:  sub   sp, sp, #0x70
    0x1a7a11178 <+8>:  stp   x24, x23, [sp, #0x30
]
    0x1a7a1117c <+12>: stp   x22, x21, [sp, #0x40
]
Target 0: (Notes) stopped.
(lldb)
```

The hitTest: breakpoint has fired. You can inspect which view was hit by inspecting the CPU register. Print it out in LLDB:

```
(lldb) po $arg1
```

This command instructs LLDB to print out the contents of the object at the memory address referenced by what's stored in the arg1 assembly register. This is a virtual register that LLDB uses because it supports multiple CPU architectures. It's equal to $x0 on Apple Silicon and $rdi on x86_64 machines.

> **Note**: Wondering why the command is po? po stands for *print object*. There's also p, which simply prints the contents of arg1. po is usually more useful as it gives the NSObject's (or Swift's SwiftObject's) description or debugDescription methods, if available.

Assembly is an important skill to learn if you want to take your debugging to the next level. It will give you insight into Apple's code — even when you don't have any source code to read from. It will give you a greater appreciation of how the Swift compiler team danced in and out of Objective-C with Swift, and it will give you a greater appreciation of how everything works on your Apple devices.

You'll learn more about registers and assembly in Chapter 11, "Assembly Register Calling Convention".

For now, simply know the $arg register in the above LLDB command contains the instance of the subclass NSView the hitTest: method was called upon.

> **Note**: The output will produce different results depending on where you clicked and what version of Notes you're using. It could give a private class specific to Notes, or it could give you a public class belonging to Cocoa.

In LLDB, type the following to resume the program:

```
(lldb) continue
```

Instead of continuing, Notes will likely hit another breakpoint for `hitTest:` and pause execution. This is due to the fact that the `hitTest:` method is recursively calling this method for all subviews contained within the parent view that was clicked. You can inspect the contents of this breakpoint, but this will soon become tedious since there are so many views that make up the Notes UI.

> **Note**: Apple uses a pattern they call the "responder chain". Since the UI is made up of views within views within views, each one of them has the opportunity to respond to a click and then pass the click along to the next one until it gets to the root window. This is another reason it's important to remember to call `super` in your view code.

Automate the hitTest:

The process of clicking on a view, stopping, po'ing the arg1 register then continuing can get tiring quickly. What if you created a breakpoint to automate all of this?

There's several ways to achieve this, but perhaps the cleanest way is to declare a new breakpoint with all the traits you want. Wouldn't that be neat?! :]

Remove the previous breakpoint with the following command:

```
(lldb) breakpoint delete
```

LLDB will ask if you sure you want to delete all breakpoints, either press enter or press 'Y' then enter to confirm.

Now, create a new breakpoint with the following:

```
(lldb) breakpoint set -n "-[NSView hitTest:]" -C "po $arg1" -G1
```

The gist of this command says to create a breakpoint on `-[NSView hitTest:]`, have it execute the "`po $arg1`" command, then automatically continue after executing the command. You'll learn more about these options in a later chapter.

Resume execution with the `c` or `continue` command:

```
(lldb) continue
```

Now, click anywhere in Note and check out the output in the LLDB console. You'll see many many `NSView`s being called to see if they should take the mouse click!

Filter Breakpoints for Important Content

Since there are so many NSViews that make up Notes, you need a way to filter out some of the noise and only stop on the NSView relevant to what you're looking for. This is an example of debugging a frequently-called method, where you want to find a unique case that helps pinpoint what you're really looking for.

Since Notes is all about saving text it has a lot of views that handle text. Some are public, and some are private like **ICMacTextView**.

Let's say you want to break only when you click an instance of ICMacTextView. You can modify the existing breakpoint to stop only on a ICMacTextView click by using **breakpoint conditions**.

Provided you still have your -[NSView hitTest:] breakpoint set, and it's the only active breakpoint in your LLDB session, you can modify that breakpoint with the following LLDB command:

```
(lldb) breakpoint modify -c '(BOOL)[NSStringFromClass((id)[$arg1
class]) containsString:@"ICMacTextView"]' -G0
```

This command modifies all existing breakpoints in your debugging session and creates a condition which gets evaluated every time -[NSView hitTest:] fires. If the condition evaluates to true, then execution will pause in the debugger. This condition checks that the instance of the NSView is of type ICMacTextView. The final -G0 says to modify the breakpoint to not automatically resume execution after the action has been performed.

After modifying your breakpoint above, use the c or continue command in LLDB to resume execution of Notes. Now click on the main note area in Notes, where you'd write text in your note.po LLDB should stop on hitTest:. Print out the instance of the class this method was called on:

```
(lldb) po $rdi
```

Your output should look something similar to the following:

```
<ICMacTextView: 0x1010cf200>
   Frame = {{0.00, 0.00}, {505.00, 604.00}}, Bounds = {{0.00,
0.00} {505.00, 604.00}}
   Horizontally resizable: NO, Vertically resizable: YES
   MinSize = {505.00, 604.00}, MaxSize = {731.00, 10000000.00}
```

This is printing out the object's **description**. You'll notice that there is a pointer reference within this. That's the location in memory where this ICMacTextView lives.

Type the following in LLDB:

```
(lldb) p/x $arg1
```

You'll get something similar to the following:

```
(unsigned long) $3 = 0x0000000110a42600
```

Since arg1 points to a valid Objective-C NSObject subclass (written in Swift), you can also get the same info just by po'ing this address instead of the register.

Type the following into LLDB while making sure to replace the address with your own:

```
(lldb) po 0x0000000110a42600
```

You'll get the same output as earlier.

You might be skeptical that this reference pointed at by the arg1 register is actually pointing to the NSView that displays your code. You can easily verify if that's true or not by typing the following in LLDB:

```
(lldb) po [$rdi setHidden:!(BOOL)[$rdi isHidden]];
[CATransaction flush]
```

Note: Kind of a long command to type out, right? In Chapter 10: "Regex Commands", you'll learn how to build convenient shortcuts so you don't have to type out these long LLDB commands. If you chose to install the LLDB repo mentioned earlier, a convenience command for this above action the **tv** command, or "toggle view".

Provided arg1 is pointing to the correct reference, your note editor view will disappear!

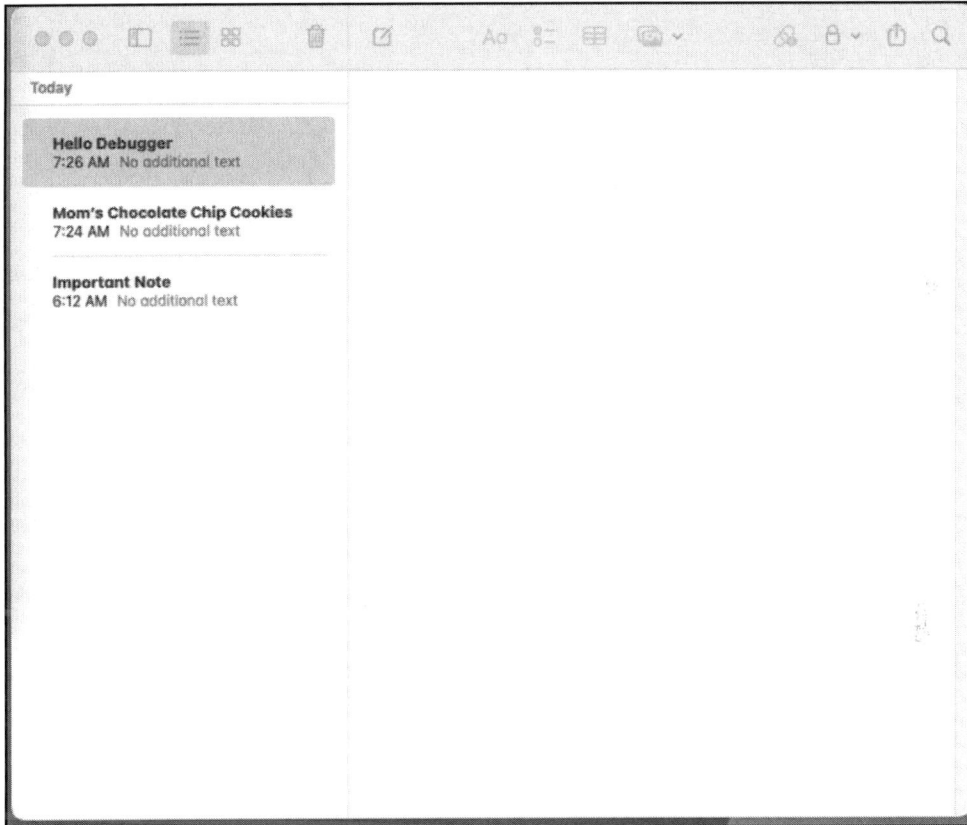

You can toggle this view on and off simply by repeatedly pressing Enter. LLDB will automatically execute the previous command.

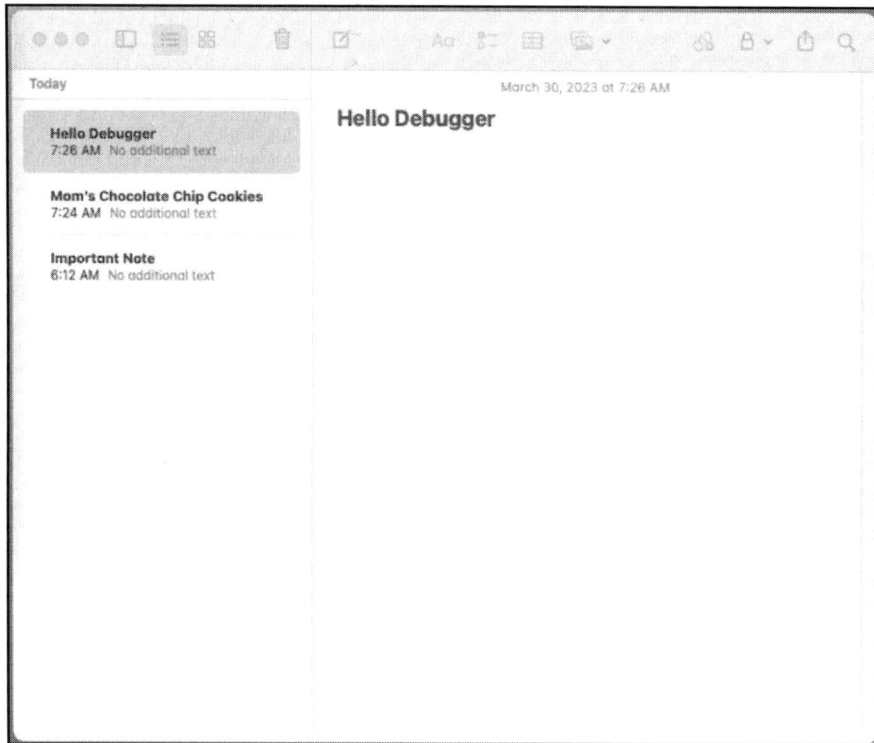

Since this is a subclass of NSView, all the methods of NSView apply. For example, the string command can query the contents of your source code through LLDB. Type the following:

```
(lldb) po [$arg1 string]
```

This will dump out the contents of your note editor. Neat!

Always remember, any APIs that you have in your development cycle can be used in LLDB. If you were crazy enough, you could create an entire app just by executing LLDB commands!

When you get bored of playing with the NSView APIs on this instance, copy the address down that arg1 is referencing (copy it to your clipboard or add it to the stickies app). You'll reference it again in a second.

Alternatively, did you notice that output preceding the hex value in the p/x $arg1 command? In my output, I got **$3**, which means that you can use $3 as a reference for that pointer value you just grabbed. This is incredibly useful when the arg1 register points to something else and you still want to reference this NSView at a later time.

Swift vs Objective-C Debugging

Wait — we're using Objective-C on a Swift class?! You bet! You'll discover that a Swift class is *mostly* all Objective-C underneath the covers (however the same can't be said about Swift structs). You'll confirm this by modifying the note's contents through LLDB using Swift!

First, import the following modules in the Swift debugging context:

```
(lldb) ex -l swift -- import Foundation
(lldb) ex -l swift -- import AppKit
```

The ex command (short for expression) lets you evaluate code and is the foundation for your p/po LLDB commands. -l swift tells LLDB to interpret your commands as Swift code. You just imported the headers to call appropriate methods in both of these modules through Swift. These are big modules, so don't be alarmed if it takes LLDB a few seconds to load each one. You'll need these in the next two commands.

Enter the following, replacing 0x0110a42600 with the memory address of your NSView subclass you recently copied to your clipboard:

```
(lldb) ex -l swift -o -- unsafeBitCast(0x0110a42600, to:
NSView.self)
```

This command prints out the ICMacTextView instance — but this time using Swift!

Now, add some text to your note via LLDB:

```
(lldb) ex -l swift -o -- unsafeBitCast(0x0110a42600, to:
NSView.self).insertText("Yay! Swift!")
```

You won't see anything right away because LLDB has suspended your app. Use the c or continue command a few times to make it appear. Depending where your cursor was in the Xcode console, you'll see the new string "Yay! Swift!" added to your source code.

When stopping the debugger out of the blue, or on Objective-C code, LLDB will default to using the Objective-C context when debugging. This means the po you execute will expect Objective-C syntax unless you force LLDB to use a different language like you did above. It's possible to alter this, but this book prefers to use Objective-C since the Swift REPL can be brutal for error-checking, has slow compilation times for executing commands, is generally much more buggy, and prevents you from executing methods the Swift LLDB context doesn't know about.

All of this will eventually go away, but we must be patient.

Key Points

- **SIP** is Apple's technology to keep processes from attaching to other processes unexpectedly.

- You can only enable/disable SIP when your Mac is in Recovery Mode.

- LLDB can attach to any process on your Mac as long as you have permissions.

- Appendix C "Helpful Python Scripts" contains a number of scripts you'll use as you work through this book.

- When an app hits a breakpoint, it is suspended. Use the `c` or `continue` command in LLDB to start it again.

- LLDB uses **arg1** as a virtual address to represent the address of the code that is impacted by a breakpoint.

Where to Go From Here?

This was a breadth-first, whirlwind introduction to using LLDB and attaching to a process where you don't have any source code to aid you. This chapter glossed over a lot of detail, but the goal was to get you right into the debugging/reverse engineering process.

To some, this first chapter might have come off as a little scary, but we'll slow down and describe methods in detail from here on out. There are lots of chapters remaining to get you into the details!

Keep reading to learn the essentials in the remainder of Section 1. Happy debugging!

If you disabled SIP, you can enable it by following the steps at the beginning of this chapter and issuing the `csrutil enable` command while in Recovery Mode. Leaving SIP disabled on your regular computer is dangerous.

Chapter 2: Overview & Getting Help

LLDB is a powerful debugger included in a suite of compiler tools and technologies known as the LLVM project (https://llvm.org). LLDB is an open source project so you can compile it and run your own version if you are so inclined. LLDB supports a number of platforms (like Linux, Windows, NetBSD), but the primary consumers of LLDB are engineers using Apple platforms such as iOS and macOS. As such, this book is primarily geared towards Apple development.

Developers building for Apple platforms will likely have little need to build LLDB from source, opting to use the precompiled LLDB version packaged in **Xcode**, located at `Xcode.app/Contents/Developer/usr/bin/lldb`. The LLDB version shipping with Xcode is in constant flux and is not associated with the public LLVM versioning. Typing `lldb --version` will give you a version internal to Apple. However, https://en.wikipedia.org/wiki/Xcode, has a table mapping the correlation of Xcode versions to the associated LLVM toolchain release. At the time of writing, Apple is shipping LLVM 15 in Xcode 14.3. Xcode's LLVM toolchain version is usually a little behind what comes from the LLVM project directly. This can be useful for tracking down bugs or expected features.

> **Note**: When referring to the program executable, *lldb is lowercase*. While referring to LLDB as a system of LLVM, uppercase is used.

Building LLDB via Xcode

You **are not** required to build LLDB for any of the chapters in this book. However, I can't give you a book about LLDB without providing instruction to the source and building it for those who are interested. If this does not interest you, feel free to skip this section.

If compiling LLDB is of interest, you'll need several tools as well as about 50GB of free space on your computer. The first tool you'll need to build LLDB is **CMake**. CMake is a program used to generate build instructions that other tools can use to actually build a project. That is, if you want to build with the command line and a GNU Makefile, you can tell CMake to do that. Or, if you're like me and want to build using Xcode, you can tell CMake to generate an xcodeproj file. The "preferred" way to build LLVM components is to use CMake and **Ninja**. Ninja is a lightweight build system that was designed for speed. But approaching a complex codebase such as LLVM, it's best to use the tools you're most experienced with, so you'll use Xcode at the price of a slightly slower build time.

Install CMake either via https://brew.sh or via https://cmake.org. If you have brew already setup, it's a simple matter of the following command:

```
brew install cmake
```

In addition to CMake, you'll need the clang compiler, which I expect you to have via Xcode 13 or higher.

After that, you're good to go. Change directories to where you want to install LLVM:

```
cd code
```

Clone the LLVM repo:

```
git clone --depth 1 --branch "release/13.x" https://github.com/
llvm/llvm-project.git
cd llvm-project
```

You are specifying a --depth of 1 as LLVM is a huge repository. This --depth flag limits the downloaded commit history and speeds up cloning (if your internet doesn't suck, you can skip the --depth 1 option). You are checking out the release/13.x branch, which will likely be the current LLVM release by the time you're reading this.

Once cloned, create a build directory, cd into that build directory and run CMake:

```
mkdir build-lldb-xcode
cd build-lldb-xcode
cmake -G Xcode -DLLVM_ENABLE_PROJECTS="clang;lldb;libcxx"
-DLLVM_BUILD_RUNTIME=Off -DLLVM_INCLUDE_TESTS=Off
-DCMAKE_BUILD_TYPE=RelWithDebInfo
-DLLVM_INCLUDE_EXAMPLES=Off ../llvm
```

The CMake command is instructed to build for an Xcode project via the -G Xcode argument. Any argument beginning with a -D is an argument that is passed into the build system. CMake uses the arguments and a file called **CMakeLists.txt** to decide what to do. With the arguments above you are telling the build system you want to build clang, LLDB, and the C++ standard library (libcxx). LLDB relies on clang, which in turn, relies on the libcxx library.

On my computer, the CMake command took 4 minutes to run. Once complete, an LLVM.xcodeproj is generated in the build-lldb directory.

If you were to list all of Xcode build targets, the output might set off alarm bells.

```
xcodebuild -list | wc -l
1281
```

The LLVM.xcodeproj is a HUUUUUGE project that will incorporate all the executables for lldb, clang, and C++ (determined by the LLVM_ENABLE_PROJECTS argument passed to CMake earlier).

Now that you've got the infastructure setup, compile lldb:

```
xcodebuild -scheme lldb
```

Running the above command on my 2020 M1 Macbook Air took about 25 minutes; your mileage may vary depending on CPU count and RAM. The compiled artifacts created by building LLDB took ~24GB of space. Again, your disk usage will vary depending on the build type, what commit you're building from and your elected CMake options.

If everything went ok, then a new lldb executable will be located in ./lldb-build/ Debug/bin/lldb.

Building LLDB via Ninja

If you've come from a more C++ background, or if you despise Xcode, you can also build the LLDB project using Ninja. This is ideal if you prefer using Visual Studio Code or CLion as an IDE.

The process is largely the same as above. Ensure that CMake installed and clone the relevant version/commit of LLVM. Install Ninja if needed:

```
brew install ninja
```

Create a build directory specific for the Ninja build and use CMake to generate the Ninja project.

```
mkdir build-lldb-ninja
cd build-lldb-ninja
cmake -G Ninja -DLLVM_ENABLE_PROJECTS="clang;lldb;libcxx"
-DLLVM_BUILD_RUNTIME=Off -DLLVM_INCLUDE_TESTS=Off
-DCMAKE_BUILD_TYPE=RelWithDebInfo
-DLLVM_INCLUDE_EXAMPLES=Off ../llvm
```

You can use **ninja -t targets** to display all the items that can be built.

Build the lldb executable with the following command:

```
ninja lldb
```

Note: A strong knowledge of CMake and its CMakeLists.txt structure is needed when making major changes to LLDB's source code. CMake is outside the scope of this book, but interested readers are advised to Google and practice some toy examples before tackling the complex intricacies of LLVM's CMake structure.

LLDB's Design

LLDB is broken down into several components in order to create a functional debugger. First, there's the lldb executable, which is responsible for coordinating everything.

Accompanying the `lldb` executable is a "special" framework. If you've ever tried executing a command in lldb via a (`lldb`) `po` `something_here`, there's hidden complexities that *might* need to occur. A compiled language like Swift *needs to be compiled*. As a result, LLDB needs a compiler to dynamically parse your expression, compile it on the fly, then return the results to lldb's output. To achieve this, LLDB uses a "watered down" clang compiler inside of a framework. If you have Xcode installed, this framework can be found at `Xcode.app/Contents/SharedFrameworks/LLDB.framework`.

This framework provides 3rd party consumer APIs discussed in Section IV of this book. These APIs are known as the **Script Bridging** code, a series of powerful C++ APIs that have remained relatively stable over the years. Since not everyone is a fan of C++, LLDB uses SWIG, a language translator, to produce Python wrappers for the C++ Script Bridging APIs. Much like a Swift Playground, using the Python Script Bridging wrappers is the preferred way to quickly play with live programs to learn and produce advanced commands in LLDB. This book primarily focuses on these APIs through the Python interface, but you can always drop down to C++ if execution speed is critical.

Finally, a "controlling process" called **debugserver** (or sometimes referred to as **lldb-server**) is responsible for manipulating a process being debugged. debugserver acts as a mindless, but powerful minion, and lldb acts as the brains, communicating its wishes to debugserver over Unix ports.

LLDB's Design + Remote Apple Devices

The above description is fine when you're debugging a process on your own computer, but what about on a remote host? What about debugging an iOS application running on an iPhone or iPad?

To achieve this, a **DeveloperDiskImage.dmg** mount (located at Xcode.app/ Contents/Developer/Platforms/iPhoneOS.platform/DeviceSupport/) is loaded onto the iOS device. This DMG includes a debugserver as well as multiple debugging executables and frameworks. But even with a lldb on your machine, and debugserver on the remote iOS device, there still needs to be a way to start the communication bridge between the 2 devices. This is where **/usr/libexec/ lockdown** (found on the iOS device) comes into play. This daemon is the gatekeeper for communicating with software requests over an iOS device's lightning/USB cable connection. Tools like Xcode initiate a request to a device for a particular "service". If lockdownd accepts the request, it will perform the required setup. For the case of debugging, lockdownd will forward the port to debugserver and set up the bridge between lldb on the computer and debugserver on the remote host.

Xcode uses a private framework called **MobileDevice** to facilitate the communication between Xcode and lockdownd. This framework has been thoroughly reversed by many and interested readers should check out the following URLs:

- https://github.com/ios-control/ios-deploy, Install and debug iOS apps from the command line.

- https://libimobiledevice.org, complete reimplementation of the MobileDevice framework.

- https://github.com/search?q=AMDeviceSecureStartService&type=code, search Github for the usage of a common MobileDevice "connection" symbol reference.

Now that you've got an overview of LLDB the project, and how lldb interacts with other components, it's time to see how you can get help when you need it.

If you've come from a more C++ background, or if you despise Xcode, you can also build the LLDB project using Ninja. This is ideal if you prefer using Visual Studio Code or CLion as your IDE.

Just like any respectable developer tool, lldb ships with a healthy amount of documentation. Knowing how to navigate through this documentation — including some of the more obscure command flags — is essential to mastering LLDB.

Open a Terminal window and type lldb. The lldb prompt will appear. From there, type the help command:

```
(lldb) help
```

This will dump out all available commands, including the custom commands loaded from your ~/.lldbinit — but more on that later.

```
Debugger commands:
  apropos             -- List debugger commands related to a word
or subject.
  breakpoint          -- Commands for operating on breakpoints
(see 'help b' for
                         shorthand.)
  command             -- Commands for managing custom LLDB
commands.
  disassemble         -- Disassemble specified instructions in the
current
                         target.  Defaults to the current function
for the
                         current thread and stack frame.
  expression          -- Evaluate an expression on the current
thread.  Displays
                         any returned value with LLDB's default
formatting.
  frame               -- Commands for selecting and examining the
current thread's
                         stack frames.
  gdb-remote          -- Connect to a process via remote GDB
server.
                         If no host is specified, localhost is
assumed.
                         gdb-remote is an abbreviation for
'process connect
                         --plugin gdb-remote connect://
<hostname>:<port>'
  gui                 -- Switch into the curses based GUI mode.
  help                -- Show a list of all debugger commands, or
give details
                         about a specific command.
  kdp-remote          -- Connect to a process via remote KDP
server.
                         If no UDP port is specified, port 41139
is
                         assumed.
                         kdp-remote is an abbreviation for
'process connect
                         --plugin kdp-remote udp://
<hostname>:<port>'
  language            -- Commands specific to a source language.
...
```

There's quite a few commands one can use with LLDB. Unfortunately, help doesn't have a pagination switch, so you have to use the scroll bars in your terminal window to read long entries.

Commands can also contain subcommands, which in turn can have sub-subcommands containing their own documentation. I told you it was a healthy amount of documentation!

Take the breakpoint command for instance. Run the documentation for breakpoint by typing the following:

```
(lldb) help breakpoint
```

You'll see the following output:

```
Commands for operating on breakpoints (see 'help b' for
shorthand.)

Syntax: breakpoint <subcommand> [<command-options>]

The following subcommands are supported:

      clear   -- Delete or disable breakpoints matching the
specified source file and line.
      command -- Commands for adding, removing and listing LLDB
commands executed when a breakpoint is hit.
      delete  -- Delete the specified breakpoint(s).  If no
breakpoints are specified, delete them all.
      disable -- Disable the specified breakpoint(s) without
deleting them.  If none are specified, disable all breakpoints.
      enable  -- Enable the specified disabled breakpoint(s). If
no breakpoints are specified, enable all of them.
      list    -- List some or all breakpoints at configurable
levels of detail.
      modify  -- Modify the options on a breakpoint or set of
breakpoints in the executable.  If no breakpoint is specified,
acts on the last created breakpoint.  With the
               exception of -e, -d and -i, passing an empty
argument clears the modification.
      name    -- Commands to manage name tags for breakpoints
      read    -- Read and set the breakpoints previously saved
to a file with "breakpoint write".
      set     -- Sets a breakpoint or set of breakpoints in the
executable.
      write   -- Write the breakpoints listed to a file that can
be read in with "breakpoint read".  If given no arguments,
writes all breakpoints.

For more help on any particular subcommand, type 'help <command>
<subcommand>'.
```

From there, you can see several supported subcommands. Look up the documentation for breakpoint name by typing the following:

```
(lldb) help breakpoint name
```

You'll see the following output:

```
Commands to manage name tags for breakpoints

Syntax: breakpoint name <subcommand> [<command-options>]

The following subcommands are supported:

      add        -- Add a name to the breakpoints provided.
      configure  -- Configure the options for the breakpoint name
provided.  If you provide a breakpoint id, the options will be
copied from the breakpoint, otherwise only the
                  options specified will be set on the name.
      delete     -- Delete a name from the breakpoints provided.
      list       -- List either the names for a breakpoint or
info about a given name.  With no arguments, lists all names

For more help on any particular subcommand, type 'help <command>
<subcommand>'.
```

If you don't understand breakpoint name at the moment, don't worry — you'll become familiar with breakpoints and all of the subsequent commands soon. For now, the help command is the most important command you can remember.

The apropos Command

Sometimes you don't know the name of the command you're searching for, but you know a certain word or phrase that might point you in the right direction. The apropos command can do this for you; it's a bit like using a search engine to find something on the web.

apropos will do a case-insensitive search for any word or string against the LLDB documentation and return any matching results. For example, try searching for anything pertaining to Swift:

```
(lldb) apropos swift
```

You'll see the following output:

```
The following commands may relate to 'swift':
  swift    -- A set of commands for operating on the Swift
Language Runtime.
  demangle -- Demangle a Swift mangled name
  refcount -- Inspect the reference count data for a Swift
object

The following settings variables may relate to 'swift':


  target.swift-extra-clang-flags -- Additional -Xcc flags to be
passed to the
                          Swift ClangImporter.
  target.swift-framework-search-paths -- List of directories to
be searched
                          when locating
frameworks for Swift.
  target.swift-module-search-paths -- List of directories to be
searched when
                          locating modules for
Swift.
  target.use-all-compiler-flags -- Try to use compiler flags for
all modules
                          when setting up the Swift
expression parser,
                          not just the main executable.
  target.experimental.swift-create-module-contexts-in-parallel
-- Create the per-module Swift AST contexts in parallel.
  symbols.swift-module-loading-mode -- The module loading mode
to use when
                          loading modules for
Swift.
  symbols.use-swift-clangimporter -- Reconstruct Clang module
dependencies from
                          headers when debugging
Swift code
  symbols.use-swift-dwarfimporter -- Reconstruct Clang module
dependencies from
                          DWARF when debugging Swift
code
  symbols.use-swift-typeref-typesystem -- Prefer Swift Remote
Mirrors over
                          Remote AST
```

This dumped everything that might pertain to the word Swift: first the commands, and then the settings which can be used to control how lldb operates.

You can also use `apropos` to search for a particular sentence. For example, if you were searching for something that can help with reference counting, you might try the following:

```
(lldb) apropos "reference count"
The following commands may relate to 'reference count':
  refcount -- Inspect the reference count data for a Swift
object
```

Notice the quotes surrounding the words `"reference count"`. `apropos` will only accept one argument to search for, so the quotes are necessary to treat the input as a single argument.

Isn't that neat? `apropos` is a handy tool for querying. It's not quite as sophisticated as modern internet search engines, but with some playing around, you can usually find what you're looking for.

Other Helpful Resources

In addition to the lldb tool itself, there's a plethora of helpful resources sprinkled around the web:

* Stack Overflow's LLDB tag (https://stackoverflow.com/search?q=lldb), including snooping responses from core LLDB developers, like Jim Ingham (http://stackoverflow.com/users/2465073/jim-ingham)

* https://www.reddit.com/r/llvm

* LLDB's source docs (https://github.com/llvm/llvm-project/blob/main/lldb/docs)

* LLDB's archives (https://lists.llvm.org/pipermail/lldb-dev/)

It's easy to forget the onslaught of LLDB commands that will soon come, but try to commit these two commands, `help` and `apropos`, to heart. They're the foundation for querying information on commands and you'll be using them all the time as you master debugging.

Chapter 3: Attaching With LLDB

Now that you've learned about the two most essential commands, help and apropos, it's time to investigate all the ways LLDB can attach itself to a process.

As used in the previous chapters, the phrase LLDB "attaching" is actually a bit misleading. A program named debugserver — found in Xcode.app/Contents/ SharedFrameworks/LLDB.framework/Resources/ for macOS — is responsible for "attaching" to a target process. It's LLDB's job to bring up and coordinate with debugserver.

Creating a Debuggee Program

To understand how LLDB attaches to a program, you need to have a simple program that you control — just in case you didn't disable SIP in the first chapter.

Open **Terminal** and navigate to the global `tmp` directory:

```
$ cd /tmp
```

The contents of this directory are erased when your computer reboots. It's a great spot for throwaway programs or making content you don't need to stick around.

Use your favorite text editor to create a file named **hello_world.swift**. For simplicity, the steps are described using the **nano** editor.

```
$ nano hello_world.swift
```

Add the following Swift code:

```
import Foundation

print("hello, world!")
CFRunLoopRun()
```

To save the file in nano, use **Control-O**. To exit, use **Control-X**.

Exit the text editor, and compile the program:

```
$ swiftc hello_world.swift
```

Upon success, you'll have an executable named `hello_world` that prints `"hello, world!"` and waits forever in a loop thanks to the `CFRunLoopRun()` call.

Test the `hello_world` program by typing:

```
$ ./hello_world
```

Your terminal window should display "hello, world!" and then nothing else. Use **Control-C** to terminate this program when the euphoria has worn off. You'll use this program in a second to discover the different ways LLDB can attach to a process.

Attaching to an Existing Process

Now, you'll see how to attach LLDB to an existing process. First, you'll need to create a process to debug, and then you'll attach to it.

In your terminal, launch hello_world in the background by typing the following:

```
$ ./hello_world &
```

The ampersand means hello_world executes as a background process. This allows you to continue using Terminal without blocking input. An alternative is to just use a different Terminal tab or window to launch the hello_world executable.

You now have a process to debug. Use LLDB to attach to this program via specifying the program name:

```
$ lldb -n hello_world
```

Your computer may ask for a password before continuing. Attaching to random processes can be dangerous, of course. Once it attaches, LLDB will pause the program and display some information about what the program was doing when you attached. For now, detach from the hello_world program by typing **quit** or simply **q**:

```
(lldb) q
```

LLDB will ask you if you're sure you want to quit. Respond that you *do* want to quit the debugger, and you'll return to the normal Terminal prompt.

Alternatively, you can attach to hello_world by providing the PID of a running program. Since you ran the program in the background earlier, the program's PID was displayed to you when it launched.

> **Note:** Just a reminder — if you didn't disable SIP on your macOS computer, you won't be able to attach LLDB to Apple applications. On more recent macOS versions, you won't be able to attach to third-party apps released from the App Store either.

If you forgot the PID or you cleared your Terminal, you can find the `hello_world` executable's PID with the process grep command:

```
$ pgrep -x hello_world
```

This will output the PID of every process named "hello_world". Note that this can be more than one process.

Next, launch LLDB using the –p argument, replacing 57086 with the number output from the command above:

```
$ lldb -p 57086
```

This tells LLDB to attach to the process with the given PID. In this case, this is your running `hello_world` process. LLDB will again pause the program and show you where it was when LLDB attached.

Attaching to a Future Process

The previous command only addresses a running process. If the process you want to debug isn't running, or is already attached to a debugger, the previous commands will fail. How can you catch a process that's about to be launched if you don't know the PID yet without directly launching the process?

You can do that with the –w argument, which causes LLDB to wait until a process launches with a PID or executable name matching the criteria supplied using the –p or –n argument.

Exit LLDB using **q** or **quit** or by pressing **Control-D** to get back to a Terminal prompt. Now, kill the `hello_world` process using the `pkill` command:

```
pkill hello_world
```

Once you're back at the command line, type the following into Terminal:

```
$ lldb -n hello_world -w
```

This tells LLDB to attach to the process named `hello_world` whenever it launches next. Next, open a new Terminal tab, and execute a new instance of the `hello_world` program:

```
$ /tmp/hello_world
```

Switch back to your first Terminal tab, and you'll notice LLDB has now attached itself to the newly created `hello_world` process.

> **Note**: Though you killed the process before using the −w argument, this wasn't completely necessary. LLDB watches for the *next launch* of the process. It just seemed like it would be less confusing this way.

Launching a Process Using LLDB

Another way to attach to a process is to specify the path to the executable and then launch the process from within LLDB:

```
$ lldb −f /tmp/hello_world
```

This launches LLDB and tells it that it will attach to the `hello_world` executable at some point.

Once you're ready to begin the debug session, simply type the following into the LLDB session:

```
(lldb) process launch
```

You should see the — now familiar — attachment confirmation in LLDB.

> **Note**: An interesting side effect is that `stderr` output — i.e., Swift's `print`, Objective-C's `NSLog`, C's `printf` and company — is automatically sent to the Terminal window when manually launching a process. Other LLDB attaching configurations don't do this automatically.

Options While Launching

The `process launch` command comes with a suite of options worth further exploration. If you're curious and want to see the full list of available options for `process launch`, simply type `help process launch` in an LLDB session.

Close previous LLDB sessions, remove any running instances of `hello_world` via `pkill hello_world`, open a new Terminal window, and type the following:

```
$ lldb -f /bin/ls
```

This tells LLDB to use `/bin/ls`, the file listing command, as the target executable.

> **Note**: If you omit the `-f` option, LLDB automatically infers the first argument as the executable to launch and debug. When debugging Terminal executables, it can be helpful to type `lldb $(which ls)` (or equivalent), which is then translated to `lldb /bin/ls`.

You'll see the following output:

```
(lldb) target create "/bin/ls"
Current executable set to '/bin/ls' (arm64e).
```

Since `ls` is a quick program — it launches, does its job, then exits — it's a good specimen for this next part since you'll run this program multiple times with different arguments to explore what each does.

On the other hand, you need to have disabled SIP using the instructions in Chapter 1, "Getting Started", because you aren't the owner of the `ls` executable. So, if you can't or don't want to disable SIP, you'll just need to follow along without executing the commands.

To launch `ls` from LLDB with no arguments, enter the following:

```
(lldb) process launch
```

You'll see the following output:

```
Process 7681 launched: '/bin/ls' (arm64e)
... # Omitted directory listing output
Process 7681 exited with status = 0 (0x00000000)
```

An ls process will launch in the directory you started in. To change the current working directory, tell LLDB where to launch with the −w option. Enter the following:

```
(lldb) process launch -w /Applications
```

This launches ls from within the /Applications directory. This is equivalent to the following:

```
$ cd /Applications
$ ls
```

There's yet *another* way to do this. Instead of telling LLDB to change to a directory and then run the program, you can pass arguments to the program directly.

Try the following:

```
(lldb) process launch -- /Applications
```

This has the same effect as the previous command, but this time it's doing the following:

```
$ ls /Applications
```

Again, this spits out all your macOS programs, but you specified an argument instead of changing the starting directory. What about specifying your desktop directory as a launch argument? Try running this:

```
(lldb) process launch -- ~/Desktop
```

You'll see the following:

```
Process 57442 launched: '/bin/ls' (arm64e)
ls: ~/Desktop: No such file or directory
Process 57442 exited with status = 1 (0x00000001)
```

Uh-oh, that didn't work. You need the shell to expand the *tilde* in the argument. Try this instead:

```
(lldb) process launch -X true -- ~/Desktop
```

The −X option expands any shell arguments you provide, such as the tilde. LLDB has a shortcut for this: Simply type run. To learn more about creating your own command shortcuts, check out Chapter 9, "Persisting & Customizing Commands".

Type the following to see the documentation for run:

```
(lldb) help run
```

You'll see the following:

```
...
Command Options Usage:
  run [<run-args>]


'run' is an abbreviation for 'process launch -X true --'
```

See? It's an abbreviation of the command you just ran! Give the command a go by typing the following:

```
(lldb) run ~/Desktop
```

Environment Variables

For Terminal programs, **environment variables** can be equally as important as the program's arguments. If you were to consult the man 1 ls, you'd see that the ls command can display output in color so long as the color environment variable, CLICOLOR, is enabled. You also have the "color palette" environment variable LSCOLORS to tell how to display certain file types.

With a target in LLDB, you can launch and set a program with any combination of environment variables.

For example, to display all the environment variables that the ls command will launch with, run the following command in LLDB:

```
(lldb) env
```

This will display all the environment variables for the target. It's important to note that LLDB won't display the environment variables until the target runs at least once. If you don't see any output, just give LLDB a simple run before executing the env command.

You can inspect and augment these environment variables before launch using the
`settings set|show|replace|clear|list target.env-vars` command. However,
you can also just specify them at launch with the −E option from the `process`
`launch` command!

Time to display the /usr/share directory in a garish color!

```
(lldb) process launch -E LSCOLORS=Db -E CLICOLOR=1  -- /usr/
share
```

```
(lldb) process launch -E LSCOLORS=Db -E CLICOLOR=1 -- /usr/share
Process 1438 launched: '/bin/ls' (arm64e)
CSI                             locale
CoreDuetDaemonConfig.bundle     man
ans2_dummy_dir                  mecabra
calendar                        misc
com.apple.languageassetd        morphun
cracklib                        pmenergy
cups                            ri
dict                            sandbox
doc                             screen
examples                        skel
file                            snmp
firmlinks                       tabset
firmware                        terminfo
germantok                       thermald.bundle
hiutil                          tokenizer
httpd                           ucupdate
icu                             vim
kdrl.bundle                     zoneinfo
kpep                            zoneinfo.default
langid                          zsh
Process 1438 exited with status = 0 (0x00000000)
(lldb) ▎
```

Wow! Doesn't that just burn the eyes? Try a different color with the following:

```
(lldb) process launch -E LSCOLORS=Af -E CLICOLOR=1  -- /usr/
share
```

This would be equivalent to you executing the following in Terminal without LLDB:

```
LSCOLORS=Af CLICOLOR=1 ls /Applications/
```

Lots of Terminal commands will contain environment variables and their
descriptions in the command's man page. Always make sure to read about how you'd
expect an environment variable to augment a program.

In addition, many commands — and Apple frameworks! — have "private"
environment variables not discussed in any documentation or man page. You'll look
at how to extract this information from executables later in this book.

stdin, stderr and stout

Using the launch options, you can control where to send the output of a program.

Type the following:

```
(lldb) process launch -o /tmp/ls_output.txt -- /Applications
```

The –o option tells LLDB to pipe stdout to the given file.

You'll see the following output:

```
Process 15194 launched: '/bin/ls' (arm64e)
Process 15194 exited with status = 0 (0x00000000)
```

Notice there's no output directly from ls.

Open another Terminal tab and run the following:

```
$ cat /tmp/ls_output.txt
```

It's your application's directory output again, as expected!

stdin, or standard input, also has a similar option, –i. To see it in action, first type the following:

```
(lldb) target delete
```

This removes ls as the target. Next, type this:

```
(lldb) target create /usr/bin/wc
```

This sets /usr/bin/wc as the new target. wc counts characters, words or lines in the input given to stdin.

You've swapped target executables for your LLDB session from ls to wc. Now, you need some data to provide to wc. Open a new Terminal tab and enter the following:

```
$ echo "hello world" > /tmp/wc_input.txt
```

You'll use this file to give wc some input.

Switch back to the LLDB session and enter the following:

```
(lldb) process launch -i /tmp/wc_input.txt
```

You'll see the following output:

```
Process 24511 launched: '/usr/bin/wc' (arm64e)
       1       2      12
Process 24511 exited with status = 0 (0x00000000)
```

This is functionally equivalent to the following:

```
$ wc < /tmp/wc_input.txt
```

Sometimes, you don't want a stdin. This is useful for GUI programs such as Xcode but doesn't really help for Terminal commands such as ls and wc.

To illustrate, run the wc target with no arguments, like so:

```
(lldb) run
```

The program will just sit there and hang because it's expecting to read something from stdin.

Give it some input by typing hello world. Press **Return**, then press **Control-D**, which is the end-of-transmission character. wc will parse the input and exit. You'll see the same output as you did earlier when using the file as the input.

Now, launch the process like this:

```
(lldb) process launch -n
```

You'll see that wc exits immediately with the following output:

```
Process 28849 launched: '/usr/bin/wc' (arm64e)
Process 28849 exited with status = 0 (0x00000000)
```

The -n option tells LLDB not to create a stdin; therefore, wc has no data to work with and exits immediately.

The curses Interface

If you've spent a lot of time debugging in Xcode, you might've become comfortable seeing the stack trace, the variables window and other data as you work with the debugger. In Terminal, you can use a `curses`-style GUI for a similar experience. At an LLDB prompt, type:

```
(lldb) gui
```

And a window will appear:

From here, you can step through code using the **N** key or step into code using **S**. You can also use the function keys to examine variables, stacks and frames.

To exit back to the regular LLDB console, press **F1** to bring up the LLDB menu, and then press **X** to exit.

Key Points

- Launch LLDB and attach to processes using −n, −p or −w switches.

- Use the −f switch to launch LLDB and then explicitly launch the process from within LLDB.

- Use `target create` and `target delete` to load and detach an executable to a running LLDB session.

- Use `process launch` to launch a process from within LLDB.

- Use −E flags to set environment variables for a target process.

- Use −i and −o to control where a target process should get its input and output.

- The `run` command is an alias for `process launch --`.

- The `gui` command gives an Xcode-esque interface for when you're using Terminal for your `lldb` session.

Where to Go From Here?

You can find more interesting options to play with via the `help` command, but that's for you to explore on your own.

For now, try attaching to GUI and non-GUI programs alike. It might seem like you can't understand much without the source code, but you'll discover in the upcoming sections how much information and control you have over these programs.

Chapter 4: Stopping in Code

Whether you're using Swift, Objective-C, C++, C, or an entirely different language in your technology stack, you'll need to learn how to create breakpoints. It's easy to click on the side panel in Xcode to create a breakpoint using the GUI, but the `lldb` console can give you much more control over breakpoints.

In this chapter, you're going to learn all about breakpoints and how to create them using LLDB.

Signals

For this chapter, you'll be looking at an Xcode project called **Signals** which you'll find in the resources bundle for this chapter.

Open up the **Signals** starter project using Xcode. Signals is a basic primary-detail project themed as an American football app that displays some rather nerdily-named offensive play calls.

The app monitors several Unix signals, handles them when received and displays them in a list.

Unix signals are a basic form of interprocess communication. For example, one of the signals, SIGSTOP, can be used to save the state and pause execution of a process, while its counterpart, SIGCONT, is sent to a program to resume execution. Both of these signals can be used by a debugger to pause and continue a program's execution.

Signals is an interesting application on several fronts, because it not only explores Unix signal handling, but also highlights what happens when a controlling process (lldb) handles the passing of Unix signals to the controlled process. By default, lldb has custom actions for handling different signals. Some signals are not passed onto the controlled process while lldb is attached.

In order to display a signal, you can either raise a Signal from within the application, or send a signal externally from a different application, like bash running in Terminal.

In addition, there's a `UISwitch` that toggles the signal handling. When the switch is toggled, it calls a C function `sigprocmask` to enable or disable the signal handlers that the Signals app is listening to.

Finally, the Signals application has a **Timeout** bar button which raises the `SIGSTOP` signal from within the application, essentially "freezing" the program. However, if `lldb` is attached to the Signals program (and by default it will be, when you build and run through Xcode), calling `SIGSTOP` will allow you to inspect the execution state with `lldb` while in Xcode.

Build and run the app on your preferred iOS Simulator running iOS 16 or greater. Once the Signals project is running, navigate to the Xcode console and pause the debugger.

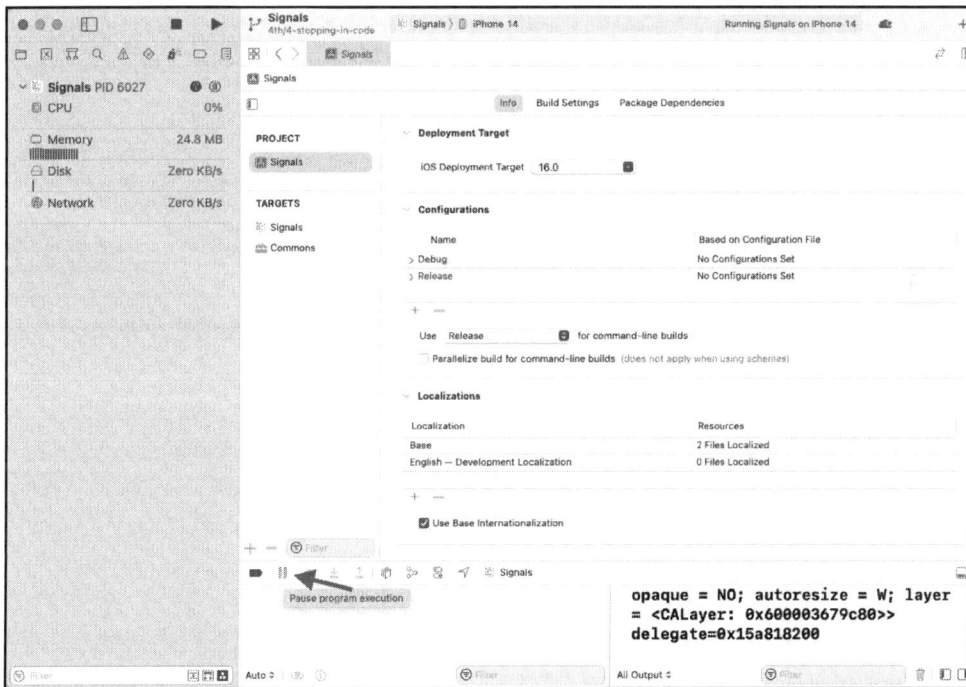

Resume Xcode by clicking the same button you used to pause and keep an eye on the Simulator. A new row will be added to the `UITableView` whenever the debugger stops then resumes execution. This is achieved by Signals monitoring the `SIGSTOP` Unix signal event and adding a row to the data model whenever it occurs. When a process is stopped, any new signals will not be immediately processed because the program is sort of, well, stopped.

Xcode Breakpoints

Before you go off learning the cool, shiny breakpoints through the lldb console, it's worth covering what you can achieve through Xcode alone.

Symbolic breakpoints are a great debugging feature of Xcode. They let you set a breakpoint on a **symbol** within your application. An example of a symbol is – [NSObject init], which refers to the init method of NSObject instances.

Symbolic breakpoints allow you to set a breakpoint on a symbol instead of a line of source code, allowing you to put breakpoints on Apple's code as well as your own. Once you create a symbolic breakpoint, you don't have to recreate it the next time the program launches.

You're now going to set a symbolic breakpoint to show all the instances of NSObject being created.

Kill the app if it's currently running.

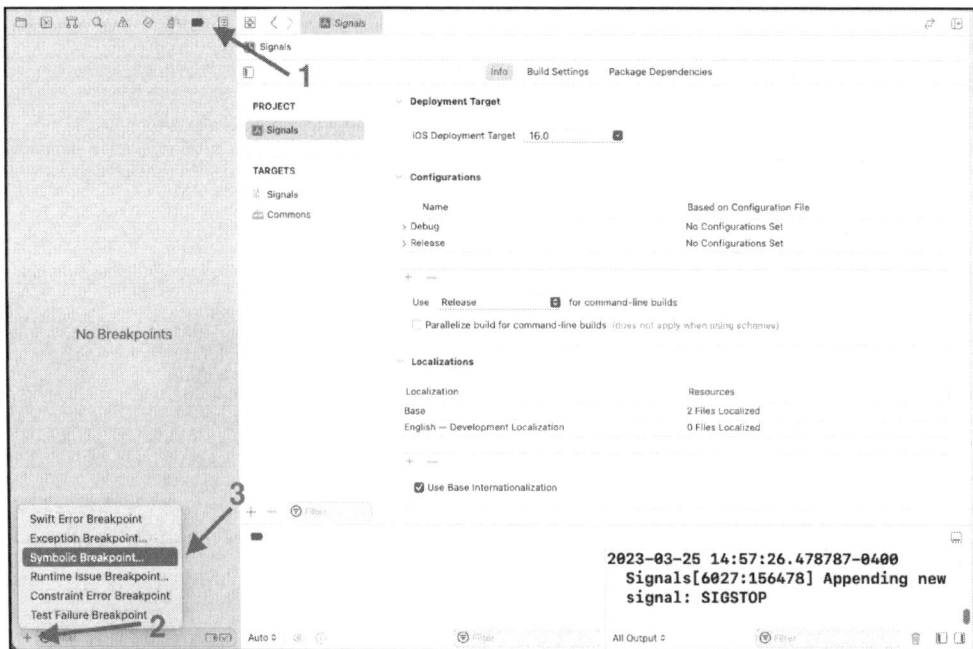

1. Switch to the **Breakpoint Navigator**.

2. In the bottom left, click the plus button to display the contextual menu.

3. Select the **Symbolic Breakpoint...** option.

A pop-up will appear. In the **Symbol** part of the popup type: `-[NSObject init]`. Under **Action**, select **Add Action** and then select **Debugger Command** from the dropdown. Next, enter `po [$arg1 class]` in the box below.

Finally, select **Automatically continue after evaluating actions**. Your popup should look similar to below:

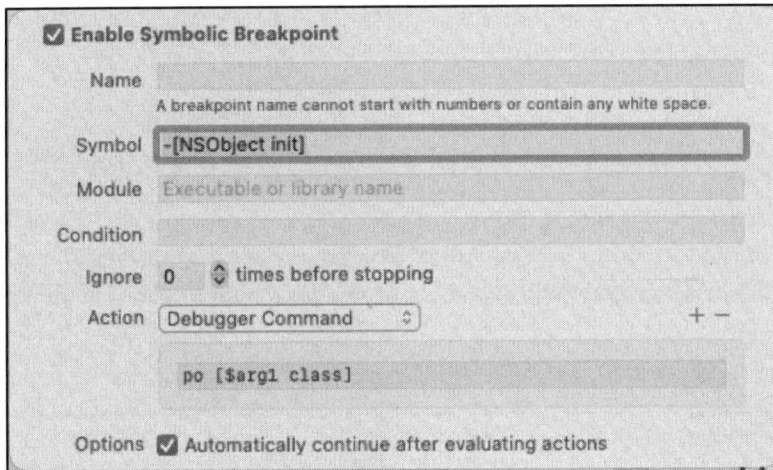

Build and run the app. Xcode will dump all the names of the classes it initializes while running the Signals app into the console pane of Xcode...which, upon viewing, is quite a lot. In fact, it's so many that my app sometimes crashed before it was done displaying class names.

What you've done here is set a breakpoint that fires each time `-[NSObject init]` is called. When the breakpoint fires, a command runs in `lldb`, and execution of the program continues automatically.

> **Note:** You'll learn how to properly use and manipulate registers in Chapter 11, "Assembly Register Calling Convention", but for now, simply know **$arg1** is synonymous to the register that's used for the first argument of a function call. Depending on your computer, this could be `$rdi` for x86_64 (Intel) machines, or `$x0` for the newer ARM64 (Apple Silicon) machines.

Once you've finished inspecting all the class names dumped out, delete the symbolic breakpoint by right-clicking the breakpoint in the breakpoint navigator and selecting **Delete Breakpoint**.

In addition to symbolic breakpoints, Xcode also supports several types of error breakpoints. One of these is the **Exception Breakpoint**. Sometimes, something goes wrong in your program and it just simply crashes. When this happens, your first reaction to this should be to enable an exception breakpoint, which will fire every time an exception is thrown. Xcode will show you the offending line, which greatly aids in hunting down the culprit responsible for the crash. Be mindful though, some older frameworks use exceptions during their normal operation and your breakpoint will get hit before it gets to your error. When this happens, just resume Xcode and eventually your real error will trigger the breakpoint.

Finally, there is the **Swift Error Breakpoint**, which stops any time Swift throws an error by essentially creating a breakpoint on the `swift_willThrow` method. This is a great option to use if you're working with any APIs that can be error-prone, as it lets you diagnose the situation quickly without making false assumptions about the correctness of your code. Swift throws errors using a different mechanism than C++ or Objective-C which is why you can't just use exception breakpoints in Swift.

lldb Breakpoint Syntax

Now that you've had a *crash* course in using the IDE debugging features of Xcode, it's time to learn how to create breakpoints through the `lldb` console. In order to create useful breakpoints, you need to learn how to query what you're looking for.

The `image` command is an excellent tool to help introspect details that will be vital for setting breakpoints.

There are two configurations you'll use in this book for code hunting. The first is the following:

```
(lldb) image lookup -n "-[UIViewController viewDidLoad]"
```

This command dumps the implementation address (the offset address of where this method is located within the framework's binary) of the function for `-[UIViewController viewDidLoad]`. The `-n` argument tells LLDB to look up either a symbol or function name. There are other arguments that tell LLDB to look up by offset or line number and more.

The output will be similar to below:

```
1 match found in /Applications/Xcode.app/Contents/Developer/
Platforms/iPhoneOS.platform/Library/Developer/CoreSimulator/
Profiles/Runtimes/iOS.simruntime/Contents/Resources/RuntimeRoot/
System/Library/PrivateFrameworks/UIKitCore.framework/UIKitCore:
        Address: UIKitCore[0x00000000004b9278]
(UIKitCore.__TEXT.__text + 4943316)
        Summary: UIKitCore`-[UIViewController viewDidLoad]
```

You can tell this is a relatively new iOS version due to the location of the –
[UIViewController viewDidLoad] method. Prior to iOS 12, this method was
located in UIKit, but has now since moved to UIKitCore likely due to the macOS/
iOS unification process.

Another useful, similar command is this:

```
(lldb) image lookup -rn test
```

This does a case-sensitive regex lookup for the word "test". If the lowercase word
"test" is found anywhere, in any function, in any of the modules (i.e. UIKit,
Foundation, Core Data, etc) loaded in the current executable, this command will spit
out the results. Because it is a regex lookup it also returns results when "test" is a
part of a longer word like "latest" or "datestamp".

> **Note**: Use the –n argument when you want exact matches (with quotes around
> your query if it contains spaces) and use the –rn arguments to do a regex
> search. The –n only command helps figure out the exact query to match a
> breakpoint which makes it unwieldy when dealing with long symbol names
> (which frequently occur in Swift). The –rn argument option will be heavily
> favored in this book since a smart regex can eliminate quite a bit of typing —
> as you'll soon find out.

Objective-C Properties

Learning how to query loaded code is essential for learning how to create
breakpoints on that code. Both Objective-C and Swift have specific naming
conventions when code is generated by the compiler. This is known as **name
mangling**.

For example, the following Objective-C class is declared in the Signals project:

```
@interface TestClass : NSObject
@property (nonatomic, strong) NSString *name;
@end
```

The compiler will generate code for both the setter and getter of the property name. The getter will look like:

```
-[TestClass name]
```

...while the setter looks like this:

```
-[TestClass setName:]
```

Build and run the Signals app if it isn't already running, then pause the program. Verify these methods do exist by typing the following into lldb:

```
(lldb) image lookup -n "-[TestClass name]"
```

In the console output, you'll get something similar to the following:

```
1 match found in /Users/lolz/Library/Developer/Xcode/
DerivedData/Signals-exknwuyeumkttfanwxtsssaetltk/Build/Products/
Debug-iphonesimulator/Signals.app/Signals:
        Address: Signals[0x0000000100002354]
(Signals.__TEXT.__text + 0)
        Summary: Signals`-[TestClass name] at TestClass.h:34
```

lldb dumps information about the function included in the executable. The output may look scary, but there are some good tidbits here.

> **Note:** The image lookup command can produce a lot of output that can be pretty hard on the eyes when a query matches a lot of code. In a later chapter, you'll build a cleaner alternative to lldb's image lookup command to save your eyes from looking at too much output.

The console output tells you lldb was able to find out this function was implemented in the Signals.app/Signals executable, at an offset of 0x0000000100002354 in the __TEXT segment of the __text section of the file (don't worry if that didn't make sense, this is a concept called Mach-O and will be explained in the "Low Level" section of this book). lldb was also able to tell that this method was declared on line 34 of TestClass.h.

You can check for the setter as well, like so:

```
(lldb) image lookup -n "-[TestClass setName:]"
```

You'll get output similar to the previous command, this time showing the implementation address and of the setter's declaration for name. Because the compiler created these methods at runtime, they don't actually exist at line 34 of **TestClass.h** until the code is run.

Stop the Signals app if it's running and open **TestClass.h**. Next, add a breakpoint to line 34 by clicking on the line number. Now open the Breakpoint Navigator. Notice that there is a single breakpoint set.

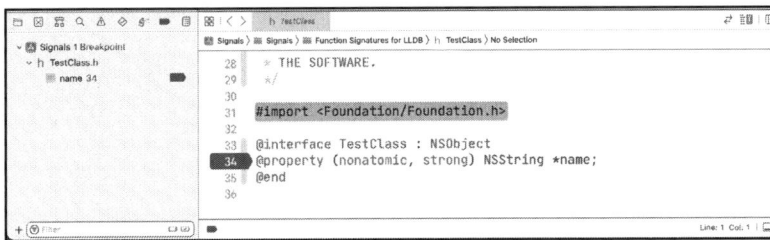

Run the app and Xcode adds two breakpoints: one for the synthesized setter and getter of the name property.

Objective-C Properties and Dot Notation

Something that is often misleading to entry level Objective-C (or Swift only) developers is the Objective-C dot notation syntax for properties.

Objective-C dot notation is a somewhat controversial compiler feature that allows properties to use a shorthand getter or setter. At compile time, though, dot notation is converted to standard syntax.

Consider the following:

```
TestClass *a = [[TestClass alloc] init];

// Both equivalent for setters
[a setName:@"hello, world"];
a.name = @"hello, world";

// Both equivalent for getters
NSString *b;
b = [a name]; // b = @"hello, world"
b = a.name;   // b = @"hello, world"
```

In the above example, the -[TestClass setName:] method is called twice, even with the dot notation. The compiler does not generate a separate -[TestClass .name] setter. The same can be said for the getter, -[TestClass name]. This is important to know if you're dealing with Objective-C code and trying to create breakpoints on the setters and getters of properties with dot notation.

Swift Properties

The syntax for a property is much different in Swift. Take a look at the code in **SwiftTestClass.swift** which contains the following:

```
class SwiftTestClass: NSObject {
  var name: String!
}
```

Make sure Signals is running and paused in lldb. Feel free to clear the lldb console by pressing **Command-K** or clicking the trashcan icon in the debug window to start fresh.

In the lldb console, type the following:

```
(lldb) image lookup -rn Signals.SwiftTestClass.name.setter
```

You'll get output similar to below:

```
1 match found in /Users/lolz/Library/Developer/Xcode/
DerivedData/Signals-exknwuyeumkttfanwxtsssaetltk/Build/Products/
Debug-iphonesimulator/Signals.app/Signals:
        Address: Signals[0x000000010000b0ec]
(Signals.__TEXT.__text + 36248)
        Summary: Signals`Signals.SwiftTestClass.name.setter :
Swift.Optional<Swift.String> at SwiftTestClass.swift:34
```

Hunt for the information after the word Summary in the output. There are a couple of interesting things to note here.

Do you see how long the function name is!? This whole thing needs to be typed out for *one* valid Swift breakpoint! If you wanted to set a breakpoint on this setter, you'd have to type the following:

```
(lldb) b Signals.SwiftTestClass.name.setter :
Swift.Optional<Swift.String>
```

This symbol is actually a *pretty*, unmangled representation of the actual function name, **$s7Signals14SwiftTestClassC4nameSSSgvs**. lldb will hide the unmangled names by default, but you can view them by adding the --verbose option, or just -v, in the image lookup command.

You can verify these two functions are the same with the following Terminal command:

```
% xcrun swift-demangle s7Signals14SwiftTestClassC4nameSSSgvs  #
note the dollar sign is removed from function
$s7Signals14SwiftTestClassC4nameSSSgvs --->
Signals.SwiftTestClass.name.setter : Swift.String?
```

Using regular expressions is an attractive alternative to typing out this monstrosity.

Apart from the length of the Swift function name you produced, note how the Swift property is formed. The function signature containing the property name has the word setter immediately following the property. Perhaps the same convention works for the getter method as well?

Search for the SwiftTestClass setter and getter for the name property, at the same time, using the following regular expression query:

```
(lldb) image lookup -rn Signals.SwiftTestClass.name
```

This uses a regex query to dump everything that contains the phrase Signals.SwiftTestClass.name.

Since this is a regular expression, the periods (.) are evaluated as wildcards, which in turn matches periods in the actual function signatures.

You'll get a fair bit of output, but hone in every time you see the word **Summary** in the console output. You'll find the output matches the getter, (Signals.SwiftTestClass.name.getter) the setter, (Signals.SwiftTestClass.name.setter), as well as some helper methods for Swift constructors and some generated methods for using key paths.

There's a pattern for the function names for Swift properties:

ModuleName.Classname.PropertyName.(getter|setter)

The ability to dump methods, find a pattern, and narrow your search scope is a great way to uncover the Swift/Objective-C language internals as you work to create smart breakpoints in your code.

Finally... Creating Breakpoints

Now that you know how to query the existence of functions and methods in your code, it's time to start creating breakpoints on them.

If you already have the Signals app running, stop and restart the application, then click the pause button to stop the application and bring up the lldb console.

There are several different ways to create breakpoints. The most basic way is to simply type the letter **b** followed by the name of your breakpoint. This is fairly easy in Objective-C and C, since the names are short and easy to type (e.g. -[NSObject init] or -[UIView setAlpha:]). As demonstrated above, they're quite tricky to type in C++ and Swift, since the compiler turns your methods into symbols with rather long names.

Since UIKit is primarily Objective-C (at the time of this writing at least!), create a breakpoint using the b argument, like so:

```
(lldb) b -[UIViewController viewDidLoad]
```

You'll see the following output:

```
Breakpoint 1: where = UIKitCore`-[UIViewController viewDidLoad],
address = 0x00000001845f0278
```

When you create a valid breakpoint, the console will spit out some information about that breakpoint. In this particular case, the breakpoint was created as **Breakpoint 1** since this was the first breakpoint in this particular debugging session. As you create more breakpoints, this breakpoint ID will increment. If lldb complains that it's unable "to resolve breakpoint to any actual locations", check the spelling and capitalization of your symbol.

Resume the debugger. Once you've resumed execution, a new SIGSTOP signal will be displayed. Tap on the cell to bring up the detail UIViewController. The program should pause when viewDidLoad of the detail view controller is called.

> **Note**: Like a lot of shorthand commands, b is an abbreviation for another, longer lldb command. Run the help with the b command to figure out the actual command yourself and learn all the cool tricks b can do under the hood.

In addition to the b command, there's another longer `breakpoint set` command, which has a slew of options available. You'll explore these options over the next couple of sections. Many of the commands will stem from various options of the `breakpoint set` command.

Regex Breakpoints

Another extremely powerful command is the regular expression breakpoint, `rbreak`, which is an abbreviation for `breakpoint set -r %1`. You can quickly create many breakpoints using smart regular expressions to stop wherever you want.

Going back to the previous example with the egregiously long Swift property function names, instead of typing:

```
(lldb) b Signals.SwiftTestClass.name.setter :
Swift.Optional<Swift.String>
```

You can simply type:

```
(lldb) rb SwiftTestClass.name.setter
```

The `rb` command will expand out to `rbreak` (provided you don't have any other LLDB commands that begin with "rb"). This will create a breakpoint on the setter property of `name` in `SwiftTestClass`

To be even more brief, you could simply use the following:

```
(lldb) rb name\.setter
```

This will produce a breakpoint on everything that contains the phrase `name.setter`. This will work if you know you don't have any other Swift properties called `name` within your project. This command will create breakpoints for every class, including classes in imported libraries, that contains a "name" property that has a setter. You'll look at filtering symbols to match specific images and namespaces later in this chapter.

Let's up the complexity of these regular expressions.

Create a breakpoint on every Objective-C instance method of `UIViewController`. Type the following into your `lldb` session:

```
(lldb) rb '\-\[UIViewController\ '
```

lldb should respond that it has set a breakpoint in about 800 or so locations.

The back slashes are regex escape characters to indicate you want the literal character to be in the regular expression search. As a result, this query breaks on every method containing the string `-[UIViewController` followed by a space.

But wait… what about Objective-C categories? They take on the form of `(-|+) [ClassName(categoryName) method]`. You'll have to rewrite the regular expression to include categories as well.

Type the following into your lldb session and when prompted type y to confirm:

```
(lldb) breakpoint delete
```

This command deletes all the breakpoints you have set.

Next, type the following:

```
(lldb) rb '\-\[UIViewController(\ |\()'
```

This regular expression is tweaked so either a space or an open parenthesis follows the symbol name. lldb should respond with more locations than before. Type `breakpoint list` to confirm that a few of the matches contain categories of `UIViewController` if you like.

Regex breakpoints let you capture a wide variety of breakpoints with a single expression.

Breakpoint Scope

You can limit the scope of your breakpoints to a certain file, using the `-f` option. For example, you could type the following:

```
(lldb) rb . -f DetailViewController.swift
```

This would be useful if you were debugging **DetailViewController.swift**. It would set a breakpoint on all the property getters/setters, blocks/closures, extensions/categories, and functions/methods in this file. `-f` is known as a **scope limitation**.

If you were completely crazy and a fan of pain (the doctors call that masochistic?), you could omit the scope limitation and simply do this:

```
(lldb) rb .
```

This will create a breakpoint on everything... Yes, everything! This will create breakpoints on all the code in the Signals project, all the code in UIKit as well as Foundation, all the event run loop code that gets fired at (hopefully) 60 hertz — everything. As a result, expect to type `continue` in the debugger a fair bit if you execute this.

There are other ways to limit the scope of your searches. You can limit to a single library using the –s option:

```
(lldb) rb . -s Commons
```

This would set a breakpoint on everything within the `Commons` library, which is a dynamic library contained within the Signals project.

This is not limited to your code; you can use the same tactic to create a breakpoint on every function in UIKitCore, like so:

```
(lldb) rb . -s UIKitCore
```

Even *that* is still a little crazy. There are a lot of UIKitCore methods in iOS 16.0, so this command should set breakpoints in over 160,000 locations. How about only stopping on the first method in UIKitCore you hit, and simply continue? The –o option offers a solution for this. It creates what is known as a "one-shot" breakpoint.

When a one-shot breakpoint gets hit, the breakpoint is deleted. So it'll only ever hit once.

To see this in action, type the following in your LLDB session:

```
(lldb) breakpoint delete
(lldb) rb . -s UIKitCore -o 1
```

Be patient while your computer executes this command, as `lldb` has to set your breakpoint in those 160,000+ locations. Also make sure you are using the Simulator, or else you'll wait for a very long time!

Next, continue the debugger, and click on a cell in the table view. The debugger stops on the first UIKitCore method this action calls. Finally, continue the debugger, and the breakpoint will no longer fire. Pause the app and type `breakpoint list` to confirm that `No breakpoints currently set`.

> **Note**: `lldb` is actually modifying memory when creating many breakpoints with this approach. That is, `lldb` will determine the address for the symbol loaded into memory, create an assembly instruction where control will stop letting `lldb` (or more precisely, `debugserver`) "catch" the program. An explanation of these internals can be found in Jonathan Levin's Make Debugging Great Again (http://newosxbook.com/articles/MDGA.html) article.

Other Cool Breakpoint Options

The –L option lets you filter by source language. So, if you wanted to only go after Swift code in the `Commons` module of the Signals project, you could do the following:

```
(lldb) breakpoint set -L swift -r . -s Commons
```

This would set a breakpoint on every Swift method within the Commons module.

What if you wanted to go after something interesting around a Swift `if let` but totally forgot where in your application it is? You can use **source regex breakpoints** to help figure locations of interest! Like so:

```
(lldb) breakpoint set -A -p "if let"
```

This will create a breakpoint on every source code location that contains `"if let"`. You can of course get waaaaaay more fancy since the –p takes a regular expression breakpoint to go after complicated expressions. The –A option says to search in all source files known to the project.

If you wanted to filter the above breakpoint query to only `MainViewController.swift` and `DetailViewController.swift`, you could do the following:

```
(lldb) breakpoint set -p "if let" -f MainViewController.swift -f
DetailViewController.swift
```

Notice how the –A has gone, and how each –f will let you specify a single filename. I am lazy, so I'll usually default to –A to give me all files and drill in from there.

Finally, you can also filter by a specific module as well. If you wanted to create a breakpoint for `if let` for anything in the Signals executable (while ignoring other frameworks like Commons), you could do this:

```
(lldb) breakpoint set -p "if let" -s Signals -A
```

This will grab all source files (–A), but filter those to only the ones that belong to the Signals executable (with the –s Signals option).

Breakpoint Actions

You can also perform actions when suspended on a breakpoint in lldb just like using Xcode's Symbolic Breakpoint window.

You will make a breakpoint which prints the UIViewController instance whenever viewDidLoad gets hit, but you'll do it via lldb console. Then, you'll export this breakpoint to a file so you can show how cool you are to your co-workers by using the breakpoint read and breakpoint write commands to share your breakpoint with them!

First off, delete all breakpoints:

```
(lldb) breakpoint delete
```

Now create the following (complex!) breakpoint:

```
(lldb) breakpoint set -n "-[UIViewController viewDidLoad]" -C
"po $arg1" -G1
```

Make sure to use a capital –C, since lldb's –c performs a different option!

This command creates a breakpoint on -[UIViewController viewDidLoad], then executes the (C)ommand "po $arg1", which prints out the instance of the UIViewController. From there, the –G1 option tells the breakpoint to automatically continue after executing the command.

Verify the console displays the expected information by triggering a viewDidLoad by tapping on one of the UITableViewCells containing a Unix signal.

Now, how can you send this to a coworker? Pause the Signals app again and in lldb, type the following:

```
(lldb) breakpoint write -f /tmp/br.json
```

This will write all the breakpoints in your session, as well as any from the Breakpoint navigator, to the /tmp/br.json file. You can specify a single breakpoint or list of breakpoints by breakpoint ID, but that's for you to determine via the help documentation on your own time.

You can verify the breakpoint data either in Terminal or via lldb by using the **platform shell** command to execute terminal commands without leaving lldb.

Use the **cat** Terminal command to display the breakpoint data.

```
(lldb) platform shell cat /tmp/br.json
```

This means that you can send over this file to your coworker and have her open it via the **breakpoint read** command.

To simulate this, delete all breakpoints again.

```
(lldb) breakpoint delete
```

You will now have a clean debugging session with no breakpoints.

Now, re-import your custom breakpoint command:

```
(lldb) breakpoint read -f /tmp/br.json
```

Once again, if you were to trigger the UIViewController's viewDidLoad method, the instance will be printed out due to your custom breakpoint logic! Using these commands, you can easily send and receive lldb breakpoint commands to help replicate a hard to catch bug!

Modifying and Removing Breakpoints

Now that you have a basic understanding of how to create these breakpoints, you might be wondering how you can alter them. What if you found the object you were interested in and wanted to delete the breakpoint, or temporarily disable it? What if you need to modify the breakpoint to perform a specific action next time it triggers?

First, you'll need to discover how to uniquely identify a breakpoint or a group of breakpoints.

Build and run the Signals app to get a clean LLDB session. Next, pause the debugger and type the following into lldb:

```
(lldb) b main
```

The output will look something similar to the following:

```
Breakpoint 1: 105 locations.
```

This creates a breakpoint with 105 locations, matching the function "main" in various modules.

In this case, the breakpoint ID is 1, because it's the first breakpoint you created in this session. If you had set any breakpoints in the Breakpoint navigator, they would already be created, so your ID would be greater than 1. To see details about this breakpoint you can use the breakpoint list subcommand.

Type the following:

```
(lldb) breakpoint list 1
```

The output will look similar to the truncated output below:

```
(lldb) br list
Current breakpoints:
1: name = 'main', locations = 105, resolved = 105, hit count = 0
   1.1: where = Signals`main at AppDelegate.swift, address =
0x000000010070122c, resolved, hit count = 0
   1.2: where = Foundation`-[NSDirectoryTraversalOperation main],
address = 0x0000000180758eb8, resolved, hit count = 0
   1.3: where = Foundation`-[NSFilesystemItemRemoveOperation
main], address = 0x000000018075a6a8, resolved, hit count = 0
   1.4: where = Foundation`-[NSFilesystemItemMoveOperation main],
address = 0x000000018075ac80, resolved, hit count = 0
   1.5: where = Foundation`-[NSOperation main], address =
0x00000001807d4554, resolved, hit count = 0
   1.6: where = Foundation`-[NSBlockOperation main], address =
0x00000001807d571c, resolved, hit count = 0
   1.7: where = Foundation`-[NSInvocationOperation main], address
= 0x00000001807d5cbc, resolved, hit count = 0
   1.8: where = Foundation`-[_NSBarrierOperation main], address =
0x00000001807d5fe4, resolved, hit count = 0
```

This shows the details of that breakpoint, including all locations that include the word "main".

A cleaner way to view this is to type the following:

```
(lldb) breakpoint list 1 -b
```

This will give you output that is a little easier on the visual senses. If you have a breakpoint ID that encapsulates a lot of breakpoints, this brief flag is a good solution.

If you want to query all the breakpoints in your lldb session, simply omit the ID like so:

```
(lldb) breakpoint list
```

You can also specify multiple breakpoint IDs and ranges:

```
(lldb) breakpoint list 1 3
(lldb) breakpoint list 1-3
```

Using breakpoint delete to delete all breakpoints is a bit heavy-handed. You can simply use the same ID pattern used in the breakpoint list command to delete a set.

You can delete a single breakpoint by specifying the ID like so:

```
(lldb) breakpoint delete 1
```

However, your breakpoint for "main" had 105 locations (maybe more or less depending on the iOS version). You can also delete a single location:

```
(lldb) breakpoint delete 1.1
```

This would delete the first sub-breakpoint of breakpoint 1, which results in only one main function breakpoint removed while keeping the remaining main breakpoints active.

Key Points

- The **Breakpoint Navigator** in Xcode is a wrapper around many of the console `breakpoint` commands.

- **Symbolic Breakpoints** can be set on symbols in your app or in any loaded library.

- Use `image lookup` with the `-n` or `-rn` switches to find out where a symbol is defined.

- The compiler synthesizes getters and setters for properties at runtime, so sometimes you have to launch an app before you can set breakpoints.

- `rbreak` is an abbreviated command for `breakpoint set -r` that lets you use regular expressions to match symbol names to breakpoint on.

- The `-s` and `-f` switches on `breakpoint set` allow you to constrain how many locations are included in a breakpoint.

- The `-p` switch allows you to set a breakpoint on an expression in your source code.

- The `read` and `write` subcommands of `breakpoint` allow you to export and import breakpoints into `.json` files for sharing or saving.

- The `breakpoint list` and `breakpoint delete` commands take breakpoint ID numbers or ranges to constrain their actions.

Where to Go From Here?

You've covered a lot in this chapter. Breakpoints are a big topic and mastering the art of quickly finding an item of interest is essential to becoming a debugging expert. You've also started exploring function searching using regular expressions. Now would be a great time to brush up on regular expression syntax, as you'll be using lots of regular expressions in the rest of this book.

You've only begun to discover how the compiler generates functions in Objective-C and Swift. Try to figure out the syntax for stopping on Objective-C blocks or Swift closures. Once you've done that, try to design a breakpoint that only stops on Objective-C blocks within the Commons framework of the Signals project. These are regex skills you'll need in the future to construct ever more complicated breakpoints.

Chapter 5: Expression

Now that you've learned how to set breakpoints, it's time to learn how to query and manipulate the software you're debugging. In this chapter, you'll learn about the **expression** command, which allows you to inspect variables and execute arbitrary code. *This is kind of a big deal*, because you can declare, initialize and inject code on the fly without recompiling your program!

Formatting With p and po

You might be familiar with the common debugging command, **po**. po is used to display information in your program or execute code. If lldb knows how to interpret the value you've po'd, it will be able to interpret that value and display meaningful information to you. For example lldb can interpret: a C int, Objective-C NSObject or a Swift struct, a variable in source code, a register's value, etc.

If you do a quick help po in the lldb console, you'll find po is actually a shorthand expression for expression -O --. The -O argument is used to print the object's **description**.

po's often overlooked sibling, **p**, is another abbreviation with the -O option omitted, resulting in expression --. The format of what p will print out is dependent on the *LLDB type system*. LLDB's type formatting helps determine a variable's description in lldb and is fully customizable.

In the following sections, you'll learn how to modify the output of both p and po to be more useful for your debugging needs.

You can influence the content of po in the source code of a debugged program. Likewise, one can control the formatting of what p displays via lldb's options/public APIs.

Modifying an Object's Description

In order to change how lldb displays an object using po, you needs to modify an object's description in the source code. You will continue using the Signals project for this chapter.

Open the **Signals** project in Xcode. Open **MainViewController.swift** and add the following code above viewDidLoad():

```
override var description: String {
  return "Yay! debugging " + super.description
}
```

In viewDidLoad, add the following line of code below super.viewDidLoad():

```
print("\(self)")
```

Put a breakpoint just after the print method you created in the viewDidLoad() of **MainViewController.swift**. Do this using the Xcode GUI breakpoint side panel.

Build and run the application.

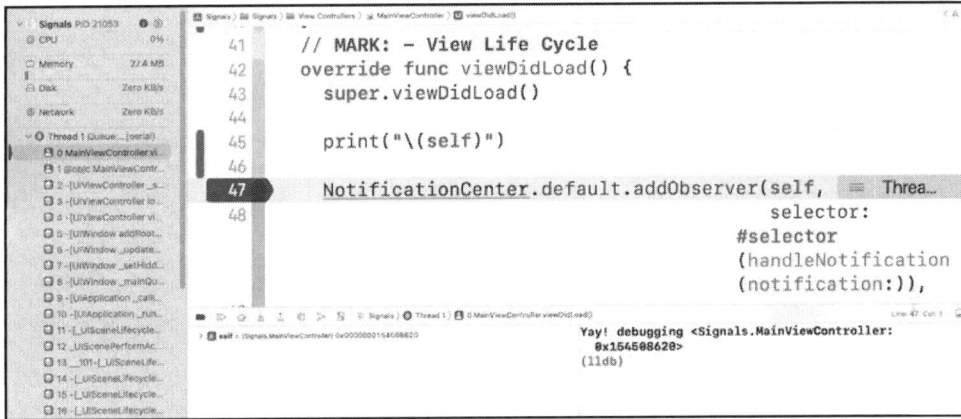

Once the Signals project stops at viewDidLoad(), type the following into the lldb console:

```
(lldb) po self
```

You'll get output similar to the following:

```
Yay! debugging <Signals.MainViewController: 0x14851c520>
```

Take note of the output of the print statement and how it matches the po self you just executed in the debugger.

You can also take it a step further. NSObject has an additional method description used for debugging called **debugDescription**. Add the following below your description variable definition:

```
override var debugDescription: String {
  return "debugDescription: " + super.debugDescription
}
```

Build and run the application. When the debugger stops at the breakpoint, print self again:

```
(lldb) po self
```

The output from the lldb console will look similar to the following:

```
debugDescription: Yay! debugging <Signals.MainViewController:
0x15c608650>
```

Notice how the po self and the output of self from the print command now differ, since you implemented debugDescription. When you print an object from lldb, it's debugDescription that gets called, rather than description. Neat!

> **Note**: The description and debugDescription actually originate from Objective-C logic integrated into lldb. Swift does provide an elegant wrapper around this idea with a public protocol called **CustomDebugStringConvertible**, which requires the adopter to implement the debugDescription method. This protocol is only required for Swift classes that don't explicitly inherit from NSObject (i.e. class A { }).

As you can see, having a description or debugDescription when working with an NSObject class or subclass will influence the output of po.

> **Note**: A surprisingly easy and simple anti-debugging measure to frustrate script kiddies is to return an empty string for description and debugDescription. r/jailbreakdeveloperss won't know what hit 'em. :]

So which NSObject classes override these description methods? Using image lookup command from the previous chapter can answer this. Your learnings from previous chapters are already coming in handy!

If, say, you wanted to know all the Objective-C classes that override debugDescription, you can query all the methods with:

```
(lldb) image lookup -rn '\ debugDescription\]'
```

Based upon the output, it seems the authors of the Foundation framework have added the debugDescription to a lot of foundation types like NSArray, to make our debugging lives easier. In addition, there are also private classes that have overridden debugDescription methods as well.

You may notice one of them in the listing is **CALayer**. This a public class used for rendering 2D UI on iOS, and performing efficient animations. Take a look at the difference between description and debugDescription in CALayer.

In your lldb console, type the following:

```
(lldb) po self.view!.layer.description
```

You'll see something similar to the following:

```
"<CALayer: 0x600002e9eb00>"
```

That's a little boring. Now type the following:

```
(lldb) po self.view!.layer
```

You'll see something similar to the following:

```
<CALayer:0x600001829a80; name = "VC:Signals.MainViewController";
position = CGPoint (195 422); bounds = CGRect (0 0; 390 844);
delegate = <UITableView: 0x131065400; frame = (0 0; 390 844);
clipsToBounds = YES; autoresize = W+H; gestureRecognizers =
<NSArray: 0x600001608960>; layer = <CALayer: 0x600001829a80>;
contentOffset: {0, 0}; contentSize: {0, 0};
adjustedContentInset: {0, 0, 0, 0}; dataSource: Yay! debugging
<Signals.MainViewController: 0x132020a70>>; sublayers =
(<CALayer: 0x600001829d40>, <CALayer: 0x600001829d80>);
masksToBounds = YES; allowsGroupOpacity = YES; name =
VC:Signals.MainViewController; backgroundColor = <CGColor
0x600003c56dc0> [<CGColorSpace 0x600003c721c0>
(kCGColorSpaceICCBased; kCGColorSpaceModelRGB; sRGB
IEC61966-2.1; extended range)] ( 0.980392 0.980392 0.980392 1 )>
```

That's much more interesting — and much more useful! Obviously the developers of Core Animation decided the plain description should be just the object reference, but if you're in the debugger, you'll want to see more information.

Next, while you're still stopped in the debugger (and if not, get back to the viewDidLoad() breakpoint), execute the p command on self, like so:

```
(lldb) p self
```

You'll get something similar to the truncated output below:

```
Signals.MainViewController) $R2 = 0x0000000132020a70 {
  UIKit.UITableViewController = {
    baseUIViewController@0 = {
      baseUIResponder@0 = {
        baseNSObject@0 = {
          isa = Signals.MainViewController
        }
      }
    }
    _overrideTransitioningDelegate = 0x0000000000000000
    _view = some {
      some = 0x0000000131065400 {
        baseUIScrollView@0 = {
...
```

This will dump the full internals of the MainViewController instance along with all the internal variables from a UIViewController. This might look scary, but break it down.

First, lldb spits out the class name of self. In this case, Signals.MainViewController.

Next follows a reference ($R2) which you can use to refer to this object from now on within this lldb session. Yours will vary as this is a number lldb increments each time you use p or po. This reference is useful if you ever want to get back to this object later in the session, perhaps when you're in a different scope and self is no longer the same object. In that case, you can refer back to this object as $R2. To see how, type the following:

```
(lldb) p $R2
```

You'll see the same information printed out again. You'll learn more about these lldb variables later in this chapter.

After the $R2 variable name is the address to this object in memory, followed by some output specific to this type of class. In this case, it shows the details relevant to UITableViewController, which is the superclass of MainViewController. The internal variables of UITableViewController are displayed as well in a higher indentation level.

> **Note**: Normally, internal variables of a class are hidden from end users when you don't have the source code. However, the nice thing about Objective-C is lldb (and other reverse engineering tools) can extract this private information to rebuild the class's internal layout. The same couldn't be said for a C struct whose names have been removed from a binary.

As you can see, the meat of the output of the p command is different to the po command. The output of p is dependent upon **type formatting**: internal data structures the lldb authors have added to every (noteworthy) data structure in Objective-C, Swift, and other languages. It's important to note the formatting for Swift is under active development with every LLVM release, so the output of p for MainViewController might be different for you when you try on your version of Xcode.

Fortunately, you have the power to change lldb's default type formatters if you so desire. In your lldb session, type the following:

```
(lldb) type summary add Signals.MainViewController --summary-
string "Wahoo!"
```

You've now told lldb you just want to return the static string, "Wahoo!", whenever you print out an instance of the MainViewController class. The Signals prefix is essential for Swift classes since Swift includes the module in the classname to prevent namespace collisions. Use lldb to print out self now:

```
(lldb) p self
```

The output should look similar to the following:

```
(lldb) (Signals.MainViewController) $R7 = 0x0000000132020a70
Wahoo!
```

This formatting will be remembered by lldb across app launches, so be sure to remove it when you're done playing with the p command. This can be done via the following:

```
(lldb) type summary clear
```

Typing p self will now go back to the default implementation created by the lldb formatting authors. Type formatting is an extensive topic and the lldb authors provide a good resource (https://lldb.llvm.org/use/variable.html) describing how to use it.

Another way to get information about an object is to insert a dump command into your source code.

In **MainViewController.swift**, replace:

```
print("\(self)")
```

With the following:

```
dump(self)
```

Finally, build and run the app. The dump command prints the debugDescription of the object as well as data about its hierarchy and variables, kind of a mixture of what you get from print, po and p.

Swift vs Objective-C Debugging Contexts

It's important to note there are two debugging contexts when debugging your program: a non-Swift debugging context and a Swift context. By default, when you stop in Objective-C code, lldb will use the non-Swift (Objective-C, C, C++) debugging context, and if you're stopped in Swift code, lldb will use the Swift context. Sounds logical, right?

If you stop the debugger out of the blue (for example, if you click the process pause button in Xcode), lldb will choose the non-Swift context by default.

Make sure the GUI Swift breakpoint you've created in the previous section is still enabled and build and run the app. When the breakpoint hits, type the following into your LLDB session:

```
(lldb) po [UIApplication sharedApplication]
```

lldb will throw a cranky error at you:

```
error: <EXPR>:8:16: error: expected ',' separator
[UIApplication sharedApplication]
               ^
               ,
```

You've stopped in Swift code, so you're in the Swift context. But you're trying to execute Objective-C code. That won't work. Similarly, in the Objective-C context, doing a po on a Swift object will not work.

You can force the expression to use the Objective-C context with the −l option to select the language. However, since the po expression is mapped to expression −0 −−, you'll be unable to use the po command since the arguments you provide come *after* the −−, which means you'll have to type out the expression. In lldb, type the following:

```
(lldb) expression -l objc -O -- [UIApplication
sharedApplication]
```

Here you've told lldb to use the objc language for Objective-C. You can also use objc++ for Objective-C++ if necessary.

lldb will now display the memory location of the shared application object. Try the same thing in Swift. Since you're already stopped in the Swift context, try to print the UIApplication reference using Swift syntax, like so:

```
(lldb) po UIApplication.shared
```

You'll get the same address as you did printing with the Objective-C context. Resume the program, by typing c or continue, then pause the Signals application out of the blue.

From there, press the up arrow to bring up the same Swift command you just executed and see what happens:

```
(lldb) po UIApplication.shared
```

Again, lldb will be cranky:

```
error: <user expression 2>:1:15: property 'shared' not found on
object of type 'UIApplication'
UIApplication.shared
```

Remember, stopping out of the blue will put lldb in the Objective-C context. That's why you're getting this error when trying to execute Swift code.

You should always be aware of which language lldb expects when you are paused in the debugger.

User Defined Variables

As you saw earlier, lldb will automatically create local variables on your behalf when printing out objects. You can create your own variables as well.

Remove all the breakpoints from the program and build and run the app. Stop the debugger out of the blue so it defaults to the Objective-C context. From there type:

```
(lldb) po id test = [NSObject new]
```

lldb will execute this code, which creates a new NSObject and stores it to the test variable. Now, print the test variable in the console:

```
(lldb) po test
```

You'll get an error like the following:

```
error: <user expression 4>:1:1: function 'test' with unknown
type must be given a function type
test
^~~~
```

This is because you need to prepend variables you want lldb to remember with the **$** character.

Declare test again with the $ in front:

```
(lldb) po id $test = [NSObject new]
(lldb) po $test
```

Now, lldb will happily display the memory location and type of your new object. This variable was created in the Objective-C object. But what happens if you try to access this from the Swift context? Try it, by typing the following:

```
(lldb) expression -l swift -O -- $test
```

So far so good. Now try executing a Swift-styled method on this Objective-C class.

```
(lldb) expression -l swift -O -- $test.description
```

You'll get an error like this:

```
error: <EXPR>:3:1: error: cannot find '$test' in scope
$test
^~~~~
```

If you create an lldb variable in the Objective-C context, then move to the Swift context, don't expect everything to "just work", as a different context is used.

So how could creating references in lldb actually be used in a real life situation? You can grab the reference to an object and execute (as well as debug!) arbitrary methods of your choosing. To see this in action, create a symbolic breakpoint on MainViewController's parent view controller, **MainContainerViewController** using an Xcode symbolic breakpoint for MainContainerViewController's viewDidLoad.

In the Symbol section, type the following:

```
Signals.MainContainerViewController.viewDidLoad
```

Your breakpoint should look like the following:

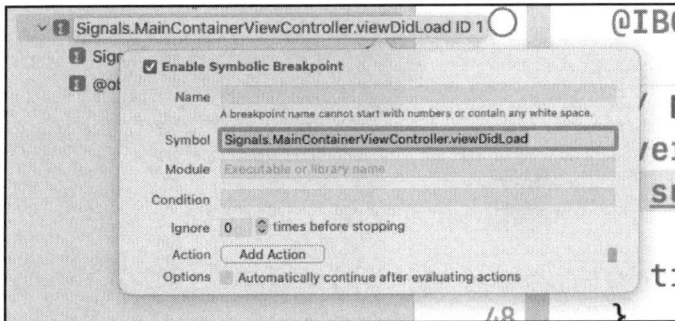

Build and run the app. Notice that Xcode creates two breakpoints for your symbol. It will first stop on the @objc
`Signals.MainContainerViewController.viewDidLoad()`. This is a little too early. Either click the continue button in Xcode or type c in the lldb window to continue execution. Xcode will now break on
`MainContainerViewController.viewDidLoad()` in the swift context. From there, type the following:

```
(lldb) p self
```

Since this is the first argument you executed in the Swift debugging context, lldb will create the variable, **$R0**. Resume execution of the program by typing c or continue in LLDB.

Note: Remember in the last chapter when you saw the compiler creating synthesized getters and setters for your breakpoints? The same thing is happening here. There is an underlying Objective-C class because this code is using UIKit and MainContainerViewController is subclassing UIViewController. So, your symbol gets two matches. You can disable the @objc version in the Breakpoint navigator by clicking on the breakpoint icon or in the lldb console by typing breakpoint disable and supplying the id number. So, if the main breakpoint was ID 1, the two child breakpoints will be ID 1.1 and 1.2. Alternatively, just remember to continue when you stop at the Objective-C breakpoint.

Now you don't have a reference to the instance of `MainContainerViewController` through the use of `self` since the execution has left `viewDidLoad()` and moved on to bigger and better run loop events.

Oh, wait, you still have that `$R0` variable! You can now reference `MainContainerViewController` and even execute arbitrary methods to help debug your code.

Pause the app in the debugger manually, then type the following:

```
(lldb) po $R0.title
```

Unfortunately, you get:

```
error: use of undeclared identifier '$R0'
```

You stopped the debugger out of the blue! Remember, LLDB will default to Objective-C; you'll need to use the –l option to stay in the Swift context:

```
(lldb) expression -O -l swift -- $R0.title
```

The output will be similar to the following:

```
▿ Optional<String>
  - some : "Quarterback"
```

Of course, this is the title of the view controller, shown in the navigation bar.

Now, type the following:

```
(lldb) expression -l swift -- $R0.title = "💩💩💩💩💩"
```

Resume the app by typing c or pressing the play button in Xcode.

> **Note**: To quickly access a poop emoji on your macOS machine, press **Command-Control-Space**. From there, you can easily hunt down the correct emoji by searching for the phrase "poop."

It's the small things in life you cherish!

As you can see, you can easily manipulate variables as you wish.

In addition, you can also create a breakpoint on code, execute the code, and cause the breakpoint to be hit. This can be useful if you're in the middle of debugging something and want to step through a function with certain inputs to see how it operates.

For example, you still have the symbolic breakpoint in viewDidLoad(), so try executing that method to inspect the code. Pause execution of the program, then type:

```
(lldb) expression -l swift -O -- $R0.viewDidLoad()
```

Nothing happened. The breakpoint didn't hit. What gives? In fact, MainContainerViewController *did* execute the method, but by default, lldb will ignore any breakpoints when executing commands. You can disable this option with the -i option.

Type the following into your lldb session:

```
(lldb) expression -l swift -O -i 0 -- $R0.viewDidLoad()
```

lldb will now break on the `viewDidLoad()` symbolic breakpoint you created earlier. This tactic is a great way to test the logic of methods. For example, you can implement test-driven debugging, by giving a function different parameters to see how it handles different input. This is a great tactic when testing complicated conditional logic!

Code Injection

You're not just limited to defining data in lldb. You can also create functions, classes, and methods on the fly through lldb! In order to persist these values, you'll need to prepend a dollar sign to the code/class just like you did with the `test` variable earlier.

Here's an example using the Swift context to create executable code:

```
(lldb) expression -l swift -- func $donothing() -> Int { return
4 }
(lldb) exp -l swift -- $donothing()
(Int) $R5 = 4
```

The above declares a Swift function called `donothing()` which returns the value 4. Upon inspecting this function, it looks perfectly valid for executable memory.

```
(lldb) exp -l swift -- $donothing
() $R6 = 0x0000000102e85770
(lldb) memory region 0x0000000102e85770
[0x0000000102e84000-0x0000000102e88000) r-x
```

Again, *this is pretty cool*. You can not only modify memory in existing code (just like with breakpoints), but you can inject executable code into an existing process. Let that idea simmer for a bit; you'll use that knowledge in an upcoming chapter for interposing code...

Type Formatting

One of the nice options lldb has is the ability to format the output of basic data types. This makes lldb a great tool to learn how the compiler formats basic C types. This is a must to know when you're exploring at the assembly level, which you'll do later in this book.

First, remove the previous symbolic breakpoint. Next, build and run the app and pause the debugger out of the blue to make sure you're in the Objective-C context.

Type the following into your lldb session:

```
(lldb) expression -G x -- 10
```

This –G option tells lldb what format you want the output in. The G stands for **GDB format**. If you're not aware, GDB is the debugger that preceded lldb. This, therefore, is saying whatever you specify is a GDB format specifier. In this case, x is used which indicates hexadecimal.

You'll see the following output:

```
(int) $0 = 0x0000000a
```

This is decimal 10 printed as hexadecimal. Wow!

But wait! There's more! lldb lets you format types using a neat shorthand syntax. Type the following:

```
(lldb) p/x 10
```

You'll see the same output as before. But that's a lot less typing!

This is great for learning the representations behind C datatypes. For example, what's the binary representation of the integer 10?

```
(lldb) p/t 10
```

The /t specifies binary format. You'll see what decimal 10 looks like in binary. This can be particularly useful when you're dealing with a bit field.

What about negative 10?

```
(lldb) p/t -10
```

Decimal 10 in two's complement. Neat!

What about the floating point binary representation of 10.0?

```
(lldb) p/t 10.0
```

That could come in handy!

How about the ASCII value of the character 'D'?

```
(lldb) p/d 'D'
```

Ah so 'D' is 68! The /d specifies decimal format.

Finally, what is the acronym hidden behind this integer?

```
(lldb) p/c 2051829580
```

The /c specifies char format. It takes the number in binary, splits into 8 bit (1 byte) chunks, and converts each chunk into an ASCII character. In this case, it's a 4 character code (FourCC), saying LoLz. :]

The full list of output formats is below (taken from GDB online docs (https://sourceware.org/gdb/onlinedocs/gdb/Output-Formats.html)):

- x: hexadecimal

- d: decimal

- u: unsigned decimal

- o: octal

- t: binary

- a: address

- c: character constant

- f: float

- s: string

If these formats aren't enough for you, you can use lldb's extra formatters, although you'll be unable to use the GDB formatting syntax.

lldb's formatters can be used like this:

```
(lldb) expression -f Y -- 2051829580
```

This gives you the following output:

```
(int) $0 = 4c 6f 4c 7a          LoLz
```

lldb uses these formatters (taken from the `lldb` online docs (https://lldb.llvm.org/use/variable.html)):

- B: boolean

- b: binary

- y: bytes

- Y: bytes with ASCII

- c: character

- C: printable character

- F: complex float

- s: c-string

- i: decimal

- E: enumeration

- x: hex

- f: float

- o: octal

- O: OSType

- U: unicode16

- u: unsigned decimal

- p: pointer

Key Points

- The po command, like Swift's `print` function, allows you to view the `description` and `debugDescription` properties of objects.

- The p command, like Swift's `dump` function, gives you information about the internals of an object.

- Variables in an `lldb` session begin with a $ and are valid for the entire session.

- Switch between language contexts in `lldb` using `expression -l <language> -O --`.

- When you pause the debugger using the button in Xcode you will probably be in an Objective-C context.

- You can use the `expression` command to add functions and inject code into an application without recompiling.

- `expression` supports GDB type formatters using –G as well as its own using –f.

Where to Go From Here?

Pat yourself on the back — this was another jam-packed round of what you can do with the `expression` command. Try exploring some of the other expression options yourself by executing `help expression` and see if you can figure out what they do.

Chapter 6: Thread, Frame & Stepping Around

You've learned how to create breakpoints, how to print and modify values, as well as how to execute code while paused in the debugger. But so far, you've been left high and dry on how to move around in the debugger and inspect data beyond the immediate scope. It's time to fix that!

In this chapter, you'll learn how to move the debugger in and out of code while lldb has suspended a program.

This is a critical skill to have since you often want to inspect values as they change over time when entering or exiting snippets of code.

Stack 101

When a computer program executes, it stores values in the **stack** and the **heap**. Both have their merits. As an advanced debugger, you'll need to have a good understanding of how these work. Right now, let's take a brief look at the stack.

You may already know the whole spiel about what a stack is in computer science terms. In any case, it's worth having an intro/refresher of how a process keeps track of code and variables when executing.

The stack is a LIFO (Last-In-First-Out) queue that stores references to your currently executing code. This LIFO ordering means that whatever is added most recently, is removed first. Think of a stack of plates. Add a plate to the top, and it will be the one you take off first.

The **stack pointer** points to the current top of the stack. In the plate analogy, the stack pointer points to that top plate, telling you where to take the next plate from, or where to put the next plate on.

Migrating the plates analogy to the stack in computer memory, now imagine the plates had Velcro and were attached to the ceiling. Each time you added a plate onto the last one, the stack would grow downwards towards the floor.

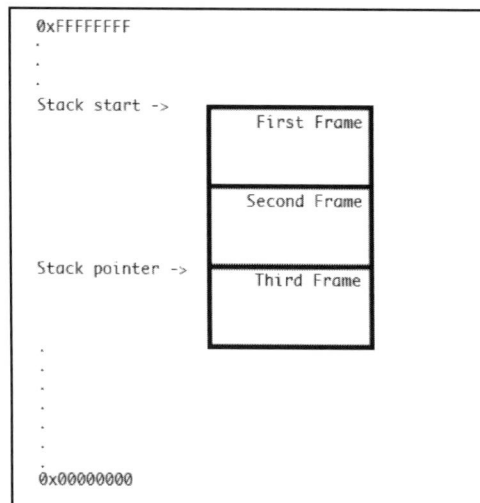

```
0xFFFFFFFF
    .
    .
    .
Stack start ->
                    +----------------+
                    |   First Frame  |
                    +----------------+
                    |  Second Frame  |
                    +----------------+
Stack pointer ->    |   Third Frame  |
                    +----------------+
    .
    .
    .
    .
    .
0x00000000
```

In this diagram, the high address is shown at the top (0xFFFFFFFF) and the low address is shown at the bottom (0x00000000) demonstrating that the stack grows downwards.

You'll take an in depth look at the stack pointer and other registers in Chapter 13, "Assembly & the Stack", but in this chapter you'll explore various ways to step through code that is on the stack.

Examining the Stack's Frames

You'll continue to use the Signals project for this chapter.

Open the **Signals** project in Xcode. Next, add a symbolic breakpoint to `MainViewController`'s `viewWillAppear(_:)` function. Be sure to honor the spaces in the function signature or else the breakpoint will not be recognized. You can always tell in the GUI if you have matched symbols, because the flag next to the name of your breakpoint will be filled in to show it's active. If the breakpoint flag is just an outline, `lldb` hasn't found a match and if it looks disabled, well, it is.

```
Signals.MainViewController.viewWillAppear
```

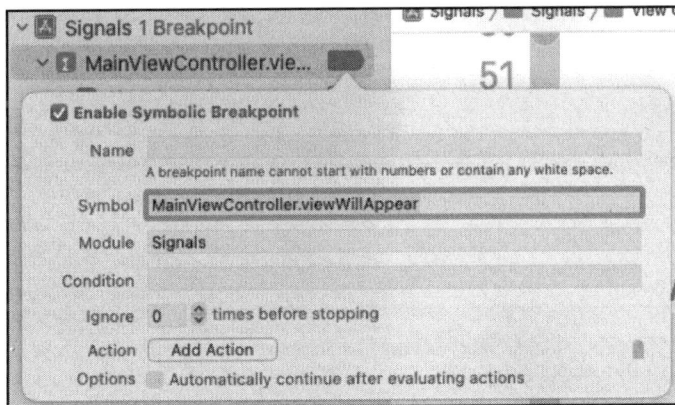

Alternatively, just set a regular breakpoint on the `viewWillAppear` signature of the **MainViewController.swift** file.

Remember from the last chapter, if you set a symbolic breakpoint it will break twice. Build and run the program. We want the break in the Swift context, so if you broke in the Objective-C context, type c or click the resume button. As expected, the debugger will pause the program on the `viewWillAppear(_:)` method of `MainViewController`. Next, take a look at the stack trace in the left panel of Xcode. If you don't see it already, click on the **Debug Navigator** in the left panel or press **Command**-7, if you have the default Xcode keymap.

Make sure the three buttons in the bottom right corner are all disabled. These help filter stack functions to only functions you have source code for. Since you're learning about public as well as private code, you should always have these buttons disabled so you can see the full stack trace.

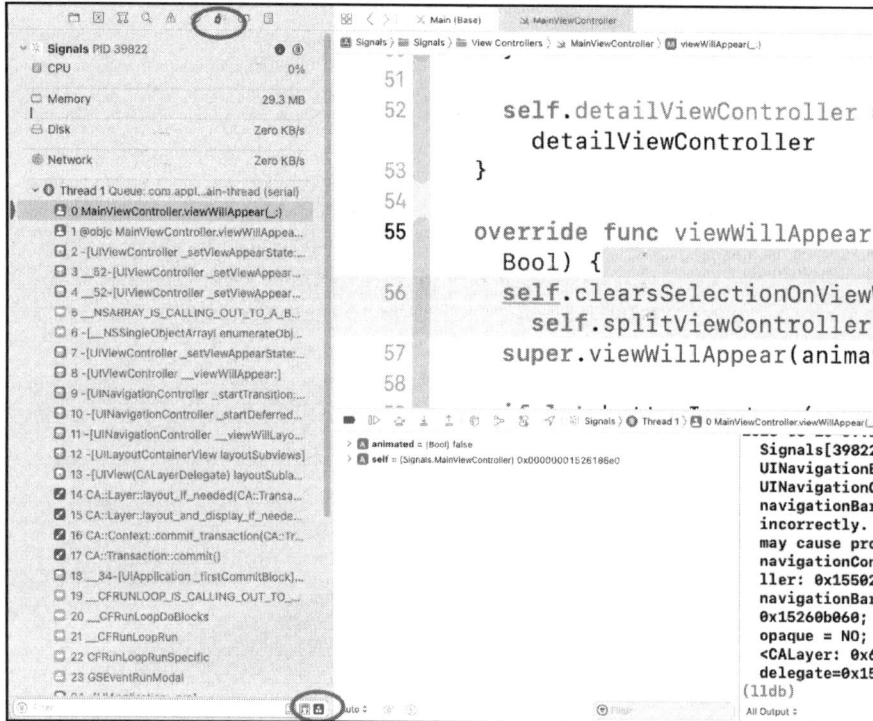

Within the Debug navigator panel, the **stack trace** will appear, showing the list of **stack frames,** the first one being viewWillAppear(_:). Following that is the Swift/Objective-C bridging method, @objc MainViewController.viewWillAppear(_:). This method is automatically generated so Objective-C can reach into Swift code. This is that place your symbolic breakpoint always hits when you are making your symbolic breakpoints.

After that, there's a few stack frames of Objective-C code coming from UIKit(Core). Dig a little deeper, and you'll see some C++ code belonging to CoreAnimation. C++ frames have lots of ::'s in their names. Even deeper, you'll see a couple of methods all containing the name CFRunLoop that belong to CoreFoundation. Finally, to cap it all off, is the **main** function (yes, Swift programs still have a main function, it's just hidden from you).

The stack trace you see in Xcode is a pretty printed version of what lldb is doing underneath Xcode's covers.

In the lldb console, type the following:

```
(lldb) thread backtrace
```

You'll see a stack trace much like you see in Xcode's Debug Navigator. You could also simply type bt if you wish, which does the same. bt is actually a different command and you can see the difference if you pull out your trusty friend, help.

bt and thread backtrace will display the entire stack trace, but you can also explore individual frames. Type the following into lldb:

```
(lldb) frame info
```

You'll get output similar to the following:

```
frame #0: 0x0000000104a7edcc
Signals`MainViewController.viewWillAppear(animated=false,
self=0x0000000000000000) at MainViewController.swift:53
```

As you can see, this output matches the content found in the Debug navigator of Xcode. Using the lldb console gives you finer-grained control of what information you want to view. Remember, lots of what Xcode shows you is just a GUI wrapper around things you can find from the command line.

Taking a look back at the Debug navigator, you'll see some numbers starting from 0 and incrementing as you go down the **call stack**. This numbering helps you associate which **stack frame** you're looking at. Select a different frame in the stack by typing the following:

```
(lldb) frame select 1
```

> **Note**: A shortcut to doing the exact same frame select 1 command is by just typing **f 1**.

Upon executing this lldb command, Xcode will jump to the @objc MainViewController.viewWillAppear(_:) **bridging method**, the method located at index 1 in the stack. A bridging method, also known as a **thunk**, is required because Swift has a different **calling convention** than Objective-C, C, C++. That is, the registers that are expected as input (or stored on the stack) need to be moved around. In order to work with non-Swift code, the compiler generates an intermediate function so Objective-C code can interact with the Swift code.

Since this method is auto compiled, you will not have the source code and will be stuck viewing the assembly of the @objc method.

> **Note**: Depending on your macOS computer, you will have either an Intel or Apple Silicon CPU. The assembly for your computer will be different based upon that hardware. Both Intel and Apple Silicon machines can compile code for each other. Intel machines can run only Intel instructions (x86_64) whereas Apple Silicon machines can run both Apple Silicon instructions (arm64) and Intel instructions (x86_64). It runs x86_64 through the Rosetta 2 translation engine.

Depending on your computer's hardware, your assembly will look similar to one of the following flavors.

Here is the ARM64 from an M1 Macbook Air:

Here is the same breakpoint in the same Xcode project with x86_64 assembly from an Intel Macbook Air:

Notice how the assembly looks different? You'll take a much deeper dive into ARM64 assembly in later chapters of this book as Apple has almost completely moved away from x86_64.

No matter the macOS computer you have, take note of the **green line in the assembly**. Right before that line is the `call[q]` (x86_64) or the **bl** (ARM664) instruction that's responsible for executing `viewWillAppear(_:)` you set a breakpoint on earlier.

Don't let the assembly blur your eyes too much. You're not out of the assembly woods just yet...

Stepping

There are 3 essential stepping actions you can do while a program is paused to execute one "chunk" of code and then re-suspend program execution. Through `lldb`, you can **step over**, **step in**, or **step out** of code.

Being able to step through code is great for understanding how variables change in your program and is a great way to verify logic is executing correctly.

Stepping Over

Stepping over allows you to step to the next code statement in a particular frame. This means if the current statement is calling another function, lldb will run until this function has completed and returned.

Let's see this in action.

Type the following in the lldb console:

```
(lldb) run
```

This will relaunch the Signals program without Xcode having to recompile. This is a great trick if you have long build times for your app and you don't want to wait for a new build to test unmodified code. :]

Replace "Signals"?

An instance of "Signals" is already running. Would you like to terminate it and launch a new instance?

> Replace

> Cancel

> ☐ Don't ask again

When the dialog box appears, click "Replace". Xcode will launch a new instance of the Signals app and stop on your symbolic breakpoint as before.

Next, type the following:

```
(lldb) next
```

The debugger will move one line forward. This is how you step over. Simple, but useful!

Stepping In

Stepping in means if the next statement is a function call, the debugger will move into the start of that function and then pause again.

Relaunch the Signals program from `lldb`:

```
(lldb) run
```

Next, type the following:

```
(lldb) step
```

No luck. The program should've stepped in, because the line it's on contains a function call (well, actually it contains a few!).

In this case, `lldb` acted more like a "step over" instead of a "step into". This is because `lldb` will, by default, ignore stepping into a function if there are no debug symbols for that function. In this case, the function calls are all going into UIKit, for which you don't have debug symbols.

There is a setting that specifies how `lldb` should behave when stepping into a function for which no debug symbols exist. Pause the app and execute the following command in `lldb` to see where this setting is held:

```
(lldb) settings show target.process.thread.step-in-avoid-nodebug
```

If true, then stepping in will act as a step over in these instances. You can either change this setting (which you'll do in the future), or tell the debugger to ignore the setting, which you'll do now. Type `run` to reload the app and when it hits your breakpoint, type the following into `lldb`:

```
(lldb) step -a0
```

This tells LLDB to step in regardless of whether you have the required debug symbols or not. Because you don't have the debug symbols for this code, you're just seeing memory addresses and assembly instructions. Don't worry, in a few chapters all of what you're seeing will make sense. Well, at least you'll know what you're looking at. :]

Stepping Out

Stepping out means a function will continue for its duration then stop when it has returned. From a stack viewpoint, execution continues until the stack frame is popped off. If you're having a hard time visualizing this, remember the plates attached to the ceiling. A plate is removed and the stack pointer is now higher as it's closer to the ceiling.

Run the Signals project again, and this time when the debugger pauses, take a quick look at the stack trace. Next, type the following into lldb:

```
(lldb) finish
```

If you're at the top of the stack, the app will just resume. With the app running, try setting a breakpoint at tableView(_:numberOfRowsInSection:), which is line 87 of **MainViewController.swift** in the Starter project. This will likely pause the application with a more interesting stack trace.

Remember, by simply pressing **Enter**, lldb will execute the last command you typed. The finish command will instruct lldb to step out of the current function.

Pay attention to the stack frames in the left panel as you step back from tableView(_:numberOfRowsInSection:) to the handleNotification(notification:) function that called it and then even into the code that was watching for the SIGSTOP.

Run the app again and this time, instead of using finish try the thread return command. Notice on the stack trace that you're popping each frame and diving down one level. Eventually you'll wind up at main.

Stepping in the Xcode GUI

Although you get much more fine-grained control using the console, Xcode already provides these options for you as buttons just above the lldb console. These buttons appear when an application is running.

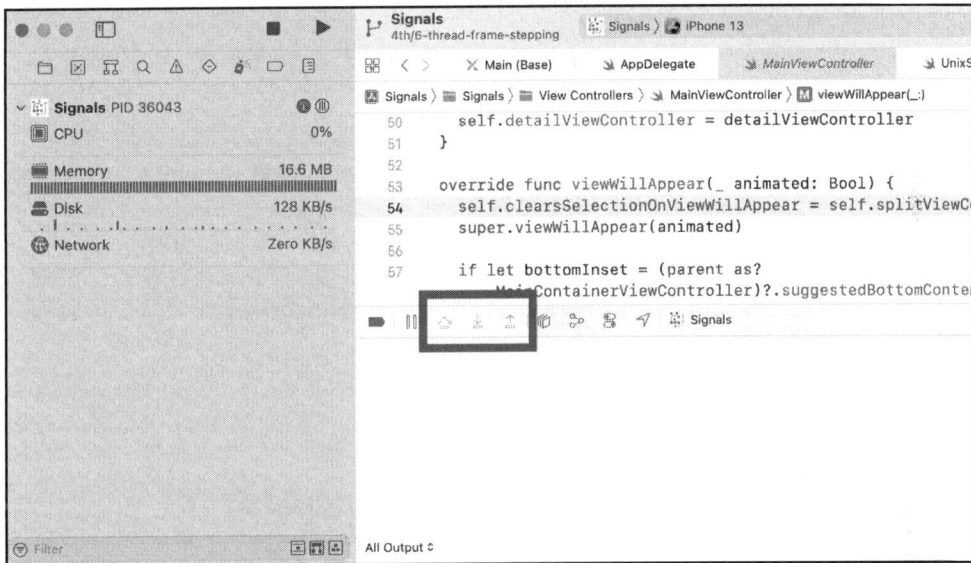

They appear, in order, as **step over**, **step in**, and **step out**.

Finally, the step over and step in buttons have one more cool trick. You can manually control the execution of different threads, by holding down **Control** and **Shift** while clicking on these buttons.

This will result in stepping through the thread on which the debugger is paused, while the rest of the threads remain paused. This is a great trick to have in your toolbox if you are working with some hard-to-debug concurrency code like networking or something with Grand Central Dispatch.

Of course lldb has the command line equivalent to do the same from the console by using the --run-mode option, or more simply -m followed by the appropriate option.

Examining Data in the Stack

A very interesting option of the `frame` command is the **`frame variable`**
subcommand. This command will take the debug symbol information found in the
headers of your executable, or a dYSM if your app is stripped... more on that later,
and dump information for that particular stack frame into the console. Thanks to the
debug information, the `frame variable` command can easily tell you the scope of
all the variables in your function as well as any global variables within your program
using the appropriate options.

Run the Signals project again and make sure you hit the `viewWillAppear(_:)`
breakpoint. Next, navigate to the top of the stack if you're not already there by either
clicking on the top stack frame in Xcode's Debug Navigator or by entering **`frame
select 0`** in the console, or use LLDB's shorthand command **f 0**.

Next, type the following:

```
(lldb) frame variable
```

You'll get output similar to the following:

```
(Bool) animated = false
(Signals.MainViewController) self = 0x0000000138f0a770 {
  UIKit.UITableViewController = {
    baseUIViewController@0 = {
      baseUIResponder@0 = {
        baseNSObject@0 = {
          isa = Signals.MainViewController
        }
      }
    }
    _overrideTransitioningDelegate = 0x0000000000000000
    _view = some {
      some = 0x000000013a016e00 {
        baseUIScrollView@0 = {
          baseUIView@0 = {
            baseUIResponder@0 = {
... etc ...
```

This dumps the variables available to the current stack frame and line of code. It'll
also dump all the instance variables, both public and private (if available), from the
current variables.

> **Note**: A shortcut for `frame variable` is v.

If you add a variable name after `frame variable`, for example `frame variable self`, then it will only print out that particular object. Just like p & po, there's a `frame variable -O --`, with a shortcut of `vo`, which prints a simplified description of a variable.

p & v default to listing all instance variables inside an object, while po & vo print a simplified description of an object.

Remember, `lldb` has to compile code based upon the expression it's executing. `vo` doesn't compile and execute code, which allows for significant boost in `lldb` speed when a developer is only interested in dumping information about an object. That is why using `vo` has gained traction for debugging in Swift over the last several years due to the fact that `vo` doesn't require code to be compiled.

To sum up: Use po when executing code and use vo when extracting information about an object.

Xcode also uses `frame variable` inside of its debugger windows. You, being the observant reader you are, might notice the output of `frame variable` also matches the content found in the **Variables view**, the panel to the left of the console window.

If it's not already, expand the Variables View by clicking on the left icon in the lower right corner of Xcode. You can compare the output of `frame variable` to the Variables View. You might notice `frame variable` will actually give you more information about the ivars of Apple's private API than the Variables view will.

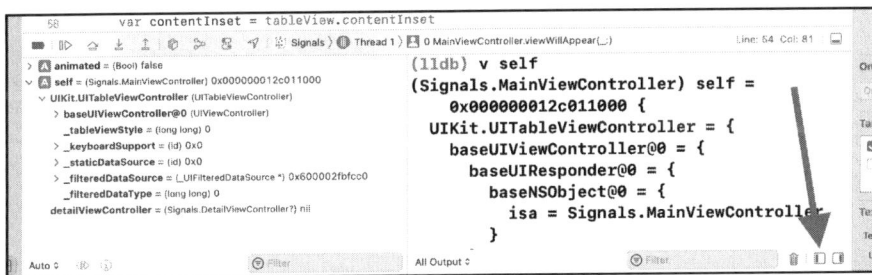

As you can see, this is an attractive way to explore public variables when working with Apple's frameworks.

You are encouraged to look at the options of `frame variable` (via a `help v`) on your own time and find an output format that is easiest for you workflow. Below are some highlighted options and their output

Key Points

- In a **stack trace**, each level is called a **frame**.

- The `thread backtrace` and `frame info` commands provide similar information to Xcode's Debug navigator pane.

- `frame select` lets you switch `lldb` to a different frame in the stack trace.

- The `run` command relaunches your application without recompiling it.

- Use the `next` command to advance your app by one line.

- The `step` command will step into a function. Add the `-a0` switch to step into functions that are not your code.

- Use `finish` or `thread return` to step out of a function.

- `frame variable`, `v` and `vo` are all ways to dump information about the current frame into the console.

Where to Go From Here?

In this chapter, you've explored stack frames and the content in them. You've also learned how to navigate the stack by stepping in, out, and over code.

There are a lot of options in the `thread` command you didn't cover. Try exploring some of them with the `help thread` command, and seeing if you can learn some cool options.

Take a look at the `thread until` and `thread jump` subcommands for navigating the stack. You'll use them later, but they are fun commands so give them a shot now to see what they do!

Chapter 7: Image

If you've read this far, you now have a solid foundation in debugging. You can find and attach to a process of interest, efficiently create regular expression breakpoints to cover a wide range of culprits, navigate the stack frame and tweak variables using the expression command.

It's time to explore one of the best tools for finding code of interest through the powers of lldb. You've already seen it a few times, but in this chapter, you'll take a deep dive into the **image** command.

The image command is an alias for the **target modules** subcommand. The image command specializes in querying information about code that lives within a **module**. "Module" is a generic term for executable code, like an executable or a shared library. Examples of shared libraries include frameworks like UIKit for iOS or dynamic libraries like libSystem.B.dylib. A module can apply to a shared library on disk or code that's loaded into a process.

Listing Modules

You'll continue using the `Signals` project. Fire up the project in Xcode and then build & run on a simulator.

> **Note**: You might be wondering why you keep running on the simulator and not a device. It's just easier and faster. You don't have to worry about certificate permissions and the connection to the device and things like that. Also, the processor on your computer is, hopefully, faster than the one on your phone, so stopping and starting the app won't take as long. If you *want* to run on device, most everything with the Signals app will work the same though. Go ahead.

At any point, suspend the program and type the following in `lldb`:

```
(lldb) image list
```

This command lists all the modules currently loaded. You'll see a lot! For such a simple program to run in memory, all those modules had to be loaded into the process!

The start of the list should look something like the following:

```
[  0] 88B10840-E223-3B24-B89F-922AFF796077 0x00000001027ac000 /
Users/lolz/Library/Developer/Xcode/DerivedData/Signals-
bugxmcyqgcvqzfdfkgoztexuneae/Build/Products/Debug-
iphonesimulator/Signals.app/Signals
[  1] 86A8BA48-8BB4-3B30-9CDA-051F73C74F44 0x0000000102a80000 /
usr/lib/dyld
[  2] CC38080D-7C09-357A-B552-DB1B456781CE 0x00000001029dc000 /
Applications/Xcode.app/Contents/Developer/Platforms/
iPhoneOS.platform/Library/Developer/CoreSimulator/Profiles/
Runtimes/iOS.simruntime/Contents/Resources/RuntimeRoot/usr/lib/
dyld_sim
[  3] 4597B93E-E778-3BB5-BB66-E4344A5F2FDB 0x00000001c7be2000 /
Applications/Xcode.app/Contents/Developer/Platforms/
iPhoneOS.platform/Library/Developer/CoreSimulator/Profiles/
Runtimes/iOS.simruntime/Contents/Resources/RuntimeRoot/usr/lib/
libBacktraceRecording.dylib
[  4] 14F79286-A67E-30FE-B786-E5A978D6DB0D 0x00000001c7bf5000 /
Applications/Xcode.app/Contents/Developer/Platforms/
iPhoneOS.platform/Library/Developer/CoreSimulator/Profiles/
Runtimes/iOS.simruntime/Contents/Resources/RuntimeRoot/usr/lib/
libMainThreadChecker.dylib
...
```

Like some other commands, there's a –b switch to make the output "brief". Enter the following command:

```
(lldb) image list -b
```

Now you just get the names of each module.

The first module is the main executable, Signals. The second module is the **dynamic link editor** or, more simply, **dyld**. dyld is responsible for loading any code into memory and executes code well before any of your code has a chance to start running.

You can filter out modules by specifying their name. Type the following into lldb:

```
(lldb) image list Foundation
```

The output will look similar to the following:

```
[  0] E14C8373-8298-3E74-AFC5-61DDDC413228 0x00000001806ea000 /
Applications/Xcode.app/Contents/Developer/Platforms/
iPhoneOS.platform/Library/Developer/CoreSimulator/Profiles/
Runtimes/iOS.simruntime/Contents/Resources/RuntimeRoot/System/
Library/Frameworks/Foundation.framework/Foundation
```

This is a useful way to find information about just the modules you want. The output has a few interesting pieces to note:

1. The module's UUID prints first: E14C8373-8298-3E74-AFC5-61DDDC413228. The UUID is important for hunting down symbolic information and uniquely identifies the version of the Foundation framework.

2. Following the UUID is the load address: 0x00000001806ea000. This identifies where the module loads into the executable's process space.

3. Finally, you have the full path to the module's location on the disk.

> **Note**: Some modules won't be at the physical location they claim to be on the disk. This is likely because they're part of the **dyld shared cache**, or dsc. dsc packs hundreds — sometimes thousands — of shared libraries together. Starting in macOS Monterey, Apple no longer includes the separated dynamic libraries on disk, leaving only dsc to explore if you're not spelunking in memory. You'll learn more about dsc at the end of this chapter.

Take a deeper dive into another common module, UIKit. Type the following into
lldb:

```
(lldb) image dump symtab -s address UIKit
Symtab, file = /Applications/Xcode.app/Contents/Developer/
Platforms/iPhoneOS.platform/Library/Developer/CoreSimulator/
Profiles/Runtimes/iOS.simruntime/Contents/Resources/RuntimeRoot/
System/Library/Frameworks/UIKit.framework/UIKit, num_symbols = 3
(sorted by address):
                Debug symbol
                |Synthetic symbol
                ||Externally Visible
                |||
Index   UserID DSX Type            File Address/Value Load
Address        Size                Flags      Name
------- ------ --- --------------- -------------------
----------------- ------------------- ----------
----------------------------------- ----------
[    0]      0   Data                0x0000000000000fc8
0x00000001ac4ebfc8 0x0000000000000030 0x001e0000
UIKitVersionString
[    1]      1   Data                0x0000000000000ff8
0x00000001ac4ebff8 0x0000000000000008 0x001e0000
UIKitVersionNumber
```

This dumps all the symbol table information available for UIKit. Remember, from a
code standpoint, UIKit is a wrapper for the private **UIKitCore** module. As you can
see, the UIKit module doesn't include many symbols due to the sharing of code for
Mac Catalyst. Repeat the same action for UIKitCore:

```
(lldb) image dump symtab UIKitCore -s address
```

It's more output than you can shake a stick at! This command sorts the output by the
addresses of each function thanks to the -s address argument. The lldb command
above is comparable to dumping the symbol table information via nm, but instead, it
happens in memory. *Although not applicable to iOS Simulator shared libraries, this is
convenient because you won't be able to run the* nm *command on libraries packed into
the* dsc *since* nm *expects an actual file on disk.*

The image dump output has a lot of useful information, but your eyes will likely hurt
scrolling through UIKitCore's symbol table in its entirety. You need a way to
effectively query the UIKitCore module.

The **image lookup** command is perfect for narrowing your search. Type the
following into lldb:

```
(lldb) image lookup -n "-[UIViewController viewDidLoad]"
```

You'll get output similar to the following:

```
1 match found in /Applications/Xcode.app/Contents/Developer/
Platforms/iPhoneOS.platform/Library/Developer/CoreSimulator/
Profiles/Runtimes/iOS.simruntime/Contents/Resources/RuntimeRoot/
System/Library/PrivateFrameworks/UIKitCore.framework/UIKitCore:
        Address: UIKitCore[0x00000000004b9278]
(UIKitCore.__TEXT.__text + 4943316)
        Summary: UIKitCore`-[UIViewController viewDidLoad]
```

This dumps out information relating solely to UIViewController's viewDidLoad instance method. The −n option searches for *functions or symbols*. On this computer, the viewDidLoad method is located at offset 0x00000000004b9278 of the UIKitCore file on the disk and is found in the UIKitCore.__TEXT.__text section of UIKitCore. The __TEXT.__text section is an R-X mapped section of memory where executable code typically lives. You'll learn about the Mach-O components in the "Low Level" section of this book.

Typing the full −[UIViewController viewDidLoad] method can be a little tedious, and this can only dump out methods where you already know the name of the symbol.

This is where regular expressions come into play again. The −r option lets you perform a regular expression query. Type the following into lldb:

```
(lldb) image lookup -rn UIViewController
```

Not only does this dump out all methods containing the phrase "UIViewController", but it also spits out results like UIViewControllerBuiltinTransitionViewAnimator since it contains "UIViewController". You can be smart with the regular expression query, just like when you were setting breakpoints, to only spit out UIViewController methods. Type the following into lldb:

```
(lldb) image lookup -rn '\[UIViewController\ '
```

This is good, but what about categories? They come in the form of (+|−) [UIViewController(CategoryName) methodName]. Search for all UIViewController category methods:

```
(lldb) image lookup -rn '\[UIViewController\('
```

Searching for the presence of the parenthesis immediately following the Objective-C class name returns category methods for that particular class. Not only does this print out both public and undocumented APIs, but it also gives you hints to the methods the UIViewController class overrides from its parent classes.

> **Note**: image lookup's output can be a little jarring to read when there are many search results. In the upcoming chapters, you'll look at ways to manipulate lldb to improve readability via command aliases and using lldb's Script Bridging interface. You can get a taste of what "pretty" output looks like with the following zinger:

```
script print("\n".join([i.GetSymbol().GetName() + "\n" for i in
lldb.target.FindGlobalFunctions("\[UIViewController\(", 0,
lldb.eMatchTypeRegex)]))
```

You can also limit your search queries to a specific module by appending the module name as the final argument to your search query. If you wanted to see all the implementations of viewDidLoad implemented in UIKitCore, you'd type the following:

```
(lldb) image lookup -rn viewDidLoad\]$ UIKitCore
```

Using the regular expression syntax, the command above looks for any viewDidLoad methods. The \]$ syntax dictates the final character in the symbol's name is a closing bracket. This is a nice addition because Objective-C blocks could be implemented in a viewDidLoad method. When that happens, the symbol name for the block's function would be the name of the symbol for the function where the block is created with the phrase __block_invoke appended, along with an increasing number if multiple blocks are implemented in the function.

> **Note**: Regarding lldb's command interface, there's a subtle difference between searching for code in a module — image lookup — versus breaking in code for a module — breakpoint set. If you wanted to search for all blocks in the Commons framework that contain the phrase _block_invoke in their symbols, you'd use image lookup -rn _block_invoke Commons. If you wanted to make a *breakpoint* for every block in the Commons framework, you'd use rb appendSignal.*block_invoke -s Commons. Take note of the -s argument versus the space.

> **Note**: It's worth mentioning that a private symbol's name can be stripped out
> of code in a shared library. A private symbol is a symbol that can't be linked to
> from another module — i.e., dictated from the private keyword in Swift or the
> static symbol declaration in C. The presence of a private symbol's name in
> the symbol table hints that Apple didn't care to remove it. If lldb can infer a
> symbol at an address but can't find a name for it, lldb names the symbol
> ___lldb_unnamed_symbol<Counter>$$<Module> where Counter increases
> for every unknown symbol name in the module. See how many stripped,
> private symbols there are with an image lookup -rn ___lldb.

Swift Symbol Naming

Swift, like C++, generates mangled symbol names depending on the context/
attributes of the originating source code. Compiling a simple C file and then
comparing it to Swift best illustrates this. In Terminal, compile and view a function
in C code:

```
% echo "void somefunction(void) {}" > /tmp/mangling_test.c
% clang -o /tmp/mangling_test /tmp/mangling_test.c -shared
% nm /tmp/mangling_test
```

If all goes well, nm will give you this output:

```
0000000000003fb4 T _somefunction
```

The nm command reads the symbol table embedded in the binary, which contains
_somefunction. It's common for all C compilers to prepend an underscore to the
function name for its symbol. Notice how somefunction appears the same in the C
source code and the symbol table.

Now, in Terminal, compare how Swift generates the same function name:

```
% echo "func somefunction() {}" > /tmp/mangling_test.swift
% swiftc -o /tmp/mangling_test /tmp/mangling_test.swift -emit-
library
% nm /tmp/mangling_test
```

This time, nm will give you longer output:

```
0000000000003fb0 t _$s13mangling_test12somefunctionyyF
0000000000003fb4 s ___swift_reflection_version
```

The resulting symbol is now named _$s13mangling_test12somefunctionyyF. The module name mangling_test was included in the somefunction symbol. In addition to an underscore, the **$s** substring appears at the beginning of the name, hinting that the stable Swift ABI was *likely* used to compile the symbol.

To view the unmangled names, pipe the output into the swift-demangle command like so:

```
% nm /tmp/mangling_test | xcrun swift-demangle
```

Now, swift-demangle undoes all of the mangling:

```
0000000000003fb0 t mangling_test.somefunction() -> ()
0000000000003fb4 s ___swift_reflection_version
```

lldb provides a similar demangling command you can use in a process to unmangle names:

```
(lldb) language swift demangle
_$s13mangling_test12somefunctionyyF
_$s13mangling_test12somefunctionyyF --->
mangling_test.somefunction() -> ()
```

This mangling is important for both searching for code via lldb's image lookup as well as setting breakpoints discussed in Chapter 4: "Stopping in Code". You can search for this Swift symbol using the mangled name or unmangled name. Although the Swift ABI has now solidified, the LLDB authors still occasionally tweak how to query the symbol. For example, with lldb-1400.0.38.17 (Xcode 14.2), the following search queries will resolve to the same s13mangling_test12somefunctionyyF symbol:

```
(lldb) image lookup -n somefunction
(lldb) image lookup -n mangling_test.somefunction
(lldb) image lookup -n $s13mangling_test12somefunctionyyF
```

More Swift Naming Conventions

Understanding how Swift mangles symbols can help you identify clever breakpoints in your source code.

Swift symbols using the stable ABI begin with a $s in the symbol name, which you can learn more about from Apple's Swift GitHub repo (https://github.com/apple/swift/blob/main/docs/ABI/Mangling.rst). Here's an example of how to look for Swift code in the Commons module of the Signal project using Swift mangled naming:

```
(lldb) image lookup -rn ^\$s Commons
```

Expanding on the regex above, you can find relevant Swift symbols in a mixed language codebase. Do this by appending a wildcard followed by class names, methods or functions to the prefix above, such as the following:

```
(lldb) image lookup -rn ^\$s.*viewDidLoad`
```

Without going into the full details of Swift symbol mangling, the *type* of object the symbol represents is *usually* encoded as a one- or two-character encoding following the symbol name. Zero or more **entities** following the type can help explain the type of symbol.

For example, imagine the Swift file **Bleh.swift** contains the following code:

```
class SomeClass {
    var heresAVariable: Int = 0
}
```

The compiler generates several methods pertaining to using and manipulating heresAVariable, such as getting/setting/modifying/initialization. Now, narrow the focus to just the mangled getter symbol, which has the following mangled name:

```
_$s4Bleh9SomeClassC14heresAVariableSivg
```

Immediately following the $s is the number 4, indicating the module length of Bleh. 9 is the length of the class, SomeClass. The C immediately following SomeClass indicates it's of type class. 14 gives the length of heresAVariable. Si is a *Swift type* of Int. The v indicates it's a variable, and the g means it's a getter function.

Using this knowledge, you can create a regular expression breakpoint on all the getters of a class/struct with the following lldb expression:

```
(lldb) rb \$s.*vg$
```

The command above uses the mangling convention to search for a getter, g, of a variable, v.

> **Note**: Earlier in this book, you used a regular expression and searched for the phrases getter or setter for breakpoints. However, that has the potential downside of false positives for breakpoints that you wouldn't want to stop on. Using the mangled names allows more precise control of your breakpoints. But this comes at the price of learning the implementation details of how the compiler generates Swift code.

It's worth repeating: Regular expression breakpoints are useful — especially when working with Swift. :]

Undocumented Debugging Methods

The image lookup command also does a great job searching for undocumented methods. Apple has included undocumented APIs for internal debugging that can also be used by those who are willing to dig through the symbol tables to find these helpful APIs.

Here are a couple interesting APIs pulled from UIKitCore for inspecting an Objective-C object's contents:

- -[NSObject(IvarDescription) _ivarDescription] dumps the raw ivars used to store values in Objective-C properties.

- -[NSObject(IvarDescription) _propertyDescription] lists the property declarations for that class.

- -[NSObject(IvarDescription) _shortMethodDescription] lists the methods implemented by that class.

- -[NSObject(IvarDescription) _methodDescription] lists the methods implemented by that class and recursively lists methods of its parent class.

You can also use APIs for inspecting the UIViews and UIViewController hierarchy:

- -[UIViewController _printHierarchy] prints the entire view hierarchy from the UIViewController's standpoint.

- +[UIViewController _printHierarchy] prints the entire view hierarchy.

Remember, these APIs are Objective-C-centric, so be sure to use the Objective-C context when executing them if you're not in an Objective-C stack frame.

For fun, execute this command in the Signals project:

```
(lldb) exp -lobjc -O -- [[UIApplication sharedApplication]
_ivarDescription]
```

You'll get a slew of output since UIApplication holds many instance variables behind the scenes. Scan carefully, and find something that interests you.

For example, the private __gestureEnvironment variable holding references to a class called UIGestureEnvironment seems interesting.

You can use what you've learned to dump information about this class with the following:

```
(lldb) image lookup -rn UIGestureEnvironment
```

Spelunk into any rabbit hole of interest and play around with the private references to an Objective-C class using -[NSObject _shortMethodDescription] and -[NSObject _ivarDescription].

Dyld Shared Cache

When working with all these shared libraries, you may have noticed something a little odd. Open Terminal and type these commands:

```
% cd /tmp
% touch some_program.swift
% swiftc some_program.swift -framework CoreAudio
```

This creates a Swift command line executable that doesn't do anything — the equivalent of an int main() { return 0; } in C — and links in the CoreAudio framework. Verify CoreAudio is linked to swift_program:

```
% otool -L some_program
```

The `otool` command should report something similar to:

```
some_program:
   /usr/lib/libobjc.A.dylib (compatibility version 1.0.0, current
version 228.0.0)
   /usr/lib/libSystem.B.dylib (compatibility version 1.0.0,
current version 1319.0.0)
   /System/Library/Frameworks/CoreAudio.framework/Versions/A/
CoreAudio (compatibility version 1.0.0, current version 1.0.0)
```

`otool`'s –L option displays the list of required dynamic dependency libraries found in the Mach-O header of `some_program`.

In macOS — or any recent version of iOS — you won't be able to find these libraries on the disk, which makes it hard to dig through them for more interesting method names and object properties.

```
% ls /usr/lib/libobjc.A.dylib
ls: /usr/lib/libobjc.A.dylib: No such file or directory
% ls /usr/lib/libSystem.B.dylib
ls: /usr/lib/libSystem.B.dylib: No such file or directory
% ls /System/Library/Frameworks/CoreAudio.framework/Versions/A/
CoreAudio
ls: /System/Library/Frameworks/CoreAudio.framework/Versions/A/
CoreAudio: No such file or directory
```

That's because Apple moved these libraries/frameworks from their expected locations into the **dyld shared cache** or **dsc**. This acts as a "super library", giving a significant optimization boost when loading processes.

The problem with `dsc` is you'll often want to explore these dynamic libraries but don't have a way to do so if they're packed away into a structure that seems to change on every major OS release. You can explore several solutions to introspect individual libraries in `dsc`:

1. Use `lldb`. `lldb` knows about the `dsc` format, allowing you to quickly query information from a loaded library.

2. Use public/private tools to extract the `dsc` shared library code so you can reinspect them on disk. Although `dyld` is available on Apple's open source site (https://opensource.apple.com/tarballs/dyld/), Apple often lags behind on releasing the current implementation. You can also check out the ipsw (https://github.com/blacktop/ipsw) tool that by @blacktop_ (https://twitter.com/blacktop_) created.

Extracting Shared Libraries Without a Third-Party Tool

Apple has shipped a special bundle located at /usr/lib/dsc_extractor.bundle since about Big Sur or so. You can link to this bundle and use it to extract dsc libraries using the publicly exported symbol **dyld_shared_cache_extract_dylibs_progress**.

The C function signature looks like:

```
extern int
dyld_shared_cache_extract_dylibs_progress(const char*
shared_cache_file_path,
                                          const char*
extraction_root_path,
                                          void (^progress)
(unsigned current, unsigned total));
```

You can link and call this function using the dlopen/dlsym APIs. You'll learn more about these APIs in the "Low Level" section of this book.

Here's the Swift code to load the bundle and call the dyld_shared_cache_extract_dylibs_progress function. This code is also available with the materials download for this book:

```
import Foundation

typealias extract_dylibs = @convention(c) (
  UnsafePointer<CChar>?,
  UnsafePointer<CChar>?, ((UInt32, UInt32) -> Void)?) -> Int32

if CommandLine.argc != 3 {
  print("\(String(utf8String: getprogname()) ?? "") <cache_path>
<output_path>")
  exit(1)
}

guard let handle = dlopen("/usr/lib/dsc_extractor.bundle",
RTLD_NOW) else {
  print("Couldn't find handle")
  exit(1)
}

guard let sym = dlsym(
  handle, "dyld_shared_cache_extract_dylibs_progress") else {

  print("Can't find dyld_shared_cache_extract_dylibs_progress")
  exit(1)
```

```
}
let extract_dylibs_func = unsafeBitCast(
  sym, to: extract_dylibs.self)
let err = extract_dylibs_func(CommandLine.arguments[1],
                              CommandLine.arguments[2])
 { cur, total in
    print("\(cur)/\(total)")
}

if err != 0 {
  print("Something went wrong")
  exit(1)
} else {
  print("success! files written at \"\(CommandLine.arguments[2])
\"")
}
```

Put this code into a file called dsc_extractor.swift and then run the following:

```
% swiftc dsc_extractor.swift
```

This produces the dsc_exctractor executable. The tool expects two arguments:

1. A path to a dyld shared cache (dsc) file.

2. The output path where it writes the extracted dsc library contents.

You can then use nm and otool to inspect the libraries it produces, outside of linking them to an app and using lldb.

For example, run it with the following:

```
% dsc_extractor /System/Volumes/Preboot/Cryptexes/OS/System/
Library/dyld/dyld_shared_cache_arm64e /tmp/dsc_payload
```

If you have not updated to macOS Ventura yet then you might not have the shared cache in the /System/Volumes/Preboot/Cryptexes/OS/System/Library/dyld/ folder. Instead, try here:

```
% dsc_extractor /System/Library/dyld/dyld_shared_cache_arm64e /
tmp/dsc_payload
```

If your terminal complains it cannot find the dsc_extractor try again but add ./ to the beginning of the command to remind terminal to look in this directory.

Note: Apple has been moving the dyld shared cache files around as they clean up the file system as part of the migration away from x86. In Ventura, the cache moved to /System/Volumes/Preboot/Cryptexes/OS/System/Library/dyld/dyld_shared_cache_arm64e. Depending on when you read this, it may have moved again. You can ask in the Kodeco forums for this book, if you cannot find it and need help.

Note: The author created the program above on an M1 Macbook Air, which has the arm64e CPU variant. You'll learn more about this CPU architecture in the assembly section. Be aware that all installs of macOS have the arm64e and the x86_64 dyld shared cache files available.

Key Points

- `image` is an alias for the `target modules` subcommand and lets you inspect the loaded libraries for an app.

- Use `image lookup -n` to search for modules by name. Add the `-r` flag to also use regex syntax to narrow your searches.

- Swift symbols get mangled by the compiler, but following a pattern, so you can still use regex to match them.

- Use `language swift demangle` in `lldb` to demangle symbols or use `xcrun swift-demangle` in terminal.

- Using `image lookup` to search Apple's code for undocumented methods that may assist you in your debugging.

- Apple combines libraries into a shared cache, but you can extract and introspect individual libraries.

Where to Go From Here?

A number of challenges in this chapter can help you get interested in symbol exploration:

- Figure out a pattern using `image lookup` to find all Swift closures within the Signals module. Once you do that, create a breakpoint on every Swift closure within the Signals module. How could you create a breakpoint for all Swift closures in a particular file?

- Use the `image lookup` command to figure out which UIKitCore method contains the most Objective-C blocks.

- Look at Swift code that can stop on **didSet**/**willSet** property helpers or do/try/catch blocks. Can you use a regex pattern to stop on code like this?

- Use `image lookup -rs "Notification$" UIKitCore` to dump all the NSNotification names you can observe through UIKitCore and see if there are any interesting undocumented ones worth playing around with.

Need Another Challenge?

Using the private UIKitCore NSObject category method _shortMethodDescription as well as your image lookup -rn command, attach to the SpringBoard process and search for the class responsible for displaying time in the upper-left corner of the status bar. Keep in mind that you'll need SIP disabled. Change the class's value to something more amusing. Drill into subviews and see if you can find it using the tools given so far.

Chapter 8: Watchpoints

You've learned how to create breakpoints on executable code; that is, memory that has read and execute permissions. But using only breakpoints leaves out an important component to debugging — you can monitor when the instruction pointer executes an address, but with breakpoints you can't monitor when memory is being read or written to. You can't monitor value changes to instantiated Swift objects on the heap, nor can you monitor reads to a particular address (say, a hardcoded string) in memory. This is where a **watchpoint** comes into play.

A watchpoint is a special type of breakpoint that can monitor reads or writes to a particular value in memory and is not limited to executable code as are breakpoints. However, there are limitations to using watchpoints: there are a finite amount of watchpoints permitted per architecture (typically 4) and the "watched" size of memory usually caps out at 8 bytes.

Watchpoint Best Practices

Like all debugging techniques, a watchpoint is a another tool in the debugging toolbox. You'll likely not use this tool very often, but it can be *extremely* useful in certain situations. Watchpoints are great for:

- Tracking an allocated Swift/Objective-C object when you don't know how a property is getting set, i.e. via direct ivar access, Swift `inout` parameter initialization, Objective-C property setter method, Swift property setter method, hardcoded offset access, or other methods.

- Monitoring when a hardcoded string is being utilized, such as in a `print/printf/NSLog/cout` function call.

- Monitoring the instruction pointer for a particular type of assembly instruction.

You should use a watchpoint when a value is getting **set**. You'll learn about a different tool in an upcoming chapter, the **MallocStackLogging** environment variable, to monitor when an object is being **allocated**.

Breakpoints Limitations

Watchpoints are great for discovering when a particular piece of memory is being read or written to. A practical example of this is when an instance variable is written to a previously allocated instance created from the heap, such as in an Objective-C/Swift class instance.

Fortunately, in Swift, you don't have direct access to the instance variable. Access is gated via the setter methods that are generated by the compiler! In addition, Swift also gives you the `didGet` and `didSet` methods which provide an attractive alternative to using watchpoints on Swift properties provided you have the source code to augment.

The same features do not get carried over to the C/ObjC/ObjC++ family, where a value in memory could be modified directly through the instance variable, through the property setter, or even through direct memory access.

Unfortunately, even with all the safety that Swift brings, there are some edge cases in Swift where a setter breakpoint will not get used, like `inout` functions modifying the underlying ivar. Take the following code as an example:

```
class SomeClass {
  var heresAVariable: Int = 0
}
```

```
func modifyVal(_ i : inout Int) { i = 4 }

var c = SomeClass()
modifyVal(&c.heresAVariable)
```

Setting a `(lldb) rb setter` breakpoint will not stop here! The generated assembly will calculate the offset of `heresAVariable` and write directly to that memory. This means you can't always rely on Objective-C's set{PropertyName}:'s breakpoint syntax, nor Swift's {Module}.{Class}.{Property}.setter methods to catch when write-able memory is being set!

Finding a Property's Offset

You'll explore how to use watchpoints in lieu of a breakpoint to catch a particular write in memory on a singleton.

Open up the **Signals** application in the starter directory for this chapter and build and run the program.

Once running, pause the application and head over to the lldb console. Type the following:

```
(lldb) language objc class-table dump UnixSignalHandler -v
```

This will dump the Objective-C class layout of `UnixSignalHandler`. The output will look similar to the following:

```
isa = 0x100acc5d8 name = UnixSignalHandler instance size = 56
num ivars = 4 superclass = NSObject
  ivar name = source type = id size = 8 offset = 24
  ivar name = _shouldEnableSignalHandling type = bool size = 1
offset = 32
  ivar name = _signals type = id size = 8 offset = 40
  ivar name = _sharedUserDefaults type = id size = 8 offset = 48
  instance method name = initPrivate type = @16@0:8
  instance method name = appendSignal:sig: type =
v28@0:8^{__siginfo=iiiiIi^v(sigval=i^v)q[7Q]}16i24
  instance method name = setShouldEnableSignalHandling: type =
v20@0:8B16
  ...
```

Check out the ivar named **_shouldEnableSignalHandling**, a bool type, whose offset is 32 bytes and whose size is 1 byte (yes, a byte, *NOT a bit*).

This means that if you know where an instance of the `UnixSignalHandler` class is located on the heap, you can add 32 bytes to that address to get the location where `_shouldEnableSignalHandling` is stored for that instance of `UnixSignalHandler`.

> **Note:** The `lldb` command "`language objc class-table dump`" isn't as fleshed out as it could be on Swift classes... even though on Apple platforms a Swift class inherits from an Objective-C class. You can alternatively try the `dsdump` tool (https://github.com/DerekSelander/dsdump), which is an up to date `class-dump` tool for finding offsets in Swift code.

Now that you know the offset to find the `_shouldEnableSignalHandling` ivar on an instance, it's time to find the instance of the `UnixSignalHandler` singleton. In Xcode:

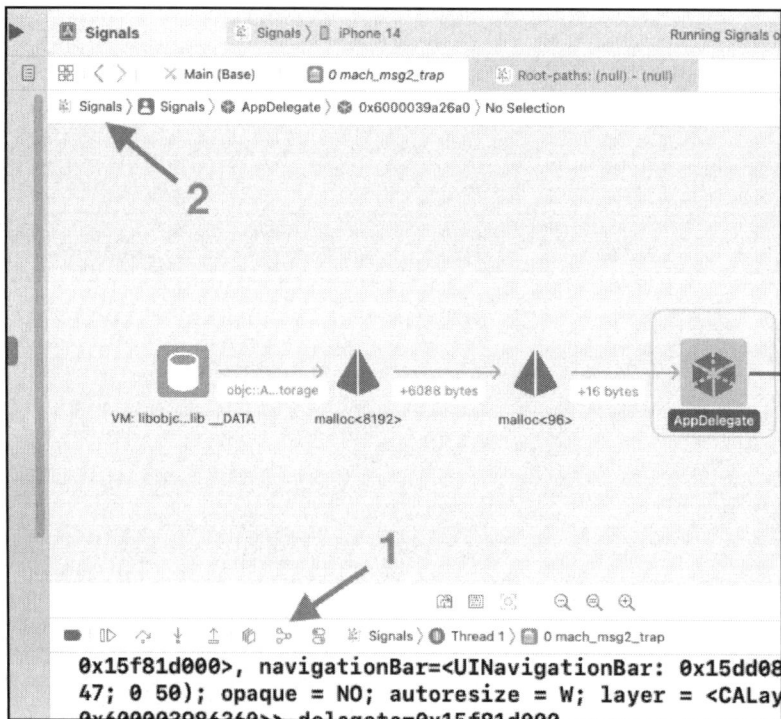

1. Click on the **Debug Memory Graph** button located on the top of the debug console.

2. Select the **Signals** project, then select the **Commons** framework (the framework responsible for implementing the `UnixSignalHandler`).

Drill down and you'll see the instance of the UnixSignalHandler both visually in Xcode and the memory address. Notice in the image below, that Xcode gives you multiple ways to see the memory address for the object. It's in the Debug navigator on the left, in the breadcrumb indicator at the top and in the **Memory Inspector** in the pane on the right.

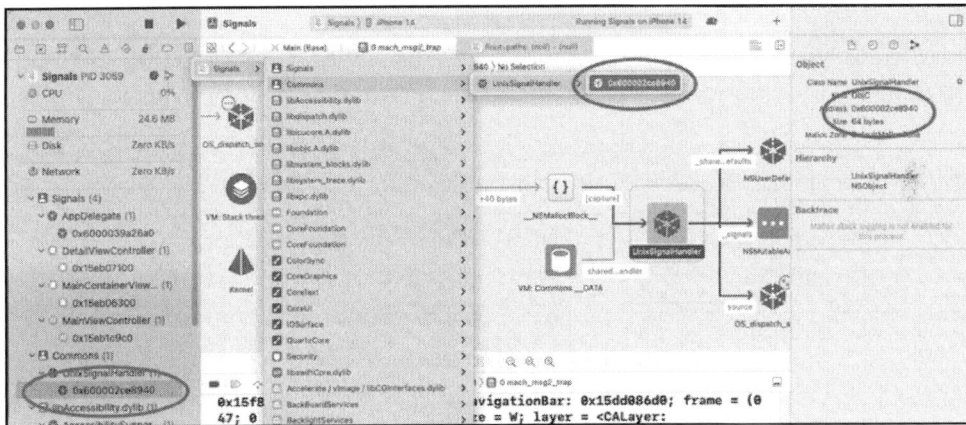

Once you have the instance, copy the memory address of the UnixSignalHandler into your clipboard or write it down somewhere.

On my particular instance of the Signals program, I can see that the singleton instance of UnixSignalHandler has a heap address value starting at **0x600002ce8940**, but note that yours will be different.

> **Note**: Without dwelling too long on the fact that the debugging scripts we provide may be a better debugging experience than what Xcode can currently deliver, if you're not a fan of all the GUI clicking you just performed, check out the **search** command from Appendix C: "Helpful Python Scripts". This command can enumerate the heap for Swift/Objective-C classes and has a few extra features rich that Xcode's GUI equivalent lacks.

Through lldb, Add your instance value to 32 to find the location of the _shouldEnableSignalHandling ivar. Format the output in hexadecimal using lldb's p/x (print hexadecimal) command.

```
(lldb) p/x 0x600002ce8940 + 32
```

lldb's with (long) $0 = 0x0000600002ce8960 which is the location of interest. Time to put a watchpoint on it!

Now you can use `watchpoint set` to place the watchpoint. If you used `lldb` to make the memory calculation the correct address is stored in the variable that `lldb` just created for you. In the example above it is `$0`. If you did the memory calculation by hand, use your calculated offset value of `UnixSignalHandler`.

```
(lldb) watchpoint set expression -s 1 -w write -- $0
```

This creates a new watchpoint that monitors a 1 byte range (thanks to the `-s 1` argument) starting at address `0x0000600002ce8960` and only stops if the value gets set (`-w write`).

The **-w** argument can be set to the following values:

- `read`: Fires when the value is read from.

- `write`: Fires when the value is written to.

- `read_write`: Fires when the value is read from or written to.

The plumbing is now set up in `lldb` to monitor this change. You'll now trigger the write to occur through the GUI of the Signals app. Resume the app if it's still paused and tap on the playbook `UISwitch` button.

The Signals app will be suspended. Take a gander over to the left hand side of Xcode to view the stack trace and see how the program got stopped.

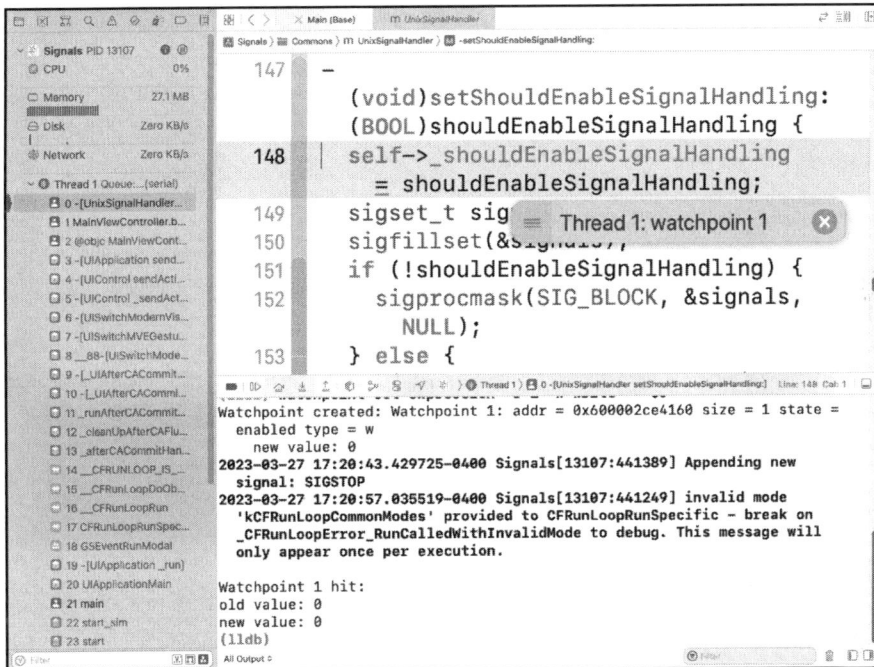

The Xcode GUI Watchpoint Equivalent

Xcode provides a GUI for setting watchpoints. You could perform the equivalent of the above methods by setting a breakpoint on the creation method of the UnixSignalHandler singleton, then set a watchpoint via the GUI. First though, you need to delete the watchpoint you just made.

In lldb, delete the watchpoint, then resume execution:

```
(lldb) watchpoint delete
About to delete all watchpoints, do you want to do that?: [Y/n]
Y
All watchpoints removed. (1 watchpoints)
(lldb) c
```

In the Signals program, make sure the Playbook UISwitch is flicked back to on. Once on, navigate to **UnixSignalHandler.m** and set a GUI breakpoint at the end of the sharedHandler constructor that returns the singleton instance. The line of code reads return sharedSignalHandler;.

Control should suspend since you've added a breakpoint to a callback function that monitors breakpoints and references that code. If not, make sure your Playbook UISwitch is active.

Once control is suspended, make sure your **Variables View** is visible. The toggle for that view is found in the lower-right corner of Xcode.

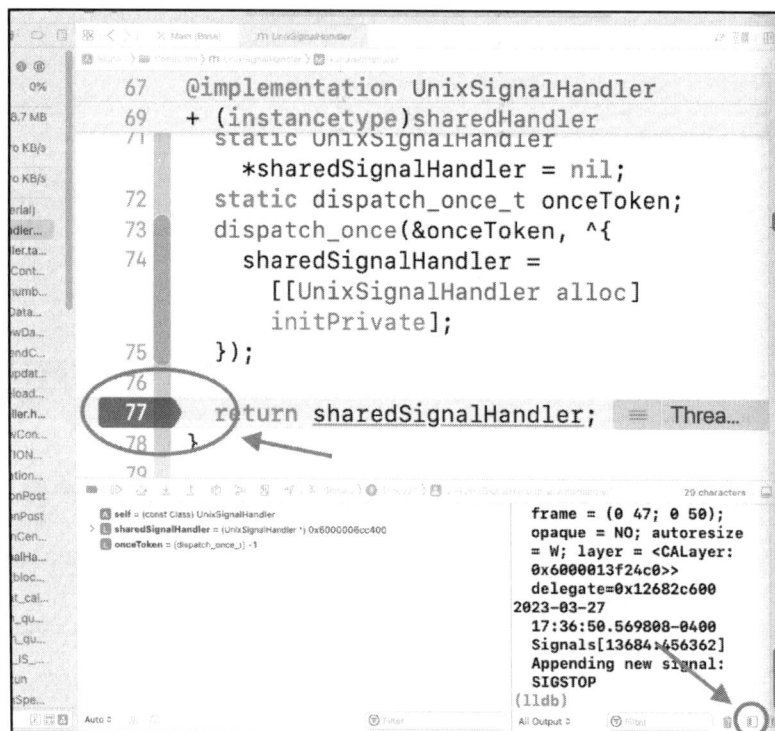

In the Variables view, drill down into the **sharedSignalHandler** instance, then right click on the **_shouldEnableSignalHandling** variable. Select **Watch _shouldEnableSignalHandling**.

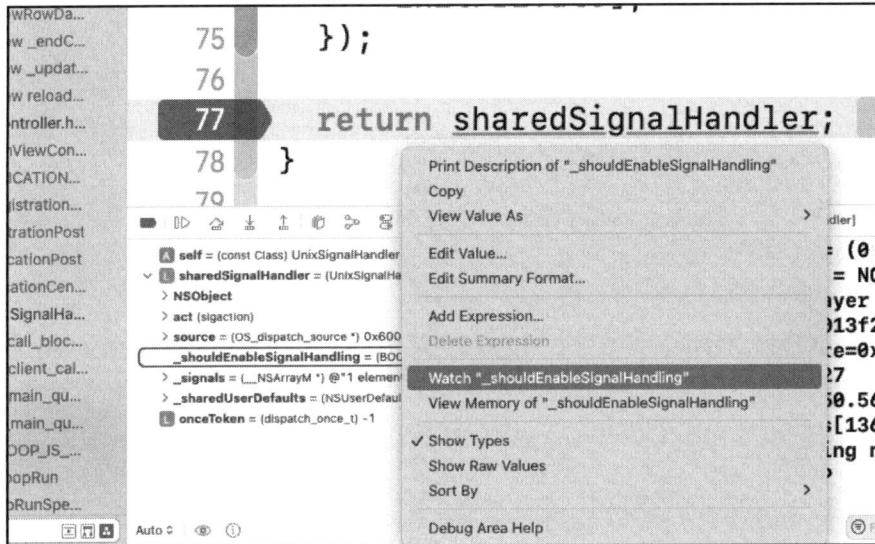

Now, remove the GUI breakpoint, you were just using it to pause the app in the right stack frame. Resume control of the program through Xcode or LLDB. Test out the newly created watchpoint by tapping the Playbook UISwitch yet again in the app. Each time you toggle the switch, the app will pause on the line where the value of _shouldEnableSignalHandling gets set.

Other Watchpoint Tidbits

Fortunately, the syntax for watchpoints is very similar to the syntax for breakpoints. You can delete, disable, enable, list, command, or modify them just as you would using lldb's breakpoint syntax.

The more interesting ones of the group are the command and modify actions. Use modify to add a condition to trigger the watchpoint only if it's true. The command action lets you perform a unique command whenever the watchpoint gets triggered.

For example, if you wanted the previous watchpoint to stop only when the new value is set to 0.

First, find the watchpoint ID to modify:

```
(lldb) watchpoint list -b
```

This says to list all the watchpoints in a "brief" (–b) format. lldb responds with information about all of the current watchpoints:

```
Number of supported hardware watchpoints: 4
Current watchpoints:
Watchpoint 2: addr = 0x60000161be60 size = 1 state = enabled
type = w   .
```

You can see the Watchpoint ID is **2**. From there modify, Watchpoint ID 2:

```
(lldb) watchpoint modify 2 -c '*(BOOL*)0x60000161be60 == 0'
```

This will modify Watchpoint ID 2 to only stop if the new value of _shouldEnableSignalHandling is set to false.

If you omit the Watchpoint ID in the above example (the 2), your modification will be applied to every valid watchpoint in the process.

One more example before you wrap this chapter up! Instead of conditionally stopping when _shouldEnableSignalHandling is set to 0, you can simply have lldb print the stack trace every time it's set.

Remove all watchpoint conditions by using the modify subcommand without supplying any new conditions:

```
(lldb) watchpoint modify 2
```

This removes the condition you previously created. Now add a command to print the backtrace, then continue.

```
(lldb) watchpoint command add 2
Enter your debugger command(s).  Type 'DONE' to end.
> bt 5
> continue
> DONE
```

Instead of conditionally stopping, the watchpoint will now print the first five stack frames in the lldb console, then continue.

Once you get bored of seeing all that output, you can remove this command by typing:

```
(lldb) watchpoint command delete 2
```

And there you have it! Watchpoints in a nutshell.

Key Points

- Watchpoints can monitor memory addresses for `read`, `write`, or `read_write` actions.

- The `watchpoint` command has similar subcommands to breakpoints such as: `list`, `delete`, and `disable`.

- Use `watchpoint modify` to add conditions to how often a watchpoint should fire.

- Use `watchpoint command` when you want triggering of the watchpoint to do more than just pause execution of the code.

- You are limited to four watchpoints at a time.

- Watchpoints shine when you are tracking a variable that seems to be changing outside of its official accessor methods.

- Find the memory addresses of variables in the instance of an object using `class-table dump`.

Where to Go From Here?

Watchpoints tend to play very nicely with those who understand how an executable is laid out in memory. This layout, known as Mach-O, will be discussed in detail in the "Low Level" section. Combining this knowledge with watchpoints, you can watch when strings are referenced, or when static pointers are initialized, without having to tediously track the locations at runtime.

But for now, just remember that you have a great tool to use when you need to hunt for how something is changing and your breakpoints don't produce any results.

Chapter 9: Persisting & Customizing Commands

With watchpoints covered, you now have an excellent foundation with the basic workflows within lldb, but there's two problems that haven't been addressed: persisting your lldb commands and creating shortcuts for them!

In this chapter, you'll learn how to create simple, custom commands and save them for future lldb sessions!

Persisting... How?

Whenever lldb is invoked, it searches several directories for special initialization files. If found, these files will be loaded into lldb as soon as lldb launches but before lldb attaches to a process. This is an important detail if you're trying to execute arbitrary code in the init file.

You can use these files to specify settings or create custom commands to do your debugging bidding.

lldb searches for an initialization file in the following places:

1. ~/**.lldbinit-[context]** where [context] is **Xcode**, if you are debugging with Xcode, or **lldb** if you are using the command line incarnation of lldb.

    For example, if you wanted commands that were only available in lldb while debugging in the Terminal, you'd add content to ~/.lldbinit-lldb, while if you wanted to have commands only available to Xcode you'd use ~/.lldbinit-Xcode.

2. Next, lldb searches for content found in ~/**.lldbinit**. This is the ideal file for most of your logic, since you want to use commands in both Xcode *and* Terminal sessions of lldb.

3. Finally, lldb will search the directory where it was invoked. Unfortunately, when Xcode launches lldb, it'll launch lldb at the / root directory. This isn't an ideal place to stick an .lldbinit file, so this particular implementation will be ignored throughout the book.

Creating the .lldbinit File

In this section you're going to create your first .lldbinit file.

First, open a Terminal window and type the following:

```
nano ~/.lldbinit
```

This uses the nano text editor to open up your .lldbinit file. If you already have an existing file in the location, nano will open the file instead of creating a new one.

> **Note**: You really should be using some form of **vi** or **emacs** for editing .lldbinit, and then angrily blog about how unconventional the other editor is. I'm suggesting nano to stay out of the great debate.

Once the file is open, add the following line of code to the end of your .lldbinit file:

```
command alias -- Yay_Autolayout expression -l objc -O --
[[[[UIApplication sharedApplication] keyWindow]
rootViewController] view] recursiveDescription]
```

You've just created an **alias** — a shortcut command for a longer expression. It's named Yay_Autolayout and it'll execute an expression command to get the root UIView (iOS only) and dump the position and layout of the root view and all of its subviews.

Save your work by pressing **Ctrl + O**, but don't exit nano just yet.

Open the Signals Xcode project — you know, the one you've been using throughout this section. Build and run the Signals application. Once running, pause execution and type the alias in the debugger:

```
(lldb) Yay_Autolayout
```

This will dump out all the views in the applications! Neat!

> **Note**: The cool thing about this command is it'll work equally well for apps you do — and don't — have source code for. You could, hypothetically, attach lldb to the Simulator's SpringBoard and dump all the views using the exact same method.

Now, use lldb to get help for this new command:

```
(lldb) help Yay_Autolayout
```

The output will look kinda meh. You can do better. Go back to the nano Terminal window and rewrite the command alias to include some helpful information, like so:

```
command alias -H "Yay_Autolayout will get the root view and
recursively dump all the subviews and their frames" -h
"Recursively dump views" -- Yay_Autolayout expression -l objc -O
-- [[[[UIApplication sharedApplication] keyWindow]
rootViewController] view] recursiveDescription]
```

Make sure nano saves the file by pressing **Ctrl + O**. Next, build and run the Signals project.

Now when you stop the debugger and type help Yay_Autolayout, you'll get help text at the bottom of the output. This is done with the -H command.

You can also get a brief summary by just typing help, which gives the -h description along with the rest of the commands.

> **Note**: You also may see a lot of extra "help" text that you didn't write. This appears to be a defect (feature?) in lldb's help as it's providing you with the help text for the command you've aliased in addition to what you specify with the -h and -H switches. For example, using the help command with the alias above, the entire help text for the expression command appears. Unfortunately, none of the options listed are usable because of how the alias is constructed...so defect? Creating an alias for breakpoint list however, the switches that help displays continue to work because they normally appear after the command anyway...so feature? The techniques you learn in later in the book to create more complex, custom commands will not have this behavior. They will only display the help text that you supply.

This may seem a bit pointless now, but when you have many, many custom commands in your .lldbinit file, you'll be thankful you provided documentation for yourself.

Command Aliases With Arguments

You've just created a standalone command alias that doesn't require any arguments. However, you'll often want to create aliases to which you can supply input.

Go back to the nano window in Terminal. Add the following at the bottom of the file:

```
command alias cpo expression -l objc -O --
```

You've just created a new command called **cpo**. The cpo command will do a normal po (print object), but it'll use the Objective-C context instead. This is an ideal command to use when you're in a Swift context, but want to use Objective-C to print out an address or register of something you know is a valid Objective-C object.

Save your work in nano, and jump over to the Signals project. Navigate to **MainViewController**'s viewDidLoad and set a breakpoint at the top of the function. Build and run the application.

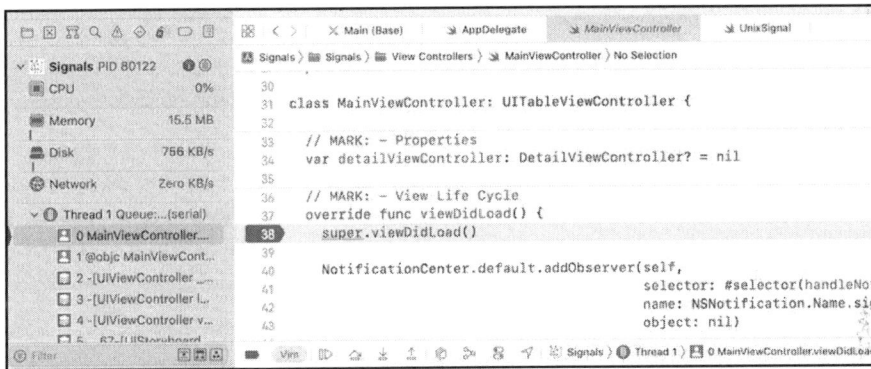

To best understand the importance of the cpo command, first get the reference to the MainViewController.

```
(lldb) po self
```

You'll get output similar to the following:

```
<Signals.MainViewController: 0x15210c180>
```

Take the memory address you get at the end of the output (as usual, yours will likely be different), and try printing that in the debugger.

```
(lldb) po 0x15210c180
```

This will not produce any meaningful output, since you've stopped in a Swift file, and Swift is a type-safe language. Simply printing an address in Swift will not do anything. This is why the Objective-C context is so useful when debugging, especially when working in assembly where there are only references to memory addresses.

Now, use the new command you've just created on the address:

```
(lldb) cpo 0x15210c180
```

You'll see the same output as you did with po self:

```
<Signals.MainViewController: 0x15210c180>
```

This is a helpful command to get a NSObject's description, whether it's created with Objective-C or Swift.

You can also add your own substitution arguments using a % substitution pattern. Here is a contrived example to illustrate. Add a new command that takes your preferred language as an argument:

```
command alias lpo expression -l %1 -O --
```

When this new lpo alias executes it will replace the %1 with the first argument provided after the command. Using %1, %2, etc. you can specify as many substitutions as you like. Now repeat the previous po self exercise but this time you'll provide the language **swift** or **objc** each time. When the Signals app pauses in viewDidLoad, it's in the Swift context, so execute the command with swift:

```
(lldb) lpo swift self
```

You should get similar output as before.

```
<Signals.MainViewController: 0x152b0bc20>
```

Now take the memory address and execute the command again and specify the Swift context.

```
(lldb) lpo swift 0x152b0bc20
```

Again, same as before, you get the uninteresting output. But switching to the objc context provides the class name and memory location again:

```
(lldb) lpo objc 0x152b0bc20
<Signals.MainViewController: 0x152b0bc20>
```

Key Points

- Use `command alias` to make shortcuts for commands you use often.

- `lldb` will load initialization commands from a contextual `.lldbinit` file for Xcode (`.lldbinit-Xcode`) or for terminal (`.lldbinit-lldb`).

- `lldb` will also load initialization commands from a generic `.lldbinit` file on launch. This file is read after the contextual one mentioned above.

- You can specify aliases within an `lldb` session, but they will only live for that session.

- For aliases, be sure to add –h and –H help text to remind future you why you made them and how to use them.

Where to Go From Here?

You've learned how to create aliases for simple commands as well as persist them in the `.lldbinit` file. This will work across both Xcode and Terminal invocations of `lldb`.

As an exercise, add help messages to your newly created `cpo` command in the `~/.lldbinit` file so you'll be able to remember how to use it when you have an onslaught of custom commands. Remember the –h option is the short help message that's displayed when you just type `help`, while the –H option is the longer help command used when you type `help command`. Remember to use the –– to separate your help input arguments from the rest of your command.

In addition, write a command alias for something you use often. Put this alias in your `~/.lldbinit` file and try it out!

Chapter 10: Regex Commands

In the previous chapter, you learned about `command alias` as well as how to persist commands through an `lldbinit` file. Unfortunately, `command alias` has some limitations because `lldb` essentially just replaces the alias with the actual command when it parses your input.

In this chapter, you'll combine the input substitution technique from the last chapter with regular expressions to create more flexible custom `lldb` commands using **command regex**.

command regex

The lldb command **command regex** acts much like command alias, except you can provide a regular expression for input which will be parsed and applied to the action part of the command.

command regex takes an input syntax that looks similar to the following:

```
s/<regex>/<subst>/
```

This is a normal regular expression. It starts with 's/', which specifies a stream editor input to use the **substitute command**. The <regex> part is the bit that specifies what should be replaced. The <subst> part says what to replace it with.

> **Note:** This syntax is derived from the **sed** Terminal command. This is important to know, because if you're experimenting using advanced patterns, you can check the **man** pages of sed to see what's possible within the substitute formatting syntax.

Time to look at a concrete example. Open up the **Signals** Xcode project. Build and run, then pause the application in the debugger. Once the lldb console is up and ready to receive input, enter the following command in lldb:

```
(lldb) command regex rlook 's/(.+)/image lookup -rn %1/'
```

This command you've entered will make your image regex searches much easier. You've created a new command called rlook. This new command takes everything after the rlook and prefixes it with image lookup -rn. It does this through a regex with a single matcher (the parentheses) which matches on one or more characters, and replaces the whole thing with image lookup -rn %1. The %1 specifies the contents of the matcher.

> **Note:** There is a subtle, but important, difference in the matching behavior of the % replacement from the last chapter. In the previous chapter, each argument got matched up with a % placeholder and the rest of the input got appended to the end of the command. Now, everything that doesn't match just gets ignored.

So, for example, if you enter this:

```
rlook FOO
```

lldb will actually execute the following:

```
image lookup -rn FOO
```

Now, instead of having to type the soul-crushingly long `image lookup -rn`, you can just type `rlook`!

But wait, it gets better. Provided there are no conflicts with the characters `rl`, you can simply use that instead. A feature of lldb is that you can specify any command, be it built-in or your own, by using any prefix which is not shared with another command.

This means you can easily search for methods like `viewDidLoad` using an *even more* convenient amount of typing. Try it out now:

```
(lldb) rl viewDidLoad
```

This will produce all the `viewDidLoad` implementations across all modules in the current executable. Try limiting it to only code in the Signals app:

```
(lldb) rl viewDidLoad Signals
```

Now that you're satisfied with the command, add the following line of code to your ~/.lldbinit file:

```
command regex rlook 's/(.+)/image lookup -rn %1/'
```

Note: The best way to implement a `regex` command is to use lldb while a program is running. This lets you iterate on the command regex (by redeclaring it if you're not happy with it) and test it out without having to relaunch lldb.

Once you're happy with the command, add it to your ~/.lldbinit file so it will be available every time lldb starts up. Now the `rlook` command will be available to you from here on out, resulting in no more painful typing of the full `image lookup -rn` command.

Remember a couple chapters back when image lookup*'s output was described as less than ideal?* You can use the following command regex instead!

```
command regex rsearch 's/(.+)/script
print("\n".join([hex(i.GetSymbol().GetStartAddress().GetLoadAddr
ess(lldb.target)) + " " +i.GetSymbol().GetName() + "\n" for i in
lldb.target.FindGlobalFunctions("%1", 0,
lldb.eMatchTypeRegex)]))/'
```

This uses lldb's script bridging (discussed in the "Custom LLDB Commands" Section) in combination with a regular expression command. Using this in the Signals project will produce a significantly cleaner display of information:

```
(lldb) rsearch viewDidLoad\]$
0x18d6ff604 -[UIDocumentBrowserViewController viewDidLoad]

0x18d70a944 -[DOCRemoteViewController viewDidLoad]

0x18d728e5c -[DOCTargetSelectionBrowserViewController
viewDidLoad]

0x18417b500 -[_UIAlertControllerTextFieldViewController
viewDidLoad]

0x1841a10b0 -[UIAlertController viewDidLoad]

0x1844bfb34 -[_UIProgressiveBlurContextController viewDidLoad]

0x1844f1fa4 -[UITabBarController viewDidLoad]
...
```

Executing Complex Logic

It still might be hard to see how this is a powerful improvement over just using command alias, well, time to take the command regex up a level! You can actually use this command to execute multiple commands for a single alias. While lldb is still paused, implement this new command:

```
(lldb) command regex -- tv 's/(.+)/expression -l objc -O --
@import QuartzCore; [%1 setHidden:!(BOOL)[%1 isHidden]]; (void)
[CATransaction flush];/'
```

This complicated, yet useful command, will create a command named **tv** (toggle view), which toggles a UIView (or NSView) on or off while the debugger is paused. This can be quite helpful when you're debugging a complex layout and want to confirm you've got a handle to the right UI element.

Packed into this command are three separate lines of code:

1. `@import QuartzCore` imports the QuartzCore framework symbols into `lldb`. This allows `lldb` to call code in the debugged process. `lldb` uses **modules** in order to call symbols within a process (you'll learn more about modules in the "Low Level" section). The code that toggles view visibility is found in the QuartzCore framework, so just in case `QuartzCore` hasn't been imported yet, you're doing it now.

2. `[%1 setHidden:!(BOOL)[%1 isHidden]];` toggles the view to either hidden or visible, depending what the previous state was. Note that `isHidden` doesn't know the return type, so you need to cast it to an Objective-C `BOOL`.

3. The final command, `[CATransaction flush]`, flushes the CATransaction queue. Manipulating the UI in the debugger normally means the screen will not reflect any updates until the debugger resumes execution.

   However, this method updates the screen immediately resulting in `lldb` not needing to `continue` in order to show visual changes.

> **Note**: Due to the limitations of the input params, specifying multiline input for `command regex` is not allowed. This means you have to join all the commands onto one line. This is ugly but necessary when crafting these regex commands. However, if you ever do this in actual Objective-C/Swift source code, may the Apple Gods punish you with extra-long app review times! :]

Pause the app if it's running and execute this newly created `tv` command. Be mindful of the number of square brackets, `lldb` and auto-complete may conspire to mess everything up.

```
(lldb) tv [[[UIApp keyWindow] rootViewController] view]
```

Bring up the Simulator to verify the view has disappeared.

Now simply press **Enter** in the `lldb` console, as `lldb` will repeat the last command you've entered. The view will flash back to normal. Keep pressing **Enter** for a nice strobe effect, whee!

Now that you're done implementing the `tv` command, add it to your `~/.lldbinit` file:

```
command regex -- tv 's/(.+)/expression -l objc -O -- @import
QuartzCore; [%1 setHidden:!(BOOL)[%1 isHidden]]; (void)
[CATransaction flush];/'
```

Chaining Regex Inputs

There's a reason why that weird sed stream editor input style was chosen for using this command: this format lets you easily specify multiple actions for the same command. When given multiple commands, the regex will try to match each input. If the input matches, that particular <subst> is applied to the command. If the input doesn't match for a particular stream, it'll go to the next command and see if the regex can match that input.

It's generally necessary to use the Objective-C context when working with objects in memory and registers. Also, anything that begins with the square open bracket or the '@' character is (likely) Objective-C. This is because Swift makes it difficult to work with memory, and Swift won't let you access registers, nor do Swift expressions usually ever begin with an open bracket or '@' character.

You can use this information to automatically detect which context you need to use for a given input.

Let's see how you'd you go about building a command which gets the class information out of an object, and honors the following requirements:

- In Objective-C, you'd use **[objcObject class]**.

- In Swift, you'd use **type(of: swiftObject)**.

In the Signals project, create a GUI breakpoint on the first line of **viewDidLoad()** in the **MainViewController**. This will ensure that lldb pauses in a Swift context with the main views of the application loaded.

Build and run, then wait for the breakpoint to be triggered. As usual, head on over to the debugger.

First, build out the Objective-C implementation of this new command, **getcls**.

```
(lldb) command regex getcls 's/(([0-9]|\$|\@|\[).*)/cpo [%1
class]/'
```

Note: This command regex assumes you have the cpo alias from the last chapter in your ~/.lldbinit.

Wow, that regex makes the eyes blur. Time to break it down:

At first, there's an inner grouping saying the following characters can be used to match the start:

- [0–9] means the numbers from 0-9 can be used.

- \$ means the literal character '$' will be matched.

- \@ means the literal character '@' will be matched.

- \[means the literal character '[' will be matched.

Any characters that start with the above will generate a match. Following that is .* which means zero or more characters will produce a match.

Overall, this means that a number, $, @, or [, followed by any characters will result in the command matching and running cpo [%1 class]. Once again, %1 is replaced with the first matcher from the regex. In this case, it's the entire command. The inner matcher (matching a number, $, or so on) would be %2.

Try throwing a couple of commands at the getcls command to see how it works:

```
(lldb) getcls @"hello world"
__NSCFString

(lldb) getcls @[@"hello world"]
__NSSingleObjectArrayI

(lldb) getcls [UIDevice currentDevice]
UIDevice

(lldb) po UIDevice.current
<UIDevice: 0x60800002b520>

(lldb) getcls 0x60800002b520
UIDevice
```

Awesome!

However, this only handles references that make sense in the Objective-C context and that match your command. For example, try the following:

```
(lldb) getcls self
```

You'll get an error:

```
error: getcls
```

This is because there was no matching regex for the input you provided.

Redefine getcls and add a regex which catches other forms of input. Type the following into lldb:

```
(lldb) command regex getcls 's/(([0-9]|\$|\@|\[).*)/cpo [%1
class]/' 's/(.+)/expression -l swift -O -- type(of: %1)/'
```

The first part of the command is the same as what you added previously, but now you've added another regex to the end. This one is a catch-all, just like the rlook command you added earlier. This catch-all simply calls type(of:) with the input as the parameter.

Try executing the command again for self while execution is stopped in the Swift context of MainViewController.swift:

```
(lldb) getcls self
```

You'll now get the expected Signals.MainViewController output. Since you made the Swift context as a catch-all, you can use this command in interesting ways.

```
(lldb) getcls self .title
```

This provides you with the class for the title property of self.

```
Swift.Optional<Swift.String>
```

Notice the space in there, and it still works. This is because you told the Swift context to quite literally take anything except newlines.

Once, you're done playing with this new and improved getcls command, be sure to add it to your ~/.lldbinit file.

And that's it for lldb's command regex! The next step up from a command regex will be lldb's full blown **script bridging** interface — a fully featured Python implementation for creating advanced lldb commands to do your debugging bidding. You'll take an in depth look at script bridging in the "Custom LLDB Commands" section of this book.

For now, simply use either command alias or command regex to suit your debugging needs.

Key Points

- `command alias` uses exact matching of your inputs and basic argument substitution.

- `command regex` allows for more powerful input matching and argument substitution.

- Join complex, multi-line commands using `;` to combine them into one `command regex` command.

- Chain multiple regex patterns to provide multiple actions for different inputs to the same command.

Where to Go From Here?

Go back to the regex commands you've created in this chapter and add **syntax** and **help** help documentation.

You'll thank yourself for this documentation about your command's functionality, when it's 11 PM on a Friday night and you just want to figure out your bleeping gosh darn bug.

Section II: Understanding Assembly

Knowing what the computer is doing with all those 1s and 0s underneath your code is an excellent skill to have when digging for useful information about a program. This section will set you up with the theory you'll need for the remainder of this book in order to create complex debugging scripts — and introduce you to the basic theory behind reverse-engineering code.

Chapter 11: Assembly Register Calling Convention

Now that you've gained a basic understanding of how to maneuver around the debugger, it's time to take a step down the executable Jenga tower and explore the 1s and 0s that make up your source code. This section will focus on the low-level aspects of debugging.

In this chapter, you'll look at registers the CPU uses and explore and modify parameters passed into function calls. You'll also learn about common Apple computer architectures and how their registers are used within a function. This is known as an architecture's **calling convention**.

Knowing how assembly works and how a specific architecture's calling convention works is an extremely important skill to have. It lets you observe function parameters you don't have the source code for and lets you modify the parameters passed into a function. In addition, it's sometimes even better to go to the assembly level because your source code could have different or unknown names for variables you're not aware of.

For example, let's say you always wanted to know the second parameter of a function call, regardless of what the parameter's name is. Knowledge of assembly gives you a great base layer to manipulate and observe parameters in functions.

Assembly 101

Wait, so what's assembly again?

Have you ever stopped in a function you didn't have source code for, and saw an onslaught of memory addresses followed by cryptic, short commands? Did you huddle in a ball and quietly whisper to yourself you'll never look at this dense stuff again? Well... that stuff is known as assembly!

Here's a picture of a backtrace in Xcode, which showcases the assembly of a function within the Simulator.

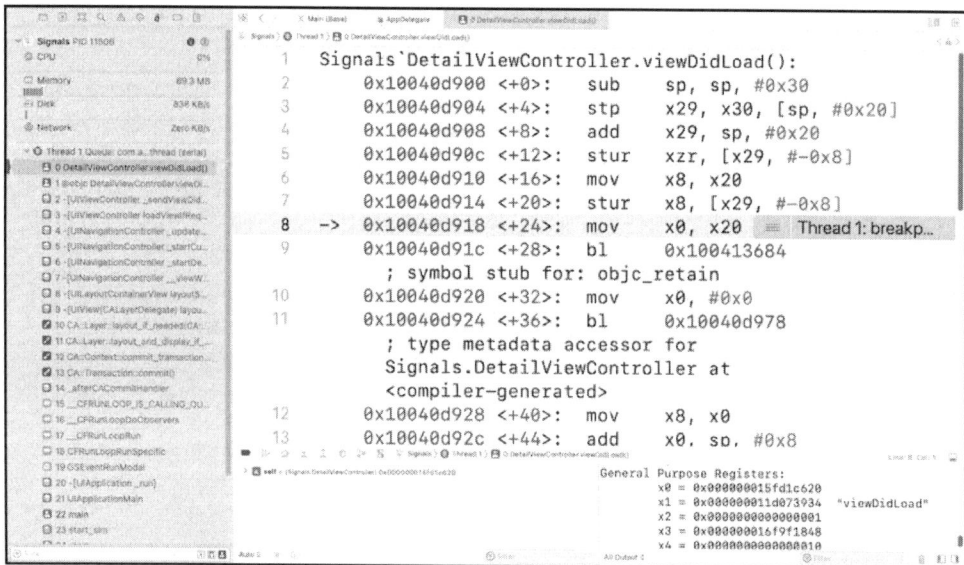

Looking at the image above, the assembly can be broken into several parts. Each line in an assembly instruction contains an **opcode**, which can be thought of as an extremely simple instruction for the computer.

So what does an opcode look like? An opcode is an instruction that performs a simple task on the computer. For example, consider the following snippet of assembly:

```
stp    x0, x1, [sp]
sub    x0, x8, #0x3
mov    x8, x20
```

In this nonsense block of assembly, you see three opcodes, **stp**, **sub**, and **mov**. Think of the opcode items as the action to perform. The things following the opcode are the source and destination labels. That is, these are the items the opcode acts upon.

In the above example, there are several **registers**, shown as **x0**, **x8**, **x1**, and **sp**. Most registers begin with **x** or **r** but there are some special use registers like **sp**, **fp** and **xzr**.

In addition, you can also find a numeric constant in hexadecimal shown as **0x3**. The **#** before this constant tells you it's an absolute number. A hexadecimal number by itself is almost always a memory location.

There's no need to know what this code is doing at the moment, since you'll first need to learn about the registers and calling convention of functions. Then you'll learn more about the opcodes and write your own assembly in a future chapter. Remember, though, the focus in this book is to be able to read and follow assembly to help in debugging, not to write a bunch of assembly.

x86_64 vs ARM64

As a developer for Apple platforms, there are two primary architectures you'll deal with when learning assembly: **x86_64** architecture and **arm64** architecture. x86_64 was the architecture used on macOS computers with "Intel" CPUs. ARM64 is the architecture used on iOS devices and macOS computers with "Apple Silicon".

arm64 is a **64-bit** architecture, which means every address can hold up to 64 1s or 0s. Alternatively, older Macs and older iOS devices use a **32-bit** architecture, but Apple stopped making 32-bit Macs at the end of the 2010's. As of the writing of this book, Apple has also almost completed its transition away from x86_64 to Apple Silicon. To assist owners of Apple Silicon computers with running older x86_64 software, Apple created the Rosetta2 technology.

If you have any doubt of what hardware architecture you're working with, you can get your computer's hardware architecture by running the following command in Terminal:

```
uname -m
```

ARM emphasizes power conservation, so it has a reduced set of opcodes compared to x86 that help facilitate energy consumption over complex assembly instructions. This is good news for you, because there are fewer instructions for you to learn on the ARM architecture.

Apple originally shipped 32-bit ARM processors in many of their devices, but have since moved to 64-bit ARM processors. 32-bit devices are basically obsolete as Apple has phased them out through various iOS versions. For example, iOS 16 does not support any 32-bit devices.

Since it's best to focus on what you'll need for the future, this book focuses primarily on arm64 assembly.

arm64 Register Calling Convention

Your CPU uses a set of registers in order to manipulate data in your running program. These are storage holders, just like the RAM in your computer. However they're located on the CPU itself very close to the parts of the CPU that need them. So these parts of the CPU can access these registers incredibly quickly. Also, there are a finite number of registers.

Most instructions involve one or more registers and perform operations such as writing the contents of a register to memory, reading the contents of memory to a register or performing arithmetic operations (add, subtract, etc.) on two registers.

In **arm64**, there are **31 general purpose registers** used by the machine to manipulate data.

These registers are **x0** through **x30**. You may also see registers referred to starting with **w**. Registers starting with w are referencing 32-bit numbers. If you're working with Metal or some floating point math, then registers might start with s, d, q, h or b depending on their size. For now, just think about registers that start with x.

When you call a function in arm64, the manner and use of the registers follows a very specific convention. This dictates where the parameters to the function should go and where the return value from the function will be when the function finishes. This is important so code compiled with one compiler can be used with code compiled with another compiler.

Take a look at this simple Swift code:

```
let fName = "Zoltan"
```

When viewing code through assembly, the computer doesn't care about names for variables; it only cares about locations in memory. Here is the assembly code to create the String object and initialize it.

```
0x1044757a8 <+124>: adrp    x0, 8
0x1044757ac <+128>: add     x0, x0, #0x770              ; "Zoltan"
0x1044757b0 <+132>: mov     w8, #0x6
0x1044757b4 <+136>: mov     x1, x8
0x1044757b8 <+140>: mov     w8, #0x1
0x1044757bc <+144>: str     w8, [sp, #0x4]
0x1044757c0 <+148>: and     w2, w8, #0x1
0x1044757c4 <+152>: bl      0x10447b3f0                ; symbol
stub for: Swift.String.init(_builtinStringLiteral:
Builtin.RawPointer, utf8CodeUnitCount: Builtin.Word, isASCII:
Builtin.Int1) -> Swift.String
```

A short string like "Zoltan" in Swift is contained in a struct with the string data at the beginning and the length of the string at the end. The code above, makes some space for the "Zoltan" string in x0 and then adds the length value of #0x6 and stores the value in x1. The bl line calls the String.init function. That function expects the given registers will contain the appropriate values as shown above. When the String.init function returns, x0 will contain the memory location of the new String.

However, as soon as the **function prologue** (the beginning section of a function that prepares the stack and registers) finishes executing, the values in these registers will likely change. The generated assembly will likely overwrite the values stored in these registers, or just simply discard these references when the code has no more need of them.

This means as soon as you leave the start of a function (through stepping over, stepping in, or stepping out), you can no longer assume these registers will hold the expected values you want to observe, unless you actually look at the assembly code to see what it's doing.

This calling convention heavily influences your debugging (and breakpoint) strategy. If you were to automate any type of breaking and exploring, you would have to stop at the start of a function call in order to inspect or modify the parameters without having to actually dive into the assembly.

Objective-C and Registers

As you learned in the previous section, registers use a specific calling convention. You can take that same knowledge and apply it to other languages as well.

When Objective-C executes a method, a special C function, **objc_msgSend**, is executed. There's actually several different types of these functions, but objc_msgSend is the most widely used, as this is the heart of message dispatch. As the first parameter, objc_msgSend takes the reference of the object upon which the message is being sent. This is followed by a **selector**, which is simply just a char * specifying the name of the method being called on the object. Finally, objc_msgSend takes a variable amount of arguments within the function if the Selector specifies there should be parameters.

Let's look at a concrete example of this in an iOS context:

```
[UIApplication sharedApplication];
```

The compiler will take this code and create the following pseudocode:

```
id UIApplicationClass = [UIApplication class];
objc_msgSend(UIApplicationClass, "sharedApplication");
```

The first parameter is a reference to the UIApplication class, followed by the sharedApplication selector. An easy way to tell if there are any parameters is to simply check for colons in the Objective-C Selector. Each colon will represent a parameter in a Selector.

Here's another Objective-C example:

```
NSString *helloWorldString = [@"Can't Sleep; "
stringByAppendingString:@"Coffee for dessert was unwise."];
```

The compiler will create the following (shown below in pseudocode):

```
NSString *helloWorldString;
helloWorldString = objc_msgSend(@"Can't Sleep; ",
 "stringByAppendingString:", @"Coffee for dessert was unwise.");
```

The first argument is an instance of an NSString (@"Can't Sleep; "), followed by the Selector, followed by a parameter which is also an NSString instance.

Using this knowledge of objc_msgSend, you can use the registers to help explore content, which you'll do very shortly.

Putting Theory to Practice

For this section, you'll be using a project supplied in this chapter's resource bundle called **Registers**.

Open this project up through Xcode and give it a run.

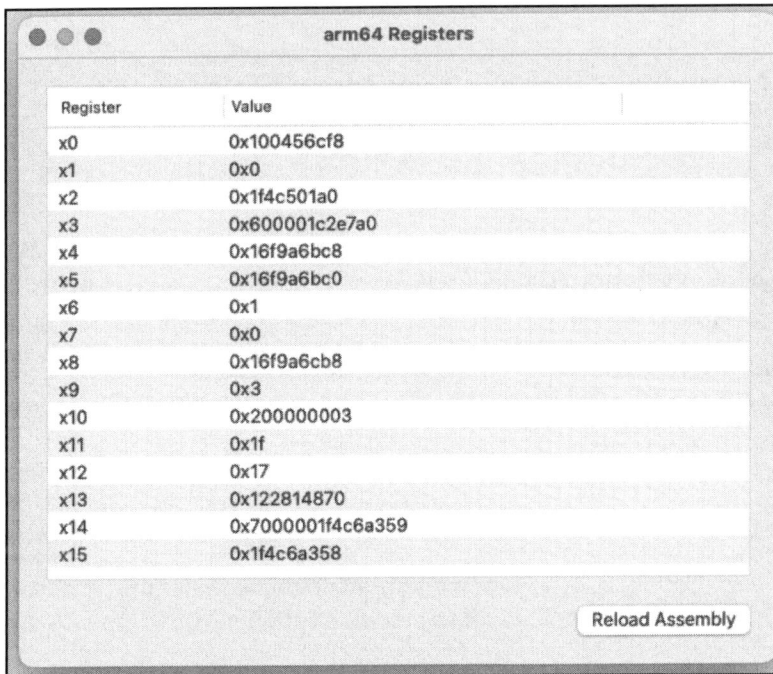

Register	Value
x0	0x100456cf8
x1	0x0
x2	0x1f4c501a0
x3	0x600001c2e7a0
x4	0x16f9a6bc8
x5	0x16f9a6bc0
x6	0x1
x7	0x0
x8	0x16f9a6cb8
x9	0x3
x10	0x200000003
x11	0x1f
x12	0x17
x13	0x122814870
x14	0x7000001f4c6a359
x15	0x1f4c6a358

arm64 Registers — **Reload Assembly**

This is a rather simple application which merely displays the contents of some registers. It's important to note that this application can't display the values of registers at any given moment; it can only display the values of registers during a specific function call. This means that you won't see too many changes to the values of these registers since they'll likely have the same (or similar) value when the function to grab the register values is called.

Now that you've got an understanding of the functionality behind the Registers macOS application, create a symbolic breakpoint for NSViewController's viewDidLoad method. Remember to use "NS" instead of "UI", since you're working on a Cocoa application.

```
☑ Symbolic Breakpoint
      Symbol    -[NSViewController viewDidLoad]
      Module    Example: "libSystem.B.dylib"
   Condition
      Ignore    0    ⌃ times before stopping
      Action    [ Add Action ]
     Options    ☐ Automatically continue after evaluating actions
```

Build and rerun the application. Once the debugger has stopped, type the following into the LLDB console:

```
(lldb) register read
```

This will list all of the main registers at the paused state of execution. However, this is too much information. You should selectively print out registers and treat them as Objective-C objects instead.

If you recall, -[NSViewController viewDidLoad] will be translated into the following assembly pseudocode:

```
x0 = UIViewControllerInstance
x1 = "viewDidLoad"
objc_msgSend(x0, x1)
```

With the arm64 calling convention in mind, and knowing how objc_msgSend works, you can find the specific NSViewController that is being loaded.

Type the following into the LLDB console:

```
(lldb) po $x0
```

You'll get output similar to the following:

```
<Registers.ViewController: 0x6080000c13b0>
```

This will dump out the NSViewController reference held in the x0 register, which as you now know, is the location of the first argument to the method. Remember that you can use $arg1 to refer to the register where the *first* argument is held.

In LLDB, it's important to prefix registers with the $ character, so LLDB knows you want the value of a register and not a variable related to your scope in the source code. Yes, that's different than the assembly you see in the disassembly view! Annoying, eh?

> **Note**: The observant among you might notice whenever you stop on an Objective-C method, you'll never see the objc_msgSend in the LLDB backtrace. This is because the objc_msgSend family of functions performs a **b**, or jump opcode command in assembly. This means that objc_msgSend acts as a trampoline function, and once the Objective-C code starts executing, all stack trace history of objc_msgSend will be gone. This is an optimization known as **tail call optimization**.

Try printing out the RSI register, which will hopefully contain the Selector that was called. Type the following into the LLDB console:

```
(lldb) po $x1
```

Unfortunately, you'll get garbage output that looks something like this:

```
8211036373
```

Why is this?

An Objective-C Selector is basically just a char *. This means, like all C types, LLDB does not know how to format this data. As a result, you must explicitly cast this reference to the data type you want.

Try casting it to the correct type:

```
(lldb) po (char *)$x1
```

You'll now get the expected:

```
"viewDidLoad"
```

Of course, you can also cast it to the Selector type to produce the same result:

```
(lldb) po (SEL)$x1
```

Now, it's time to explore an Objective-C method with arguments. Since you've stopped on `viewDidLoad`, you can safely assume the `NSView` instance has loaded. A method of interest is the **mouseUp:** Selector implemented by `NSView`'s parent class, `NSResponder`.

In LLDB, create a breakpoint on `NSResponder`'s `mouseUp:` Selector and resume execution. If you can't remember how to do that, here are the commands you need:

```
(lldb) b -[NSResponder mouseUp:]
(lldb) continue
```

Now, click on the application's window. Make sure to click on the outside of the NSScrollView as it will gobble up your click and the `-[NSResponder mouseUp:]` breakpoint will not get hit.

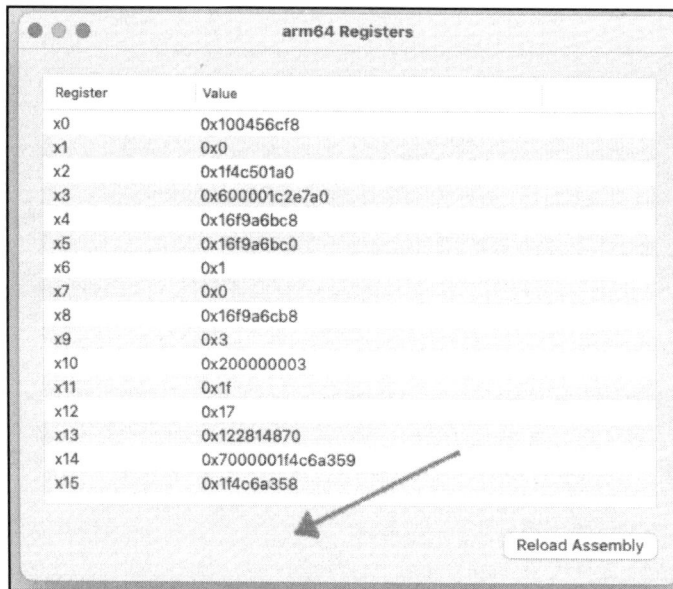

As soon as you let go of the mouse or the trackpad, LLDB will stop on the `mouseUp:` breakpoint. Print out the reference of the `NSResponder` by typing the following into the LLDB console:

```
(lldb) po $x0
```

You'll get something similar to the following:

```
<NSView: 0x11d62e010>
```

However, there's something interesting with the Selector. There's a colon in it, meaning there's an argument to explore! Type the following into the LLDB console:

```
(lldb) po $x2
```

You'll get the description of the NSEvent:

```
NSEvent: type=LMouseUp loc=(351.672,137.914) time=175929.4
flags=0 win=0x6100001e0400 winNum=8622 ctxt=0x0 evNum=10956
click=1 buttonNumber=0 pressure=0 deviceID:0x300000014400000
subtype=NSEventSubtypeTouch
```

How can you tell it's an NSEvent? Well, you can either look online for documentation on –[NSResponder mouseUp:] or, you can simply use Objective-C to get the type:

```
(lldb) po [$x2 class]
```

Pretty cool, eh?

Sometimes it's useful to use registers and breakpoints in order to get a reference to an object you know is alive in memory.

For example, what if you wanted to change the front NSWindow to red, but you had no reference to this view in your code, and you didn't want to recompile with any code changes? You can simply create a breakpoint you can easily trip, get the reference from the register and manipulate the instance of the object as you please. You'll try changing the main window to red now.

> **Note**: Even though NSResponder implements mouseDown:, NSWindow overrides this method since it's a subclass of NSResponder. You can dump all classes that implement mouseDown: and figure out which of those classes inherit from NSResponder to determine if the method is overridden without having access to the source code. An example of dumping all the Objective-C classes that implement mouseDown: is image lookup -rn '\ mouseDown:'

First remove any previous breakpoints using the LLDB console:

```
(lldb) breakpoint delete
About to delete all breakpoints, do you want to do that?: [Y/n]
```

Then type the following into the LLDB console:

```
(lldb) b "-[NSWindow mouseDown:]"
(lldb) continue
```

This sets a breakpoint for mouseDown

Tap on the application. Immediately after tapping, the breakpoint should trip. Then type the following into the LLDB console:

```
(lldb) po [$x0 setBackgroundColor:[NSColor redColor]]
(lldb) continue
```

Upon resuming, the NSWindow will change to red!

Swift and Registers

When exploring registers in Swift you'll hit three hurdles that make assembly debugging harder than it is in Objective-C.

1. First, registers are **not** available in the Swift debugging context. This means you have to get whatever data you want and then use the Objective-C debugging context to print out the registers passed into the Swift function. Remember that you can use the expression -l objc -O -- command, or alternatively use the cpo custom command you made in Chapter 9, "Persisting & Customizing Commands". Fortunately, the register read command is available in the Swift context.

2. Second, Swift is not as dynamic as Objective-C. In fact, it's sometimes best to assume that Swift is like C, except with a very, very cranky and bossy compiler. If you have a memory address, you need to explicitly cast it to the object you expect it to be; otherwise, the Swift debugging context has no clue how to interpret a memory address.

3. When Swift calls a function, it has no need to use `objc_msgSend`, unless you mark up a method to use **@objc**. In addition, Swift will oftentimes opt to remove the `self` register (x0) as the first parameter and instead place it on the stack.

This means that the x0 register, which originally held the instance to `self`, and the x1 register, which originally held the Selector in Objective-C, are freed up to handle parameters for a function. This is done in the name of "optimization", but the compiler's inconsistency results in incompatible code and tools which struggle to analyze Swift generated assembly.

It has also resulted in version updates for this book to be a major PITA, since the Swift authors seem to come up with a new calling convention each year for Swift.

In the Registers project, navigate to **ViewController.swift** and add the following function below `viewDidLoad`:

```
func executeLotsOfArguments(one: Int, two: Int, three: Int,
                           four: Int, five: Int, six: Int,
                           seven: Int, eight: Int, nine: Int,
                           ten: Int) {
    print("arguments are: \(one), \(two), \(three),
          \(four), \(five), \(six), \(seven),
          \(eight), \(nine), \(ten)")
}
```

Note: The `print` command should be one line, if it's on multiple lines above, it's just beacause of page geometry, enter it as one line.

Next, add the following to the end of `viewDidLoad` to call this new function with the appropriate arguments:

```
self.executeLotsOfArguments(
    one: 31, two: 32, three: 33, four: 34,
    five: 35, six: 36, seven: 37,
    eight: 38, nine: 39, ten: 40)
```

Put a breakpoint on the very same line as of the declaration of
executeLotsOfArguments so the debugger will stop at the very beginning of the
function. This is important, or else the registers might get clobbered if the function
is actually executing.

Finally, remove the symbolic breakpoint you set on -[NSViewController
viewDidLoad].

Build and run the app, then wait for the executeLotsOfArguments breakpoint to
stop execution.

Again, a good way to start investigating is to dump the list registers. In LLDB, type
the following:

```
(lldb) register read -f d
```

This will dump the registers and display the format in decimal by using the -f d
option.

The output will look similar to the following:

```
General Purpose Registers:
        x0 = 1
        x1 = 8419065840  libswiftCore.dylib`type metadata for
Any + 8
        x2 = 33
        x3 = 34
        x4 = 35
        x5 = 36
        x6 = 37
        x7 = 38
        x8 = 1
        x9 = 40
       x10 = 39
       x11 = 32
       x12 = 8419006000  libswiftCore.dylib`protocol witness
table for Swift.Int : Swift.CustomStringConvertible in Swift
       x13 = 105553126854192
       x14 = 2161727825501079277 (0x000000010411c6ed) (void
*)0x01f4c6b578000000
       x15 = 8401620944  (void *)0x00000001f4c71400: NSResponder
       x16 = 8401620944  (void *)0x00000001f4c71400: NSResponder
       x17 = -424042045551510852 (0x0000000199127abc)
libobjc.A.dylib`-[NSObject release]
       x18 = 0
       x19 = 105553139451872
       x20 = 6103686920
       x21 = 105553160866960
       x22 = 0
```

```
        x23 = 4294967300
        x24 = 1
        x25 = 8434082064  @"Found circular dependency when
loading dependencies for %@ and %@"
        x26 = 5192684800
        x27 = 21474836484
        x28 = 8359120896
AppKit`_OBJC_PROTOCOL_REFERENCE_$_NSSecureCoding
         fp = 6103687040
         lr = 4363202980
Registers`Registers.ViewController.viewDidLoad() -> () + 192 at
ViewController.swift:61:3
         sp = 6103686528
         pc = 4363203312
Registers`Registers.ViewController.executeLotsOfArguments(one:
Swift.Int, two: Swift.Int, three: Swift.Int, four: Swift.Int,
five: Swift.Int, six: Swift.Int, seven: Swift.Int, eight:
Swift.Int, nine: Swift.Int, ten: Swift.Int) -> () + 228 at
ViewController.swift:67:13
       cpsr = 1610616832
```

As you can see things aren't in quite the order you'd expect. In the console, now type:

```
(lldb) disassemble
```

Scroll back up to the top of the function and look for a number of stur commands. This is the function placing all of the numbers onto the stack. Notice that things are already kind of crazy. Register x0 gets placed on the stack first, then x11 contains the second value. Then things look ok, but x10 seems to be in the place of x8. This is all because of how swift uses the stack more for storage and how registers like x8 in addition to x0 and x1 have special uses, so you can't just store regular values in there.

You may (or may not depending on the Swift version) also notice other parameters are stored in some of the other registers. While this is true, it's simply a leftover from the code that sets up the stack for the remaining parameters. Remember, parameters after the sixth one go on the stack.

The Return Register

But wait — there's more! So far, you've seen how registers are called in a function, but what about return values?

Fortunately, there is only one designated register for return values from functions: **x0**. Go back to executeLotsOfArguments and modify the function to return an Int:

```
func executeLotsOfArguments(one: Int, two: Int, three: Int,
                            four: Int, five: Int, six: Int,
                            seven: Int, eight: Int, nine: Int,
                            ten: Int) -> Int {
    print("arguments are: \(one), \(two), \(three), \(four),
          \(five), \(six), \(seven), \(eight), \(nine), \(ten)")
    return 100
}
```

In viewDidLoad, modify the function call to receive and ignore the String value.

```
override func viewDidLoad() {
    super.viewDidLoad()
    _ = self.executeLotsOfArguments(one: 1, two: 2,
        three: 3, four: 4, five: 5, six: 6, seven: 7,
        eight: 8, nine: 9, ten: 10)
}
```

Create a breakpoint somewhere in executeLotsOfArguments. Build and run again, and wait for execution to stop in the function. Next, type the following into the LLDB console:

```
(lldb) finish
```

This will finish executing the current function and pause the debugger again. At this point, the return value from the function should be in x0. Type the following into LLDB:

```
(lldb) re re x0 -fd
```

You'll get something similar to the following:

```
     x0 = 100
```

Boom! Your return value!

Knowledge of the return value in x0 is extremely Important as it will form the foundation of debugging scripts you'll write in later sections.

Changing Around Values in Registers

In order to solidify your understanding of registers, you'll modify registers in an already-compiled application.

Close Xcode and the Registers project. Open a Terminal window and launch the iPhone X Simulator. Do this by typing the following:

```
xcrun simctl list
```

You'll see a long list of devices. Search for the latest iOS version for which you have a simulator installed. Underneath that section, find your favorite device. The one that you've been using to run the examples in this book will work best.

It will look something like this:

```
iPhone 14 (DE1F3042-4033-4A69-B0BF-FD71713CFBF6) (Shutdown)
```

The UUID is what you're after. Use that to open the iOS Simulator by typing the following, replacing your UUID as appropriate:

```
open /Applications/Xcode.app/Contents/Developer/Applications/
Simulator.app --args -CurrentDeviceUDID DE1F3042-4033-4A69-B0BF-
FD71713CFBF6
```

Make sure the simulator is launched and is sitting on the home screen. You can get to the home screen by pressing **Command + Shift + H**. Once your simulator is set up, head over to the Terminal window and attach LLDB to the SpringBoard application:

```
lldb -n SpringBoard
```

This attaches LLDB to the SpringBoard instance running on the iOS Simulator! SpringBoard is the program that controls the home screen on iOS.

> **Note**: Attaching to the `SpringBoard` requires that SIP, System Integrity Protection, is disabled. The procedure for disabling this was outline in Chapter 1. If you can't or don't want to disable SIP, launch a program you own in the simulator. Then in terminal use the `pgrep` command to find the process id for your app. Next, use `lldb -p <the process id you found>` and continue with the chapter. Choose an app with some Objective-C in it, like the `Signals` app.

Once attached, type the following into LLDB:

```
(lldb) p/x @"Yay! Debugging"
```

You should get some output similar to the following:

```
(__NSCFString *) $3 = 0x0000618000644080 @"Yay! Debugging!"
```

Take a note of the memory reference of this newly created NSString instance as you'll use it soon. Now, create a breakpoint on UILabel's setText: method in LLDB:

```
(lldb) br set -n "-[UILabel setText:]" -C "po $x2 =
0x0000618000644080" -G1
```

The above breakpoint will stop on the -[UILabel setText:] Objective-C method. When that happens, it will assign the RDX register the value 0x0000618000644080, thanks to the -C or --command option. In addition, you've told LLDB to resume execution immediately after executing this command via the -G or --auto-continue option, which expects a boolean to determine if it should auto continue.

Take a step back and review what you've just done. Whenever UILabel's setText: method gets hit, you're replacing what's in RDX — the third parameter — with a different NSString instance that says **Yay! Debugging!**.

Resume the debugger by using the **continue** command:

```
(lldb) continue
```

Explore the SpringBoard Simulator app and see what content has changed. Swipe up and down and observe the changes:

Try exploring other areas where modal presentations can occur, as this will likely result in a new `UIViewController` (and all of its subviews) being lazily loaded, causing the breakpoint action to be hit.

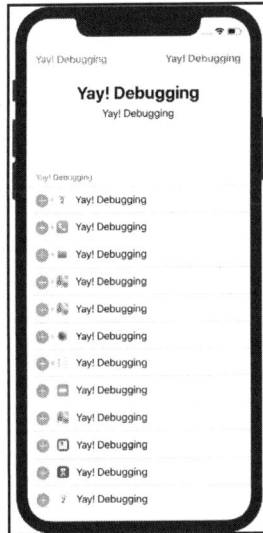

Although this might seem like a cool gimmicky programming trick, it provides an insightful look into how a limited knowledge of registers and assembly can produce big changes in applications you don't have the source for.

This is also useful from a debugging standpoint, as you can quickly visually verify where the `-[UILabel setText:]` is executed within the SpringBoard application and run breakpoint conditions to find the exact line of code that sets a particular `UILabel`'s text.

To continue this thought, any `UILabel` instances whose text did not change also tells you something. For example, the `UIButtons` whose text didn't change to `Yay! Debugging!` speaks for itself. Perhaps the `UILabel`'s `setText:` was called at an earlier time? Or maybe the developers of the SpringBoard application chose to use `setAttributedText:` instead? Or maybe they're using SwiftUI or a private method that is not publicly available to third-party developers?

As you can see, using and manipulating registers can give you a lot of insight into how an application functions.

Key Points

- Architectures define a calling convention which dictates where parameters to a function and its return value are stored.

- In Objective-C, the x0 register is the reference of the calling NSObject, x1 is the Selector, x2 is the first parameter and so on.

- In Swift, there's still not a consistent register calling convention. For right now, the reference to "self" in a class is passed on the stack allowing the parameters to start with the x2 register. But who knows how long this will last and what crazy changes will take place as Swift evolves.

- The x0 register is used for return values in functions regardless of whether you're working with Objective-C or Swift.

- Make sure you use the Objective-C context when printing registers with $.

Where to Go From Here?

Whew! That was a long one, wasn't it? Sit back and take a break with your favorite form of liquid; you've earned it.

There's a lot you can do with registers. Try exploring apps you don't have the source code for; it's a lot of fun and will build a good foundation for tackling tough debugging problems.

Try attaching to an application on the iOS Simulator and map out the UIViewControllers as they appear using assembly, a smart breakpoint, and a breakpoint command.

Chapter 12: Assembly & Memory

You've begun the journey and learned the dark arts of the calling convention in the previous chapter. When a function is called, you now know how parameters are passed to functions, and how function return values come back. What you haven't learned yet is how code is executed when it's loaded into memory.

In this chapter, you'll explore how a program executes. You'll look at a special register used to tell the processor where it should read the next instruction from, as well as how different sizes and groupings of memory can produce *very* different results.

Reviewing Reading Assembly

As you saw in the previous chapter, assembly instructions contain an opcode, a source and a destination. During the course of history, there have been two formats for the assembly code, called **Intel** and **AT&T**. They changed around the order of source and destination, and used different leading characters to denote registers, constants, etc. The default format for LLDB is Intel. It places the destination as the first argument after the opcode.

```
opcode   destination source
```

If you ever encounter a disassembly where those things are reversed, or where the registers are all prefixed with % symbols, you are reading AT&T format. Depending on what system you're using at the time, there should be a setting to swap formats.

Before you move forward, another change to your LLDB setup will make some things a little easier. Before your code can be executed, functions need to make space in memory and get all of the values into the right registers or into the right order on the stack. This is called the **function prologue**. After completing its work, a function needs to put everything back and clean up. This is the **function epilogue**.

Because these two parts aren't particularly relevant to the logic of a function, LLDBs default is to skip over them when you've set a breakpoint. However, as you're learning, seeing how the prologue moves things around is important. So, you'll change this setting.

Add the following line to the bottom of your ~/**.lldbinit** file:

```
settings set target.skip-prologue false
```

This line tells LLDB to not skip the function prologue. You came across this earlier in this book, and from now on it's prudent to not skip the prologue since you'll be inspecting assembly right from the first instruction in a function.

Note: When editing your ~/**.lldbinit** file, make sure you don't use a program like TextEdit for this, as it will add unnecessary characters into the file that could result in LLDB not correctly parsing the file. An easy (although dangerous) way to add this is through a Terminal command like so: echo `"settings set target.skip-prologue false" >> ~/.lldbinit`.

Make sure you have two '>>' in there or else you'll overwrite all your previous content in your ~/**.lldbinit** file. If you're not comfortable with the Terminal, editors like nano (which you've used earlier) are your best bet.

Creating the cpx Command

First of all, you're going to create your own LLDB command to help later on.

Open ~/.lldbinit again in your favorite text editor (vim, right?). Then add the following to the bottom of the file:

```
command alias -H "Print value in ObjC context in hexadecimal" -h
"Print in hex" -- cpx expression -f x -l objc --
```

This command, **cpx**, is a convenience command you can use to print out something in hexadecimal format, using the Objective-C context. This will be useful when printing out register contents.

Remember, registers aren't available in the Swift context, so you need to use the Objective-C context instead.

Now you have the tools needed to explore memory in this chapter through an assembly point of view!

Bits, Bytes and Other Terminology

Before you begin exploring memory, you need to be aware of some vocabulary about how memory is grouped. A value that can contain either a 1 or a 0 is known as a **bit**. You can say there are 64 bits per address in a 64-bit architecture. Simple enough.

When there are 8 bits grouped together, they're known as a **byte**. How many unique values can a byte hold? You can determine that by calculating 2^8 which will be 256 values, starting from 0 and going to 255.

Lots of information is expressed in bytes. For example, the C `sizeof()` function returns the size of the object in bytes.

If you are familiar with ASCII character encoding, you'll recall all ASCII characters can be held in a single byte.

It's time to take a look at this terminology in action and learn some tricks along the way.

Open up the **Registers** macOS application, which you'll find in the resources folder for this chapter. Next, build and run the app. Once it's running, pause the program and bring up the LLDB console. As mentioned previously, this will result in the non-Swift debugging context being used.

```
(lldb) p sizeof('A')
```

This will print out the number of bytes required to make up the A character:

```
(unsigned long) $0 = 1
```

Next, type the following:

```
(lldb) p/t 'A'
```

You'll get the following output:

```
(char) $1 = 0b01000001
```

This is the binary representation for the character A in ASCII.

Another more common way to display a byte of information is using hexadecimal values. Two hexadecimal digits are required to represent a byte of information in hexadecimal.

Print out the hexadecimal representation of A using your new command, or just use p/x if you decided not to add it:

```
(lldb) cpx 'A'
```

You'll get the following output:

```
(char) $2 = 0x41
```

Hexadecimal is great for viewing memory because a single hexadecimal digit represents exactly 4 bits. So if you have 2 hexadecimal digits, you have 1 byte. If you have 8 hexadecimal digits, you have 4 bytes. And so on.

Here are a few more terms for you that you'll find useful in the chapters to come:

- **Nybble**: 4 bits, a single value in hexadecimal

- **Half word**: 16 bits, or 2 bytes

- **Word**: 32 bits, or 4 bytes

- **Double word** or **Giant word**: 64 bits or 8 bytes.

With this terminology, you're all set to explore the different memory chunks.

The Program Counter Register

When a program executes, code to be executed is loaded into memory. The location of which code to execute next in the program is determined by one magically important register: the **pc** , **program counter** or **instruction pointer** register.

You'll now see this register in action. Open the **Registers** application again and navigate to **AppDelegate.swift**. Modify the file so it contains the following code:

```swift
@NSApplicationMain
class AppDelegate: NSObject, NSApplicationDelegate {

  func applicationWillBecomeActive(
    _ notification: Notification) {
    print("\(#function)")
    self.aBadMethod()
  }

  func aBadMethod() {
    print("\(#function)")
  }

  func aGoodMethod() {
    print("\(#function)")
  }
}
```

Build and run the application. Unsurprisingly, the method name, `applicationWillBecomeActive(_:)`, appears in the debug console, followed by the `aBadMethod`. There will be no execution of `aGoodMethod`.

Create a breakpoint at the very beginning of the `aBadMethod` using the Xcode GUI:

```
 9  import Cocoa
10
11  @NSApplicationMain
12  class AppDelegate: NSObject, NSApplicationDelegate {
13
14    func applicationWillFinishLaunching(_ notification: Notification) {
15      print("\(#function)")
16      self.aBadMethod()
17    }
18
19    func aBadMethod() {
20      print("\(#function)")
21    }
22
23    func aGoodMethod() {
24      print("\(#function)")
25    }
26  }
27
28
```

Build and run again. Once the breakpoint hits at the beginning of the `aBadMethod`, use the **Debug** menu in Xcode to **Debug ▸ Debug Workflow ▸ Always Show Disassembly**. You'll now see the actual assembly of the program!

Next, type the following into the LLDB console:

```
(lldb) cpx $pc
```

This prints out the instruction pointer register using the `cpx` command you created earlier.

You'll notice the output LLDB spits out will match the address highlighted by the green line in Xcode:

```
(unsigned long) $1 = 0x0000000100dfda78
```

It's worth noting your address could be different than the above output, but the address of the green line and the pc console output will match. If they don't match then you likely didn't adjust the prologue setting from the beginning of this chapter and your green line is just before the bl opcode. Now, enter the following command in LLDB:

```
(lldb) image lookup -vrn ^Registers.*aGoodMethod
```

This is the tried-and-true image lookup command with the typical regular expression arguments plus an added argument, -v, which dumps the verbose output.

You'll get a fair bit of content. Search for the content immediately following range = [; pressing **Command-F** may prove useful here. It's the first value in the range brackets that you're looking for.

This address is known as the **load address**. This is the actual physical address of this function in memory.

This differs from the usual output you've seen in the image lookup command, in that it only displays the offset of the function relative to the executable, also known as the **implementation offset**. When hunting for a function's address, it's important to differentiate the load address from the implementation offset in an executable, as it will differ.

Copy this new address at the beginning of the range brackets. For this particular example, the load address of aGoodMethod is located at 0x0000000100dfdc48. Now, write this address which points the beginning of the aGoodMethod method to the pc register.

```
(lldb) register write $pc 0x0000000100dfdc48
```

Click **continue** using the Xcode debug button. It's important you do this instead of typing `continue` in LLDB, as there is a bug that will trip you up when modifying the pc register and continuing in the console.

After pressing the Xcode continue button, you'll see that aBadMethod() is not executed and aGoodMethod() is executed instead. Verify this by viewing the output in the console log.

> **Note**: Modifying the pc register is actually a bit dangerous. According to the ARM documentation, the pc register is read-only on 64-bit systems. You need to make sure the registers holding data for a previous value in the pc register do not get applied to a new function which would make an incorrect assumption with the registers. Since aGoodMethod and aBadMethod are very similar in functionality, you've stopped at the beginning, and as no optimizations were applied to the Registers application, this is not a worry.

Registers and Breaking Up the Bits

As mentioned in the previous chapter, arm64 has 31 general purpose registers: x0 - x30. In order to maintain compatibility with previous architectures, such as a 32-bit architecture, registers can be broken up into their 32, 16, or 8-bit values.

For registers that have had a history across different architectures, the frontmost character in the name given to the register determines the size of the register. For example, the x0 register starts with x, which signifies 64 bits. If you wanted the 32 bit equivalent of the x0 register, you'd swap out the x character with an w, to get the w0 register.

Additionally, ARM64 has a set of vector or floating point registers. These registers are 128-bits each. The floating point registers begin with v. They can be broken into 64-bits by prefixing with a d or 32-bits by prefixing with an s. For now, just think about the integer registers, and x or w.

Why is this useful? When working with registers, sometimes the value passed into a register does not need to use all 64 bits. For example, consider the Boolean data type.

All you really need is a 1 or a 0 to indicate `true` or `false`, right? Based upon the languages features and constraints, the compiler knows this and will sometimes only write information to certain parts of a register.

Let's see this in action.

Remove all breakpoints in the Registers project. Build and run the project. Now, pause the program out of the blue.

Once stopped, type the following:

```
(lldb) register write x0 0x0123456789ABCDEF
```

This writes a value to the x0 register.

Let's halt for a minute. A word of warning: You should be aware that writing to registers could cause your program to tank, especially if the register you write to is expected to have a certain type of data. But you're doing this in the name of science, so don't worry if your program does crash!

Confirm that this value has been successfully written to the x0 register:

```
(lldb) cpx $x0
```

Since this is a 64-bit program, you'll get a double word, i.e. 64 bits, or 8 bytes, or 16 hexadecimal digits.

Now, try printing out the w0 register:

```
(lldb) cpx $w0
```

The w0 register is the least-significant half of the x0 register. So you'll only see the least-significant half of the double word, i.e., a word. You should see the following:

```
0x89abcdef
```

Keep an eye out for registers with different sizes when exploring assembly. The size of the registers can give clues about the values contained within.

Breaking Down the Memory

Now that you've taken a look at the program counter, it's time to explore further the memory behind it.

The counter is actually a **pointer**. It's not executing the instructions stored in the pc register — it's executing the instructions pointed to in the pc register.

Seeing this in LLDB will perhaps describe it better. Back in the Registers application, open **AppDelegate.swift** and once again set a breakpoint on aBadMethod. Build and run the app.

Once the breakpoint is hit and the program is stopped, navigate back to the assembly view. If you forgot, and haven't created a keyboard shortcut for it, it's found under **Debug ▸ Debug Workflow ▸ Always Show Disassembly**.

You'll be greeted by the onslaught of opcodes and registers. Take a look at the location of the pc register, which should be pointing to the very beginning of the function.

For this particular build, the beginning address of aBadMethod begins as **0x100685a78**. As usual, your address will likely be different.

In the LLDB console, type the following:

```
(lldb) cpx $pc
```

As you know by now, this prints out the contents of the program counter register.

As expected, you'll get the address of the start of aBadMethod. But again, the pc register points to a value in memory. What is it pointing to?

Well... you could dust off your mad C coding skillz (you remember those, right?) and dereference the pointer, but there's a much more elegant way to go about it using LLDB.

Type the following, replacing the address with the address of your aBadMethod function:

```
(lldb) memory read -fi -c1 0x100685a78
```

Wow, what the heck does that command do?!

`memory read` takes a value and reads the contents pointed at by the memory address you supply. The `-f` command is a formatting argument; in this case, it's the assembly **instruction** format. Finally you're saying you only want one assembly instruction to be printed out with the **count**, or `-c` argument.

You'll get output that looks similar to this:

```
->  0x100685a78: 0xd10383ff    sub    sp, sp, #0xe0
```

This here is some gooooooooood output. It's telling you the assembly instruction, as well as the opcode, provided in hexadecimal (**0xd10383ff**) that is responsible for the `sub` operation.

Look at that "d10383ff" there in the output some more. This is an encoding of the entire instruction, i.e. the whole `pushq rbp`. Don't believe me? You can verify it. Type the following into LLDB:

```
(lldb) expression -f i -l objc -- 0xd10383ff
```

The `i` format asks LLDB to decode `0xd10383ff` into an opcode format. You'll get the following output:

```
(unsigned int) $1 = 0xd10383ff    sub    sp, sp, #0xe0
```

That command is a little long, but it's because you need the required switch to Objective-C context if you are in the Swift debugging context. However, if you move to the Objective-C debugging context, you can use a convenience expression that is a lot shorter.

Try clicking on a different frame in the left panel of Xcode to get into an Objective-C context which doesn't contain Swift or Objective-C/Swift bridging code.

Click on any frame which is in an Objective-C function.

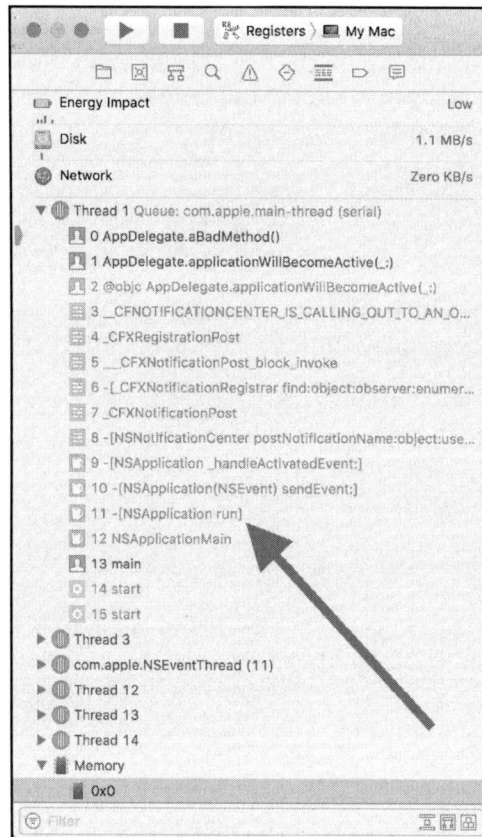

Next, type the following into the LLDB console:

```
(lldb) p/i 0xd10383ff
```

Much better, right?

Now, back to the application in hand. Type the following into LLDB, replacing the address once again with your aBadMethod function address:

```
(lldb) memory read —fi —c4 0x1005eda78
```

You'll get 10x the output! That's something worthy to put on that LinkedIn résumé...

By the way, there's a shorthand convenience way to execute the above command. You can simply type the following to achieve the same result.

```
(lldb) x/4i 0x1005eda78
```

With either command you choose, you'll get something similar to following output:

```
0xd10383ff    sub    sp, sp, #0xe0
0xa90c4ff4    stp    x20, x19, [sp, #0xc0]
0xa90d7bfd    stp    x29, x30, [sp, #0xd0]
0x910343fd    add    x29, sp, #0xd0
```

There's something interesting to note here: arm64 instructions can have variable lengths when decoded, but are always encoded to 4 bytes. Also, based on the way you've been working, you might think that the byte stored at memory address 0x1005eda78 is d1, the first part of the first instruction encoding.

Narrator: it's not.

Perhaps now would be a good time to talk about **endianness**.

Endianness... This Stuff Is Reversed?

The ARM family architecture devices all use **little-endian**, which means that data is stored in memory with the least significant byte first. If you were to store the number 0xabcd in memory, the 0xcd byte would be stored first, followed by the 0xab byte.

Back to the instruction example, this means that the instruction 0xd10383ff will be stored in memory as 0xff, followed by 0x83, followed by 0x03 and finally 0xd1.

Thinking about opcode encoding, if you'd been reading the memory and tried to decode the opcode without remembering endianness, you might type:

```
(lldb) p/i 0xff8303d1
```

You'd now get a most unhelpful opcode:

```
0xff8303d1    .long    0xff8303d1 ; unknown opcode
```

Let's see some more examples of little-endian in action. Type the following into LLDB:

```
(lldb) memory read -s1 -c20 -fx 0x1005eda78
```

This command reads the memory at address 0x1005eda78. It reads in size chunks of 1 byte thanks to the -s1 option, and a count of 20 thanks to the -c20 option.

You'll see something like this:

```
0x1005eda78: 0xff 0x83 0x03 0xd1 0xf4 0x4f 0x0c 0xa9
0x1005eda80: 0xfd 0x7b 0x0d 0xa9 0xfd 0x43 0x03 0x91
0x1005eda88: 0xe8 0x03 0x14 0xaa
```

Now, double the size and half the count like so:

```
(lldb) memory read -s2 -c10 -fx 0x1005eda78
```

You will see something like this:

```
0x1005eda78: 0x83ff 0xd103 0x4ff4 0xa90c 0x7bfd 0xa90d 0x43fd
0x9103
0x1005eda88: 0x03e8 0xaa14
```

Notice how when the memory values are grouped together, they are reversed thanks to being in little-endian.

Now double the size and half the count again:

```
(lldb) memory read -s4 -c5 -fx 0x1005eda78
```

And now you'll get something like this:

```
0x1005eda78: 0xd10383ff 0xa90c4ff4 0xa90d7bfd 0x910343fd
0x1005eda88: 0xaa1403e8
```

Once again the values are reversed compared to the previous output.

This is *very* important to remember and also a source of confusion when exploring memory. Not only will the size of memory give you a potentially incorrect answer, but also the order. Remember this when you start yelling at your computer when you're trying to figure out how something should work!

Key Points

- The default format for assembly in LLDB is `opcode destination source` which is referred to as "Intel" format.

- LLDB skips the function prologue when a breakpoint drops into assembly. You can change this using the `target.skip-prologue` setting.

- A **bit** is a single 0 or 1 value. Bits are grouped into larger chunks called **nibbles** (4 bits), **bytes** (8 bits0), **words** (32 bits) and **double words** (64 bits).

- Use `register read` and `register write` to manipulate the values in the registers during an LLDb session.

- The `pc` register is technically read-only, but you can write to it at the risk of crashing everything.

- ARM64 uses a `w` prefix to refer to the lower 32-bits of any `x` register.

- Assembly opcodes and parameters are encoded into 4-byte groups regardless of how long they are.

- ARM64 uses **little-endian** encoding where the least significant byte is stored first.

Where to Go From Here?

Good job getting through this one. Memory layout can be a confusing topic. Try exploring memory on other devices to make sure you have a solid understanding of the little-endian architecture and how assembly is grouped together.

In the next chapter, you'll explore the stack frame and how a function gets called.

Chapter 13: Assembly & the Stack

When parameters passed into a function, sometimes they are passed in registers, and sometimes they are passed through the stack, and sometimes both! But what does *being passed on the stack* mean exactly? It's time to take a deeper dive into what happens when a function is called from an assembly standpoint by exploring some "stack related" registers as well as the contents in the stack.

Understanding how the stack works is useful when you're reverse engineering programs, since you can help deduce what parameters are being manipulated in a certain function when no debugging symbols are available.

Let's begin.

The Stack, Revisited

As discussed previously in Chapter 6, "Thread, Frame & Stepping Around", when a program executes, the memory is laid out so the stack starts at a "high address" and grows downward, towards a lower address; that is, towards the heap.

> **Note**: In some architectures, the stack grows upwards. But for all Apple devices, the stack grows downwards.

Confused? Here's an image to help clarify how the stack moves.

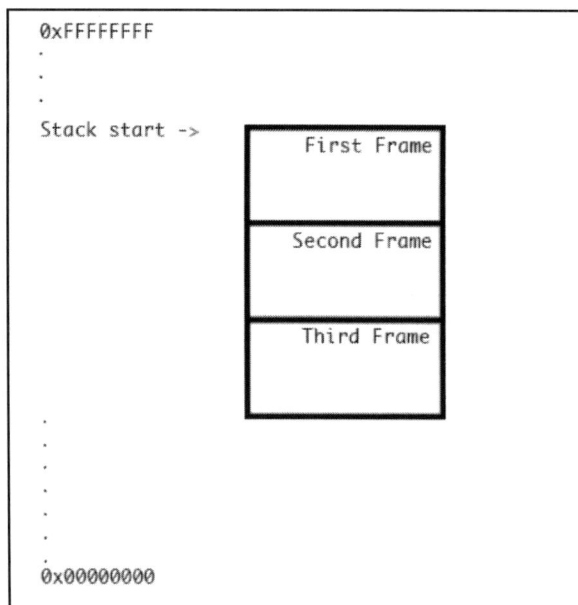

```
0xFFFFFFFF
  .
  .
  .
Stack start ->    ┌──────────────────┐
                  │     First Frame  │
                  │                  │
                  ├──────────────────┤
                  │   Second Frame   │
                  │                  │
                  ├──────────────────┤
                  │    Third Frame   │
                  │                  │
                  └──────────────────┘
  .
  .
  .
  .
  .
0x00000000
```

The stack starts at a high address. How high, exactly, is determined by the operating system's kernel. The kernel gives stack space to each running program (well, each thread).

The stack is finite in size and increases by growing downwards in memory address space. As space on the stack is used up, the pointer to the "top" of the stack moves down from the highest address to the lowest address.

Once the stack reaches the finite size given by the kernel, or if it crosses the bounds of the heap, the stack is said to *overflow*. This is a fatal error, often referred to as a *stack overflow*. Now you know where your favorite website gets its name from!

Stack Pointer, Frame Pointer and Link Register

Two very important registers you've yet to learn about are the **sp** and **lr**. The stack pointer register, sp, points to the head of the stack for a particular thread. The head of the stack will grow downwards, so the sp will decrement when it's time to make more space in the stack. The sp will *always* point to the head of the stack.

Here's a visual of the stack pointer changing when a function is called.

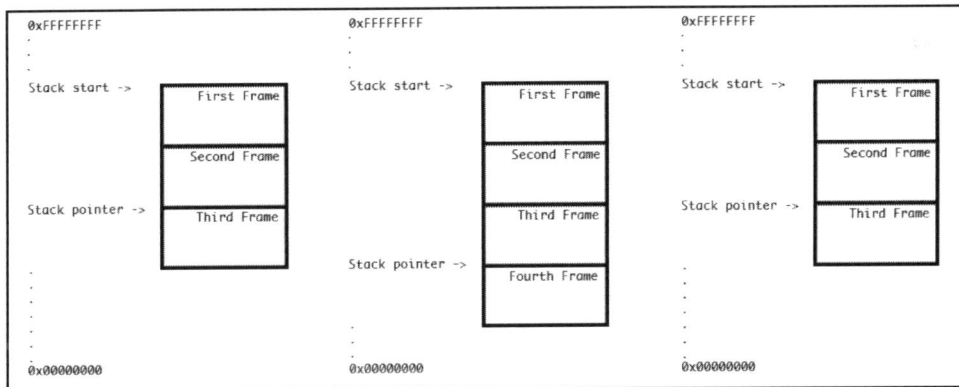

In the above image, the sequence of the stack pointer follows:

1. The stack pointer currently points to Frame 3.

2. The code pointed to by the instruction pointer register calls a new function. The stack pointer gets updated to point to a new frame, Frame 4, which is potentially responsible for scratchspace and data inside this newly called function from the instruction pointer.

3. Execution is completed in Frame 4 and control resumes back in Frame 3. The stack pointer's previous reference to Frame 4 gets popped off and resumes pointing to Frame 3.

The frame pointer is another important register and is related to the stack pointer. While the stack pointer points to where the head of the stack currently is, the frame pointer points to a location above the stack pointer just below any space the function used for saving registers in the prologue.

The other important register, the link register, lr. It points to the next line to be executed after this function is done. lr is actually just a convenience name for the x30 register.

The interesting thing here is the previous contents of the x29 and x30 are stored on the stack *before* it's set to the value of the current function. This is the first thing that happens in the function prologue. You can traverse the stack just by knowing the value in the link register. A debugger does this when it shows you the stack trace.

> **Note:** Some systems don't use a link register, and it's possible to compile your application to omit using the link register. The logic is it might be beneficial to have an extra register to use. But this means you can't unwind the stack easily, which makes debugging much harder.

> **Note:** When you jump to a different stack frame by clicking on a frame in Xcode or using LLDB, both the sp & lr registers will change values to correspond to the new frame! This is expected because local variables for a function use offsets of sp to get their values.
>
> If the sp didn't change, you'd be unable to print local variables to that function, and the program might even crash. This might result in a source of confusion when exploring the lr & sp registers, so always keep this in mind. You can verify this in LLDB by selecting different frames and typing cpx $lr or cpx $sp in the LLDB console.

So why are these two registers important to learn about? When a program is compiled with debug information, the debug information references offsets from the stack pointer register to get a variable. These offsets are given names, the same names you gave your variables in your source code.

When a program is compiled and optimized for release, the debug information that comes packaged into the binary is removed. Although the names to the references of these variables and parameters are removed, you can still use offsets of the stack pointer and base pointer to find the location of where these references are stored.

Stack Related Opcodes

So far, you've learned about the calling convention and how the memory is laid out, but haven't really explored what the many opcodes actually *do* in arm64 assembly. It's time to focus on several stack related opcodes in more detail.

The str and stp Opcode

When anything such as an int, Objective-C instance, Swift class or a reference needs to be saved onto the stack, the **str** opcode is used, or its cousin the **stp** opcode. The str opcode puts a single register on the stack while stp puts a pair of registers onto the stack.

To see at a concrete example, consider the following opcode:

```
str 0x00000005, [sp]
```

This stores the value of 5 at the location pointed to by the stack pointer. It's your responsibility as the coder to ensure there is room on the stack for the value.

The ldr and ldp Opcodes

The **ldr** opcode is the exact opposite of the str opcode. ldr takes the value from the stack and stores it to a destination. You can guess what ldp is for, right? Unlike some other instruction sets, in ARM64, you don't move the stack pointer to reclaim the space until the end of the function.

Below is an example of ldr:

```
ldr x0, [sp, #0x8]
```

This stores the value of the sp register offset by 0x8 into the x0. The ARM64 layout really wants things to stay in alignment for efficiency, so you'll often see offsets of 0x8, 0x10, 0x20 as different values are pulled from the stack.

The 'bl' Opcode

The **bl** opcode is responsible for executing a function. bl stands for "branch with link". It sets the lr register to the location of the next instruction in the calling function. Then bl jumps to the function memory location. When it returns, any return value from that function is in register x0. After bl jumps, the first thing you would expect the new function to do is to store the values of x29 and x30 to keep the stacks and frames all in sync.

Imagine a function at 0x7fffb34df410 in memory like so:

```
0x7fffb34de913 <+227>: call   0x7fffb34df410
0x7fffb34de918 <+232>: mov    edx, eax
```

When an instruction is executed, first the pc register (program counter) is incremented, then the instruction is executed. So, when the call instruction is executed, the pc register will increment to 0x7fffb34de918, then execute the instruction pointed to by 0x7fffb34de913. Since this is a call instruction, the pc register is pushed onto the stack (just as if a push had been executed) then the pc register is set to the value 0x7fffb34df410, the address of the function to be executed.

From there, execution continues at the location 0x7fffb34df410.

Computers are pretty cool, aren't they?

The 'ret' Opcode

The **ret** opcode is the opposite of the bl opcode, in that it jumps to x30 or the link register. Thus execution goes back to where the function was called from.

Now that you have a basic understanding of these four important opcodes, it's time to see them in action.

It's *very* important to have all stp opcodes in your function prologue match your ldp opcodes in your function epilogue, or else the stack will get out of sync. For example, if there was no corresponding ldp for a stp, when the ret happened at the end of the function it would jump to the wrong location. Execution would return to some random place, potentially not even a valid place in the program.

Fortunately, the compiler will take care of synchronizing your stp and ldp opcodes when it compiles your Swift or Objective-C into assembly. You only need to worry about this when you're writing your own assembly.

Observing Registers in Action

Now that you have an understanding of the sp and lr registers, as well as some opcodes that manipulate the stack, it's time to see it all in action.

In the Registers application lives a function named **StackWalkthrough(int)**. This C function takes one integer as a parameter and is written in assembly and is located in **StackWalkthrough.s**. Open this file and have a look around; there's no need to understand it all just now. You'll learn how it works in a minute.

This function is made available to Swift through a bridging header **Registers-Bridging Header.h**, so you can call this method written in assembly from Swift.

Now to make use of this.

Open **ViewController.swift**, and add the following below viewDidLoad():

```
override func awakeFromNib() {
    super.awakeFromNib()
    StackWalkthrough(42)
}
```

This will call StackWalkthrough with a parameter of 42. The 42 is simply a value used to show how the stack works. 42 in hex is 0x2a, so you'll be looking for that in the memory dumps.

Before you begin, here is Stackwalkthrough's code:

```
sub   sp, sp, #0x20          ; 1
stp   x29, x30, [sp, #0x10]  ; 2
add   x29, sp, #0x10         ; 3
str   xzr, [sp, #0x8]
str   xzr, [sp]              ; 4
                             ; end of the function prologue
str   x0, [sp]               ; 5
mov   x0, #0xF0              ; 6
ldr   x0, [sp]               ; 7
                             ; start the epilogue
ldp x29, x30, [sp, #0x10]    ; 8
add sp, sp, #0x20            ; 9
ret                          ; 10
```

Here's what's going on in the code:

1. Make room in the stack to store four 8-byte things. Notice you're subtracting from the pointer value.

2. Now, store a pair of values, the old frame pointer and the link register to the stack at the end of the room you've just made for things.

3. Add 0x10 to the stack pointer and store it in x29, the frame pointer. This therefore sets the frame pointer to the end of where registers were saved to.

4. Clear out the space in the remainder of the allocated stack space. Remember you just moved the stack pointer, who knows what values existed at these locations. zxr is equal to 0x0 but makes the code easier to reason. You are clearing out the space, you're not setting a value of zero to be used in some maths.

5. Store our function argument to the tip of the stack.

6. Put the value of 0xF0 into register x0, overwriting whatever was there.

7. Now put the value from head of the stack into register x0, overwriting whatever was there.

8. Replace the frame pointer and the link register.

9. Remove the room in the stack for the four 8-byte things (Opposite of what you did on the first line)

10. Jump to the value of the link register.

Read it through and try to understand it if you can. You're already familiar with the mov instruction, and the rest of the assembly consists of function related opcodes you've just learned about.

This function takes the integer parameter passed into it as you'll recall, the first parameter is passed in x0, and pushes this parameter onto the stack. x0 is then set to 0xF0, then the value popped off the stack is stored back into the x0 register. It'll be a sure hit in the App Store. :]

Make sure you have a good mental understanding of what is happening in this function, as you'll be exploring the registers in LLDB next.

Back in Xcode, create a breakpoint using Xcode's GUI on the StackWalkthrough(42) line in the awakeFromNib function of **ViewController.swift**. Also create a symbolic breakpoint on StackWalkthrough, since you'll want to stop at the beginning of the StackWalkthrough function when exploring the registers.

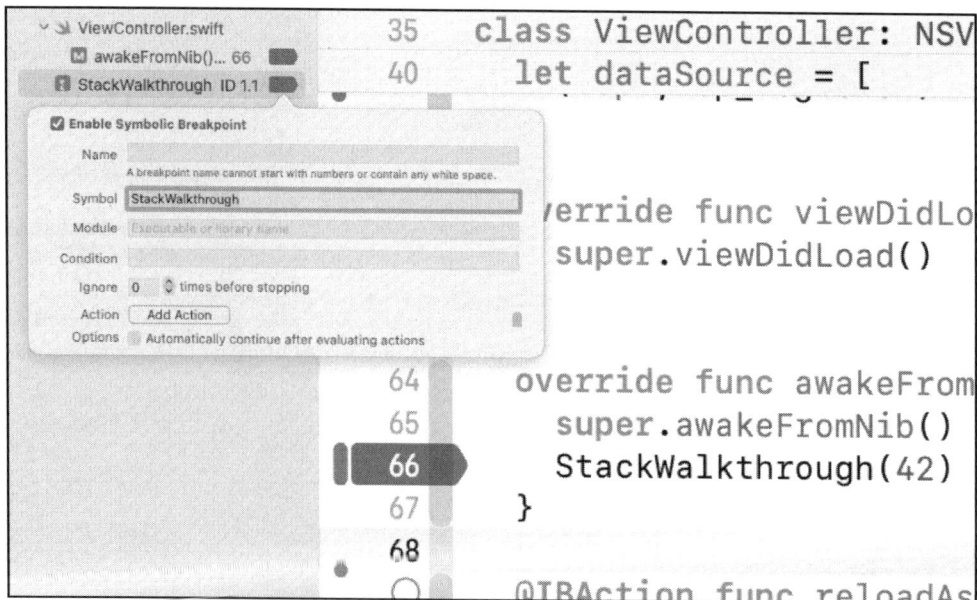

Build and run and wait for the GUI breakpoint to trigger.

Now click **Debug ▸ Debug Workflow ▸Always Show Disassembly**, to show the disassembly. You'll be greeted with exciting looking stuff!

```
 Registers   Thread 1    0 ViewController.awakeFromNib()
 1    Registers`ViewController.awakeFromNib():
 2        0x1041ef51c <+0>:    sub     sp, sp, #0x30
 3        0x1041ef520 <+4>:    stp     x29, x30, [sp, #0x20]
 4        0x1041ef524 <+8>:    add     x29, sp, #0x20
 5        0x1041ef528 <+12>:   str     x20, [sp]
 6        0x1041ef52c <+16>:   stur    xzr, [x29, #-0x8]
 7        0x1041ef530 <+20>:   mov     x8, x20
 8        0x1041ef534 <+24>:   stur    x8, [x29, #-0x8]
 9        0x1041ef538 <+28>:   mov     x0, x20
10        0x1041ef53c <+32>:   bl      0x1041f212c              ; symbol stub for:
             objc_retain
11        0x1041ef540 <+36>:   mov     x0, #0x0
12        0x1041ef544 <+40>:   bl      0x1041ef4c0              ; type metadata accessor
             for Registers.ViewController at <compiler-generated>
13        0x1041ef548 <+44>:   mov     x8, x0
14        0x1041ef54c <+48>:   add     x0, sp, #0x8
15        0x1041ef550 <+52>:   str     x20, [sp, #0x8]
16        0x1041ef554 <+56>:   str     x8, [sp, #0x10]
17        0x1041ef558 <+60>:   adrp    x8, 9
18        0x1041ef55c <+64>:   ldr     x1, [x8, #0x600]
19        0x1041ef560 <+68>:   bl      0x1041f2108              ; symbol stub for:
             objc_msgSendSuper2
20        0x1041ef564 <+72>:   ldr     x0, [sp]
21        0x1041ef568 <+76>:   bl      0x1041f2120              ; symbol stub for:
             objc_release
22        0x1041ef56c <+80>:   mov     w0, #0x2a
23   ->   0x1041ef570 <+84>:   bl      0x1041edcf8            ; StackWalkthrough
24        0x1041ef574 <+88>:   ldp     x29, x30, [sp, #0x20]
25        0x1041ef578 <+92>:   add     sp, sp, #0x30
```

Wow! Look at that! You've landed right on a `bl` opcode instruction. Do you wonder what function you're about to enter?

> **Note**: If you didn't land right on the `bl` instruction using the Xcode GUI breakpoint, you can either use LLDB's **thread step-inst** or more simply, **si** to single step through assembly instructions. Alternatively, you can create a GUI breakpoint on the memory address that `bl`s the `StackWalkthrough` function.

Recall that `Stackwalkthrough` takes an argument and that simple arguments get passed in using the registers. Confirm that `x0` contains the value of 42, or anything you changed it to:

```
(lldb) register read x0 lr sp
```

You should get some output like this:

```
x0 = 0x000000000000002a
lr = 0x4f238001044cb56c (0x00000001044cb56c)
Registers`Registers.ViewController.awakeFromNib() -> () + 80 at
ViewController.swift:65:11
sp = 0x000000016b936170
```

The x0 register contains the argument for the function, sp is pointing to the top of the stack for *the current function* and lr is pointing to where this frame will return.

In LLDB, type the following:

```
(lldb) si
```

This is an alias for thread step-inst, which tells LLDB to execute the next instruction and then pause the debugger. You've now stepped into StackWalkthrough.

From here on out, you'll step through every assembly instruction while monitoring the stack memory. You'll also check the values of some of the registers. To help with this, type the following into LLDB:

```
(lldb) command alias dumpstack memory read $sp
```

This creates the command **dumpstack** that will dump the top four addresses of the stack. Execute dumpstack now:

```
(lldb) dumpstack
```

```
0x16b936170: b0 41 51 03 00 60 00 00 b0 41 51 03 00 60 00 00
0x16b936180: f0 46 4d 04 01 00 00 00 b0 41 51 03 00 60 00 00
```

Since you are at the very beginning of the function, sp is still pointing to the location it had back in awakeFromNib.

Now type si in the lldb console to make some room on the stack for this function to work.

Type dumpstack again. Notice that the memory addresses have decreased by 20.

```
0x16b936150: b0 41 51 03 00 60 00 00 00 e1 91 02 00 60 00 00
0x16b936160: 90 61 93 6b 01 00 00 00 6c b5 4c 04 01 80 23 4f
```

What's in the memory addresses is meaningless. Sometimes you'll see zeros, sometimes repeating patterns of noise, sometimes recognizable data. As the stack pointer moves up and down during program execution, the same parts of memory get used over and over.

Execute si again to store the old lr and sp values to the stack. Recall that x29 holds the frame pointer and local changes to the stack pointer are done with offsets from sp.

Type dumpstack again and then confirm that the lr and sp values are stored safely away. Use register read to match up the values.

The next step in the function prologue is to put the local sp value into x29, the frame pointer, so that if another bl happens somewhere in this function, the chain of frames will maintain references to each other. Type si again to execute that command. Then type:

```
register read sp x29
```

You should see something similar to the following:

```
sp = 0x000000016ce76150
fp = 0x000000016ce76160
```

The x29 register is pointing to the end of the stack for this frame and sp is pointing to the working area. The last part of the prologue is to clean any old bits out of the stack. Type si two times to execute the two str xzr commands. Then type dumpstack again. Look at this nice stack, ready to work:

```
0x16ce76150: 00 00 00 00 00 00 00 00 00 00 00 00 00 00 00 00
0x16ce76160: 90 61 e7 6c 01 00 00 00 74 b5 f8 02 01 00 00 00
```

Your green line breakpoint should be pointing to the str x0, [sp] which is the first line of actual work for the function. Type si to store the argument from x0 into the stack. Then type dumpstack and look for your argument.

```
0x16ce76150: 2a 00 00 00 00 00 00 00 00 00 00 00 00 00 00 00
0x16ce76160: 90 61 e7 6c 01 00 00 00 74 b5 f8 02 01 00 00 00
```

The str command made a copy of the value. You could look in register x0 and it would still hold 2a. Type si again to execute the next command and replace the value in x0 with the constant, 0xF0. Now type register read x0 to confirm it holds the new value. Type si again to pull the value off of the stack and put it in x0.

Type `register read x0` and confirm that `0xF0` has been replaced with `2a` from the stack. The work is done in the function, now on to the epilogue to clean everything up. Type `register read x29 sp x30` to see where things are now:

```
fp = 0x000000016ce76160
sp = 0x000000016ce76150
lr = 0x0000000102f8b574
Registers`Registers.ViewController.awakeFromNib() -> () + 88 at
ViewController.swift:67:3
```

Now type `si` again and then execute the `register read x29 sp 30` command again.

```
fp = 0x000000016ce76190
sp = 0x000000016ce76150
lr = 0x0000000102f8b574
Registers`Registers.ViewController.awakeFromNib() -> () + 88 at
ViewController.swift:67:3
```

The frame pointer is now pointing to where it was when this function started. The last step is to reset the `sp` value. Type `si` again to execute the command to reset the `sp`. Before you type `si` one last time to leave this function, notice that we're not going to do anything to clean up changes we made to the stack. But, type `si` a final time and jump back to `awakeFromNib`.

Wowza! That was fun! A simple function, but it illustrates how the stack works through `stp`, `ldp` and `ret` instructions.

The Stack and Extra Parameters

As described in Chapter 11, the calling convention for arm64 will use registers `x0 - x7` for function parameters. When a function requires more parameters, the stack needs to be used.

> **Note:** The stack may also need to be used when a large struct is passed to a function. Each parameter register can only hold 8 bytes (on 64-bit architecture), so if the struct needs more than 8 bytes, it will need to be passed on the stack as well. There are strict rules defining how this works in the calling convention, which all compilers must adhere to.

Open **ViewController.swift** and find the function named
executeLotsOfArguments(one:two:three:four:five:six:seven:eight:nine:t
en:). You used this function in Chapter 11 to explore the registers. You'll use it again
now to see how parameters 7 and beyond get passed to the function.

Add the following code to the end of viewDidLoad:

```
_ = self.executeLotsOfArguments(one: 1, two: 2, three: 3,
                                four: 4, five: 5, six: 6,
                                seven: 7, eight: 8, nine: 9,
                                ten: 10)
```

Next, using the Xcode GUI, create a breakpoint on the line you just added. Delete the
other breakpoints if you don't want to experience the glory of StackWalkthrough
again. Build and run the app, and wait for this breakpoint to hit. You should see the
disassembly view again, but if you don't, use the **Always Show Disassembly** option.

```
          stub for: objc_release
22  ->  0x102b3aed8 <+80>:  mov    x9, sp              ≡ Thread 1: breakpoint 1.1 (1)
23      0x102b3aedc <+84>:  mov    w8, #0x9
24      0x102b3aee0 <+88>:  str    x8, [x9]
25      0x102b3aee4 <+92>:  mov    w8, #0xa
26      0x102b3aee8 <+96>:  str    x8, [x9, #0x8]
27      0x102b3aeec <+100>: mov    w8, #0x1
28      0x102b3aef0 <+104>: mov    x0, x8
29      0x102b3aef4 <+108>: mov    w8, #0x2
30      0x102b3aef8 <+112>: mov    x1, x8
31      0x102b3aefc <+116>: mov    w8, #0x3
32      0x102b3af00 <+120>: mov    x2, x8
33      0x102b3af04 <+124>: mov    w8, #0x4
34      0x102b3af08 <+128>: mov    x3, x8
35      0x102b3af0c <+132>: mov    w8, #0x5
36      0x102b3af10 <+136>: mov    x4, x8
37      0x102b3af14 <+140>: mov    w8, #0x6
38      0x102b3af18 <+144>: mov    x5, x8
39      0x102b3af1c <+148>: mov    w8, #0x7
40      0x102b3af20 <+152>: mov    x6, x8
41      0x102b3af24 <+156>: mov    w8, #0x8
42      0x102b3af28 <+160>: mov    x7, x8
43      0x102b3af2c <+164>: bl     0x102b3af5c                ;
          Registers.ViewController.executeLotsOfArguments(one: Swift.Int,
          two: Swift.Int, three: Swift.Int, four: Swift.Int, five:
```

As you've learned in the **Stack Related Opcodes** section, bl is responsible for the
execution of a function. There's only one bl opcode between where the app is paused
right now and the start of viewDidLoad's function epilogue, this means this bl must
be the one responsible for calling
executeLotsOfArguments(one:two:three:four:five:six:seven:
eight:nine:ten:).

But what are all the rest of the instructions before bl? Let's find out.

These instructions set up the stack as necessary to pass the additional parameters. You have your parameters being put into the appropriate registers, as seen by the mov instructions for each of the values. Notice that because you're passing small values for the Int that the compiler is using w sized registers so it can go faster.

But parameters nine and ten need to be passed on the stack. This is done with the following instructions:

```
0x102b3aed8 <+80>:    mov    x9, sp
0x102b3aedc <+84>:    mov    w8, #0x9
0x102b3aee0 <+88>:    str    x8, [x9]
0x102b3aee4 <+92>:    mov    w8, #0xa
0x102b3aee8 <+96>:    str    x8, [x9, #0x8]
```

Looks scary, doesn't it? I'll explain.

The brackets containing x9 and an optional value indicate reading from a memory location, just like *, the de-referencing operator would do in C programming. The first line above says "put sp into x9." The second line says "put 0x9 into the lower part of x8, w8". The third line says "put x8 into the memory address pointed to by x9". The process then repeats but puts x8 into the memory address pointed to by x9 plus 0x8. And so on. ARM uses x8 and x9 as scratch space as it's moving things around. x9 gets assigned the value of sp because the compiler doesn't want to accidentally move sp.

You can easily determine if extra scratch space is allocated for a stack frame by looking for the very first instruction in the function prologue. For example, click on the viewDidLoad stack frame and scroll to the top. Observe how much scratch space has been created:

```
Registers`ViewController.viewDidLoad():
    0x102b3ae88 <+0>:     sub    sp, sp, #0x40
    0x102b3ae8c <+4>:     stp    x29, x30, [sp, #0x30]
    0x102b3ae90 <+8>:     add    x29, sp, #0x30
    0x102b3ae94 <+12>:    stur   xzr, [x29, #-0x8]
    0x102b3ae98 <+16>:    mov    x8, x20
    0x102b3ae9c <+20>:    stur   x8, [x29, #-0x8]
```

The compiler has allocated 64 bytes. 16 of those bytes will be used to store the sp and lr, which leaves 48 bytes of space for it to work with.

Time to look at this scratch space in more depth.

The Stack and Debugging Info

The stack is not only used when calling functions, but it's also used as a scratch space for a function's local variables. Speaking of which, how does the debugger know which addresses to reference when printing out the names of variables that belong to that function?

Let's find out!

Clear all the breakpoints you've set and create a new Symbolic breakpoint on executeLotsOfArguments.

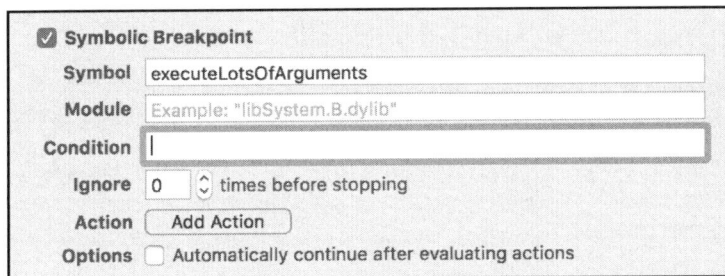

Build and run the app, then wait for the breakpoint to hit.

As expected, control should stop at the ever-so-short name of a function: executeLotsOfArguments(one:two:three:four:five:six:seven:eight:nine:ten:), from here on, now referred to as executeLotsOfArguments, because its full name is a bit of a mouthful!

In the lower right corner of Xcode, click on **Show the Variables View**:

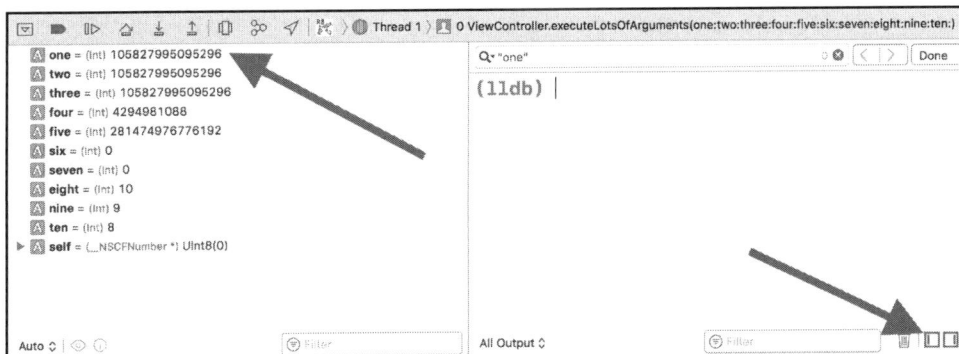

From there, look at the value pointed at by the one variable... it definitely ain't holding the value of 0x1 at the moment. This value seems to be gibberish!

Why is one referencing a seemingly random value?

The answer is stored by the **DWARF Debugging Information** embedded into the debug build of the Registers application. You can dump this information to help give you insight into what the one variable is referencing in memory.

In LLDB, type the following:

```
(lldb) image dump symfile Registers
```

You'll get a crazy amount of output. Search for (Cmd + F) the word **"one"**; include the quotes within your search.

Below is a (very) truncated output that includes the relevant information:

```
0x106aa0758:    Block{0x3000007db}, ranges =
[0x100002f5c-0x100003404)
0x4f875cd88:     Variable{0x3000007f8}, name = "one", type =
{0000000300001126} 0x0000600008E87BA0 (Swift.Int), scope =
parameter, decl = ViewController.swift:92, location =
DW_OP_fbreg −24
```

Based upon the output, the variable named one is of type **Swift.Int**, found in executeLotsOfArguments, whose location can be found at **DW_OP_fbreg -24**. This rather obfuscated code actually means frame pointer minus 24, i.e. x29 − 24. Or in hexadecimal, x29 − 0x18.

This is important information. It tells the debugger the variable called one can always be found in this memory address. Well, not always, but always when that variable is valid, i.e. it's in scope.

You may wonder why it can't just be x0, since that's where the value is passed to the function, and it's also the first parameter. Well, x0 may need to be reused later on within the function, so using the stack is a safer bet for storage.

The debugger should still be stopped on executeLotsOfArguments. Make sure you're viewing the **Always Show Disassembly** output and hunt for the assembly:

```
stur   x0, [x29, #−0x18]
```

Once you've found it in the assembly output of executeLotsOfArguments, create a breakpoint on this line of assembly. You may have found a false hit a little earlier that contains xzr. Can you remember why that might be?

Continue execution so LLDB will stop on this line of assembly.

```
41        0x10475eff8 <+156>:  sub    x20, x29, #0x78
42        0x10475effc <+160>:  str    x20, [sp, #0xd8]
43        0x10475f000 <+164>:  stur   xzr, [x29, #-0x78]
44        0x10475f004 <+168>:  stur   xzr, [x29, #-0x70]
45   ->   0x10475f008 <+172>:  stur   x0, [x29, #-0x18]
46        0x10475f00c <+176>:  stur   x11, [x29, #-0x20]
47        0x10475f010 <+180>:  stur   x2, [x29, #-0x28]
48        0x10475f014 <+184>:  stur   x3, [x29, #-0x30]
49        0x10475f018 <+188>:  stur   x4, [x29, #-0x38]
```

Try printing out the output of one in LLDB:

```
(lldb) po one
```

Gibberish, still. Hmph.

Remember, x0 will contain the first parameter passed into the function. So to make the debugger be able to see the value that one should be, x0 needs to be written to the address where one is stored. In this case, x29 – 0x18.

Now, perform an assembly instruction step in LLDB:

```
(lldb) si
```

Print the value of one again.

```
(lldb) po one
```

Awwww.... yeah! It's working! The value one is referencing is correctly holding the value 0x1.

You may be wondering what happens if one changes. Well, x29 – 0x18 needs to change in that case too. This would potentially be another instruction needed to write it there as well as wherever the value is used. This is why debug builds are so much slower than release builds.

Key Points

- Stack addresses go down towards zero. The function prologue will move the stack pointer down far enough to make room for the needs of the function.

- When each new function begins, it stores sp and lr onto the stack so that it can get back to the right place when it's done working.

- The str and stp are odd in that the destination is at the end of the line of parameter registers. For most other opcodes, the first register after the opcode is the destination.

- The function prologue and the function epilogue must match in how much the move the sp or the stack will become corrupt.

- Look for xzr as a sign that the compiler is zeroing out some space so that new values that get stored don't pick up any stray bits.

- Xcode stores variables on the stack during a debug build so that the variables view values don't accidentally get changed as the register values change.

Section III: Low Level

With a foundation of assembler theory solidly below you, it's time to explore other aspects of how programs work. This section is an eclectic grab-bag of weird and fun studies into reverse engineering, seldom-used APIs and debugging strategies.

Chapter 14: System Calls & Ptrace

As alluded to in the introduction to this book, debugging is not entirely about just fixing stuff. Debugging is the process of gaining a better understanding of what's happening behind the scenes. In this chapter, you'll explore the foundation of how debugging works, namely, 2 powerful APIs that enable lldb to attach and control a process. They are the **mach exception setter** APIs and the system call, **ptrace**.

In addition, you'll learn some common security tricks developers use with ptrace to prevent a process from attaching to their programs. You'll also learn some easy workarounds for these developer-imposed restrictions.

System Calls

Wait, wait, wait... ptrace is a system call. What's a *system* call?

A **system call** is an entry point into code handled by the kernel. System calls are the foundation for userland code to do anything of interest, like opening a file, launching a process, consulting the value of a process identifier, etc.

From the userland side, a system call will marshal the appropriate arguments and send them over to the kernel. Userland code is not able to see the implementation details (i.e. the assembly) of what's happening in the kernel. A userland function takes the arguments and executes a **trap**, think of it as a arm64 bl or x86_64 call instruction, to a function in the kernel. The kernel takes the arguments, determines if the arguments are well formed and if the process has permission to do the action. The kernel will then carry out that system call or deny accordingly.

For example, **getpid**, which gets the process identifier for the current process is actually a system call. The userland "source" to this is handwritten assembly found in xnu's libsyscall/custom/__getpid.s (https://github.com/apple/darwin-xnu/blob/main/libsyscall/custom/__getpid.s). On the kernel side, the getpid call is picked up and eventually calls getpid(proc_t p, __unused struct getpid_args *uap, int32_t *retval) found in xnu's bsd/kern/kern_prot.c (https://github.com/apple/darwin-xnu/blob/main/bsd/kern/kern_prot.c).

> **Note**: There are many unique system call wrappers that will call into the kernel, but there's also a generic API to make system calls via the **syscall(int, ...)** function. One supplies an integer available from the <sys/syscall.h> header (or finds a private syscall number that's in use) and passes in the expected arguments to that function. For example to mimic the __exit(int status) system call, you'd execute the syscall(SYS_exit, status); where status is the return value you'd pass into __exit.

Finding System Calls

To get a list of system calls, you can peruse the sources of xnu on opensource.apple.com. Alternatively, you can use **DTrace** to dynamically find them at runtime.

macOS Ventura has about 557 system calls. Open a Terminal window and run the following command to get the number of systems calls available in your system:

```
sudo dtrace -ln 'syscall:::entry' | wc -l
```

Note: Remember, you'll need to disable SIP (See Chapter 1) if you want to use DTrace. In addition, you'll also need sudo for the DTrace command since DTrace can monitor processes across multiple users, as well as perform some incredibly powerful actions. With great power comes great responsibility — that's why you need sudo. You'll learn more about how to bend DTrace to your will in the 5th section of this book. For now you'll use simple DTrace commands to get system call information out of ptrace.

ptrace

With system calls explained, you're now going to take a look at the ptrace system call in more depth. The easiest way to describe ptrace is that it enables setting certain debugging related flags for a process that are only accessible from the kernel side. This allows the debugger to catch the debugee if the debugee were to crash. For those interested at exploring the source, look at the ptrace kernel code (https://github.com/apple/darwin-xnu/blob/main/bsd/kern/mach_process.c) to see what's happening and search for references to **P_LTRACED**.

It's time to use ptrace for yourself. Open a Terminal console. Before you start, make sure to clear the Terminal console by pressing **Command-K**. Next execute this DTrace inline script to see how ptrace is called:

```
sudo dtrace -qn 'syscall::ptrace:entry { printf("%s(%d, %d, %d, %d) from %s\n", probefunc, arg0, arg1, arg2, arg3, execname); }'
```

Open up the **helloptrace** application, which you'll find in the resources folder for this chapter. This is a macOS Terminal command application that does not do much at the moment.

The only thing of interest in this project is a bridging header used to import the ptrace system call API into Swift.

Open **main.swift** and add the following code to the end of the file:

```
while true {
    sleep(2)
    print("Hello ptrace!")
}
```

Next, position Xcode and the DTrace Terminal window you can see them both at the same time. Build and run the application. Once your app has launched observe the output generated by the DTrace script.

Remember from way back in the beginning of the book, that debugserver is the process that LLDB uses to attach to processes. The actual process you're attaching to is the second parameter of the output, 915 in the screen shot.

Use **Open Quickly** to read the header for **ptrace.h**. Press **Command-Shift-O** and type ptrace.h. Compare the first parameter to **ptrace.h** header and you'll see the first parameter, 14, actually stands for **PT_ATTACHEXC**. What does this PT_ATTACHEXC mean? To get information about this parameter, first, open a Terminal window. Finally, type **man ptrace** and search for PT_ATTACHEXC.

> **Note:** You can perform case-sensitive searches on man pages by pressing /, followed by your search query. You can search downwards to the next hit by pressing **N** or upwards to the previous hit by pressing **Shift-N**.

You'll find some relevant info about PT_ATTACHEXC with the following output obtained from the ptrace man page:

```
This request allows a process to gain control of an otherwise
unrelated process and begin tracing it. It does not need any
cooperation from the to-be-traced process, but the kernel does
require the parent process to contain the right privileges. In
this case, `pid` specifies the process ID of the to-be-traced
process, and the other two arguments are ignored.
```

With this information, the reason for the first call of ptrace should be clear. This call says "Hey, attach to this process", and attaches to the process provided in the second parameter.

Onto the next ptrace call from your DTrace output:

```
ptrace(13, 915, 5635, 0) from debugserver
```

This one is a bit trickier to understand, since Apple decided to not give any man documentation about this one. This call relates to the internals of a process attaching to another one.

If you look at the ptrace API header, 13 stands for **PT_THUPDATE** and relates to how the controlling process, in this case, debugserver, handles UNIX signals and Mach messages passed to the controlled process; in this case, helloptrace. The kernel needs to know how to handle signal passing from a process controlled by another process, as in the Signals project from Section 1. The controlling process could say it doesn't want to send any signals to the controlled process.

This specific ptrace action is an implementation detail of how the Mach kernel handles ptrace internally; there's no need to dwell on it. Fortunately, there are other *documented* signals definitely worth exploring through man. One of them is the **PT_DENY_ATTACH** action, which you'll learn about now.

Creating Attachment Issues

A process can actually specify it doesn't want to be attached to by calling ptrace and supplying the PT_DENY_ATTACH argument. This is often used as an anti-debugging mechanism to prevent unwelcome reverse engineers from discovering a program's internals.

You'll now experiment with this argument. Open **main.swift** and add the following line of code before the `while` loop:

```
ptrace(PT_DENY_ATTACH, 0, nil, 0)
```

Build and run, keep on eye on the debugger console and see what happens.

The program will exit and output the following to the debugger console:

```
Program ended with exit code: 45
```

> **Note**: You may need to open up the debug console by clicking **View ▸ Debug Area ▸ Activate Console** or pressing **Command-Shift-Y** if you're one of those cool, shortcut devs.

This happened because Xcode launches the `helloptrace` program by default with LLDB automatically attached. If you execute the `ptrace` function with `PT_DENY_ATTACH`, LLDB will exit early and the program will stop executing.

If you were to try and execute the `helloptrace` program, and tried later to attach to it, LLDB would fail in attaching and the `helloptrace` program would happily continue execution, oblivious to `debugserver`'s attachment issues.

There are numerous macOS (and iOS) programs that perform this very action in their production builds. However, it's rather trivial to circumvent this security precaution. Ninja debug mode activated!

Getting Around PT_DENY_ATTACH

Once a process executes `ptrace` with the `PT_DENY_ATTACH` argument, making an attachment greatly escalates in complexity. However, there's a *much* easier way of getting around this problem.

Typically a developer will execute `ptrace(PT_DENY_ATTACH, 0, 0, 0)` somewhere in the main executable's code — oftentimes, right in the main function.

Since LLDB has the –w argument to wait for the launching of a process, you can use LLDB to "catch" the launch of a process and perform logic to augment or ignore the `PT_DENY_ATTACH` command before the process has a chance to execute `ptrace`!

Open a new Terminal window and type the following:

```
sudo lldb -n "helloptrace" -w
```

This starts an lldb session and attaches to the helloptrace program, but this time -w tells lldb to wait until a new process with the name helloptrace has started.

You need to use sudo due to an ongoing bug with LLDB and macOS security when you tell LLDB to wait for a Terminal program to launch.

Next, go to the **Product** menu and select **Product ▸ Show Build Folder in Finder**.

Next, drag the helloptrace executable into a new Terminal tab. Finally, press **Enter** to start the executable.

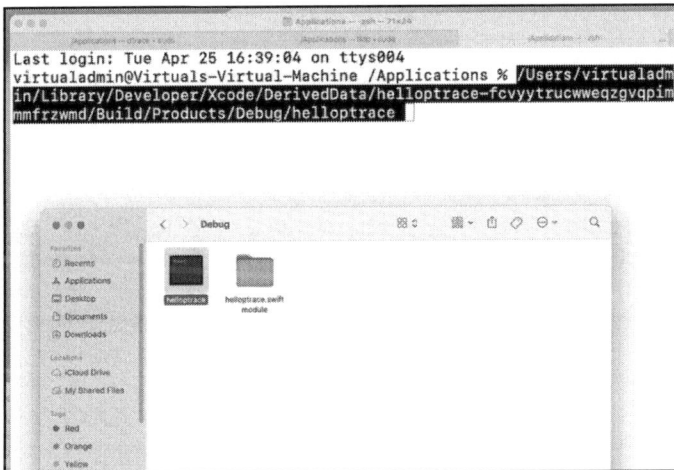

Now, open the previously created Terminal tab, where you had LLDB sit and wait for the helloptrace executable.

If everything went as expected, LLDB will see helloptrace has started and will launch itself, attaching to this newly created helloptrace process.

In LLDB, create the following regex breakpoint to stop on any type of function containing the word ptrace:

```
(lldb) rb ptrace -s libsystem_kernel.dylib
```

This will add a breakpoint on the userland gateway to the actual kernel ptrace function. Next, type continue into the Terminal window.

```
(lldb) continue
```

You'll break right before the ptrace function is about to be executed. However, you can simply use LLDB to return early and not execute that function. Do that now like so:

```
(lldb) thread return 0
```

Next, simply just continue:

```
(lldb) continue
```

Although the program entered the ptrace userland gateway function, you told LLDB to return early and not execute the logic that will execute the kernel ptrace system call.

> **Note**: The "defending" programming side can up the ante and hide the ptrace API by using syscall (i.e. syscall(SYS_ptrace, PT_DENY_ATTACH, 0, nil, 0)). The syscall API is called at a much higher frequency compared to ptrace, which would make breaking on the code of interest more difficult. However, code referencing calls to syscall might also "pop out" to a researcher when dumping the symbol table. One can hide this by dynamically resolving the syscall symbol through dlopen/dlsym, or use less obvious means by resolving syscall. An even better method would be to replicate the required assembly needed to make the ptrace call, completely sidestepping any suspicious references in the symbol table.

Navigate to the Hello ptrace! output tab and verify it's outputting "helloptrace" over and over. If so, you've successfully bypassed PT_DENY_ATTACH and are running lldb while still attached to the helloptrace command!

In a couple chapters, you'll explore an alternative method to crippling external functions like ptrace by inspecting Mach-O's __DATA.__la_symbol_ptr section along with the lovely DYLD_INSERT_LIBRARIES environment variable.

Other Anti-Debugging Techniques

Since we're on the topic of anti-debugging, let's put iTunes on the spot: for the longest time, iTunes actually used the ptrace's PT_DENY_ATTACH. However, more recent versions of iTunes has opted for a different technique to prevent debugging: iTunes will now check if it's being debugged using the powerful **sysctl** function, then kill itself if true. sysctl is another kernel function (like ptrace) that gets or sets kernel values. iTunes repeatedly calls sysctl while it's running using a NSTimer to call out to the logic.

Below is a simplified code example in Swift of what iTunes is doing:

```swift
let mib = UnsafeMutablePointer<Int32>.allocate(capacity: 4)
mib[0] = CTL_KERN
mib[1] = KERN_PROC
mib[2] = KERN_PROC_PID
mib[3] = getpid()

var size: Int = MemoryLayout<kinfo_proc>.size
var info: kinfo_proc? = nil

sysctl(mib, 4, &info, &size, nil, 0)

if (info.unsafelyUnwrapped.kp_proc.p_flag & P_TRACED) > 0 {
  exit(1)
}
```

The details of the expected params for sysctl are outside the scope of this chapter that interested readres can explore, but know there's more than one way to skin a cat.

Key Points

- `ptrace` is a system call that attaches to other processes.

- Apps can deny `ptrace` attachments using the `PT_DENY_ATTACH` argument.

Where to Go From Here?

With the DTrace dumping script you used in this chapter, explore parts of your system and see when `ptrace` is called.

If you're feeling cocky, read up on the `ptrace` man pages and see if you can create a program that will automatically attach itself to another program on your system.

Still have energy? Go `man sysctl`. That will be some good night-time reading.

Remember, having attachment issues is not always a bad thing!

Chapter 15: Shared Libraries

Shared libraries are essential for any program to run. This chapter focuses on the compilation and linking process, highlighting how to write code that uses public and private APIs.

A shared library is a bundle of code loaded into a program at runtime instead of being included at compile time. Shared libraries can't run by themselves — they need to be loaded in by an executable. Examples of shared libraries in iOS include UIKit and the Foundation frameworks. These are first-party shared libraries provided by Apple that you can link against. You can also create your own frameworks and package them inside your app bundle.

Creating your own shared libraries is an attractive development option. They provide encapsulation of code that can be shared between different projects. It can also lead to a more rigorous testing strategy, where you can test the shared library in isolation and be sure it works as intended.

Shared Libraries 101

Several types of shared libraries can be loaded in at runtime: **dynamic libraries**, **frameworks** and **plugins**.

A dynamic library, or **dylib**, is a shared executable that only contains executable code.

On the other hand, a framework is more of a directory that *can* contain executable code — as well as other content, like images and JSON files — almost anything! In fact, a framework doesn't even need to contain *any* code for it to be classified as a framework. A framework ends in a `*.framework` extension and contains the directory for the encapsulated resources.

Finally, there are plugins. These are a bit like frameworks, except they should be self-contained as much as possible. That is, if someone gave you a framework, you'd expect to call those APIs implemented in the framework. A plugin should do as much as possible on its own without having another entity have to call on its APIs.

This chapter's focus is primarily on dynamic libraries because it's the simplest option to showcase a shared library and an executable calling code from it.

To appreciate how dynamic libraries, linking and loading work, you'll build a dynamic library and an executable that references it. You'll compile all of this using `clang` without Xcode to appreciate what's happening. For this example, you'll create a C executable that calls code from a Swift dynamic library. You're using Swift with C on purpose — instead of Swift with Swift — as it emphasizes the concept of resolving symbol names. You'll learn how to import Swift code from a Swift dylib later when you learn about TBDs and module maps.

Building a Swift Dynamic Library

In the following section, you're encouraged to write the code yourself, but the source is available in the `starter` directory for copy/pasters.

In Terminal, navigate to the `/tmp` directory, and use your favorite text editor to add the following code to **/tmp/SwiftSharedLibrary.swift**:

```swift
@_cdecl("swift_function")
public func swift_function() {
    print("hello from \(#function)")
}

public func mangled_function() {
```

```
    print("!!!!!! \(#function)")
}
```

Compile this code into a dylib with the following command:

```
$ swiftc SwiftSharedLibrary.swift -emit-library -o
libSwiftSharedLibrary.dylib
```

The swiftc command is an integrated front end for the clang compiler. That's fancy, technical speak for saying it'll compile Swift code. :]

-emit-library instructs swiftc to create a dynamic library instead of an executable. The -o flag lets you specify the output filename, which will be libSwiftSharedLibrary.dylib. By default, Swift generates this name for you. However, it's nice to be explicit in case Apple decides to change this in the future.

The SwiftSharedLibrary.swift source code declares three functions (yes, three). The Swift compiler front end creates two mangled functions:

- swift_function, whose symbol mangled name is $s18SwiftSharedLibrary14swift_functionyyF.

- mangled_function, whose mangled name is s18SwiftSharedLibrary16mangled_functionyyF.

In addition, the compiler generates a **C-like unmangled function** called swift_function, which, in turn, calls the mangled equivalent. This is all done thanks to the **@_cdecl("swift_function")** attribute in the Swift source.

This is best seen by dumping the symbol table and greping for the word "function":

```
$ nm -U libSwiftSharedLibrary.dylib | grep function
0000000000003954 T _$s18SwiftSharedLibrary14swift_functionyyF
0000000000003c3c T _$s18SwiftSharedLibrary16mangled_functionyyF
0000000000003940 T _swift_function
```

nm's -U option filters for local symbols, meaning it displays symbols implemented in libSwiftSharedLibrary.dylib instead of symbols referenced elsewhere. From the output, the capital T indicates that a symbol is **public**. This lets code in other modules reference this symbol. If you didn't include the public keyword in the Swift source code, the t would be lowercase, indicating the symbol is private and can't be referenced from another module — at least not with public APIs like dlsym.

From the output, observe the unmangled _swift_function symbol generated via the @_cdel("swift_function") attribute. Note how the compiler prepends an underscore to (almost) all symbols when compiling code.

You can also get Swift to demangle the names in any output like the one above. You can pipe any output to `swift demangle`, and you'll see the demangled names:

```
$ nm -U libSwiftSharedLibrary.dylib | grep function | swift
demangle
0000000000003a48 T SwiftSharedLibrary.swift_function() -> ()
0000000000003cf4 T SwiftSharedLibrary.mangled_function() -> ()
0000000000003a34 T _swift_function
```

This can be useful if you need to see what each function is in an nm output.

Building a C Executable

You'll now create the executable to reference the unmangled `swift_function` implemented in `libSwiftSharedLibrary.dylib`. Add the following code to **/tmp/exe.c**:

```
extern void swift_function(void);

int main() {
  swift_function();
  return 0;
}
```

The code above externally declares the `swift_function()` and attempts to execute it. Compile exe.c while linking `libSwiftSharedLibrary.dylib`:

```
$ clang exe.c -o exe libSwiftSharedLibrary.dylib
```

This time, you're using `clang` to compile the exe.c file. Remember, `swiftc` is essentially a wrapper for `clang` with some additional flag handling baked in for Swift.

You've just compiled the executable to exe. `clang` was smart enough to infer that the `libSwiftSharedLibrary.dylib` was a dynamic library and automatically linked it into your executable. An alternative way to execute the above command is the following:

```
$ clang exe.c -o exe -lSwiftSharedLibrary -L./
```

This format uses `clang`'s `-l` option to tell the linker that it needs to link against the `SwiftSharedLibrary`. When specifying the `-l` option for a dynamic library, `ld` will take that name, prepend a `lib`, and append `.dylib` to its search query. So, if you passed in `-lPumpkinLatte`, `ld` would search for `libPumpkinLatte.dylib` in its dynamic library search paths.

But how does one specify the search paths to ld? That's the −L./ flag's job. This flag can be used multiple times, and it instructs ld of all the possible locations to look for a dynamic library. It's important you know both ways to link a dynamic library, as developers and developer tools use both methods interchangeably.

Give the exe program a run:

```
$ ./exe
```

The expected output from swift_function appears!

```
hello from swift_function()
```

Symbols and Dependencies

When linking dynamic frameworks, it's insightful to be able to inspect dependencies from a particular module. Use otool −L on the exe executable to display the shared libraries exe needs in order to run:

```
$ otool −L exe
```

This shows that exe needs the standard system library and your SwiftSharedLibrary.dylib in order to run.

```
exe:
    libSwiftSharedLibrary.dylib (compatibility version 0.0.0,
current version 0.0.0)
    /usr/lib/libSystem.B.dylib (compatibility version 1.0.0,
current version 1319.100.3)
```

The −L option displays framework load commands that are embedded near the beginning of the exe executable, which will be thoroughly discussed in an upcoming chapter. The referenced libSwiftSharedLibrary.dylib is listed as a requirement.

Using the same otool −L option, inspect the libSwiftSharedLibrary.dylib dependencies:

```
$ otool −L libSwiftSharedLibrary.dylib
libSwiftSharedLibrary.dylib:
    libSwiftSharedLibrary.dylib (compatibility version 0.0.0,
current version 0.0.0)
    /usr/lib/libSystem.B.dylib (compatibility version 1.0.0,
current version 1319.100.3)
    /usr/lib/swift/libswiftCore.dylib (compatibility version
1.0.0, current version 5.8.0)
```

The library that *is* important is `libswiftCore.dylib`, the library that provides the APIs to use `print` and friends referenced by the Swift source code. Remember the name `libswiftCore.dylib`, as you'll use it later when working with static libraries. The final linked library is `libSystem.B.dylib`, which is imported by pretty much every shared library and isn't relevant for this example.

At runtime, `dyld` will take these libraries, resolve exe's dependencies, then recursively resolve all of the shared library dependencies. This process repeats to the next layer until there are no more dependencies to load in. You can see this in action by setting the **DYLD_PRINT_LIBRARIES** environment variable. Here's a partial excerpt from my computer:

```
• /tmp DYLD_PRINT_LIBRARIES=1 /tmp/exe
dyld[4368]: <F60CC8B7-8D5B-3676-BC08-0C2CDE2A775A> /private/tmp/exe
dyld[4368]: <F86A0A66-54BF-34F4-A1B5-E05374ABD3D2> /private/tmp/libSwiftSharedLibrary.dylib
dyld[4368]: <81F154EC-CC94-3E43-848B-57273FA17DB2> /usr/lib/libobjc.A.dylib
dyld[4368]: <52AA13E2-567C-36C2-9494-7B892FDBF245> /usr/lib/libc++abi.dylib
dyld[4368]: <31B81CC9-A726-377E-9D2C-929F81A9DE10> /usr/lib/liboah.dylib
dyld[4368]: <54E8FBE1-DF0D-33A2-B8FA-356565C12929> /usr/lib/libc++.1.dylib
dyld[4368]: <7F800990-E44E-316C-B806-3FC633A41FF0> /usr/lib/libSystem.B.dylib
dyld[4368]: <F6E1922F-64B5-3DCB-8AE0-68C642D42727> /usr/lib/system/libcache.dylib
dyld[4368]: <08AB48F3-EF56-335F-B515-BD3F76C06849> /usr/lib/system/libcommonCrypto.dylib
dyld[4368]: <92C8AE9C-2DA6-31A4-B5F6-AA0BF31D6967> /usr/lib/system/libcompiler_rt.dylib
dyld[4368]: <77F49B3E-AF36-3F26-82C7-FDC86A6FA38F> /usr/lib/system/libcopyfile.dylib
dyld[4368]: <A776108D-9975-3DD0-BDDB-121895BC59D1> /usr/lib/system/libcorecrypto.dylib
dyld[4368]: <78FF427C-107B-33C3-A3C2-577AA588DFF1> /usr/lib/system/libdispatch.dylib
dyld[4368]: <2E996E2D-9BFB-3902-8B61-8B59B17B02EA> /usr/lib/system/libdyld.dylib
dyld[4368]: <AD80F96F-0270-3BFF-B0AA-90CA91F5DEA6> /usr/lib/system/libkeymgr.dylib
dyld[4368]: <B4E3D7D5-6BBE-3523-8484-A51997EA595B> /usr/lib/system/libmacho.dylib
dyld[4368]: <9633325A-5800-3CAE-83EB-D9DF9BBBDF6E> /usr/lib/system/libquarantine.dylib
dyld[4368]: <82072196-79C1-3B58-8C4B-A155C3B54F7B> /usr/lib/system/libremovefile.dylib
dyld[4368]: <6E29A67D-D59D-35DD-98DA-B21D49650DFA> /usr/lib/system/libsystem_asl.dylib
dyld[4368]: <251FF0F0-CED3-3510-9E2E-AB9C126A32DA> /usr/lib/system/libsystem_blocks.dylib
dyld[4368]: <43293DF3-305B-3F92-8EDD-02C96CCE1719> /usr/lib/system/libsystem_c.dylib
dyld[4368]: <8C220825-4BB7-31C9-9883-BEE69F9836A4> /usr/lib/system/libsystem_collections.dylib
dyld[4368]: <2BC4BB20-5784-392A-B2D0-49EEFDDE0FA5> /usr/lib/system/libsystem_configuration.dylib
dyld[4368]: <7421F3BC-37C0-3701-B2DC-5BA589EBC135> /usr/lib/system/libsystem_containermanager.dylib
dyld[4368]: <223749C5-6055-3282-BE22-1FC86C203229> /usr/lib/system/libsystem_coreservices.dylib
dyld[4368]: <EAEFCDCC-EAC4-3F9A-9718-93BE0B8D061C> /usr/lib/system/libsystem_darwin.dylib
dyld[4368]: <E65960EC-867C-38EB-ABBC-EC37D0BB9EDB> /usr/lib/system/libsystem_dnssd.dylib
dyld[4368]: <FB39342B-097D-317A-B3AE-E1A178A8D69F> /usr/lib/system/libsystem_featureflags.dylib
dyld[4368]: <D45F0DCA-D5A3-38D9-B495-06B89C5D2ED7> /usr/lib/system/libsystem_info.dylib
dyld[4368]: <1CD554B5-1597-300C-9F41-E4E522A3E7A9> /usr/lib/system/libsystem_m.dylib
dyld[4368]: <12387488-3523-3A4A-99F6-6A32F43B4022> /usr/lib/system/libsystem_malloc.dylib
dyld[4368]: <C95F7781-68C5-3383-B8C4-A703DA3753A2> /usr/lib/system/libsystem_networkextension.dylib
dyld[4368]: <2342897E-0E05-3E5B-86C3-0302018C8785> /usr/lib/system/libsystem_notify.dylib
dyld[4368]: <7D206D8C-24DC-38A5-B2E9-184CBDADF5B9> /usr/lib/system/libsystem_sandbox.dylib
dyld[4368]: <B5E69256-74BC-3151-AA97-48A4B610A7F6> /usr/lib/system/libsystem_secinit.dylib
dyld[4368]: <222F8841-2BFD-3804-AA0C-F6D80A73FBDF> /usr/lib/system/libsystem_kernel.dylib
dyld[4368]: <61D6CE46-BF8C-34EA-B81A-879743AD4063> /usr/lib/system/libsystem_platform.dylib
```

Note: If you were to look at these shared libraries on disk, you'll notice something peculiar: These libraries don't exist on disk at the specified location! You may recall from Chapter 7, "Image", that Apple has combined them into a shared cache. You'll do a much deeper dive into what's happening and why by the end of this chapter.

When a dynamic library is linked, it's typically — but not always! — due to the fact that at least one symbol is needed from that library. Display the external symbols of exe with nm:

```
$ nm -mu ./exe
  (undefined) external _swift_function (from
libSwiftSharedLibrary)
```

The –m option shows which module a symbol is referenced from. The lowercase –u will only display symbols that are external. Remember, –U for symbols implemented in the module, –u for symbols *not* implemented in the module.

When compiling, the linker searched for the swift_function symbol in libSwiftSharedLibrary.dylib and found a reference there. You're not required to replicate this on your end, but if you were to change around the C source code to call a nonexistent function like bad_function(), you'd get the following error because the symbol can't be resolved:

```
$ sed  's/swift_function/bad_function/g'  exe.c > bad_exe.c
$ clang exe.c /tmp/libSwiftSharedLibrary.dylib
UUndefined symbols for architecture arm64:
  "_bad_function", referenced from:
      _main in bad_exe-d1e251.o
ld: symbol(s) not found for architecture arm64
clang: error: linker command failed with exit code 1 (use -v to
see invocation)
```

Linking Tricks

The @_cdecl() attribute is a common trick to read Swift symbols in non-Swift code because it's typically not possible to reference mangled Swift symbols whose names begin with a dollar sign, like $s18SwiftSharedLibrary16mangled_functionyyF.

However, there are some nifty tricks to get around this! You'll explore several tricks for executing the mangled $s14SwiftSharedLibrary16mangled_functionyyF.

Compile Time Linking

One way to call the mangled Swift function is with an option from ld to make an alias for the desired function.

```
$ clang exe.c libSwiftSharedLibrary.dylib -Xlinker -alias
-Xlinker '_$s18SwiftSharedLibrary16mangled_functionyyF' -Xlinker
_swift_function  -o ./exe
```

The -Xlinker command passes an argument to the linker, ld, one argument at a time. It might seem weird having to pass -Xlinker multiple times, but consider that clang needs to run several executables — in different processes! — and report the results. If you want to see the full list of options ld has, use man ld. Just remember that every argument has to be preceded by -Xlinker if being called from clang. An alternative way of doing this is via the **-Wl** flag, which expects commas in place of spaces, like in clang exe.c libSwiftSharedLibrary.dylib '-Wl,-alias,_$s18SwiftSharedLibrary16mangled_functionyyF,_swift_function' -o ./exe. This is nice because you only need to type -Wl once. Either method is fine — take your pick.

The -alias option replaces all references of _swift_function with _$s18SwiftSharedLibrary16mangled_functionyyF. Be careful with supplying the correct symbol, as this won't report any errors on failure. Running the exe now gives the following:

```
$ ./exe
!!!!!!! hello from mangled_function()
```

Runtime Linking

Another alternative is to use runtime linking via the **dlsym** API. You'll explore this function and dlopen in depth in the next chapter. But for now, you'll just take a quick look.

Enter the following code snippet into a file called exe2.c:

```
#include <dlfcn.h>
#include <stdlib.h>

int main() {
  void (*mangled_function)(void) = NULL;
  mangled_function = dlsym(
    RTLD_NEXT, "$s18SwiftSharedLibrary16mangled_functionyyF");
```

```
  if (mangled_function) {
    mangled_function();
  }
  return 0;
}
```

dlsym will attempt to find the symbol at runtime. If successful, the mangled_function function pointer will contain the address.

Be aware that no underscore precedes the symbol when resolving a symbol at runtime.

Then, run the following:

```
clang exe2.c libSwiftSharedLibrary.dylib -o exe2
```

Executing it, you see the same thing again:

```
$ ./exe2
!!!!!!! hello from mangled_function()
```

Note: The dlsym API only works for public symbols — or, more technically, symbols that contain the N_EXT flag in its corresponding nlist. That means if the source code has a C static or Swift private attribute, the symbol won't be exported as public. You easily see which symbols are public by observing the uppercase character on the nm output, like the T in 0000000000003894 T _swift_function.

Linking Symbols? Meh!!! Symbols

If you know that a dynamic library would **never** change (i.e., would never be updated, never recompiled), you can hardcode offsets to that library based on the module's load address.

For example, if you wanted to call the mangled mangled_function() in libSwiftSharedLibrary.dylib without using the symbol at all, you can find the offset of where the code is located on disk:

```
$ nm ./libSwiftSharedLibrary.dylib | grep mangled
0000000000003cf4 T _$s18SwiftSharedLibrary16mangled_functionyyF
```

On my machine, the mangled_function() is located at offset 0000000000003cf4. This is a hexadecimal value and needs a 0x prepended to it.

From there, one can find the starting load address of
libSwiftSharedLibrary.dylib and then add the offset to get the function. Here's
the source code for dontdothis.c:

```c
#include <mach-o/dyld.h> // _dyld.* APIs
#include <string.h>      // strcmp
#include <libgen.h>      // basename

int main() {
  uintptr_t base = 0;
  // iterate over loaded images
  for (int i = 0; i < _dyld_image_count(); i++) {
    if (strcmp(basename((char*)_dyld_get_image_name(i)),
"libSwiftSharedLibrary.dylib") == 0) {
      // we found the load address for
libSwiftSharedLibrary.dylib
      base = (uintptr_t)_dyld_get_image_header(i);
      break;
    }
  }

  // execute mangled_function
  if (base) {
    void (*mangled_function)(void) = (void*)(base +
0x00000000003cf4);
    mangled_function();
  }

  return 0;
}
```

Compiling and running produces the following on my machine:

```
clang dontdothis.c libSwiftSharedLibrary.dylib -o ./dontdothis
&& ./dontdothis
!!!!!!! hello from mangled_function()
```

This is only here to show you that it can be done. This is a *bad* idea — don't do this!
Do as I say, not as I do. :]

Defensive Linking

One final trick is to use a **weak** attribute for a symbol. A weak attribute won't crash
the program if the symbol can't be resolved.

Add the following to a file called exe3.c:

```
#include <stdio.h>

__attribute__((weak))
extern void swift_function(void);

__attribute__((weak))
extern void bad_function(void);

int main() {
  swift_function ? swift_function() : printf("swift_function not
found!\n");
  bad_function ? bad_function() : printf("bad_function not
found!\n");
  return 0;
}
```

Compile with the —undefined dynamic_lookup option, which tells ld to ignore unresolved symbols at compile time and attempt to link them at runtime:

```
$ clang exe3.c -o exe3 libSwiftSharedLibrary.dylib -undefined
dynamic_lookup && ./exe3
hello from swift_function()
bad_function not found!
```

Note: Xcode has an annoying warning that complains when using the —undefined flag on iOS. You can get around this by explicitly listing which symbols you want undefined via the —U option, like so: -Wl,-U,_bad_function,-U,_swift_function.

Notice how swift_function was called, but bad_function wasn't found. Repeat compiling, but compile without linking libSwiftSharedLibrary.dylib and run exe3:

```
$ clang exe3.c -o exe3 -undefined dynamic_lookup && ./exe3
swift_function not found!
bad_function not found!
```

Without the __attribute__((weak)), a symbol's address is assumed to be non-zero, resulting in a runtime crash from dyld.

Static Libraries

Discussing dynamic libraries wouldn't be complete without mentioning their counterpart — static libraries!

Sometimes, having a separate entity for symbols isn't the ideal solution. The current dynamic library setup makes libSwiftSharedLibrary.dylib and its path a required dependency for the executable to run. To observe this, change the name of libSwiftSharedLibrary.dylib to something different:

```
$ mv libSwiftSharedLibrary.dylib libMovedSharedLibrary.dylib
$ ./exe
dyld: Library not loaded: libSwiftSharedLibrary.dylib
  Referenced from: /private/tmp/exe
  Reason: image not found
[1]    6074 abort       exe
```

If you're following along with the examples using Terminal, be sure to rename the library back to its original name:

```
$ mv libMovedSharedLibrary.dylib libSwiftSharedLibrary.dylib
```

Having this external libSwiftSharedLibrary.dylib dependency requirement might be undesirable — especially if there's only one consumer using it (which is exe in this example).

> **Note**: There are several ways to resolve finding dependency locations for shared frameworks. A dynamic library can be referenced via an absolute path or a relative path from the calling module. Check out ld's rpath option if you're interested in exploring this.

An alternative to compiling a dynamic library is to compile the SwiftSharedLibrary.swift code as a **static library**. A static library is a chunk of sharable compiled code that acts a bit like a dynamic library but is packaged inside the calling module.

Recompile SwiftSharedLibrary.swift as a static library:

```
$ swiftc SwiftSharedLibrary.swift -static -emit-library -o
SwiftSharedLibrary.a
```

Using the −static option along with −emit-library creates a static library at SwiftSharedLibrary.a. Using a *.a is the typical naming convention for static libraries.

Now, compile the exe.c C source file while including the SwiftSharedLibrary.a static library:

```
$ clang SwiftSharedLibrary.a exe.c -o exe
```

The compiler will present some errors — OK, lots of errors:

```
ld: warning: Could not find or use auto-linked library
'swiftSwiftOnoneSupport'
ld: warning: Could not find or use auto-linked library
'swiftCore'
Undefined symbols for architecture arm64:
  "Swift.String.init(stringInterpolation:
Swift.DefaultStringInterpolation) -> Swift.String", referenced
from:
      SwiftSharedLibrary.swift_function() -> () in
SwiftSharedLibrary.a(SwiftSharedLibrary-c49738.o)
      SwiftSharedLibrary.mangled_function() -> () in
SwiftSharedLibrary.a(SwiftSharedLibrary-c49738.o)
... snip ...
```

Uh-oh! You've included a static library that has external symbols that you're not linking against. Remember when you used otool −L on libSwiftSharedLibrary.dylib and saw that it had a dependency, libswiftCore.dylib, to use Swift's print APIs? Since libSwiftSharedLibrary.a's code is being compiled directly into exe, exe now needs to link to its dependencies, like /usr/lib/swift/libswiftCore.dylib.

Build again, but now include libSwiftSharedLibrary.a's dependency of libswiftCore.dylib:

```
$ clang SwiftSharedLibrary.a exe.c -L/usr/lib/swift -lswiftCore
-o exe
```

Run the executable, then check the compiled local symbols and referenced frameworks included in exe with nm and otool:

```
$ ./exe
```

Displays your expected output:

```
hello from swift_function()
```

Now, use the −L flag to show the shared libraries with otool:

```
$ otool −L exe
```

The symbols that were once separately packaged in libSwiftSharedLibrary.dylib are now implemented directly in exe!

```
exe:
    /usr/lib/swift/libswiftCore.dylib (compatibility version
1.0.0, current version 1205.0.24)
    /usr/lib/libSystem.B.dylib (compatibility version 1.0.0,
current version 1292.100.5)
```

```
$ nm −mU exe | grep function
0000000100003908 (__TEXT,__text) external
_$s14SwiftSharedLibrary14swift_functionyyF
0000000100003bf0 (__TEXT,__text) external
_$s14SwiftSharedLibrary16mangled_functionyyF
00000001000038f4 (__TEXT,__text) external _swift_function
```

That's because a static library is essentially just a bunch of object files that get added into the final binary at link time. When examining the code with nm, the functions that come from the library appear alongside the rest of the code. The fact that they started in a separate file is no longer obvious.

Be aware: You don't need a static library if you're compiling code into only one module. If you're just doing that, you should add the code directly since, in this case, creating a static library is a superfluous step. A static library is designed to be shareable, multi-architecture compiled code you can hand out to consumers, which is a great option for SDK makers.

Static libraries are great if you're packaging code that should only be called in one spot. Sometimes, vendors opt for a static library over a dynamic library as it can allow developers more integration flexibility. For example, a consuming codebase can embed the static library directly into the main executable or, instead, integrate the static library into a dynamic library so multiple modules can use it.

Text-Based Dynamic Library Files

In the example above, you created a main executable and a dynamic library. When compiling, the linker had to look into libSwiftSharedLibrary.dylib, parse its symbol table, and ensure that the appropriate symbol was there for the linking to succeed.

When you take a step back and think about this, the linker shouldn't need to do all that heavy lifting. The linker could be told the same thing just by reading a text file. That's what a **text-based dynamic library stub** or ***.tbd** file does.

Having knowledge of how text-based dynamic library — TBD for short — files work and how to use them is essential for referencing both public and private APIs. *If you plan on utilizing and linking against APIs in private frameworks on a remote host, like iOS, using a TBD file is extremely useful!* This is because you're not likely to have physical access to the shared library on your development machine. As of Xcode 7, Apple no longer packages shared libraries for remote platforms, which is understandable given this adds significant bloat to the Xcode bundle size.

Run the find Terminal command:

```
$ find /Applications/Xcode.app -name "*.tbd"
```

This dumps all the *.tbd files packaged within Xcode. These files are used in place of shared libraries when referencing symbols. Check out any one of these files that looks interesting to you via an open or a cat Terminal command. Here's one of my favorites:

```
$ cat /Applications/Xcode.app/Contents/Developer/Platforms/
MacOSX.platform/Developer/SDKs/MacOSX.sdk/System/Library/
PrivateFrameworks/CoreSymbolication.framework/
CoreSymbolication.tbd
```

TBD Format and TAPI

The text-based dynamic library stubs need to have an agreed-upon format for ld to know how to utilize the TBD file. An open-source implementation called Text-based Application Programming Interface, or **TAPI**, can generate TBD files from headers or compiled code. tapi has source code found in the LLVM repo and is also part of opensource.apple.com. You can also check out additional documentation of the TBD parameters (https://opensource.apple.com/source/tapi/tapi-1100.0.11/docs/TBD.rst.auto.html).

To explore how to work with these, you'll compile some code and treat this as a private dynamic library you don't have the source to but *do* have the header for (via reverse engineering or stumbling upon someone else's work on GitHub). The starter project directory includes Private.m and Private.h, which contain an Objective-C class called **PrivateObjcClass**, an NSString constant called **SomeStringConstant** and a C function called **SomeCode**.

In Terminal, navigate to where you've saved the demo code for this chapter. Using your favorite method, inspect the contents of `Private.h` and `Private.m`. Now, compile this code as a shared library, and treat it as a private library.

```
$ clang -shared -o /tmp/PrivateFramework.dylib Private.m
-fmodules -arch arm64e -arch arm64 -arch x86_64
```

This creates the `/tmp/PrivateFramework.dylib` shared library for all currently supported macOS hardware. `-fmodules` is required since the `Private.h` header imported a module instead of a C `#include` header (see `@import Foundation;` in `Private.h`). Using the version of `tapi` packaged in Xcode, generate a TBD file for the newly created `/tmp/PrivateFramework.dylib`.

```
$ /Applications/Xcode.app/Contents/Developer/Toolchains/
XcodeDefault.xctoolchain/usr/bin/tapi stubify /tmp/
PrivateFramework.dylib -o /tmp/libPrivateFramework.tbd
```

This creates the TBD file called **libPrivateFramework.tbd** (remember, the `lib` part of the name is important for linking!). `tapi` has several options that can be observed with `tapi --help`. One of those options is **stubify**, which extracts symbols from an already compiled module. The `-o` argument specifies the file's destination (if you supplied `-o -`, it will go to standard out).

The TBD file created with the above command has the following contents on my machine:

```
--- !tapi-tbd
tbd-version:      4
targets:          [ x86_64-macos, arm64-macos, arm64e-macos ]
flags:            [ not_app_extension_safe ]
install-name:     '/tmp/PrivateFramework.dylib'
current-version: 0
compatibility-version: 0
exports:
  - targets:          [ x86_64-macos, arm64-macos, arm64e-macos ]
    symbols:          [ _SomeCode, _SomeStringConstant ]
    objc-classes:     [ PrivateObjcClass ]
...
```

The TBD above uses a YAML-style way of declaring values. Some of the important values from above:

- **targets**: The supported executable slices that the shared library includes. You supplied three architectures earlier when compiling the library, which are reflected here.

- **install-name**: The actual path to the shared library where it's expected to be. This should match what `otool -L` would display.

- **symbols**: A subkey under `exports`. Declares any "C-like" symbols, including any public code and data.

- **objc-classes**: A subkey under `exports`. Declares any Objective classes.

The TBD file above declares `_SomeCode` and `_SomeStringConstant` symbols and an Objective-C class called **PrivateObjcClass**. Along with a corresponding `Private.h` header, you now have all the components required to compile the executable.

The TBD file will act as a stand-in to the `PrivateFramework.dylib` compiled module for linking. You'll create an executable that will reference these symbols and link code via the TBD file.

The starter project includes a file called `tbdpoc.m`. Compile this file and link it with the TBD file.

```
$ clang tbdpoc.m -I. -L/tmp/ -lPrivateFramework -fmodules -o /
tmp/tbdpoc
$ /tmp/tbdpoc
2023-04-06 14:42:56.710 tbdpoc[9757:587074] much wow, stuff of
doing!
2023-04-06 14:42:56.710 tbdpoc[9757:587074] SomeStringConstant
is: com.kodeco.tbd.example
```

The `-L/tmp/ -lPrivateFramework` combo worked on the TBD file just like a real image should. `-I.` instructed `clang` to search the current directory for headers and include files. This is needed so `tbdpoc` could reference `Private.h`, found in the same directory.

Instead of the −l/−L flags, you can also specify the TBD file directly, and the compiler will read the file and link to the framework specified in install-name.

This will produce the exact same result:

```
$ clang tbdpoc.m -I. libPrivateFramework.tbd -fmodules -o /tmp/
tbdpoc
ld: warning: text-based stub file libPrivateFramework.tbd and
library file libPrivateFramework.tbd are out of sync. Falling
back to library file for linking.
```

It's worth noting that you can get an annoying little warning because the module's UUID (which you've omitted via the −−no-uuids) doesn't match, making ld complain. Browsing the source code to the linker https://opensource.apple.com/source/ld64/ reveals that the linker will try to match the UUIDs in the TBD file with the ones on disk — see ld64/src/ld/Options.cpp. This can be suppressed with the **LD_PREFER_TAPI_FILE** environment variable.

Modules and Module Maps

You've played with Swift code mangling names and importing them into C, and you've created a TBD file importing Objective-C/C code into an Objective-C/C executable. Now, it's time to take an Objective-C dynamic library and import it into Swift. This is the final piece of the linking puzzle, as Swift requires one additional component to properly import symbols from an external library.

This component is called a **module**. This term conflicts with the typical meaning of module — compiled code — used throughout this book. The LLVM linker's version of the module is a "precompiled" grouping of headers that greatly speeds up the compilation process compared to traditional C #include headers. LLVM has a detailed writeup (https://clang.llvm.org/docs/Modules.html) of a module and the parameters one can use.

You've executed code before that's had modules in it with @import SomeModule; in Objective-C code and have told clang to compile modules with the −fmodules argument.

You have several ways to create a usable module in Swift. One way is through the swiftc command utility with the –emit–module flag, which creates a *.swiftmodule that can be linked and referenced in Swift code. Another way is to use a **module map,** which is a text file that's understood by clang and serves as the link between C include headers and a module. This method allows you to call private APIs from Swift because you can declare the APIs in a header, include the header in a module, then import that module into Swift code.

First, navigate to the starter directory for the code for this chapter and copy over the Private.h header file to /tmp/:

```
$ cp Private.h /tmp/
```

Now, create a module map file using your favorite text editor. Write the following contents to **/tmp/module.modulemap:**

```
module YayModule {
    header "Private.h"
    export *
}
```

The module.modulemap file is important! The compiler will look for this file in the specified include directories. If it exists, clang will automatically pick it up.

This module.modulemap defines a module called YayModule, which exports the C/ObjC symbols declared in Private.h. This will allow your soon-to-be-created Swift source code to use the symbols referenced in Private.h. The poorly chosen YayModule module name is to highlight that you can choose any arbitrary name so long as you import the same module name in the Swift source code.

The export * declaration indicates YayModule should export all of its imported declarations. This is a bit cryptic, so an example will better describe this: YayModule imports Objective-C headers in Private.h in order to declare the Objective-C class. If you didn't export these declarations, you'd have to manually import an Objective-C module in addition to the YayModule module. *You should default to always including an export * statement unless you know what you're doing.*

You're almost there. Create a Swift source file named `/tmp/mmpoc.swift` with the following code:

```
import YayModule

print("calling external: \(SomeStringConstant)")
SomeCode();
let c = PrivateObjcClass()
c.doStuff()
```

As a reminder, you should now have the following files in the `/tmp` directory, which will be required to compile `mmpoc.swift`:

- **mmpoc.swift**: The file that you'll compile.

- **libPrivateFramework.tbd**: The TBD file used by `ld` to resolve symbols referenced by `mmpoc.swift`.

- **PrivateFramework.dylib**: The actual compiled framework that's loaded at runtime whose symbols will be referenced. Also used by `libPrivateFramework.tbd` to indicate who implements the APIs.

- **module.modulemap**: The Swift header file equivalent used to import the symbols.

- **Private.h**: The header file referenced by `module.modulemap` and also for declaring code in `Private.m`.

After ensuring the above files are present, give the compilation a go. If successful, run `mmpoc`:

```
$ swiftc mmpoc.swift -I. -L/tmp -lPrivateFramework -o /tmp/mmpoc
&& /tmp/mmpoc
calling external: com.kodeco.tbd.example
2023-04-06 15:22:45.109 mmpoc[10164:605856] SomeStringConstant
is: com.kodeco.tbd.example
2023-04-06 15:22:45.110 mmpoc[10164:605856] much wow, stuff of
doing!
```

Excellent! You can now call, link to and execute "private" APIs in Swift or Objective-C.

Xcode Equivalent

You jumped down to the command line to do all this work. It's worth going back up to Xcode to see how to achieve the same thing.

If you want to link to a library — `-lDynamicLibrary` or `-framework FrameworkName` — select your desired Xcode target, and then click the plus button in Xcode's **Framework and Libraries** under **General**. Alternatively, you can specify a library to link with under **Build Phases** and then **Link Binary With Libraries**.

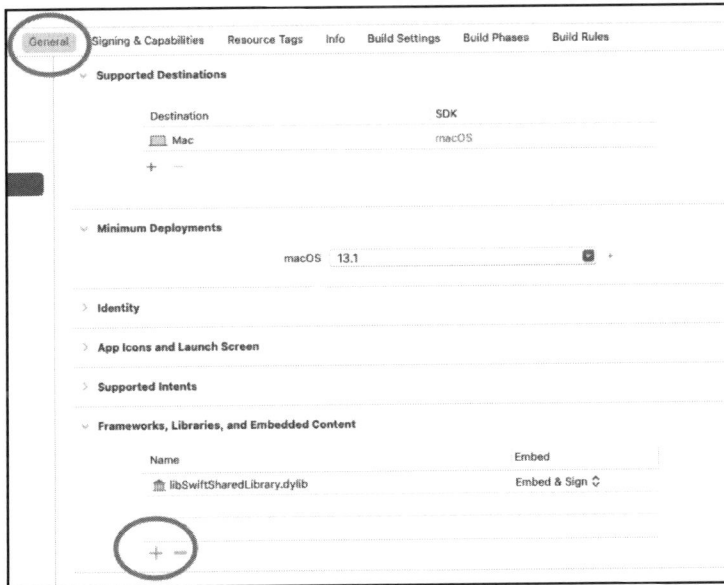

After compiling the module, `otool -L` shows that your library has been added to the executable:

```
→  MacOS otool -L sillytest | head -9
sillytest:
        libSwiftSharedLibrary.dylib (compatibility version 0.0.0, current version 0.0.0)
        /tmp/PrivateFramework.dylib (compatibility version 0.0.0, current version 0.0.0)
        /System/Library/Frameworks/Foundation.framework/Versions/C/Foundation (compatibility version 300.0.0, current
        /usr/lib/libobjc.A.dylib (compatibility version 1.0.0, current version 228.0.0)
        /usr/lib/libSystem.B.dylib (compatibility version 1.0.0, current version 1319.0.0)
        /System/Library/Frameworks/AppKit.framework/Versions/C/AppKit (compatibility version 45.0.0, current version
        /usr/lib/swift/libswiftAppKit.dylib (compatibility version 1.0.0, current version 111.0.0)
        /usr/lib/swift/libswiftCore.dylib (compatibility version 1.0.0, current version 5.7.1)
→  MacOS
```

Hopefully, all the *.a/*.tbd/*.framework/*.dylibs now make a little bit more sense when linking in a library.

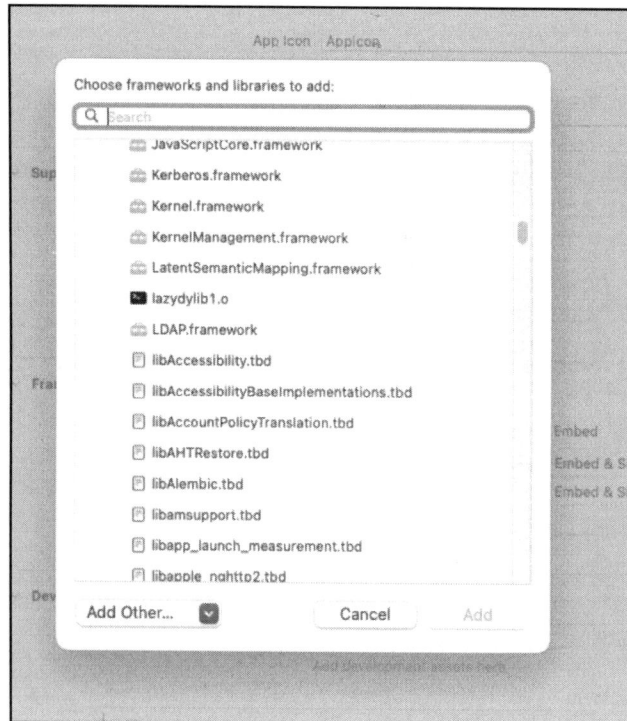

dyld Shared Cache

If you were to inspect *any* executable's linked frameworks, you'd notice that libSystem.B.dylib is included in pretty much everything.

For example, building a Swift file with no source code will still link to libSystem.B.dylib:

```
$ touch /tmp/anexample.swift && swiftc /tmp/anexample.swift -o /
tmp/anexample && otool -L /tmp/anexample
/tmp/anexample:
    /usr/lib/libobjc.A.dylib (compatibility version 1.0.0,
current version 228.0.0)
    /usr/lib/libSystem.B.dylib (compatibility version 1.0.0,
current version 1292.100.5)
```

But if you were to try and inspect this file...

```
$ file /usr/lib/libSystem.B.dylib
/usr/lib/libSystem.B.dylib: cannot open '/usr/lib/
libSystem.B.dylib' (No such file or directory)
```

You'll notice that this file doesn't exist on disk. That's because Apple aggressively caches frequently used libraries into a "mega library bundle" known as the **dyld shared cache**. This cache provides a significant speed boost, as referencing resident memory is so much faster than querying the disk hundreds of times to load libraries.

The internals of dyld and the cache are complex and outside the scope of this book (see http://newosxbook.com/index.php for excellent writing on this), but you do need to at least be able to list what modules are packed into the shared cache to be able to link to and explore their symbols in memory.

You'll use your insights gained in this chapter by compiling a Swift executable that lists all the modules packed into the dyld shared cache. You'll achieve this via private C APIs that are referenced in the source code of dyld (https://opensource.apple.com/tarballs/dyld/) under dyld_priv.h. A header with the same dyld_priv.h name has been provided in the starter project and includes a watered-down selection of these APIs. You'll use the same module.modulemap to import this dyld_priv.h header and reference these APIs via Swift.

In Terminal, open the module.modulemap in the starter directory, and add header "dyld_priv.h" between header "Private.h" and export *. The module.modulemap file now looks like this:

```
module YayModule {
    header "Private.h"
    header "dyld_priv.h"
    export *
}
```

The source code has already been written in dyldlist.swift, available in the starter directory.

```
import YayModule

let cache_uuid =
    UnsafeMutablePointer<UInt8>.allocate(capacity: 16)
let manager = FileManager.default

if _dyld_get_shared_cache_uuid(cache_uuid) {
    let cachePath = String(
        cString: dyld_shared_cache_file_path())
```

```
print("Inspecting dyld cache at \"\(cachePath)\"")

dyld_shared_cache_iterate_text(cache_uuid) { info in
    if let module = info?.pointee {
        let uuid = UUID(uuid: module.dylibUuid).uuidString
        let path = String(cString: module.path)
        let exists = manager.fileExists(atPath: path)

        print("\(exists ? "*" : " ") \(uuid) - \(path)")
    }
}
}
```

The details of these APIs will be left as an exercise for you to explore on your own. What matters is the compilation.

In Terminal, while in the starter directory, compile dyldlist.swift. If you get errors, make sure that the version of the module.modulemap you updated is the one in the starter directory and not the one in tmp.

```
$ swiftc -I. -o /tmp/dyldlist dyldlist.swift
```

You're referencing APIs, but you didn't have to explicitly link to a library when compiling via clang. Why is that? Do you remember libSystem and how it's implicitly included in *every process*? libSystem will **reexport** these symbols, which belong to /usr/lib/system/libdyld.dylib. Since libSystem automatically imports libdyld.dylib, it tells the linker, "Don't worry, I've got this".

Consulting Xcode's libSystem TBD file, you can verify all the *_dyld* symbols it handles:

```
$ cat $(xcrun --show-sdk-platform-path)/Developer/SDKs/
MacOSX.sdk/usr/lib/libSystem.tbd | grep _dyld
```

Give the dyldlist executable a run. You'll see a significant number of libraries held in the dyld shared cache:

```
$ /tmp/dyldlist  | wc -l
  2500
```

The source code adds an asterisk to any file it can find in the cache and also on disk. grep for an asterisk at the beginning of the output:

```
$ /tmp/dyldlist  | grep -E "^\*" | wc -l
4
$ /tmp/dyldlist  | grep -E "^\*"
* AED7DD2C-0325-3172-83E7-3BE31F6D4069 - /usr/lib/dyld
* 222F8841-2BFD-3804-AA0C-F6D80A73FBDF - /usr/lib/system/
libsystem_kernel.dylib
* 7AF7B500-9A6E-3121-A66A-397C209B5C83 - /usr/lib/system/
libsystem_pthread.dylib
* 61D6CE46-BF8C-34EA-B81A-879743AD4063 - /usr/lib/system/
libsystem_platform.dylib
```

Key Points

- **Shared libraries** are code external to your code that are loaded at runtime or compile time.

- Unless you're planning to actually share the code with multiple clients, making a library is often not worth the overhead.

- The `nm` and `otool` commands let you inspect shared libraries to find function names.

- The `swift demangle` command converts mangled function names into the form you can use in your code to call them.

- The linker will resolve dependencies for dynamic frameworks automatically. You need to do the resolution yourself for static libraries.

- The linker has a `weak` attribute you can use when linking so that a program won't crash if a symbol can't be resolved.

- A text-based dynamic library, or TBD, file with the `.tbd` extension can stand in for a shared library when compiling code.

- A **module map** file serves as a bridge between Swift and Objective-C code.

Where to Go From Here?

Does your head hurt? In this chapter, you learned more than you ever wanted to know about dynamic frameworks. You explored the compiling and linking process while realizing it's not about the language, but more about the linker needing to resolve symbols. You've learned how to generate `\*.tbd` files to link to a library you don't physically have on your computer's disk. You've learned how to use `clang`'s modules to import private code to use in Swift. Finally, you've learned about the dyld shared cache and how to list its libraries in Swift.

Don't forget to refer back to Chapter 7, "Image", for strategies to dump things out of the shared cache. Now, you can inspect them and link to them as you explore.

Although mentioned earlier, you really should check out the `man` pages for `ld`. Some fascinating options can be performed with the linker that could save you hours of headaches and looking at half-baked answers on Stack Overflow (https://stackoverflow.com).

Chapter 16: Hooking & Executing Code With dlopen & dlsym

Using LLDB, you've seen how easy it is to create breakpoints and inspect things of interest. You've also seen how to create classes you wouldn't normally have access to. Unfortunately, you've been unable to wield this power at development time because you can't get a public API if the framework, or any of its classes or methods, are marked as private. However, all that is about to change.

It's time to learn about the complementary skills of developing with these frameworks. In this chapter, you're going to learn about methods and strategies to "hook" into Swift and C code as well as execute methods you wouldn't normally have access to while developing.

This is a critical skill to have when you're working with something such as a private framework and want to execute or augment existing code within your own application. To do this, you're going to call on the help of two awesome functions: `dlopen` and `dlsym`.

The Objective-C Runtime vs. Swift & C

Objective-C, thanks to its powerful runtime, is a truly dynamic language. Even when compiled and running, not even the program knows what will happen when the next `objc_msgSend` comes up.

There are different strategies for hooking into and executing Objective-C code; you'll explore these in later chapters, but this chapter focuses on how to hook into and use these frameworks under Swift.

Swift acts a lot like C or C++. If it doesn't need the dynamic dispatch of Objective-C, the compiler doesn't have to use it. This means when you're looking at the assembly for a Swift method that doesn't need dynamic dispatch, the assembly can simply call the address containing the method. This "direct" function calling is where `dlopen` and `dlsym` really shine. This is what you're going to learn about in this chapter.

Setting Up Your Project

For this chapter, you're going to use a starter project named **Watermark**, located in the **starter** folder.

This project is very simple. All it does is display a watermarked image in a `UIImageView`.

However, there's something special about this watermarked image. The actual image displayed is hidden away in an array of bytes compiled into the program. That is, the image is not bundled as a separate file inside the application. Rather, the image is actually located within the executable itself. Clearly the author didn't want to hand out the original image, anticipating people would reverse engineer the **Assets.car** file, which is a common place to hold images within an application. Instead, the data of the image is stored in the __TEXT section of the executable, which is encrypted by Apple when distributed through the App Store. If that __TEXT section sounded alien, you'll learn about it in Chapter 17: "Hello, Mach-O".

First, you'll explore hooking into a common C function. Once you've mastered the concepts, you'll execute a private Swift method that's unavailable to you at development time thanks to the Swift compiler. Using dlopen and dlsym, you'll be able to call and execute this private method inside a framework with zero modifications to the framework's code.

Now that you've got more theory than you've ever wanted in an introduction, it's finally time to get started.

Easy Mode: Hooking C Functions

When learning how to use the dlopen and dlsym functions, you'll be going after the getenv C function. This simple C function takes a char * (null terminated string) for input and returns the environment variable for the parameter you supply.

This function is actually called quite a bit when your executable starts up.

Open and launch the **Watermark** project in Xcode. Create a new symbolic breakpoint, putting getenv in the **Symbol** section. Next, add a custom action with the following:

```
po (char *)$arg1
```

Now, make sure the execution automatically continues after the breakpoint hits.

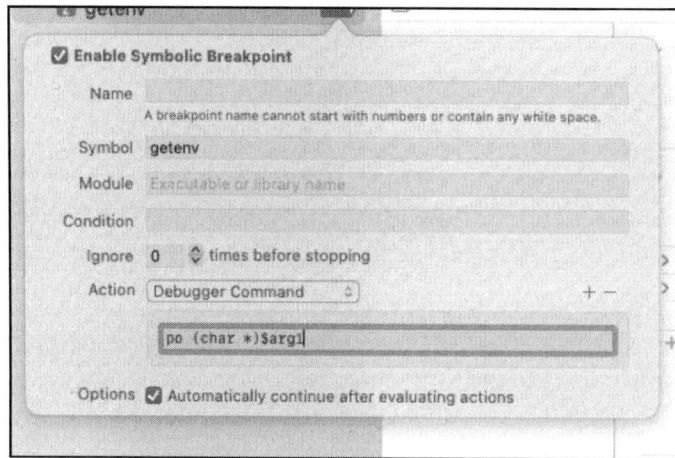

Finally, build and run the application on the iPhone Simulator, then watch the console. You'll get a slew of output indicating this method is called quite frequently.

It'll look similar to the following:

```
"DYLD_INSERT_LIBRARIES"
"NSZombiesEnabled"
"OBJC_DEBUG_POOL_ALLOCATION"
"MallocStackLogging"
"MallocStackLoggingNoCompact"
"OBJC_DEBUG_MISSING_POOLS"
"LIBDISPATCH_DEBUG_QUEUE_INVERSIONS"
"LIBDISPATCH_CONTINUATION_ALLOCATOR"
... etc ...
```

> **Note**: A far more elegant way to dump all environment variables available to your application is to use the DYLD_PRINT_ENV. To set this up, go to **Product ▸ Scheme ▸ Edit Scheme…**, and then add this in the Environment Variables section of the Run arguments. You can simply add the name, **DYLD_PRINT_ENV**, with no value, to dump out all environment variables at runtime.

However, an important point to note is all these calls to getenv are happening before your executable has even started. You can verify this by putting a breakpoint on getenv and looking at the stack trace. Notice main is nowhere in sight. This means you'll not be able to alter these function calls until your code starts executing.

Since C doesn't use dynamic dispatch, hooking a function requires you to intercept the function before it loads. On the plus side, C functions are relatively easy to grab. All you need is the name of the C function without any parameters along with the name of the dynamic framework that implements the function.

However, since C is all-powerful and used pretty much everywhere, there are different tactics of varying complexity you can explore to hook a C function. If you want to hook a C function inside your own executable, that's not a lot of work. However, if you want to hook a function called before your code (main executable or frameworks) is loaded in by dyld, the complexity definitely goes up a notch.

As soon as your executable executes main, it's already imported all the dynamic frameworks specified in the load commands, as you learned in previous chapters. The dynamic linker will recursively load frameworks in a depth-first manner. If you were to call an external framework, it can be lazily loaded or immediately loaded upon module load by dyld. Typically, most external functions are lazily loaded unless you specify special linker flags.

With lazily loaded functions, the first time the function is called, a flurry of activity occurs as dyld finds the module and location responsible for the function. This value is then put into a specific section in memory (__DATA.__la_symbol_ptr, but we'll talk about that later). Once the external function is resolved, all future calls to that function will not be resolved by dyld.

This means if you want to have the function hooked before your application starts up, you'll need to create a dynamic framework to put the hooking logic in so it'll be available before the main function starts. You'll explore this easy case of hooking a C function inside your own executable first.

Back to the Watermark project!

Open **AppDelegate.swift**, and replace application(_:didFinishLaunchingWithOptions:) with the following:

```swift
func application(
  _ application: UIApplication,
  didFinishLaunchingWithOptions launchOptions:
  [UIApplication.LaunchOptionsKey : Any]? = nil)
  -> Bool {
  if let cString = getenv("HOME") {
    let homeEnv = String(cString: cString)
    print("HOME env: \(homeEnv)")
  }
  return true
}
```

This creates a call to getenv to get the HOME environment variable.

Next, remove the symbolic getenv breakpoint you previously created and build and run the application.

The console output will look similar to the following:

```
HOME env: /Users/wtyree/Library/Developer/CoreSimulator/Devices/
53BD59A2-6863-444C-8B4A-6C2E8159D81F/data/Containers/Data/
Application/839B711F-0FB2-42B0-BC93-018868852A31
```

This is the HOME environment variable set for the Simulator you're running on.

Say you wanted to hook the getenv function to act completely normally, but return something different to the output above if and only if HOME is the parameter.

As mentioned earlier, you'll need to create a framework that's relied upon by the Watermark executable to grab that address of getenv and change it before it's resolved in the main executable.

In Xcode, navigate to **File ▸ New ▸ Target** and select **Framework** from the "Framework & Library" section. Choose **HookingC** as the product name, and set the language to **Objective-C**.

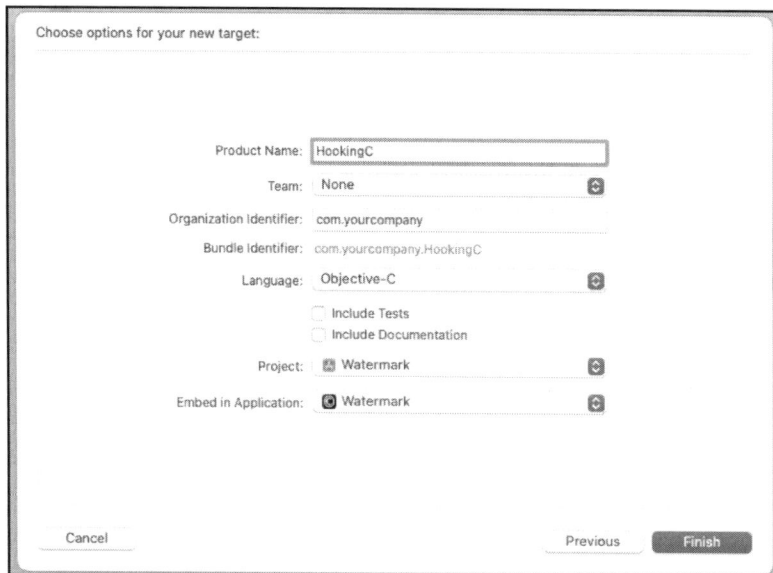

Once this new framework is created, create a new C file. In Xcode, select **File ▸ New ▸ File**, then select **C file**. Name this file **getenvhook**. Uncheck the checkbox for **Also create a header file**. Save the file with the rest of the project.

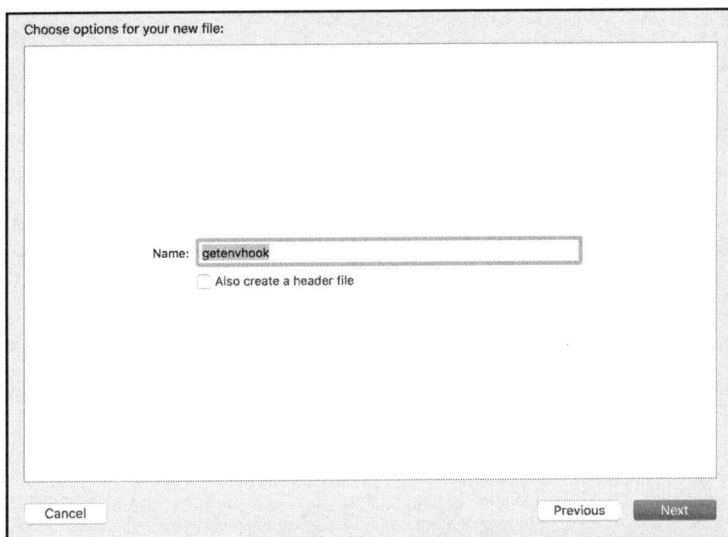

Make sure this file belongs to the **HookingC** framework that you've just created, and **not Watermark**.

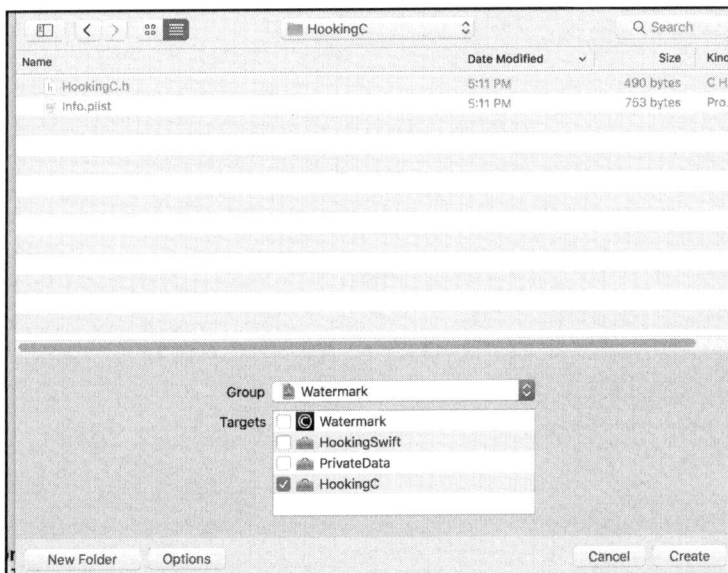

OK... you're finally about to write some code... I swear.

Open **getenvhook.c** and replace its contents with the following:

```
#include <dlfcn.h>
#include <assert.h>
#include <stdio.h>
#include <dispatch/dispatch.h>
#include <string.h>
```

- `dlfcn.h` is responsible for two very interesting functions: `dlopen` and `dlsym`.

- `assert.h` tests that the library containing the real `getenv` is correctly loaded.

- `stdio.h` will be used temporarily for a C `printf` call.

- `dispatch.h` will be used to to properly set up the logic for GCD's `dispatch_once` function.

- `string.h` will be used for the `strcmp` function, which compares two C strings.

Next, redeclare the `getenv` function with the hard-coded stub shown below:

```
char * getenv(const char *name) {
    return "YAY!";
}
```

Finally, build and run your application to see what happens. You'll get the following output:

```
HOME env: YAY!
```

Awesome! You replaced this method with your own function. However, this isn't quite what you want. You want to call the original `getenv` function and augment the return value if `"HOME"` is supplied as input.

What happens if you try to call the original `getenv` function inside your `getenv` function? Try it out now. Add some temporary code so the `getenv` looks like the following:

```
char * getenv(const char *name) {
    return getenv(name);
    return "YAY!";
}
```

You might see a warning like this one, but build and run anyway. In the name of research.

```
char * getenv(const char *name) {
    return getenv(nam  ⚠  All paths through this function will call    ⊗
    return "YAY!";          itself
}
```

Your program will... sort of... run and then eventually crash. This is because you've just created a stack overflow. All references to the previously linked getenv have disappeared now that you've created your own getenv function.

Undo that previous line of code. That idea won't work. You're going to need a different tactic to grab the original getenv function.

First things first though, you need to figure out which library holds the getenv function. Make sure that problematic line of code is removed, and build and run the application again. Pause execution and bring up the LLDB console.

Once the console pops up, enter the following:

```
(lldb) image lookup -s getenv
```

You'll get output similar to the following:

```
1 symbols match 'getenv' in /Users/wtyree/Library/Developer/
Xcode/DerivedData/Watermark-dlayapbfrqyqcyeehrxxaiewhkma/Build/
Products/Debug-iphonesimulator/Watermark.app/Frameworks/
HookingC.framework/HookingC:
        Address: HookingC[0x0000000000003f60]
(HookingC.__TEXT.__text + 0)
        Summary: HookingC`getenv at getenvhook.c:15
1 symbols match 'getenv' in /Applications/Xcode.app/Contents/
Developer/Platforms/iPhoneOS.platform/Library/Developer/
CoreSimulator/Profiles/Runtimes/iOS.simruntime/Contents/
Resources/RuntimeRoot/usr/lib/system/libsystem_c.dylib:
        Address: libsystem_c.dylib[0x0000000000056378]
(libsystem_c.dylib.__TEXT.__text + 347788)
        Summary: libsystem_c.dylib`getenv
1 symbols match 'getenv' in /Applications/Xcode.app/Contents/
Developer/Platforms/iPhoneOS.platform/Library/Developer/
CoreSimulator/Profiles/Runtimes/iOS.simruntime/Contents/
Resources/RuntimeRoot/System/Library/PrivateFrameworks/
AppleAccount.framework/AppleAccount:
```

You'll get a few hits. One of them will be the `getenv` function you created yourself. More importantly, you'll get the location of the `getenv` function you actually care about. It looks like this function is located in **libsystem_c.dylib**, and its full path is at `/usr/lib/system/libsystem_c.dylib`. Remember, the simulator prepends that big long path to these directories, but the dynamic linker is smart enough to search in the correct areas. Everything after `RuntimeRoot` is where this framework is actually stored on a real iOS device.

Now you know exactly where this function is loaded, it's time to call on the first of the amazing "dl" duo, `dlopen`. Its function signature looks like:

```
extern void * dlopen(const char * __path, int __mode);
```

`dlopen` expects a full path in the form of a `char *` and a second parameter, which is a mode expressed as an integer that determines how `dlopen` should load the module. If successful, `dlopen` returns an opaque handle (a `void *`), or `NULL` if it fails.

After `dlopen` (hopefully) returns a reference to the module, you'll use `dlsym` to get a reference to the `getenv` function. `dlsym` has this function signature:

```
extern void * dlsym(void * __handle, const char * __symbol);
```

`dlsym` expects to take the reference generated by `dlopen` as the first parameter and the name of the function as the second parameter. If everything goes well, `dlsym` will return the function address for the symbol specified in the second parameter or `NULL` if it failed.

Replace your `getenv` function with the following:

```c
char * getenv(const char *name) {
  void *handle = dlopen("/usr/lib/system/libsystem_c.dylib",
                        RTLD_NOW);
  assert(handle);
  void *real_getenv = dlsym(handle, "getenv");
  printf("Real getenv: %p\nFake getenv: %p\n",
          real_getenv,
          getenv);
  return "YAY!";
}
```

You used the `RTLD_NOW` mode of `dlopen` to say, "Hey, don't wait or do any cute lazy loading stuff. Open this module right now." After making sure the handle is not `NULL` through a C `assert`, you call `dlsym` to get a handle on the "real" `getenv`.

Build and run the application. You'll get output similar to the following:

```
Real getenv: 0x1018fe373
Fake getenv: 0x100d57e40
HOME env: YAY!
```

Your function pointers will be different than my output, but take note of the difference in address between the real and fake getenv.

You're starting to see how you'll go about this. However, you'll need to make a few touch-ups to the above code first. For example, you can cast function pointers to the exact type of function you expect to use. Right now, the real_getenv function pointer is void *, meaning it could be anything. You already know the function signature of getenv, so you can simply cast it to that.

Replace your getenv function one last time with the following:

```
char * getenv(const char *name) {
    static void *handle;         // 1
    static char * (*real_getenv)(const char *); // 2

    static dispatch_once_t onceToken;
    dispatch_once(&onceToken, ^{  // 3
        handle = dlopen("/usr/lib/system/libsystem_c.dylib",
                        RTLD_NOW);
        assert(handle);
        real_getenv = dlsym(handle, "getenv");
    });

    if (strcmp(name, "HOME") == 0) { // 4
        return "/WOOT";
    }

    return real_getenv(name); // 5
}
```

You might not be used to this amount of C code, so let's break it down:

1. This creates a static variable named handle. It's static so this variable will survive the scope of the function. That is, this variable will not be erased when the function exits, but you'll still only be able to access it inside the getenv function.

2. You're doing the same thing here as you declare the real_getenv variable as static, but you've made other changes to the real_getenv function pointer. You've cast this function pointer to match the signature of getenv. This allows you to call the real getenv function through the real_getenv variable. Cool, right?

3. You're using GCD's `dispatch_once` because you really only need to call the setup once. This nicely complements the `static` variables you declared a couple lines above. You don't want to be doing the lookup logic every time your augmented `getenv` runs!

4. You're using C's `strcmp` to see if you're querying the `"HOME"` environment variable. If it's true, you're simply returning `"/WOOT"` to show yourself that you can change around this value. Essentially, you're overriding what the `getenv` function returns.

5. If `"HOME"` is not supplied as an input parameter, then just fall back on the default `getenv`.

Open **AppDelegate.swift**, and replace
`application(_:didFinishLaunchingWithOptions:)` with the following:

```
func application(
  _ application: UIApplication,
  didFinishLaunchingWithOptions launchOptions:
  [UIApplication.LaunchOptionsKey : Any]? = nil)
  -> Bool {
  if let cString = getenv("HOME") {
    let homeEnv = String(cString: cString)
    print("HOME env: \(homeEnv)")
  }

  if let cString = getenv("PATH") {
    let homeEnv = String(cString: cString)
    print("PATH env: \(homeEnv)")
  }
  return true
}
```

Build and run the application. Provided everything went well, you'll get output similar to the following:

```
HOME env: /WOOT
PATH env: /Applications/Xcode.app/Contents/Developer/Platforms/
iPhoneOS.platform/Library/Developer/CoreSimulator/Profiles/
Runtimes/iOS.simruntime/Contents/Resources/RuntimeRoot/usr/bin:/
Applications/Xcode.app/Contents/Developer/Platforms/
iPhoneOS.platform/Library/Developer/CoreSimulator/Profiles/
Runtimes/iOS.simruntime/Contents/Resources/RuntimeRoot/bin:/
Applications/Xcode.app/Contents/Developer/Platforms/
iPhoneOS.platform/Library/Developer/CoreSimulator/Profiles/
Runtimes/iOS.simruntime/Contents/Resources/RuntimeRoot/usr/
sbin:/Applications/Xcode.app/Contents/Developer/Platforms/
iPhoneOS.platform/Library/Developer/CoreSimulator/Profiles/
Runtimes/iOS.simruntime/Contents/Resources/RuntimeRoot/sbin:/
```

```
Applications/Xcode.app/Contents/Developer/Platforms/
iPhoneOS.platform/Library/Developer/CoreSimulator/Profiles/
Runtimes/iOS.simruntime/Contents/Resources/RuntimeRoot/usr/
local/bin
```

As you can see, your hooked getenv augmented the HOME environment variable, but defaulted to the normal getenv for PATH.

Although annoying, it's worth driving this point home one last time. If you call a UIKit method, and UIKit calls getenv, your augmented getenv function will not get called because getenv's address had already been resolved when UIKit's code loads.

In order to change around UIKit's call to getenv, you would need knowledge of the indirect symbol table and to modify the getenv address stored in the __DATA.__la_symbol_ptr section of the UIKit module. This is something you'll learn about in a later chapter.

Hard Mode: Hooking Swift Methods

Going after Swift code that isn't dynamic is a lot like going after C functions. However, there are a couple of complications with this approach that make it a bit harder to hook into Swift methods.

First off, Swift often uses classes or structs in typical development. This is a unique challenge because dlsym will only give you a C function. You'll need to augment this function so the Swift method can reference self if you're grabbing an instance method, or reference the class if you're calling a class method. When accessing a method that belongs to a class, the assembly will often reference offsets of self or the class when performing the method. Since dlysm will grab you a C-type function, you'll need to utilize your knowledge of assembly, parameters and registers to turn that C function into a Swift method.

The second issue you need to worry about is that Swift mangles the names of its methods. The happy, pretty name you see in your code is actually a long name in the module's symbol table. You'll need to find this method's correct mangled name in order to reference the Swift method through dlysm.

As you know, this project produces and displays a watermarked image. Here's the challenge for you: using only code, display the original image in the UIImageView. You're not allowed to use LLDB to execute the command yourself, nor are you allowed to modify any contents in memory once the program is running.

Are you up for this challenge? Don't worry, I'll show you how it's done!

First, open **AppDelegate.swift** and remove the two `if` statements you added before in `application(_:didFinishLaunchingWithOptions:)`. Next, open **CopyrightImageGenerator.swift**.

Inside this class is a `private` computed property containing the `originalImage`. In addition, there's a public computed property containing the `watermarkedImage`. It's this method that calls the `originalImage` and superimposes the watermark. It's up to you to figure out a way to call this `originalImage` method, without changing the `HookingSwift` dynamic library at all.

Open **ViewController.swift** and add the following code to the end of `viewDidLoad()`:

```
if let handle = dlopen("", RTLD_NOW) {}
```

You're using Swift this time, but you'll use the same `dlopen` & `dlsym` trick you saw earlier. You now need to get the correct location of the `HookingSwift` framework. The nice thing about `dlopen` is you can supply relative paths instead of absolute paths.

Time to find where that framework is relative to the `Watermark` executable.

In Xcode, make sure the **Project Navigator** is visible, press **Command-1**. Next, open the **Products** directory and right-click the `Watermark.app`. Next, select **Show in Finder**.

> **Note**: Xcode has been hiding the **Products** folder in recent versions. If you don't see it in the Project navigator, use **Product ▸ Show Build Folder in Finder**.

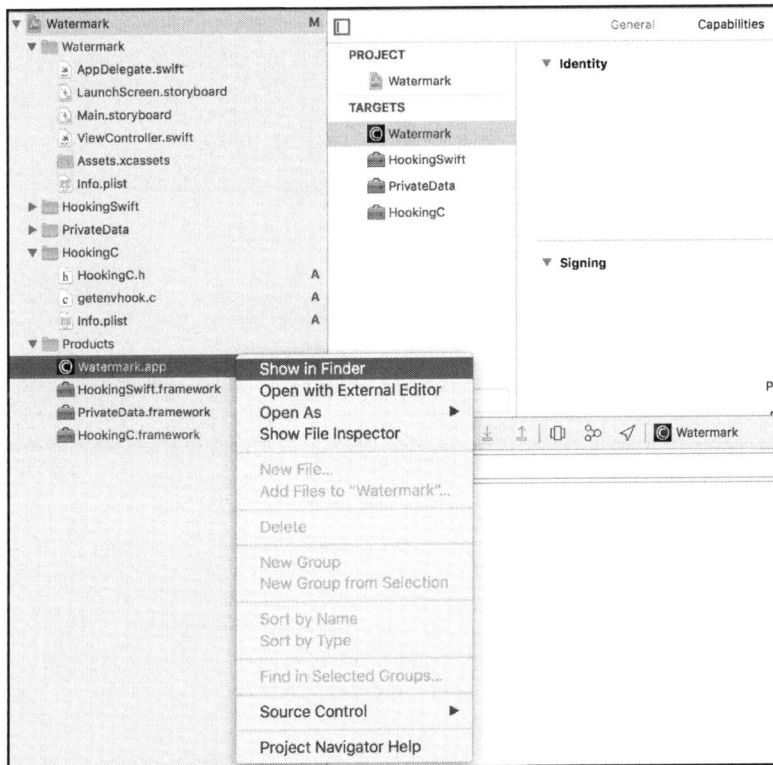

Once the Finder window pops up, right click the `Watermark` bundle and select **Show Package Contents**.

It's in this directory the actual `Watermark` executable is located, so you simply need to find the location of the `HookingSwift` framework's executable relative to this `Watermark` executable.

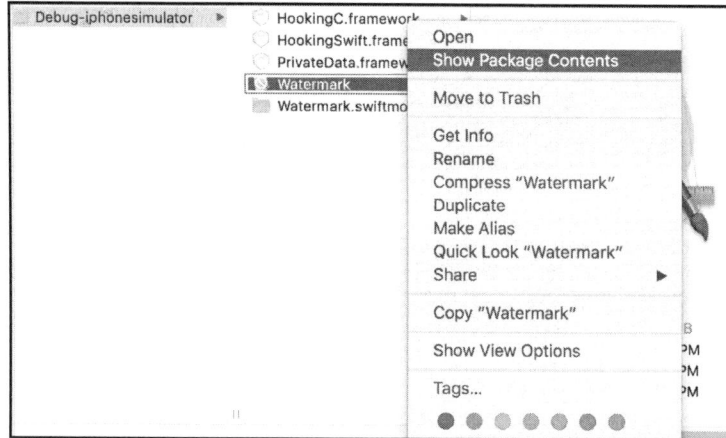

Next, select the Frameworks directory. Finally select the **HookingSwift.framework**. Within this directory, you'll come across the `HookingSwift` binary.

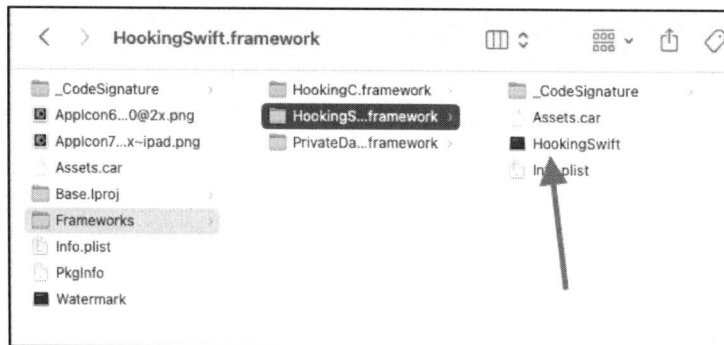

This means you've found the relative path you can supply to `dlopen`. Modify the `dlopen` function call you just added so it looks like the following:

```
if let handle =
  dlopen("./Frameworks/HookingSwift.framework/HookingSwift",
       RTLD_NOW) {
}
```

Now to the hard part. You want to grab the name of the method responsible for the `originalImage` property inside the `CopyrightImageGenerator` class. By now, you know you can use the `image lookup` LLDB function to search for method names compiled into an executable.

Since you know `originalImage` is implemented in Swift, use a "Swift style" type of search with the `image lookup` command. Make sure the app is running, then type the following into LLDB:

```
(lldb) image lookup -rn HookingSwift.*originalImage
```

You'll get output similar to the following:

```
1 match found in /Users/wtyree/Library/Developer/Xcode/
DerivedData/Watermark-dlayapbfrqyqcyeehrxxaiewhkma/Build/
Products/Debug-iphonesimulator/Watermark.app/Frameworks/
HookingSwift.framework/HookingSwift:
   Address: HookingSwift[0x0000000000003264]
(HookingSwift.__TEXT.__text + 328)
   Summary:
HookingSwift`HookingSwift.CopyrightImageGenerator.originalImage.
getter : Swift.Optional<__C.UIImage> at
CopyrightImageGenerator.swift:45
```

In the output, search for the line containing `Address:` `HookingSwift[0x0000000000003264]`. This is where this method is implemented inside the `HookingSwift` framework. This will likely be a different address for you.

For this particular example, the function is implemented at offset `0x0000000000003264` inside the `HookingSwift` framework. Copy this address and enter the following command into LLDB:

```
(lldb) image dump symtab -m HookingSwift
```

This dumps the symbol table of the `HookingSwift` framework. In addition to dumping the symbol table, you've told LLDB to show the mangled names of the Swift functions. There will be quite a few symbols that pop up in the display. You can use that address you copied into the LLDB filter bar so the amount of output becomes manageable.

You'll get an address that matches the address you copied:

```
        Address: HookingSwift[0x0000000000003264] (HookingSwift.__TEXT.__text +
        328)
        Summary:
          HookingSwift`HookingSwift.CopyrightImageGenerator.imageData.getter :
          Swift.Optional<Foundation.Data> at CopyrightImageGenerator.swift:40
            Address: HookingSwift[0x0000000000003264]
            (HookingSwift.__TEXT.__text + 328)
[    8]     54 D X Code             0x0000000000003264 0x0000000100e73264
    0x00000000000000d4 0x000f0000
    $s12HookingSwift23CopyrightImageGeneratorC08originalD033_71AD57F3ABD678B113CF3AD
    05D01FF41LLSo7UIImageCSgvg
(lldb)
```

All Output ⌄   ⬤ 003264   3 ⊗ 🗑 ▯ ◲

Here's the line that interests you.

```
[    8]     54 D X Code             0x0000000000003264
0x0000000100e73264 0x00000000000000d4 0x000f0000
$s12HookingSwift23CopyrightImageGeneratorC08originalD033_71AD57F
3ABD678B113CF3AD05D01FF41LLSo7UIImageCSgvg
```

Yep, that huge alphanumeric chunk at the end is the Swift mangled function name. It's this monstrosity you'll stick into `dlsym` to grab the address of the `originalImage` getter method.

Open **ViewController.swift** and add the following code inside the `if let` you just added:

```
let sym = dlsym(handle,
  "$S12HookingSwift23CopyrightImageGeneratorC08originalD033_71AD57
F3ABD678B113CF3AD05D01FF41LLSo7UIImageCSgvg")!
print("\(sym)")
```

> **Note:** Don't forget to clear any values from the LLDB filter window, or you won't see any output.

You've opted for an implicitly unwrapped optional since you want the application to crash if you got the wrong symbol name. Build and run the application. If everything worked out, you'll get a memory address at the tail end of the console output (yours will likely be different):

```
0x00000001005df264
```

This address is the location to `CopyrightImageGenerator`'s `originalImage` method that `dlsym` provided. You can verify this by creating a breakpoint on this address in LLDB:

```
(lldb) b 0x0000000103105770
```

LLDB creates a breakpoint on the following function:

```
Breakpoint 2: where =
HookingSwift`HookingSwift.CopyrightImageGenerator.originalImage.
getter : Swift.Optional<__C.UIImage> at
CopyrightImageGenerator.swift:45, address = 0x00000001005df264
```

Great! You can bring up the address of this function at runtime, but how do you go about calling it? Thankfully, you can use the `typealias` Swift keyword to cast function signatures.

Open **ViewController.swift**, and add the following directly under the `print` call you just added:

```
typealias privateMethodAlias = @convention(c) (Any) ->
UIImage? // 1
let originalImageFunction = unsafeBitCast(sym, to:
privateMethodAlias.self) // 2
let originalImage = originalImageFunction(imageGenerator) // 3
self.imageView.image = originalImage // 4
```

Here's what this does:

1. This declares the type of function that is syntactically equivalent to the Swift function for the `originalImage` property getter. There's something very important to notice here. `privateMethodAlias` is designed so it takes one parameter type of `Any`, but the actual Swift function expects no parameters. Why is this?

    It's due to the fact that by looking at the assembly to this method, the reference to `self` is expected in the `x0` register. This means you need to supply the instance of the class as the first parameter into the function to trick this C function into thinking it's a Swift method. If you don't do this, there's a chance the application will crash!

2. Now you've made this new alias, you're casting the `sym` address to this new type and calling it `originalImageFunction`.

3. You're executing the method and supplying the instance of the class as the first and only parameter to the function. This will cause the x0 register to be properly set to the instance of the class. It'll return the original image without the watermark.

4. You're assigning the UIImageView's image to the original image without the watermark.

With these new changes in, build and run the application. As expected, the original, watermark-free image will now be displayed in the application.

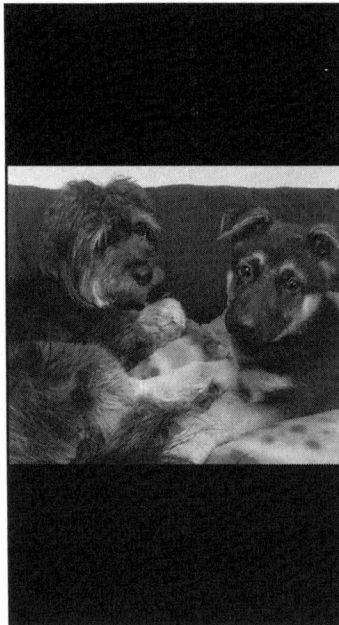

Congratulations — you've discovered two new amazing functions and how to use them properly. Grabbing the location of code at runtime is a powerful feature that lets you access hidden code the compiler normally blocks from you. In addition, it lets you hook into code so you can perform your own modifications at runtime.

Key Points

- The `getenv` function is called well before your `main` function is. `getenv` is therefore a good place to set breakpoints when you want to hook into the beginning of the app.

- Create frameworks when you want to hook into libraries, as once your `main` loads all symbol addresses will be bound and your application won't perform symbol lookup or loads again.

- Use `dlopen` to explicitly load a module, then `dlsym` to get a handle to a function in the module.

- Working with Swift methods requires the mangled name but you can find those using `image dump symtab`.

- In Swift, you can use a `typealias` to cast function signatures.

Where to Go From Here?

You're learning how to play around with dynamic frameworks. The previous chapter showed you how to dynamically load them in LLDB. This chapter showed you how to modify or execute Swift or C code you normally wouldn't be able to. In the next chapter, you're going to play with the Objective-C runtime to dynamically load a framework and use Objective-C's dynamic dispatch to execute classes you don't have the APIs for.

This is one of the most exciting features of reverse engineering — so get prepared, and caffeinated, for your foray into the next chapter!

Chapter 17: Hello, Mach-O

Mach-O is the file format used for a compiled program running on any of your Apple operating systems. Knowledge of the format is important for both debugging and reverse engineering, since the layout Mach-O defines is applicable to how the executable is stored on disk as well as how the executable is loaded into memory.

Knowing which area of memory an instruction is referencing is useful on the reverse engineering side, but there are a number of useful hidden treasures on the debugging front when exploring Mach-O. For example:

- You can introspect an external function call at runtime.

- You can quickly find the reference to a singleton's memory address without having to trip a breakpoint.

- You can inspect and modify variables in your own app or other frameworks

- You can perform security audits and make sure no internal, secret messages are being sent out into production in the form of strings or methods.

This chapter introduces the concepts of Mach-O, while the next chapter, **Mach-O Fun** will show the amusing things that are possible with this knowledge. Make sure you have that caffeine on board for this chapter since the theory comes first, followed by the fun in the following chapter.

Terminology

Before diving into the weeds with all the different C structs you're about to view, it would be best to take a high level view of the Mach-O layout.

This is the layout of every compiled executable; every main program, every framework, every kernel extension, *everything that's compiled on an Apple platform.*

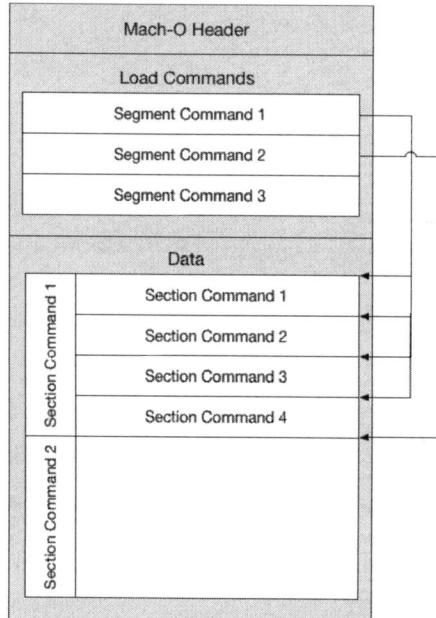

At the start of every compiled Apple program is the **Mach-O header** that gives information about the CPU this program can run on, the type of executable it is (A framework? A standalone program?) as well as how many **load commands** immediately follow it.

Load commands are instructions on how to load the program and are made up of C structs, which vary in size depending on the type of load command.

Some of the load commands provide instructions about how to load **segments**. Think of segments as areas of memory that have a specific type of memory protection. For example, executable code should only have read and execute permissions; it doesn't need write permissions.

Other parts of the program, such as global variables or singletons, need read and write permissions, but not executable permissions. This means that executable code and the address to global variables will live in separate segments.

Segments can have 0 or more subcomponents called **sections**. These are more finely-grained areas bound by the same memory protections given by their parent segment.

Take another look at the above diagram. Segment Command 1, points to an offset in the executable that contains four section commands, while Segment Command 2 points to an offset that contains 0 section commands. Finally, Segment Command 3 doesn't point to *any* offset in the executable.

It's these sections that can be of profound interest to developers and reverse engineerers since they each serve a unique purpose to the program. For example, there's a specific section to store hard-coded UTF-8 strings, there's a specific section to store references to statically defined variables and so on.

The ultimate goal of these two Mach-O chapters is to show you some interesting load commands in this chapter, and reveal some interesting sections in the next chapter.

In this chapter, you'll be seeing a lot of references to system headers. If you see something like mach-o/stab.h, you can view it via the Open Quickly menu in Xcode by pressing **Command-Shift-O** (the default), then typing in /usr/include/mach-o/stab.h.

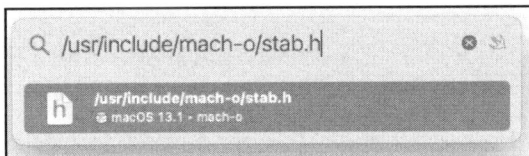

I'd recommend adding a /usr/include/ to the search query since Xcode isn't all that smart at times.

If you want to view this header without Xcode, then the physical location will be at:

```
${PATH_TO_XCODE}/Contents/Developer/Platforms/$
{SYSTEM_PLATFORM}.platform/Developer/SDKs/$
{SYSTEM_PLATFORM}.sdk/usr/include/mach-o/stab.h
```

Where ${SYSTEM_PLATFORM} can be MacOSX, iPhoneOS, iPhoneSimulator, WatchOS, etc.

Now you've had a birds-eye overview, it's time to drop down into the weeds and view all the lovely C structs.

The Mach-O Header

At the beginning of every compiled Apple executable is a special `struct` that indicates if it's a Mach-O executable. This `struct` can be found in **mach-o/loader.h**.

Remember the name of this header file, as it will be referenced quite a bit in this chapter.

There are two variants to this `struct`: one for 32-bit operating systems (mach_header), and one for 64-bit operating systems (mach_header_64). This chapter will talk about 64-bit systems by default, unless otherwise stated.

Let's take a look at the layout of the `struct mach_header_64`.

```
struct mach_header_64 {
    uint32_t   magic;       /* mach magic number identifier */
    cpu_type_t cputype;     /* cpu specifier */
    cpu_subtype_t cpusubtype; /* machine specifier */
    uint32_t   filetype;   /* type of file */
    uint32_t   ncmds;       /* number of load commands */
    uint32_t   sizeofcmds;  /* the size of all the load commands */
    uint32_t   flags;       /* flags */
    uint32_t   reserved;   /* reserved */
};
```

The first member, **magic**, is a hard-coded 32-bit unsigned integer that indicates this is the beginning of a Mach-O header.

What is the value of this `magic` number? A little further down in the `mach-o/loader.h` header, you'll find the following:

```
/* Constant for the magic field of the mach_header_64 (64-bit
architectures) */
#define MH_MAGIC_64 0xfeedfacf /*the 64-bit mach magic number*/
#define MH_CIGAM_64 0xcffaedfe /*NXSwapInt(MH_MAGIC_64)*/
```

This means that every 64-bit Mach-O executable will begin with either `0xfeedfacf`, or `0xcffaedfe` if the byte ordering is swapped. On 32-bit systems, the `magic` value is `0xfeedface`, or `0xcefaedfe` if byte-swapped.

It's this value that will let you quickly determine if the file is a Mach-O executable as well as if it's been compiled for a 32-bit or 64-bit architecture.

After the `magic` number are **cputype** and **cpusubtype**, which indicates on which type of cpu this Mach-O executable is allowed to run.

`filetype` is useful to know which type of executable you're dealing with.

Again, consulting **mach-o/loader.h** shows you the following definitions...

```
#define MH_OBJECT 0x1    /* relocatable object file */
#define MH_EXECUTE  0x2 /* demand paged executable file */
#define MH_FVMLIB 0x3    /* fixed VM shared library file */
#define MH_CORE    0x4   /* core file */
... // there's way more below but ommiting for brevity...
```

So for a main executable (i.e. not a framework), the `filetype` will be `MH_EXECUTE`.

After the `filetype`, the next most interesting aspects of the header are **ncmds** and **sizeofcmds**. The load commands indicate the attributes and how the executable is loaded into memory.

Time to take break from theory and see this in the wild by examining the raw bytes of an executable's Mach-O header in Terminal.

Mach-O Header in grep

Open up a **Terminal** window. I'll pick on the **grep** executable command, but you can pick on any Terminal command that suits your interests. Type the following:

```
xxd -l 32 /usr/bin/grep
```

This command says to dump just the first 32 raw bytes of the fullpath to the location of the grep executable. Why 32 bytes? In the `struct mach_header_64` declaration, there are 8 variables, each 4 bytes long.

You'll get something similar to the following:

```
00000000: cffa edfe 0700 0001 0300 0080 0200
0000  ..............
00000010: 1300 0000 4007 0000 8500 2000 0000
0000  ....@..... .....
```

Now is a good time to remind yourself that Apple Silicon, arm64, systems use **little-endian** format. That means that the bytes are reversed.

If your magic number doesn't match what's above and also doesn't match the other choice mentioned, you may have a **fat** executable. The next section goes into more detail about fat executable structure, but it will build on this section, so don't completely skip to the next section, read on!

Note: Even though modern Apple architecture is little-endian, Apple can store Mach-O information in big-endian or little-endian format, which is partly due to historical reasons dating back to the PPC architecture.

iOS doesn't do this, so every iOS file's Mach-O header will be little-endian on disk and in memory.

In contrast, the Mach-O header ordering on disk can be found in either format on macOS, but will be little-endian in memory.

Later in this section, you'll look at macOS's `CoreFoundation` module, whose Mach-O header is stored in big-endian format. Standards, eh?

Note: If you didn't get any proper output, make sure that your `grep` is actually at `/usr/bin/grep` with things like homebrew and oh-my-zsh improving your experience, sometimes basic utilities get moved or aliased.

Take a closer look at those first 4 bytes from the xxd output.

```
cffa edfe
```

This can be split out into individual bytes...

```
cf fa ed fe
```

Then reversed, byte-wise...

```
fe ed fa cf
```

And now, the `MH_MAGIC_64`, a.k.a. the `0xfeedfacf` magic variable, should be evident, indicating this was compiled for a 64-bit system.

Fortunately, the xxd Terminal command has a special option for little-endian architectures: the **-e** option. Add the −e option to your previous terminal command.

```
xxd −e −l 32 /usr/bin/grep
```

You'll get something similar to the following:

```
00000000: feedfacf 01000007 80000003 00000002  ................
00000010: 00000013 00000740 00200085 00000000  ....@..... ......
```

Let's put all of those values into the `struct mach_header_64`:

```
struct mach_header_64 {
    uint32_t       magic       = 0xfeedfacf
    cpu_type_t     cputype     = 0x01000007
    cpu_subtype_t  cpusubtype  = 0x80000003
    uint32_t       filetype    = 0x00000002
    uint32_t       ncmds       = 0x00000013
    uint32_t       sizeofcmds  = 0x00000740
    uint32_t       flags       = 0x00200085
    uint32_t       reserved    = 0x00000000
};
```

Here you can see the `magic` number of **0xfeedfacf** for the first value. That's a little easier than doing the reversing of the bytes in your head!

After the `0xfeedfacf`, there's a `0x01000007`. To figure this value out, you must consult **mach/machine.h**, which contains the following values:

```
#define CPU_ARCH_ABI64    0x01000000  /* 64 bit ABI */
...
#define CPU_TYPE_X86    ((cpu_type_t) 7)
```

The machine type is `CPU_ARCH_ABI64` ORed together with `CPU_TYPE_X86` producing `0x01000007` in hex (or 16777223 in decimal).

> **Note**: Depending on your computer model, and the version of `grep`, you might receive some different output but the format of the Mach-O will remain the same. Use this as a reference and decipher your own unique values.

Likewise, the `cpusubtype` value of `0x80000003` can be determined from the same header file with `CPU_SUBTYPE_LIB64` and `CPU_SUBTYPE_X86_64_ALL` ORed together. `filetype` has a value of `0x00000002`, or more precisely, `MH_EXECUTE`.

There are 19 load commands (`0x00000013` in hex, whose size is `0x00000740`). The **flags** value of `0x00200085` contains a series of options ORed together, but I'll let you jump into **mach-o/loader.h** to figure those out on your own.

If you need a specific homework task, find the significance of the `0x00200000` value in the `flags` variable.

And finally, there is the `reserved` value, which is just a bunch of boring zeros, and means nothing here!

The Fat Header

Some executables are actually a group of one or more executables "glued" together. For example, many apps compile both a 32-bit and 64-bit executable and place them into a "fat" executable. This "gluing together" of multiple executables is indicated by a **fat header**, which also has a unique magic value differentiating it from a Mach-O header.

Immediately following the fat header are structs, which indicate the CPU type and the offset into the file to where the fat header is stored.

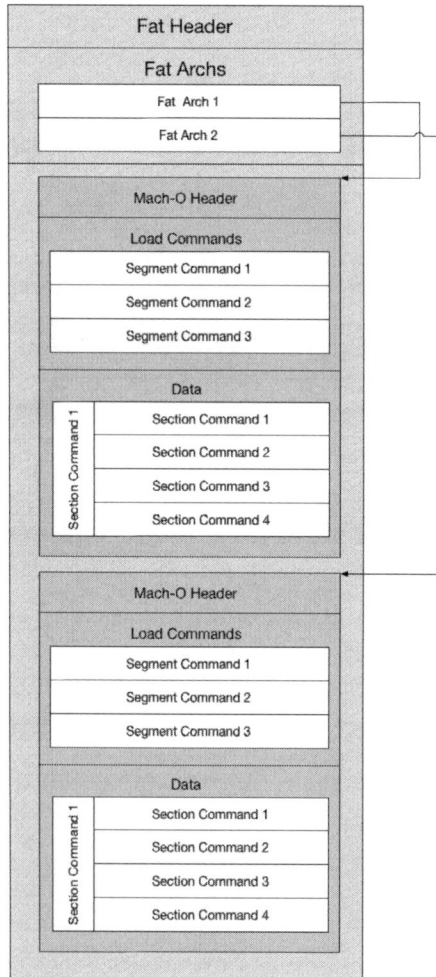

Looking at **mach-o/fat.h** gives the following struct:

```
#define FAT_MAGIC 0xcafebabe
#define FAT_CIGAM 0xbebafeca  /* NXSwapLong(FAT_MAGIC) */

struct fat_header {
  uint32_t  magic;     /* FAT_MAGIC or FAT_MAGIC_64 */
  uint32_t  nfat_arch; /* number of structs that follow */
};

...
#define FAT_MAGIC_64  0xcafebabf
#define FAT_CIGAM_64  0xbfbafeca  /* NXSwapLong(FAT_MAGIC_64) */
```

Although there's a 64-bit equivalent to the fat header, the 32-bit is still widely used in 64-bit systems. The 64-bit fat header is really only used if the offset of the executable slices is greater than 4MB. This is unlike the Mach-O 64-bit variant header you saw in the previous section, which is used only in 64-bit systems.

The fat header contains a number of **fat architecture** structs in the value nfat_arch that immediately follow the fat header.

Here's the 64-bit version of the fat architecture:

```
struct fat_arch_64 {
  cpu_type_t  cputype;    /* cpu specifier (int) */
  cpu_subtype_t cpusubtype; /* machine specifier (int) */
  uint64_t  offset;    /* file offset to this object file */
  uint64_t  size;    /* size of this object file */
  uint32_t  align;    /* alignment as a power of 2 */
  uint32_t  reserved; /* reserved */
};
```

And here's the 32-bit version of the fat architecture:

```
struct fat_arch {
  cpu_type_t  cputype;  /* cpu specifier (int) */
  cpu_subtype_t cpusubtype; /* machine specifier (int) */
  uint32_t  offset;    /* file offset to this object file */
  uint32_t  size;    /* size of this object file */
  uint32_t  align;    /* alignment as a power of 2 */
};
```

The magic value in the fat header will indicate which of these 32-bit or 64-bit structs to use.

Want to see a real life example of an executable with a fat header? Check out macOS's **WebKit** framework. In Terminal, type this:

```
file /System/Library/Frameworks/WebKit.framework/Frameworks/
libWebKitSwift.dylib
```

You'll see something similar to the following:

```
/System/Library/Frameworks/WebKit.framework/Frameworks/
libWebKitSwift.dylib: Mach-O universal binary with 2
architectures: [x86_64:Mach-O 64-bit dynamically linked shared
library x86_64] [arm64e:Mach-O 64-bit dynamically linked shared
library arm64e]
/System/Library/Frameworks/WebKit.framework/Frameworks/
libWebKitSwift.dylib (for architecture x86_64):  Mach-O 64-bit
dynamically linked shared library x86_64
/System/Library/Frameworks/WebKit.framework/Frameworks/
libWebKitSwift.dylib (for architecture arm64e):  Mach-O 64-bit
dynamically linked shared library arm64e
```

This says the WebKit consists of two architectures sliced and glued together: **x86_64**, **arm64e**. On your own time, you can see which architecture is loaded by using LLDB on a program that loads the WebKit module.

For example, the following would work when debugging a macOS app that linked to dyld. The example snippets will be from the fat binary of grep on my computer. Open a Terminal window and launch lldb for the executable:

```
lldb /usr/bin/grep
```

This will open an LLDB session for the grep application, which is a little tool shipped with macOS finding and replacing text.

Then inside the LLDB session, type the following:

```
(lldb) image list -h dyld
[  0] 0x000000019607e000
```

This will dump the load address of the dyld module. After you've obtained the load address, dump the memory containing the Mach-O header.

```
(lldb) x/8wx 0x000000019607e000
0x19607e000: 0xfeedfacf 0x0100000c 0x80000002 0x00000007
0x19607e010: 0x0000000f 0x00000838 0x80000085 0x00000000
```

On my computer, `cpusubtype` contains the value `0x80000002`, which equates to the following in `mach/machine.h`:

```
#define CPU_SUBTYPE_LIB64           0x80000000       /* 64 bit
libraries */
#define CPU_SUBTYPE_PTRAUTH_ABI 0x80000000       /* pointer
authentication with versioned ABI */
....
#define CPU_SUBTYPE_ARM64E                     ((cpu_subtype_t) 2)
```

So I can tell that the Arm64e slice of `dyld` was loaded into my process as the two values are merged together.

Jumping over to the on-disk representation of `dyld`, dump the raw bytes. Exit out of LLDB or open a new Terminal tab and type the following:

```
xxd -l 68 -e /usr/lib/dyld
```

This will produce output similar to the following:

```
00000000: bebafeca 03000000 07000000 03000000   ................
00000010: 00400000 f0570d00 0e000000 07000001   ..@...W.........
00000020: 03000000 00c00d00 d0e80f00 0e000000   ................
00000030: 0c000001 02000080 00c01d00 50620f00   ............bP
00000040: 0e000000                              ....
```

`0xbebafeca` or `FAT_CIGAM` is a 32-bit fat header in byte swapped (big-endian) format. This means that the −e is not necessary. Why is 68 bytes used for a length? Let's do the math...

• There's a `struct fat_header` right at the beginning containing two, 4-byte members called `magic` and `nfat_arch`. The `nfat_arch` has a value of `0x03000000`, but since you know it's byte-swapped, the actual value is `0x00000003`. This brings the total count to 8 bytes so far from this header.

• Immediately following the `fat_header` are three `struct fat_archs` (because `nfat_arch` is 3). The `fat_arch` is the 32-bit equivalent which contains 5, 4-byte members. That means there's an additional 60 bytes (20-bytes × 3) of interest, which brings the total byte count to 68.

Augment the above Terminal command by replacing the −e argument with the byte size argument (−g), saying to display output in 4-byte groupings.

```
xxd -l 68 -g 4 /usr/lib/dyld
```

Now the raw fat header data should be more viewable.

```
00000000: cafebabe 00000003 00000007 00000003  ................
00000010: 00004000 000d57f0 0000000e 01000007  ..@...W.........
00000020: 00000003 000dc000 000fe8d0 0000000e  ................
00000030: 0100000c 80000002 001dc000 000f6250  ..............bP
00000040: 0000000e                              ....
```

> **Note**: If the fat header was the 64-bit variant, the –g 4 option wouldn't have worked since there are a couple of 8-byte variables mixed with 4-byte ones in struct fat_arch_64.

The first two values — 0xcafebabe and 0x00000003 — are the struct fat_header, while the remaining bytes will belong to one of the three struct fat_archs. Examining the first struct fat_arch, we can see it's for i386 due to the cputype 0x00000007 and cpusubtype 0x00000003 that you saw previously. The offset to the start of the i386 slice is 0x00004000 (16384) and whose size is 0x000d57f0.

To prove that the i386 slice is at offset 16384 from the start of the file, dump the i386 header using xxd's **-s** option.

```
xxd -l 32 -e -s 16384 /usr/lib/dyld
```

As you can guess, the –s option specifies an offset to start at. You'll see the i386 slice's Mach-O header with feedface that matches the magic entry in loader.h.

```
00004000: feedface 00000007 00000003 00000007  ................
00004010: 00000012 000006d4 00000085 00000001  ................
```

Looking at the header for /usr/lib/dyld can you decipher what the other two slices are? In a terminal window you can check your guesses by typing **file /usr/lib/dyld**.

Now that the headers are discussed, time to jump into the load commands.

The Load Commands

Immediately following the Mach-O header are the load commands providing instructions on how an executable should be loaded into memory, as well as other miscellaneous details. This is where it gets interesting. Each load command consists of a series of structs, each varying in struct size and arguments.

Fortunately, for each Load Command `struct`, the first two variables are always consistent, the **cmd** and the **cmdsize**.

cmd will indicate the type of load command and the `cmdsize` will give you the size of the `struct`. This lets you iterate over the load commands and then jump by the appropriate `cmdsize`.

The Mach-O authors anticipated this situation and provided a generic load command `struct` named **struct load_command**.

```
struct load_command {
    uint32_t cmd;     /* type of load command */
    uint32_t cmdsize; /* total size of command in bytes */
};
```

This lets you start with each load command as this generic `struct load_command`. Once you know the `cmd` value, you can cast the memory address into the appropriate `struct`.

So what are the values that `cmd` can have? Again, we put our faith in **mach-o/loader.h**.

```
#define LC_SEGMENT_64 0x19  /*64-bit segment of this file to be
mapped*/
#define LC_ROUTINES_64  0x1a  /* 64-bit image routines */
#define LC_UUID    0x1b  /* the uuid */
```

If you see a constant that begins with LC, then you know that's a load command. There are 64-bit and 32-bit equivalents to load commands, so make sure you use the appropriate one. 64-bit load commands will end in a "_64" in the name. That being said, 64-bit systems can still use 32-bit load commands. For example, the LC_UUID load command doesn't contain the _64 in the name but is included in all executables.

LC_UUID is one of the simpler load commands, so it's a great example to start out with. The LC_UUID provides the **Universal Unique Identifier** to identify a specific version of an executable. This load command doesn't provide any specific segment information, as it's all contained in the LC_UUID struct.

In fact, the load command struct for the LC_UUID load command is the **struct uuid_command** found in **mach-o/loader.h**:

```
/*
 * The uuid load command contains a single 128-bit unique random
number that
 * identifies an object produced by the static link editor.
```

```
  */
struct uuid_command {
    uint32_t  cmd;      /* LC_UUID */
    uint32_t  cmdsize;  /* sizeof(struct uuid_command) */
    uint8_t uuid[16]; /* the 128-bit uuid */
};
```

Going back to grep, you can view grep's UUID using the **otool** command with the -l (load command) option.

```
otool -l /usr/bin/grep | grep LC_UUID -A2
```

This will dump the two lines following any hits that contain the phrase LC_UUID.

```
      cmd LC_UUID
  cmdsize 24
     uuid F6870A1F-5337-3CF8-B7F5-2573A085C90E
```

otool has translated the cmd from 0x1b to LC_UUID, displays the cmdsize to sizeof(struct uuid_command) (aka 24 bytes) and has displayed the UUID value in a pretty format. If you're using the same macOS version as me, then you'll have the same UUID!

Segments

The LC_UUID is a simple load command since it's self-contained and doesn't provide offsets into the executable's segments/sections. It's now time to turn your attention to **segments**.

A segment is a grouping of memory that has specific permissions. A segment can have 0 or more subcomponents named **sections**.

Before going into the load command structs that provide instructions for segments, let's talk about some segments that are typically found in a program.

- The **__PAGEZERO segment** is a section in memory that is essentially a "no man's land." This segment contains 0 sections. This memory region doesn't have read, write, or execute permissions and occupies the lower 32-bits in a 64-bit process. This is useful in case the developer screws up a pointer, or dereferences NULL; if this happens, the program will crash since there's no read permissions on that memory region (bits 0 to 2^32). Only the main executable (i.e. not a framework) will contain a __PAGEZERO load command.

- The **__TEXT segment** stores readable and executable memory. This is where the application's code lives. If you want to store something that shouldn't be changed around in memory (like executable code or hard-coded strings), then this is the segment to put content in. Typically the __TEXT segment will have multiple sections for storing various immutable data.

- The **__DATA segment** stores readable and writable memory. This is where the majority of Objective-C data goes (since the language is dynamic and can change at runtime) as well as mutable variables in memory. Typically the __DATA segment will have multiple sections for storing various mutable data.

- The **__LINKEDIT Segment** is a grab-bag of content that only has readable permissions. This segment stores the symbol table, the entitlements file (if not on the Simulator), the codesigning information and other essential information that enables a program to function. Even though this segment has lots of important data packed inside, it has no sections.

Let's hammer this information in by looking at a real-life example. Use LLDB and attach to any process. Yes, any process! I'll choose the Simulator's **SpringBoard** for the example.

After starting up Simulator, type the following:

```
lldb -n SpringBoard
```

Once attached, type the following:

```
(lldb) image dump sections SpringBoard
```

This will dump the sections (and segments) for the SpringBoard module.

```
Sections for '/Users/wtyree/vmShare/Xcode.app/Contents/
Developer/Platforms/iPhoneOS.platform/Library/Developer/
CoreSimulator/Profiles/Runtimes/iOS.simruntime/Contents/
Resources/RuntimeRoot/System/Library/CoreServices/
SpringBoard.app/SpringBoard' (arm64):
  SectID     Type              Load Address
Perm File Off.  File Size  Flags      Section Name
  ---------- ----------------- 
  ---------------------------------------------------  ---- ----------
  ---------- ---------- ---------------------------------------
  0x00000100 container
[0x0000000000000000-0x0000000100000000)* ---  0x00000000
0x00000000 0x00000000 SpringBoard.__PAGEZERO
  0x00000200 container
[0x0000000102bc0000-0x0000000102bd0000)  r-x  0x00000000
0x00010000 0x00000000 SpringBoard.__TEXT
```

```
  0x00000001 code
[0x0000000102bc15cc-0x0000000102bc15d0)  r-x  0x000015cc
0x00000004 0x80000400 SpringBoard.__TEXT.__text
  ... etc ...
```

Again, this is the in memory breakdown of the different Segments and Sections. If you wanted to see the on disk Mach-O layout instructions, you can use the following command:

```
(lldb) image dump objfile SpringBoard
```

This will give you a fair bit of information since it spits out the Mach-O load commands as well as all the symbols found in the module. If you scroll to the top, you'll find all the load commands.

It's important to note the difference between the on-disk location of the segment and sections, versus the actual memory location of the segment and sections, since they will have different values once loaded into memory.

> **Note**: And, as usual, I've written a LLDB command that displays the output in a much nicer format and has more advanced options for getting information out of specific sections in an executable. It's called **section** You can find it in the Appendix C: "Helpful Code Snippets" materials for this book.

Programmatically Finding Segments and Sections

For the demo part of this chapter, you'll build a macOS executable that iterates through the loaded modules and prints all the segments and sections found in each module.

Open Xcode, create a new project, select **macOS** then **Command Line Tool**, and name this program **MachOSegments**. Make sure the **Swift** language is selected.

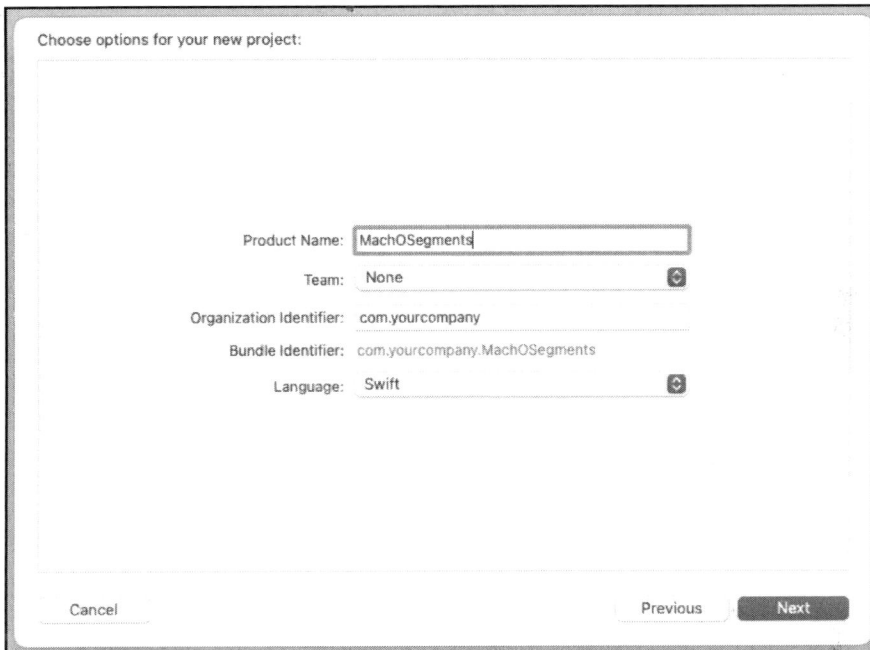

Open **main.swift** and replace its contents with the following:

```
import Foundation
import MachO // 1

for i in 0..<_dyld_image_count() { // 2
  let imagePath =
    String(validatingUTF8: _dyld_get_image_name(i))! // 3
  let imageName = (imagePath as NSString).lastPathComponent
  let header = _dyld_get_image_header(i)! // 4
  print("\(i) \(imageName) \(header)")
}

CFRunLoopRun() // 5
```

Breaking this down:

1. Although Foundation will indirectly import the MachO module, you are explicitly importing the MachO module just to be safe and for code clarity. You'll be using several of the structs found in **mach-o/loader.h** in a second.

2. The **_dyld_image_count** function will return the total count of all the loaded modules in the process. You'll use this to iterate over all the modules in a for loop.

3. The **_dyld_get_image_name** function will return the full path of the image.

4. The **_dyld_get_image_header** will return the load address of the Mach-O header (mach_header or mach_header_64) for that current module.

5. The **CFRunLoopRun** will prevent the app from exiting. This is ideal, because I'll have you inspect the process with LLDB after the output is done.

Build and run the program. You'll see a list of modules and their load addresses spit out to the console. These load addresses are the location to where that particular Mach-O header resides in memory for that module. This is almost the exact same as doing a image list -b -h in LLDB! If you're curious and want one of these values to take a peek the Mach-O header, copy one of the values and use LLDB to dump the memory.

For example, in my output I see the following:

```
8 CoreFoundation 0x00007fff33cf6000
```

You can view the raw bytes of CoreFoundations Mach-O Header by pausing execution and typing the following in LLDB:

```
(lldb) x/8wx 0x00007fff33cf6000
```

And then you'll see something similar to the following:

```
0x7fff33cf6000: 0xfeedfacf 0x01000007 0x00000008 0x00000006
0x7fff33cf6010: 0x00000013 0x00001100 0xc2100085 0x00000000
```

Now that you have the basic output in the MachOSegments program, add the following code to the end of the for loop:

```
var curLoadCommandIterator = Int(bitPattern: header) +
  MemoryLayout<mach_header_64>.size // 1
for _ in 0..<header.pointee.ncmds {
  let loadCommand =
```

```
    UnsafePointer<load_command>(
      bitPattern: curLoadCommandIterator)!.pointee // 2

  if loadCommand.cmd == LC_SEGMENT_64 {
    let segmentCommand =
      UnsafePointer<segment_command_64>(
        bitPattern: curLoadCommandIterator)!.pointee // 3

    print("\t\(segmentCommand.segname)")
  }

  curLoadCommandIterator =
    curLoadCommandIterator + Int(loadCommand.cmdsize) // 4
}
```

This is where the ugliness of Swift and C interoperability really starts to rear its ugly head. Again with the numbers breakdown:

1. Load commands start immediately after the Mach-O header, so the header address is added to the size of the load address of the mach_header_64 to determine where the load commands start. A good program would check if it's running a 32-bit mode by determining the magic value, but it's fun to walk on the wild side occasionally...

2. Using Swift's UnsafePointer to cast the load command to the "generic" load_command struct that you saw earlier. If this struct contains the correct cmd value, you'll cast this memory address to the appropriate segment_command_64 struct.

3. Here you know that the load_command struct should actually be a segment_command_64 struct, so we're using Swift's UnsafePointer object again.

4. At the end of each loop, we need to increment the curLoadCommandIterator variable by the size of the current loadCommand, which is determined by its cmdsize variable.

> **Note**: How did I know to cast the segment_command_64 struct when I saw the value LC_SEGMENT_64? In the mach-o/loader.h header, search for all references to LC_SEGMENT_64. There's the declaration that defines LC_SEGMENT_64 and then there's the segment_command_64 which states its cmd is LC_SEGMENT_64.
>
> Finding all references to the load command will give you the appropriate C struct.

Build and run.

Upon execution, you'll get some rather ugly output like the one truncated one below.

```
0 MachOPOC 0x0000000100000000
   (95, 95, 80, 65, 71, 69, 90, 69, 82, 79, 0, 0, 0, 0, 0, 0)
   (95, 95, 84, 69, 88, 84, 0, 0, 0, 0, 0, 0, 0, 0, 0, 0)
   (95, 95, 68, 65, 84, 65, 0, 0, 0, 0, 0, 0, 0, 0, 0, 0)
   (95, 95, 76, 73, 78, 75, 69, 68, 73, 84, 0, 0, 0, 0, 0, 0)
```

This is because Swift is really terrible when working with C.
segmentCommand.segname is declared as a Swift tuple of Int8s. This means you get
to build a helper function to convert these values to an actual readable Swift String.

Jump to the top part **main.swift** and declare the following function.

```
func convertIntTupleToString(name : Any) -> String {
  var returnString = ""
  let mirror = Mirror(reflecting: name)
  for child in mirror.children {
    guard let val = child.value as? Int8,
      val != 0 else {
        break
    }
    returnString.append(Character(UnicodeScalar(UInt8(val))))
  }

  return returnString
}
```

Using the **Mirror** object, you can take a tuple of any size and iterate over it. It's much
cleaner than hard coding to a parameter of type Tuple with 16 Int8's.

Jump back down to the main body, and replace print("\t\
(segmentCommand.segname)") with the following:

```
let segName = convertIntTupleToString(
  name: segmentCommand.segname)
print("\t\(segName)")
```

Build and run.

```
0 libBacktraceRecording.dylib 0x0000000100118000
   __TEXT
   __DATA_CONST
   __DATA
   __LINKEDIT
1 libMainThreadChecker.dylib 0x0000000100214000
   __TEXT
```

```
    __DATA_CONST
    __DATA
    __LINKEDIT
  2 MachOSegments 0x0000000100000000
    __PAGEZERO
    __TEXT
    __DATA_CONST
    __DATA
    __LINKEDIT
...
```

Much better, right? Now each module will print out its containing Segments.

You're almost there! The final hurdle with print out the remaining Sections for each Segment.

Right below the new print command you just created, add the following code:

```
for j in 0..<segmentCommand.nsects { // 1
  let sectionOffset = curLoadCommandIterator +
    MemoryLayout<segment_command_64>.size // 2
  let offset = MemoryLayout<section_64>.size * Int(j) // 3
  let sectionCommand =
    UnsafePointer<section_64>(
      bitPattern: sectionOffset + offset)!.pointee

  let sectionName =
    convertIntTupleToString(name: sectionCommand.sectname) // 4
  print("\t\t\(sectionName)")
}
```

The final round of numeric explanations:

1. In each `struct segment_command_64`, there's a member that specifies the number of `section_64` commands immediately following it. You'll use another `for` loop to iterate over all the sections found in each segment.

2. To start, you're grabbing the base address of the first `struct section_64` in memory.

3. For each iteration in the `for` loop, you'll start with the offset address then add the size of the `struct section_64` multiplied by the iterator variable j. If you add the `sectionOffset + offset`, you'll get the correct `section_64` address to reference.

4. A `struct section_64` also has a **sectname** variable that's a tuple of Int8's. You'll throw the same function you created earlier to get a pretty Swift String out of it.

That's it for code. Build and run. Included is a tiny snippet of the output you'll get.

```
2 MachOSegments 0x0000000100000000
  __PAGEZERO
  __TEXT
    __text
    __stubs
    __swift5_typeref
    __cstring
    __objc_methname
    __swift5_entry
    __const
    __swift5_builtin
    __swift5_reflstr
    __swift5_fieldmd
    __swift5_types
    __unwind_info
    __eh_frame
  __DATA_CONST
    __got
    __const
    __objc_imageinfo
  __DATA
    __objc_selrefs
    __data
  __LINKEDIT
```

As you can see, only the main executable has the __PAGEZERO segment, which has 0 Sections. There's a slew of sections that contain swift5 in them. There's a bunch of Objective-C related sections in the __DATA segment since Swift can't survive without Objective-C on Apple platforms.

In the next chapter, you'll look at some of these sections more closely and do some much more amusing things with the knowledge you got from this chapter.

Key Points

- All Apple executables and libraries conform to the Mach-O format.

- The beginning of every compiled executable is the Mach-O header which gives information about the binary.

- Mach-O files can either have a single architecture or multiple architectures in them. Files with multiple architectures are called **fat**.

- Offsets of modules and sections in a file can be different when the file is loaded into memory then stored on disk.

Where to Go From Here?

If I haven't indirectly hinted it enough, go check out **mach-o/loader.h**. I've read that header many times myself, and each time I read it I still learn something new. There's a lot there, so don't get frustrated if this chapter knocked you back into your chair.

Play with all the variables with the structs you created. Check out the other load commands and match them with the appropriate structs. Add these commands to the demo project you created and see what information you can pull out of them.

Chapter 18: Mach-O Fun

Hopefully you're not too burnt out from dumping raw bytes and comparing them to `structs` in the previous chapter, because here comes the real fun!

To hammer in the different Mach-O section types, you'll build a series of examples across this chapter. You'll start with a "scanner" that looks for any insecure `http:` hardcoded strings loaded into the process. After that, you'll learn how to cheat those silly, gambling or freemium games where you never win the loot.

Commence funtime *meow*.

Mach-O Refresher

Just so you know what's expected of you, you'll start with a brief refresher from the previous chapter.

Segments are groupings on disk and in memory that have the same memory protections. Segments can have zero or more sections found inside a grouping.

Sections are sub-components found in a segment. They serve a specific purpose to the program. For example, there's a specific section for compiled code and a different section for hard-coded strings.

Sections and segments are dictated by the **load commands**, which are at the beginning of the executable, immediately following the **Mach-O Header**

You saw a couple of the important segments in the previous chapter, notably the **__TEXT**, **__DATA**, and **__LINKEDIT** segments.

The Mach-O Sections

Included in this chapter is an iOS project called **MachOFun**. Open it up and take a look around.

It's a simple `UITabBarController` application which breaks up the different examples you'll implement in this chapter.

One tab showcases a `UITableViewController` with some placeholder data. You'll first build a data source that finds all hardcoded insecure HTTP URLs in memory and then you'll display them in the `UITableView` as a "public shaming".

The other tab shows a rather ugly implementation of a slot machine for gambling purposes, for which you'll use your Mach-O knowledge to cheat the system and always win.

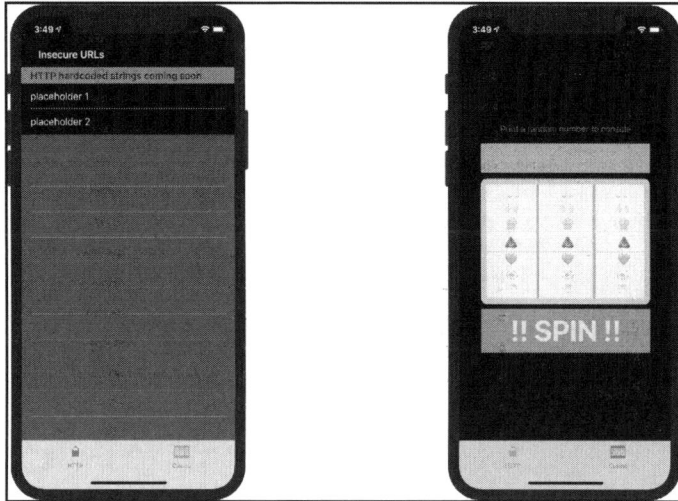

Build and run. At any point, suspend the program via LLDB and run the following command.

```
(lldb) image dump sections MachOFun
```

As you learned in the previous chapter, this will dump all the segments and corresponding sections found in the MachOFun module.

Search for the **MachOFun.__TEXT.__text**, section which stores executable code in the MachOFun application.

> **Note**: I am not the biggest fan of the image dump sections [modulename] LLDB command, since it produces an overload of output and is hard on the eyes. Also, if you forget to provide a module, LLDB will default to every module loaded into the process, which is a huge amount of output. But that command is the default and requires no extra setup. If you have trouble visually parsing the sections, use the LLDB console filter on the lower right of Xcode to make your life easier. Just remember to turn it off when you're done.

In the console output, you'll see something similar to the following, though your memory addresses may be different.

```
   0x00000001 code
 [0x00000001006e0240-0x00000001006e8b34)  r-x  0x00004240
 0x000088f4 0x80000400 MachOFun.__TEXT.__text
```

Breaking down this output:

- The **0x00000001** is LLDB's way to identify the section.

- LLDB has identified the content as **code**.

- The addresses in brackets is where this section is located in memory.

- The **0x00004240** is the offset on disk, while the **0x000088f4** value is the size of the section on disk.

- Finally, the flags have the value **0x80000400** which are S_ATTR_SOME_INSTRUCTIONS and S_ATTR_PURE_INSTRUCTIONS OR'd together. Once again, I'll leave that to you to research in **mach-o/loader.h**.

> **Note**: The size of a section or segment on disk could be different when compared to the size when loaded into memory. This will be determined by the Mach-O load command. For example, the **__PAGEZERO** segment takes up 0 bytes on disk, but when loaded into memory, it takes up the first 2^32 bits in a 64-bit process. You can verify this on any executable (I use the ls as an example) by inspecting the Load Commands: **otool -l $(which ls) | grep "Load command 0" -A11**, The **filesize** variable is 0, while the **vmsize** variable is 0x0000000100000000, or 2^32.

Now that you know how to parse the LLDB output, it's time to turn your attention back to __TEXT.__text section.

Using LLDB, take any method or function you can think of and find the section that it's located in. I'll use my go-to default, -[UIViewController viewDidLoad], but you should pick something different.

```
(lldb) image lookup -n "-[UIViewController viewDidLoad]"
```

You'll see output similar to the following:

```
1 match found in /Applications/Xcode.app/Contents/Developer/
Platforms/iPhoneOS.platform/Developer/Library/CoreSimulator/
Profiles/Runtimes/iOS.simruntime/Contents/Resources/RuntimeRoot/
System/Library/PrivateFrameworks/UIKitCore.framework/UIKitCore:
        Address: UIKitCore[0x0000000000abb3f8]
(UIKitCore.__TEXT.__text + 11243624)
        Summary: UIKitCore`-[UIViewController viewDidLoad]
```

The method –[UIViewController viewDidLoad] is located in **UIKitCore**. As
mentioned previously, if you're running a version of iOS earlier than 12, then this
method will be located in UIKit. The output above gives the full path to the
UIKitCore module. The offset on disk is shown, via
UIKitCore[0x0000000000abb3f8]; it's contained in UIKitCore.__TEXT.__text
section at offset 11243624. If you wanted the load address to be displayed in the
output, then you could supply the ––verbose option (or just –v) to LLDB.

Clear the screen and run the image dump sections MachOFun LLDB command
again. This time, search for the **MachOFun.__TEXT.__cstring** Section.

In my output, I got the following:

```
0x00000006 data-cstr
[0x0000000109e6a320-0x0000000109e6b658)   r-x   0x0000c320
0x00001338 0x00000002 MachOFun.__TEXT.__cstring
```

This is where the UTF-8 hardcoded strings are stored for your print statements, key-
value coding/observing, or anything else that's between quotation marks in your
source code. Using LLDB, dump the memory in this section by referencing the size
and the start load address.

```
(lldb) memory read -r -fC -c 0x00001338 0x0000000109e6a320
```

This prints the memory starting at address 0x0000000109e6a320, format the output
as printable characters (-fC), repeat the process 0x00001338 times, and force (-r) to
print the entire count, since LLDB defaults to an upper limit of 1024 bytes. You'll see
a load of familiar strings in here, such as "Unexpectedly found nil while
unwrapping an Optional value". Take a look through the strings and see what
you can find.

Alternatively, you can use Xcode's graphical memory viewer from the **Debug ▸ Debug Workflow ▸ View Memory** menu. Then paste or type `0x0109e6a320` into the **Address** text box. Then select a value in the **Number of Bytes** dropdown that is greater than `0x1338`. You can use the LLDB command `p/d 0x1338` to convert the value to decimal. Then just choose a number greater than that.

Numerous other sections contain UTF-8 strings for different purposes. For example, the `__TEXT.__objc_methname` section contains Objective-C method names that are referenced directly by your application. The `__TEXT.__swift4_reflstr` section contains references to Swift's reflected items. A candidate for Swift runtime reflection would be references to `IBOutlet` or `IBInspectable` variables.

I highly recommend exploring these sections further on your own.

Finding HTTP Strings

Now that you know hardcoded UTF-8 strings are stored in the `__TEXT.__cstring` module, you'll use that knowledge to search every module in the process to see if any string begins with the characters `"http:"`

Open up **InsecureNetworkRequestsTableViewController.swift** and add the following below `import UIKit`:

```
import MachO
```

Next, navigate to the **setupDataSource** function.

The logic is all setup to display any hits from the **dataSource** variable, but it only contains placeholder data for now. The `dataSource` variable is a typealiased array of (`module: String, strings: [String]`)'s. That means for every element in the array, there will be a module name, plus an array of strings for that module that contain any insecure `"http:"` strings.

Remove the code in **setupDataSource** and replace it with the following:

```
for i in 0..<_dyld_image_count() {
    let imagePath = _dyld_get_image_name(i)!
    let name = String(validatingUTF8: imagePath)!
    let basenameString = (name as NSString).lastPathComponent

    var module : InsecureHTTPRequestsData = (basenameString, [])
    var rawDataSize: UInt = 0
    guard let rawData =
      getsectdatafromFramework(basenameString,
```

```
                                    "__TEXT",
                                    "__cstring",
                                    &rawDataSize) else {
        continue
    }

    print(
        "__TEXT.__cstring data: \(rawData), \(basenameString)")
}
```

The main point of interest in this code is the **getsectdatafromFramework** API. This function takes the name of the module, the name of the containing segment as well as the section and gives the pointer to the location of the section in memory! In addition, there's an `inout` variable called `rawDataSize` which gives the size of the section in memory.

Build and run. You'll see every module that contains a __TEXT.__cstring section as well as the appropriate load address of where in memory it can be found.

From the console output, you'll can see the lots of output. I got 360 hits including:

```
__TEXT.cstring data: 0x0000000102bae5e0,
libBacktraceRecording.dylib
__TEXT.cstring data: 0x0000000102b82688, libRPAC.dylib
__TEXT.cstring data: 0x0000000102bedf88,
libViewDebuggerSupport.dylib
__TEXT.cstring data: 0x0000000102a6a0a0, MachOFun
...
```

Pause the application. Then take any address you find and use LLDB to query information about. I'll take the __TEXT.__cstring load address for libViewDebuggerSupport.dylib in my process. As always, your output for load addresses will likely be different.

Grabbing the __TEXT.__cstring load address of `libViewDebuggerSupport.dylib`, query info about it using LLDB:

```
(lldb) image lookup -a 0x0000000102bedf88
```

I get the following output:

```
Address: libViewDebuggerSupport.dylib[0x000000000002df88]
(libViewDebuggerSupport.dylib.__TEXT.__cstring + 0)
Summary: "numberOfSections"
```

The `libViewDebuggerSupport.dylib[0x000000000002df88]` shows the offset on disk to where the `__TEXT.__cstring` location is stored. Remember, that might not be the finalized offset on disk if the executable is a fat executable with multiple architecture slices. The `Summary` part of the output might seem a little misleading with `"numberOfSections"`, but remember, this is the location of where hardcoded UTF-8 strings are stored. Using LLDB, print out the first string at `libViewDebuggerSupport.dylib.__TEXT.__cstring`, like so:

```
(lldb) x/s 0x0000000102bedf88
```

You'll get:

```
0x102bedf88: "numberOfSections"
```

The first hardcoded string compiled into the `libViewDebuggerSupport.dylib` module is the string "numberOfSections". This is the output of the compiled version of `libViewDebuggerSupport.dylib` on my machine, and the first string could be different in other versions of `libViewDebuggerSupport.dylib`.

Now that you've found the start address of the `__TEXT.__cstring` sections, it's time to parse that whole buffer of memory to search for any strings that begin with `"http:"`.

Remember, this buffer of memory is a bunch of UTF-8 C strings. That means you need to parse a string for as long as you can until you hit a NULL byte.

Open **InsecureNetworkRequestsTableViewController.swift** and in `setupDataSource()`, remove the `print` statement you made earlier and replace with the following:

```
var index = 0
while index < rawDataSize {
  let cur = rawData.advanced(by: index)
  let length = strlen(cur)
  index = index + length + 1

  guard let str = String(utf8String: cur),
    length > 0 else {
      continue
  }

  if str.hasPrefix("http:") {
    module.strings.append(str)
  }
}

if module.strings.count > 0 {
```

```
    dataSource.append(module)
}
```

This code will grab the `rawData` pointing to a `__TEXT.__cstring` section in memory. The `while` loop performs several checks, making sure a valid UTF-8 string of length greater than 0 exists. If so, then the beginning of the string is checked to see if it contains the characters `"http:"`. If so, then the string is added to the `strings` array. Finally, if a module has any strings that contain `"http:"`, then that is added to the `dataSource` variable.

Finally, make sure you have a controlled test in the `MachOFun` module to make sure this is correctly working.

In `viewDidLoad`, add the following code right after `super.viewDidLoad()`:

```
let _ = "https://www.google.com"
let _ = "http://www.altavista.com"
```

If everything works as expected, the `https://www.google.com` string will not be displayed (since it begins with "https"), while the `http://www.altavista.com` string will (hopefully?) be displayed.

Build and run.

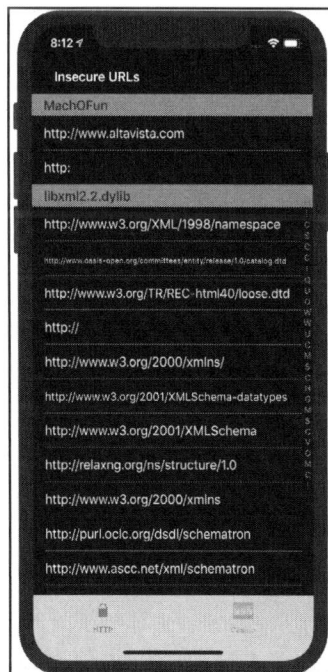

As you can see, there are a number of insecure hardcoded URLs not only in the MachOFun module, but modules like `libxml2.2dylib`, `GeoServices`, `CFNetwork`, etc.

Sections in the __DATA Segment

Now that you've got your public insecure URL shaming out of the way, it's time to shift the attention to the writeable __DATA segment and explore some interesting sections.

Suspend the MachOFun app and use LLDB to query the data sections. Execute the good ol' following LLDB command:

```
(lldb) image dump sections MachOFun
```

Search for the **__DATA_CONST.__objc_classlist** section in the output. In my process, I got the following...

```
0x00000015 data-ptrs
[0x000000010213c7a8-0x000000010213c7c8)  rw-  0x000107a8
0x00000020 0x10000000 MachOFun.__DATA_CONST__objc_classlist
```

This section stores `Class` pointers to Objective-C or Swift classes. This section is an array of `Class` pointers that point to the actual `Classes` stored into **__DATA.__objc_data**. Think of the __DATA.__objc_data section as a buffer of Objective-C data packed together, just as how the hardcoded UTF-8 strings are stored in the __TEXT.__cstring section.

Jumping back to the __DATA_CONST.__objc_classlist section, you can quickly determine that there are four classes implemented by the MachOFun module. How can you determine this? The segment size is 0x00000020 divided by the size of a pointer in a 64-bit process (8 bytes), which leaves you with four Objective-C/Swift classes.

Use LLDB to dump the raw pointers from the __DATA_CONST.__objc_classlist section to prove this is correct.

```
(lldb) x/4gx 0x0000010dcae8e0
0x10dcae8e0: 0x000000010dcb0580 0x000000010dcb0690
0x10dcae8f0: 0x000000010dcb0758 0x000000010dcb0800
```

Then for each pointer:

```
(lldb) exp -l objc -O -- 0x000000010dcb0580
```

```
MachOFun.CasinoContainerView

(lldb) exp -l objc -O -- 0x000000010dcb0690
MachOFun.CasinoViewController

(lldb) exp -l objc -O -- 0x000000010dcb0758
MachOFun.InsecureNetworkRequestsTableViewController

(lldb) exp -l objc -O -- 0x000000010dcb0800
MachOFun.AppDelegate
```

Inside MachOFun, there are four Swift classes, due to the fact the module and period precedes the class name.

Tools like **class-dump** (http://stevenygard.com/projects/class-dump/) use this information along with numerous other Mach-O sections to display Swift/Objective-C classes.

The __bss, __common and __const Sections

Sometimes a module needs to keep references to data that lives past a function call. As you've learned earlier, if you were to declare a constant such as let v = UIView() inside of a function, the pointer v is stored on the stack which points to allocated memory on the heap. But as soon as the instruction pointer leaves the function, the reference to the v variable is long gone. That's why there are several sections in the __DATA segment designed to store variables across the lifetime of a process.

When you declare a **global variable**, which is a variable outside the scope of any method or function, it will typically be placed into the **__DATA.__common** section. This section expects to share information across the module and even across other modules.

What if a developer wanted to have a variable survive across function calls, but not have it accessible to any other modules, or even from other source files within the same module? This is typically achieved by storing variables in the **__DATA.__bss** section. The C/Objective-C family does this via a **static** declaration to a variable. In Swift, this can be achieved with a **private** declaration on a Swift variable.

Finally, there are global variables that you want declared as unchanging for the life of the program. You can mark these as **const** in C/Objective-C to store variables in the **__DATA.__const** section. From a developers standpoint, Swift mostly doesn't need you to touch the __DATA.__const section due to the let keyword and checking for changes to a variable at compile time.

Cheating Freemium Games

The __DATA segment not only stores references to data in the module, but it also provides references to external variables, classes, methods, and functions that are not defined within the module.

Think about why this is the case for a second. If, in theory, a module can be loaded at any address, a reference point must be used to indicate where to start looking when calling out to that code. Since this location is not known until runtime, this starting reference point *must* be writable from the calling module.

This applies to external C functions, Swift/Objective-C classes, global variables, etc.

The **__DATA_CONST.__got** is a rather interesting section as it stores references to external functions that are lazily resolved at runtime when called. For this complex dance to work, the __DATA_CONST.__got section stores a series of function pointers that point to offsets in the **__TEXT.__stub_helper** section in the calling module. This sets off a flurry of activity as dyld resolves the location of this external function. I'll stay out of the gory details of this, but just know that external functions by default are referenced through the __DATA_CONST.__got section and are "resolved" if the function pointer doesn't point to an address in the __TEXT.__stub_helper section. This whole process is called a **fixup**.

Resume execution of the MachOFun program and navigate the app to the Casino tab. Once at the slot machine, give it a couple of spins.

For you intermediate to advanced readers out there, see if you can recall the API or APIs to generate a random number. Remember your guess and see if it's true below. Suspend the program and type the following in LLDB:

```
(lldb) exp -l objc -O -- [[NSBundle mainBundle] executablePath]
```

This will give you the full path to the running application. Copy the full path to the clipboard and type the following in LLDB, replacing `${APP_PATH} with the path you copied:

```
(lldb) platform shell dyld_info -fixups ${APP_PATH}
```

You're running the Terminal command **dyld_info**, searching for all symbols inside the MachOFun executable that dyld is going to have to bind.

Now use the filter or find or just scroll through the output to find your best guess for the random number generator function.

Did you guess the function correctly? I found:

```
__DATA_CONST __got              0x1000102D0              bind
libSystem.B.dylib/_arc4random_uniform
```

This means that **arc4random_uniform** is being called somewhere in the MachOFun code. This function will generate a random number with a range given by the first parameter.

This **0x1000102D0** value is the calculated offset in memory without the ASLR slide. This 0x1000102D0 value includes the __PAGEZERO offset (given by the 0x100000000) with the actual *real* offset on disk with the value 0x102D0.

How can you translate this 0x1000102D0 value into memory? You can use the **_dyld_get_image_vmaddr_slide** API to get the address slide! Remember, earlier in the chapter when you printed out all of the _dyld_get_image_name(i)! when looking for __cstring sections?

In LLDB, type the following, replacing the 3 with whatever index for you matches up with the MachOFun image:

```
(lldb) po (char *)_dyld_get_image_name(3)
```

This is to make sure you are referencing the correct index into the modules. Make sure the output references the MachOFun executable.

```
/Users/virtualadmin/Library/Developer/CoreSimulator/Devices/
53BD59A2-6863-444C-8B4A-6C2E8159D81F/data/Containers/Bundle/
Application/D62A2699-1881-4BC5-BD11-ACAD2479D057/MachOFun.app/
MachOFun
```

After that, use LLDB with the same index number with the _dyld_get_image_vmaddr_slide API and add it to the value you retrieved from **objdump** command:

```
(lldb) p/x (intptr_t)_dyld_get_image_vmaddr_slide(3) +
0x1000102D0
```

For me, I got the value **0x00000001005ec2d0**. This value is the resolved load address to the location to the external stub reference of arc4random_uniform *in memory*. Dereference the value of this address and examine it with LLDB:

```
(lldb) x/gx 0x00000001005ec2d0
```

This will produce something similar to the following:

```
0x1005ec2d0: 0x00000001800d8bc4
```

Query this new address and see what it resolved to:

```
(lldb) image lookup -a 0x00000001800d8bc4
```

And lo and behold you'll get the in-memory address to arc4random_uniform:

```
Address: libsystem_c.dylib[0x0000000000023bc4]
(libsystem_c.dylib.__TEXT.__text + 141016)
Summary: libsystem_c.dylib`arc4random_uniform
```

This means that the arc4random_uniform function has already been resolved, since the function pointer in __DATA_CONST.__got is pointing to arc4random_uniform instead of an offset in the __TEXT.__stub_helper section.

Hell, you're not even going to set a breakpoint on arc4random_uniform since you're so confident that this slot machine is calling arc4random_uniform to generate random numbers. You'll change around the pointer in memory just to see what can happen!

In LLDB, create a global function that always returns the value 5.

```
(lldb) exp -l objc -p -- int lolzfunc()  { return 5; }
```

The out-of-the-ordinary -p option says to execute this code outside of any stack frame. This is necessary since you can't declare functions inside other C code. This means there's a global function named **lolzfunc** floating around somewhere in memory.

Grab the address of the lolzfunc via LLDB:

```
(lldb) p/x lolzfunc
(int (*)()) $0 = 0x00000001018209b0
```

The plan of attack should be clear now. You will change around the external stub's pointer of arc4random_uniform to the address of the newly created function, lolzfunc.

In LLDB, type the following:

```
(lldb) memory write -s8 0x00000001005ec2d0 0x00000001018209b0
```

The first pointer is the original address of `arc4random_uniform` that you found earlier. The second pointer is the new `lolzfunc` address.

This tells LLDB to write 8 bytes (−s8) at location `0x00000001005ec2d0`, with value `0x00000001018209b0`.

You just followed a very complex set of instructions. To recap the steps:

1. Use `ex -l objc -O -- [[NSBundle mainBundle] executablePath]` to get the path of the running executable.

2. Use `platform shell dyld_info -fixups <the_path_from_step_1>` to dump out all of the symbols that need fixups.

3. Find the entry for `_arc4random_uniform` and copy the memory address.

4. Use `(char *)_dyld_get_image_name(<index>)` to figure out the index of the main executable.

5. Use `p/x (intptr_t)_dyld_get_image_vmaddr_slide(<the_index_from_step_4>) + <the_memory_address_from_step_3>` to get the resolved address.

6. Create the cheating function with `exp -l objc -p -- int lolzfunc() { return 5; }`.

7. Get the address of the cheating function with `p/x lolzfunc`.

8. Insert the cheating function `memory write -s8 <resolved_address_from_step_5> <memory_address_from_step_7>`.

Resume the application, then give the game another spin and see what happens.

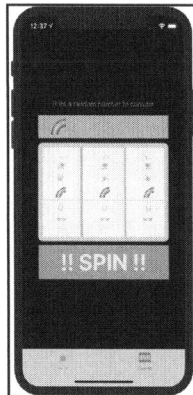

You're winning... every time... what are the odds of that? Crazy, eh?

Objective-C Swizzling vs Function Interposing

Unlike Objective-C method swizzling, lazy pointer loading occurs on a **per-module basis**. That means that the trick you just performed will only work when the MachOFun module calls out to arc4random_uniform. It wouldn't work if, say, CFNetwork called out to arc4random_uniform.

Going back to the MachOFun app, do you see that "Print a random number to console" button?

That code resolves to an IBAction method which calls SomeClassInAFramework.printARandomNumber(). That code is implemented in a different framework creatively called **AFramework**. Inside the static **printARandomNumber()** function, arc4random_uniform is being called.

Press the button a couple of times and observe how arc4random_uniform works normally. This means that if you wanted to swap all arc4random_uniform stubs, you'd have to iterate through each module, find the arc4random_uniform location stub in memory and replace it with the address of the new function.

On your own time, you may want to explore a macro from dyld called DYLD_INTERPOSE, or else Facebook's Fishhook (https://github.com/facebook/fishhook). It will allow you to add a new DATA__interpose section to a Mach-O file to swizzle a dyld symbol and do for your entire executable what you just did for the one instance of arc4random.

Key Points

- Use `image dump sections` to find all of the segments and sections for a module.

- `TEXT.__cstring` holds hard coded utf8 strings in an executable. Where do you think the other strings are?

- Explore the `__DATA` sections to find links to other modules as well as symbol names and metadata.

- The terminal apps `nm`, `otool` and `dyld_info` can help you discover symbols in applications.

Where to Go From Here?

Oh my! There is so much more for you to learn about Mach-O, but the road ends here for now.

- Check out Jonathan Levin's work on describing Mach-O (http://newosxbook.com/articles/DYLD.html).

- I also haven't even started on the complexity and power of the `__LINKEDIT` segment. A surprisingly good reference is Facebook's Fishhook (https://github.com/facebook/fishhook), a runtime library for modifying external stubs, found here. You will have a brief glimpse into the `__LINKEDIT`'s symbol table in later chapters, but there will be a lot of information that can be learned elsewhere.

Chapter 19: Code Signing

Ah, code signing: an iOS developer's nemesis. Code signing is hardly at the top of every iOS developer's agenda, but a strong knowledge of how code signing works can be extremely useful for solving problems, as well as establishing yourself as a linchpin in your development team. There's nothing more "ask-for-a-raise-worthy" than a developer who can re-sign an outdated Swift 2.2 iOS app, instead of having to fix the potentially thousands of Swift compiler errors when time is against you.

This chapter will give you a basic overview of how code signing works by having you pick apart the open-source iOS Wordpress v10.9 application (https://github.com/wordpress-mobile/WordPress-iOS/releases/tag/10.9).

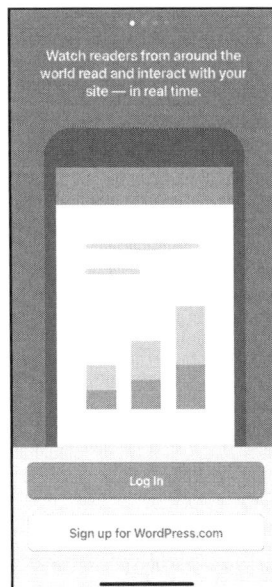

You'll explore the stages of the app's code signature before being sent to App Store Connect. In addition, you'll re-sign the Wordpress app so it can run on your very own iOS device!

Setting Up

In order to complete everything in this chapter, you'll need a number of items. First, you'll need a proper **iOS Apple Developer account** to generate Provisioning Profiles. You'll also need a physical iOS device to install the Wordpress iOS application.

Terminology

To really appreciate how code signing works, you need to understand three key components: **public/private keys**, **entitlements**, and **provisioning profiles**. You'll start with a breadth-first look, then dive into a depth-first look at each.

The **public/private key** is used to sign your application. This is your digital signature which Apple knows about and how Apple verifies you as, well, you. The private key is used to cryptographically sign the app as well as its capabilities, or **entitlements**. The entitlements are really just an XML string embedded in your app which says what the app can, and can't, do.

The grouping of the entitlements, the list of approved devices, and the public key to verify the code signature are all bundled together in a **provisioning profile** in your application. All the information is enforced through the signature created by your private key and can be verified by your public key.

That is a lot to take in, and it gets more confusing from here. So let's investigate each component of the profile separately.

Public/Private Keys

This is probably the hardest thing to understand when learning about the code signing process, since public/private keys introduce cryptography, which quickly becomes a rabbit hole of knowledge, formats, formatting, and gotchas.

Simply put, there's two different types of cryptography: **symmetric cryptography**, and **asymmetric cryptography**.

Symmetric cryptography is a type of cryptography that contains only one key. If person A tries to send a secret message to person B, they both must know that shared secret in order to encrypt and decrypt the message.

In asymmetric cryptography, there are two keys: a public key (which can be known by everyone) and a private key (which is kept secret to you). Both person A and B have their own unique private key and their own unique public key. That way, they can share information without either person knowing the other person's private key. The implementation of this is beyond the scope of this chapter, but you should learn more about this concept on your own time if this is new to you.

If you can remember when you set up your Apple developer account, you went through the process of **Requesting a Certificate From A Certificate Authority**. You created a public/private key, sent up the public key to Apple servers (by the `.csr` file). The end result of this process created a signature that is signed by Apple and is how Apple uniquely recognizes you. This means that Apple — and by extension, you — use asymmetric cryptography for distributing applications.

You can view the names, or **identities**, of your public/private key pairs used for signing your applications with the following Terminal command:

```
security find-identity -p codesigning -v
```

This command queries the macOS system keychain, looking for valid identities that contain a private key (-v) and whose type can codesign (-p codesigning).

This output will display identities that are valid, which can produce a code signed application. If you look for identities that contain the phrase "Apple Development", it's likely that this identity can be used to sign an iOS application on your device.

For example, I got the following output for identities that contained the term "Apple Development":

```
4) 61940D752C3E5CDD3C20FFE498B86E5B78D0078F "Apple Development:
walter@tyreeapps.com (78L6PC9H2P)"
```

If you got something similar, your computer is properly set up to sign a valid iOS application on your macOS machine.

You can view this identity in the GUI-equivalent program **Keychain Access**. Open Keychain Access, navigate to **My Certificates**, then search for your equivalent string by omitting the quotes.

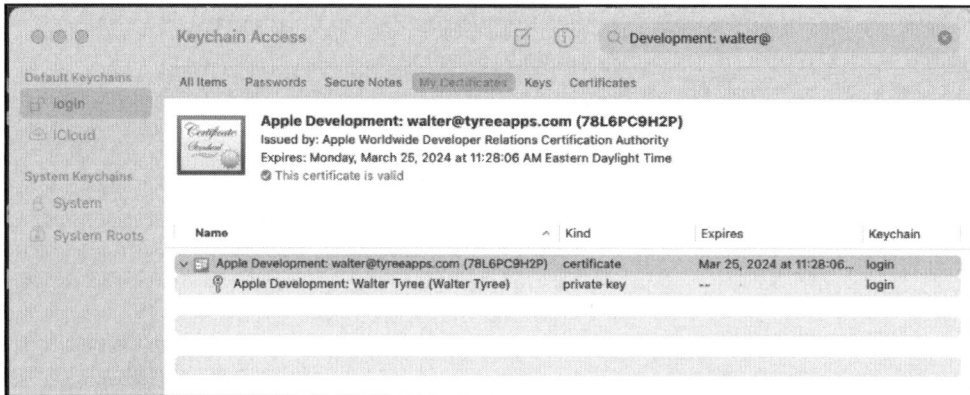

Notice that you have a public key, or a **certificate**, as well as the **private key** found below. Certificates can be recreated, but private keys are worth more than gold. Never, ever, delete a private key! If you do, you forfeit your proof that you're you, and you'll need to recreate a new identity through Apple.

Let me revisit a point you might have missed in the above paragraph. A certificate, in this sense, is only the **public key**. So if you were to use Keychain Access to export your identity, and you wanted to format it in a **.cer** (certificate) format, you'd only be exporting the public key. If you want to export the private key as well, you must use the PKCS12 format (**.p12**) to properly export the full identity, private key and all.

This is important to know if you wanted to export the identity so another developer could, say, generate a build with a matching distribution (i.e. App Store) identity. But be careful: whoever has the private key can assume the full identity for that company, at least from Apple's perspective!

Jumping back to the Terminal equivalent, you can export the public certificates using the following command:

```
security find-certificate -c "Apple Development:
walter@tyreeapps.com (78L6PC9H2P)" -p
```

This will output the public, x509 certificate of **Apple Development: walter@tyreeapps.com (78L6PC9H2P)** to stdout and format it in **PEM** format. There's two ways to display a certificate: DER and PEM. PEM can be read by the Terminal (since it's in base64 encoding) while DER, in highly professional coding terms, will produce gobbledygook and make the Terminal beep a lot.

Repeat the above command and write the output to /tmp/public_cert.cer. Be sure to replace the identity with your own identity:

```
security find-certificate  -c "Apple Development:
walter@tyreeapps.com (78L6PC9H2P)"  -p > /tmp/public_cert.cer
```

Use the Terminal command to cat this newly created file:

```
cat /tmp/public_cert.cer
```

You'll see something similar to the following:

```
-----BEGIN CERTIFICATE-----
MIIFnDCCBISgAwIBAgIIFMKm2AG4HekwDQYJKoZIhvcNAQELBQAwgZYxCzAJBgNV
BAYTAlVTMRMwEQYDVQQKDApBcHBsZSBJbmMuMSwwKgYDVQQLDCNBcHBsZSBXb3Js
ZHdpZGUgRGV2ZWxvcGVyIFJlbGF0aW9uczFEMEIGA1UEAww7QXBwbGUgV29ybGR3
...
```

This is how you can tell this certificate is in PEM. Terminal isn't cranky, and the header -----BEGIN CERTIFICATE----- is included. This would not be the case if the certificate was in DER format.

From here, you can use the openssl Terminal command to query your public, x509 certificate:

```
openssl x509 -in /tmp/public_cert.cer -inform PEM -text -noout
```

Yes, that's a lot of params!

- The x509 option says that the openssl command should be able to work with a x509 certificate.

- You provide the -in to the path of **public_cert.cer** with the decoding format of PEM (-inform PEM).

- You specify you don't want to output a certificate with the -noout param.

- But instead, you do want the certificate in a (somewhat) readable "text" format with the -text option.

The information about this public certificate will be displayed in the Terminal.

Remember this openssl command, as you'll revisit the concept of x509 certificates when you read about the provisioning profiles which embed these public certificates inside of them.

Entitlements

Embedded in (almost) every compiled application is a set of **entitlements**: again, this is an XML string embedded in the application saying what an app can and can't do. Other programs will check for permissions (or lack thereof) in the entitlements and grant or deny a request accordingly. Think of the **capabilities** section found in Xcode.

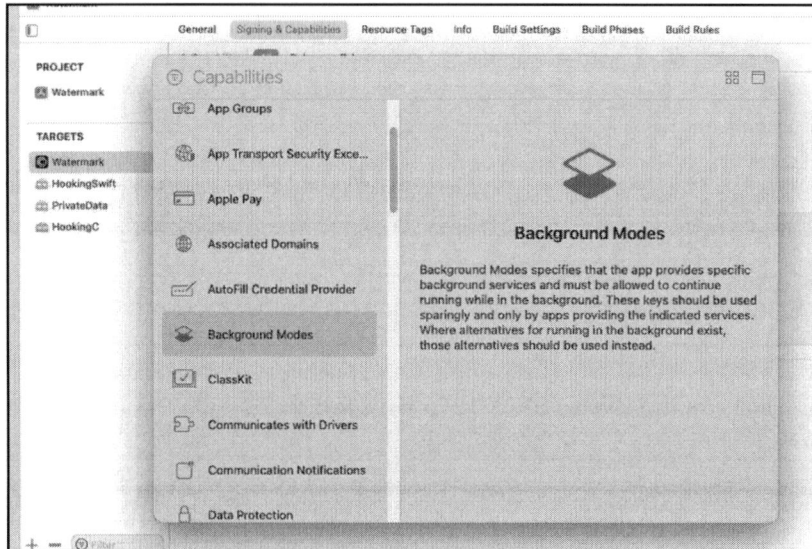

Many of these permission checks are carried out by other daemons which check your programs entitlements. For example, **App Groups**, **iCloud Services**, **Push Notifications**, **Associated Domains** all will modify the entitlements to your app. These capabilities shown in Xcode are but a small piece of the entitlements on Apple platforms as the majority of them are private to Apple and enforced through code signing.

You can see a complete list of entitlements found in the wild thanks to Jonathan Levin's entitlement database (http://newosxbook.com/ent.jl).

Probably the most important entitlement, at least in this book, is the **get-task-allow** entitlement, found on all your software compiled with a developer certificate. This allows the program in question to be attached to a debugger.

On macOS, you can get around the lack of this entitlement by disabling SIP for any applications that don't have the t rue value for this key. On iOS, you'll be out of luck trying to debug an application that doesn't have this entitlement, unless code verification has been disabled through jailbreaking.

You can view the entitlements of an application through the **codesign** Terminal command.

Find the entitlements of the macOS **Finder** application:

```
codesign -d --entitlements :- /System/Library/CoreServices/
Finder.app/Contents/MacOS/Finder
```

The -d option says to display the option immediately following in the command, which is the --entitlements. You also have that weird looking :-, which does two things:

- The - says to print to stdout

- The : says to omit the blob header and length.

Just as in Mach-O, the code signature information is stored with a magic header, immediately followed by a length. The ":" says to strip this header information out of the output and *only* display the actual XML string of entitlements.

Provisioning Profiles

Finally, the provisioning profiles are up for discussion. A provisioning profile includes the public x509 certificate, the list of approved devices, as well as the entitlements all embedded into one file.

The default location for provisioning profiles can be found here:

```
~/Library/MobileDevice/Provisioning Profiles/
```

Unfortunately, provisioning profiles are named by their UUID instead of by the name you (or Xcode) made up for them. This gives you a list of files that don't give you a lot of context, at first glance, if you were to execute an ls in the directory.

```
ls ~/Library/MobileDevice/Provisioning\ Profiles/
```

Fortunately, you can use the security command again to dump the raw info. Pick any one of your .mobileprovision files and execute the security command, like this:

```
PP_FILE=$(ls ~/Library/MobileDevice/Provisioning\ Profiles/
*mobileprovision | head -1)
security cms -D -i "$PP_FILE"
```

The first command grabs one of the provisioning profiles and assigns it to the PP_FILE variable.

The PP_FILE variable is passed into the `security` command which decodes (-D) the cryptographic message syntax (cms) format of the provisioning profile, specifying the input path via the -i option.

The output will be in plist XML form. Your content will be *very* different from mine due to the different nature of the apps you've developed, the entitlements you've specified, the devices and code signatures you've used, as well as the environment you've used (i.e. development/distribution) to generate the provisioning profile.

I'll discuss the output of one of my provisioning profiles as a guide to help explore your own. If you want to follow along word-for-word, the exact provisioning profile is included in the resource directory for this chapter. Its filename starts with 6da7f785.

From the output, here are some of the highlights:

- **AppIDName** contains the value **XC com razeware woot**. This is the name of the Application ID that is tied to this provisioning profile, which can be found in your developer portal (https://developer.apple.com/account/resources/identifiers/list).

- **Entitlements**, unsurprisingly, contains the Entitlements of what the app can and can't do with this signature. This is often the cause of problems in Xcode generated provisioning profiles since Xcode needs to update the App ID configuration (which is essentially the entitlements), and then generate a new provisioning profile with the correct values.

- **IsXcodeManaged** is a Boolean value that indicates if Xcode manages this provisioning profile. The whole code-signing process has caused so many developer headaches that Apple is trying to do more of the work on their end, including signing an app with your distribution certificate. This is a double-edged sword since it's easier to let Xcode manage this for you, but if Xcode does something you didn't expect, the underlying error can be much more difficult to track down.

- **Name** contains the value **DS Twitter PP**, which is the name of the provisioning profile that Apple displays to identify the provisioning profiles on the developer portal (https://developer.apple.com/account/resources/profiles/list).

- **ProvisionedDevices** contains an array of approved devices this provisioning profile can install on, given by a device's UDID.

- **DeveloperCertificates** is an array that contains base64-encoded x509 certificates. This will contain the same public certificate that was extracted earlier via the `security find-certificate` command. These certificates are also encoded into the actual executables themselves when code signing an application. My provisioning profile contains two different certificates with the exact same name, with one certificate expired in 2019, and one having expired in 2018.

Phew! That was a lot of theory, but now you can move on to some actual codesigning work.

Exploring the WordPress App

Just like your typical debugging workflow on your iOS device, before an app is sent up to the Apple AppStore Connect mothership, you must compile an app with a provisioning profile. This provisioning profile is included in every *pre-App Store* `.app` under the name **embedded.mobileprovision**. It's this provisioning profile that tells iOS the application is valid and came from you.

Head over to the resources for this chapter. Then open up the **WordPress.app** container found in the **Pre App Store** directory. If you're using Finder, you can open up the container by right-clicking it and selecting the **Show Package Contents**.

Now head back over to your Terminal window. For the purpose of this tutorial, assign a Terminal variable, **WORDPRESS** to the fullpath to the WordPress.app, like so:

```
WORDPRESS="/full/path/to/WordPress.app/"
```

The Provisioning Profile

Find the **embedded.mobileprovision** provisioning profile inside of the WordPress application and use the **security** command on it.

```
security cms -D -i "$WORDPRESS/embedded.mobileprovision"
```

In this particular provisioning profile, you can see the following:

- Apple has given the **Automattic, Inc.** company the team identifier of **3TMU3BH3NK**.

- The Wordpress app makes use of iCloud services, given the **com.apple.developer.icloud*** keys in the entitlements dictionary. It also looks to make use of certain extension like "App Groups".

- **get-task-allow** is `false`, meaning a debugger can't be attached, as this was app was signed with a distribution signing identity.

Copy the base64-encoded data from the **DeveloperCertificates** key. It should begin with `MIIFozCCBIu...`, and make sure you copy the trailing equals signs if there are any.

Via Terminal, assign this value to a variable named **CERT_DATA**:

```
CERT_DATA=MIIFozCCBIu...
```

The variable `CERT_DATA` now contains the base64-encoded x509 certificate that was used to sign the application.

Now, decode this base64 data and pipe it to **/tmp/wordpress_cert.cer**:

```
echo "$CERT_DATA" | base64 -D > /tmp/wordpress_cert.cer
```

You now have the Wordpress certificate in DER format at **/tmp/wordpress_cert.cer**. You can now execute the following `openssl` command:

```
openssl x509 -in /tmp/wordpress_cert.cer -inform DER -text -noout
```

You'll see the following output:

```
Certificate:
    Data:
        Version: 3 (0x2)
        Serial Number: 786948871528664923 (0xaebcdd447dc4f5b)
    Signature Algorithm: sha256WithRSAEncryption
        Issuer: C=US, O=Apple Inc., OU=Apple Worldwide Developer
Relations, CN=Apple Worldwide Developer Relations Certification
Authority
        Validity
            Not Before: Jan 17 13:26:41 2018 GMT
            Not After : Jan 17 13:26:41 2019 GMT
        Subject: UID=PZYM8XX95Q, CN=iPhone Distribution:
```

```
Automattic, Inc. (PZYM8XX95Q), OU=PZYM8XX95Q, O=Automattic,
Inc., C=US
... truncated ...
```

This means that someone working at "Automattic, Inc" has an identity named "iPhone Distribution: Automattic, Inc. (PZYM8XX95Q)" on their keychain that was used to sign this application.

Embedded Executables

Provided an application contains extensions (i.e. share extension, today widgets, or others), there will be even more signed packaged bundles found in the **./Plugins** directory that contain their own application identifier and **embedded.mobileprovision** provisioning profile.

These give the application additional functionality outside the application.

You can verify this on your own time using the same `security` command while drilling into the containers in the `./Plugins` directory, exploring each **embedded.mobileprovision** file respectively.

The _CodeSignature Directory

Included in a real iOS application bundle (but not in the Simulator) is a folder named **_CodeSignature** that includes a single file named **CodeResources**. This is an XML plist file which is a checksum of every non-executable file found in this directory.

For example, if you were to execute:

```
cat "$WORDPRESS/_CodeSignature/CodeResources"  | head -10
```

you'll see there is a checksum of value **rSZAWMReahogETtlwDpstztW6Ug=** for the file **AboutViewController.nib**

This can be calculated yourself via `openssl`:

```
openssl sha1 -binary "$WORDPRESS/AboutViewController.nib"  |
base64
```

This will produce the matching rSZAWMReahogETtlwDpstztW6Ug= value.

Apple has begun the transition from SHA-1 checksums to SHA-256 for iOS applications with Xcode 10 producing checksums for both algorithms.

This `CodeResources` file itself has a checksum performed on the file, which is embedded in the actual WordPress application! This means that if a user were to modify any of the files, or even add a directory in the .app directory without resigning the WordPress app, the iOS application will fail to install on the user's phone.

Resigning the WordPress App

Time for some codesigning fun!

You'll now install the WordPress application onto your iOS device by re-signing the application with your Apple signature.

From a high level standpoint, you'll need to do the following:

1. Copy a valid provisioning profile to the **embedded.mobileprovision** in the WordPress `.app` directory.

2. Change the `Info.plist` key **CFBundleIdentifier** to the new application identifier provided in the new provisioning profile.

3. Re-sign the WordPress application via the identity included in the embedded provisioning profile with the proper entitlements (which is also included in the provisioning profile).

You can search for valid provisioning profiles at `~/Library/MobileDevice/ Provisioning Profiles/` or you can download a valid provisioning profile from the Developer Portal (https://developer.apple.com/).

If you have a valid provisioning profile with the above qualifications, you can skip the next step. You can determine if you have a valid provisioning profile by running the same `security cms` command as discussed above.

If you don't have a valid provisioning profile that contains your device and is not expired, you'll need to create a new provisioning profile in the Apple developer portal.

(Optional) Generate a Valid Provisioning Profile

If you don't have a provisioning profile that met the above requirements (UDID, not expired), you'll need to head on over to the Developer Portal (https://developer.apple.com/) and create a new one.

Although Apple changes the UI/UX on this site from time to time, head on over to the closest equivalent to **Identifiers**. Once there, create a new ID using the + button, select **App ID** and follow the steps.

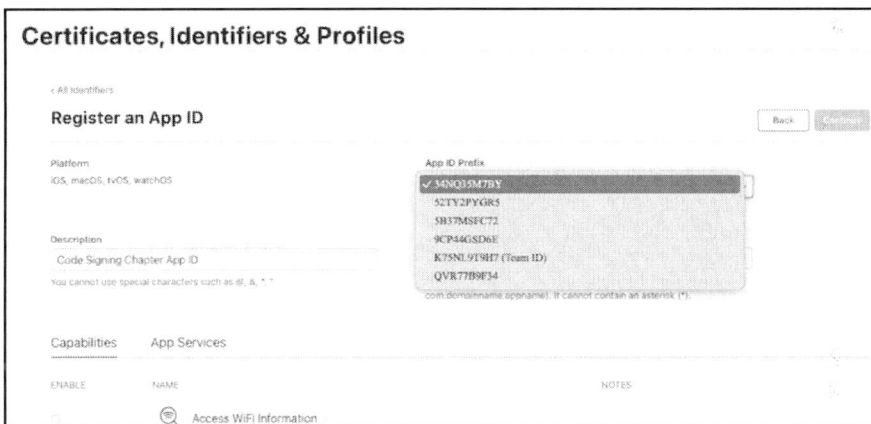

You might be confused if you have multiple App ID prefixes (like me).

To resolve this, remember that everything stems from your signing identity. You can query this information yourself from the commands you performed earlier.

Provided you have a valid `signing identity`, you can use the following Terminal query:

```
security find-certificate -c "Apple Development:
walter@tyreeapps.com (78L6PC9H2P)" -p > /tmp/public_cert.PEM
```

This extracts the public certificate from the identity. Now you can use `openssl` to search for the App ID prefix which is stored in the **Organizational Unit** (abbreviated as **OU**) in the x509 certificate.

```
openssl x509 -in /tmp/public_cert.PEM -inform pem -noout -text |
grep OU=
```

I got the following output:

```
Issuer: C=US, O=Apple Inc., OU=Apple Worldwide Developer
Relations, CN=Apple Worldwide Developer Relations Certification
Authority

Subject: UID=V969KV7V2B, CN=Apple Development:
walter@tyreeapps.com (78L6PC9H2P), OU=K75NL9T9H7, O=Derek
Selander, C=US
```

In my case, the signing identity I want to use has the App Prefix **K75NL9T9H7**, so I'll select that in the Apple Developer portal.

After creating the new App ID in the Developer Portal, head on over to the **Profiles** section. Click on the + to add a new provisioning profile.

Select **iOS App Development**, the click **Continue**.

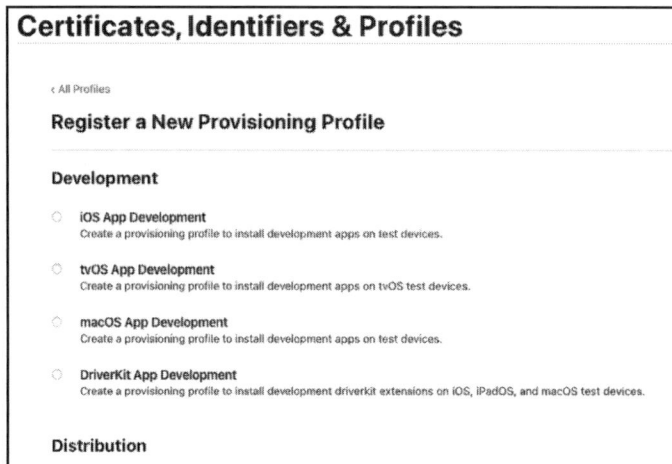

At the next page, select the App ID you just created, then click **Continue** again.

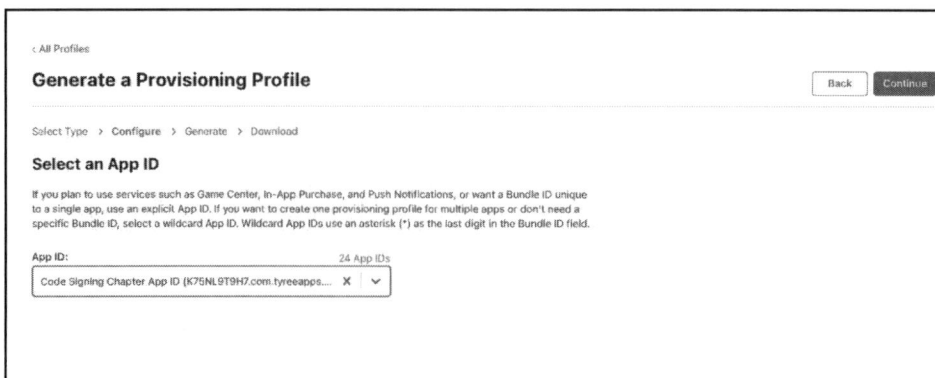

Select all the valid iOS certificates that can be used to sign the iOS application.

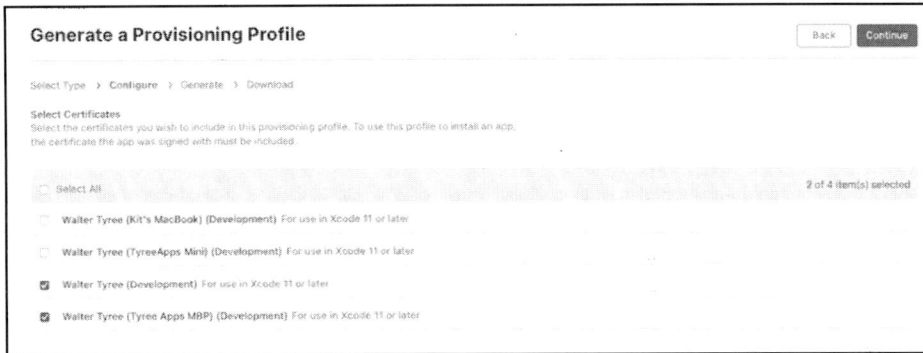

Finally, select all the devices you would like this provisioning profile to be installed on.

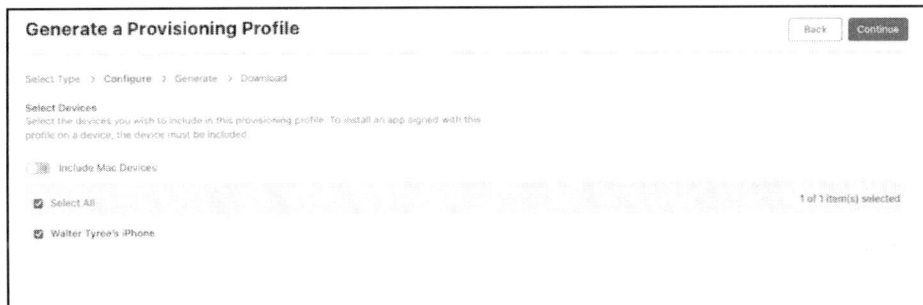

Give the provisioning profile a valid name.

A general word of advice: If you work on a team of iOS developers, and you're generating a Distribution provisioning profile, I would put your initials and date in the name. That way, people know who to track down in case something goes wrong, or if the provisioning profile is expiring.

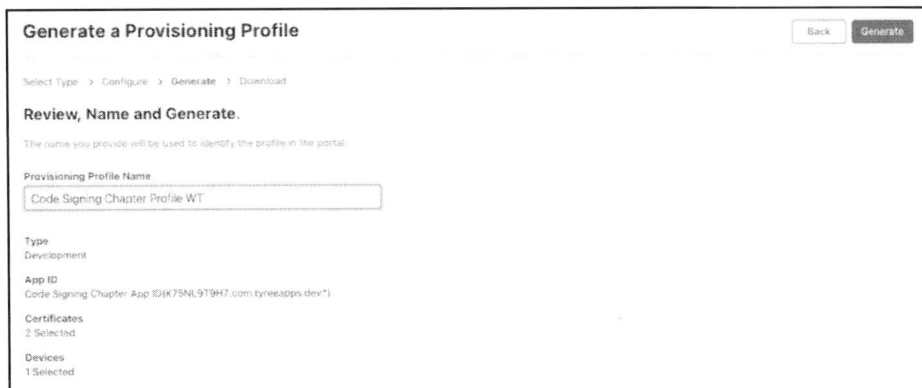

Once complete, download your newly created provisioning profile. Be sure to save it in a location that you'll remember since you'll be referencing it in a moment.

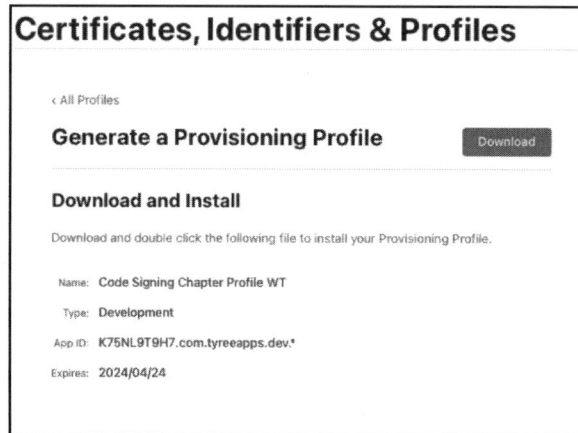

Certificates, Identifiers & Profiles

‹ All Profiles

Generate a Provisioning Profile   [Download]

Download and Install

Download and double click the following file to install your Provisioning Profile.

Name: Code Signing Chapter Profile WT

Type: Development

App ID: K75NL9T9H7.com.tyreeapps.dev.*

Expires: 2024/04/24

Copying the Provisioning Profile

At this point, you should have a valid provisioning profile, which you'll use to resign the WordPress application either by creating a new provisioning profile or by using an existing provisioning profile. Assign the **PP_PATH** Terminal variable to the fullpath of the provisioning profile you expect to use for this experiment.

Your path will be different than mine:

```
PP_PATH=~/Downloads/
Code_Signing_Example_ProvisProfile_92618.mobileprovision
```

Copy the provisioning profile at PP_PATH to the embedded.mobileprovision file in the WordPress app.

In Terminal, execute:

```
cp "$PP_PATH" "$WORDPRESS/embedded.mobileprovision"
```

Deleting the Plugins

The WordPress application has several extension applications embedded into the main app found in the ./Plugins directory. Each of these contains a unique provisioning profile with a unique application identifier. You could sign each of these extensions itself with a unique provisioning profile, but that will get way too complicated for this demo.

Instead, you'll cripple part of the Wordpress functionality and not use these extensions. Delete the entire Plugins directory for the WordPress app.

So now the new, re-signed application will not have functionality for the iOS Today Extension, but that's acceptable for this demo.

Modifying the Info.plist

I hope you've remembered the name of the App ID of the provisioning profile! You'll need to plug that into the Info.plist's key **CFBundleIdentifier** If you don't remember it, you can query it from the provisioning profile.

Here's how to grab that information:

```
security cms -D -i "$PP_PATH" | grep application-identifier -A1
```

This gave me the application identifier I need to plug into the Info.plist.

```
<key>application-identifier</key>
<string>H4U46V6494.com.selander.code-signing</string>
```

For me, my application identifier is **H4U46V6494.com.selander.code-signing**.

When you have your application identifier, replace this value in the WordPress's Info.plist for the **CFBundleIdentifier** key.

```
plutil -replace CFBundleIdentifier -string
H4U46V6494.com.selander.code-signing "$WORDPRESS/Info.plist"
```

While you're at it, change the display name to further highlight that this is in fact something you can completely tweak to your will. Change around WordPress's visual display name:

```
plutil -replace CFBundleDisplayName -string "Woot" "$WORDPRESS/
Info.plist"
```

This will change around the visual display name to Woot instead of WordPress, provided you can install the application on your iOS device.

Extracting the Entitlements

You're almost there!

Your next task is to resign the app with valid entitlements found in the provisioning profile. Since the entitlements get embedded as a dictionary and not as XML in the provisioning profile, it might be easier to extract the entitlements from the main executable first, then patch that file with the new entitlements found in the provisioning profile.

Extract the entitlements to **/tmp/ent.xml**:

```
codesign -d --entitlements :/tmp/ent.xml "$WORDPRESS/WordPress"
```

Note: The above command *appends* to the file — it does not overwrite the file. If you execute this command multiple times, you'll have an incorrectly formatted file, since there will be multiple entitlements at /tmp/ent.xml. If you execute this command multiple times, make sure to rm the file before executing it again.

Verify the entitlements are valid with a `cat`:

```
cat /tmp/ent.xml
```

Provided the entitlements work, you can extract the entitlements from the current provisioning profile and place them into this new file.

First, write out the provisioning profile XML to a file named **/tmp/scratch**:

```
security cms -D -i "$PP_PATH" > /tmp/scratch
```

Now use the **xpath** Terminal command to extract only the entitlement information to the clipboard.

By the way, you should play around with this command first before piping it to the clipboard (with pbcopy) so you understand the content it's grabbing. Just remove the | pbcopy part to inspect the actual values you're extracting.

```
xpath -e '//*[text() = "Entitlements"]/following-
sibling::dict' /tmp/scratch | pbcopy
```

You now have the valid entitlements in your clipboard. Open up **/tmp/ent.xml**, remove the enclosing <dict>'s contents and replace with the contents of your clipboard.

Your finalized /tmp/ent.xml file should look similar to the following entitlements:

```
<?xml version="1.0" encoding="UTF-8"?>
<!DOCTYPE plist PUBLIC "-//Apple//DTD PLIST 1.0//EN" "http://
www.apple.com/DTDs/PropertyList-1.0.dtd">
<plist version="1.0">
<dict>
    <key>keychain-access-groups</key>
    <array>
        <string>H4U46V6494.*</string>
    </array>
    <key>get-task-allow</key>
    <true />
    <key>application-identifier</key>
    <string>H4U46V6494.com.selander.code-signing</string>
    <key>com.apple.developer.team-identifier</key>
    <string>H4U46V6494</string>
</dict>
</plist>
```

This file is also included in the chapter directory in case you want to start with that instead.

> **Note**: Recently, Apple has switched how Booleans get rendered in XML files. The <true /> won't parse on some versions of macOS. You can either remove the space by hand so that it is <true/> or execute this command: plutil -convert xml1 /tmp/ent.xml if you run into errors about AMFIUnserializeXML: syntax error when you're working through this example.

Finally, Signing the WordPress App

You now have performed all the setup. You have a valid signing identity; you have a valid provisioning profile embedded in the WordPress application at embedded.mobileprovision; you have removed the Plugins directory; and you have the entitlements of the new provisioning profile found at **/tmp/ent.xml**.

You can now sign the application with your signing identity!

Before you do that, make a duplicate backup of the WordPress app, because it's easy to screw this part up, and it's tricky to undo the action if you do screw up.

> **Note**: The codesign tool wants to use the "Common Name" for your certificates and will silently fail if you have duplicates. Most people don't have duplicates, so it's not an issue and as you renew and update certificates over the years you don't have to worry about updating any codesign arguments. If you have duplicate names, codesign can work using the fingerprint. At the beginning of the chapter, when you executed the security find-identity command, that long string before the common name was the SHA-1 fingerprint.

Once you have a duplicate of your WordPress application, use the **codesign** command with your signing identity on the WordPress applications **Frameworks** directory:

```
codesign -f -s "Apple Development: walter@tyreeapps.com
(78L6PC9H2P)" "$WORDPRESS"/Frameworks/*
```

You need to sign this directory first.

```
codesign --entitlements /tmp/ent.xml -f -s "Apple Development:
walter@tyreeapps.com (78L6PC9H2P)" "$WORDPRESS"
```

Now for the moment of truth! See if you can install the WordPress application. Open Xcode and navigate to **Window ▸ Devices and Simulators**. Either drag and drop the **Wordpress.app** into the list with the other apps, or use the + to get a File dialog.

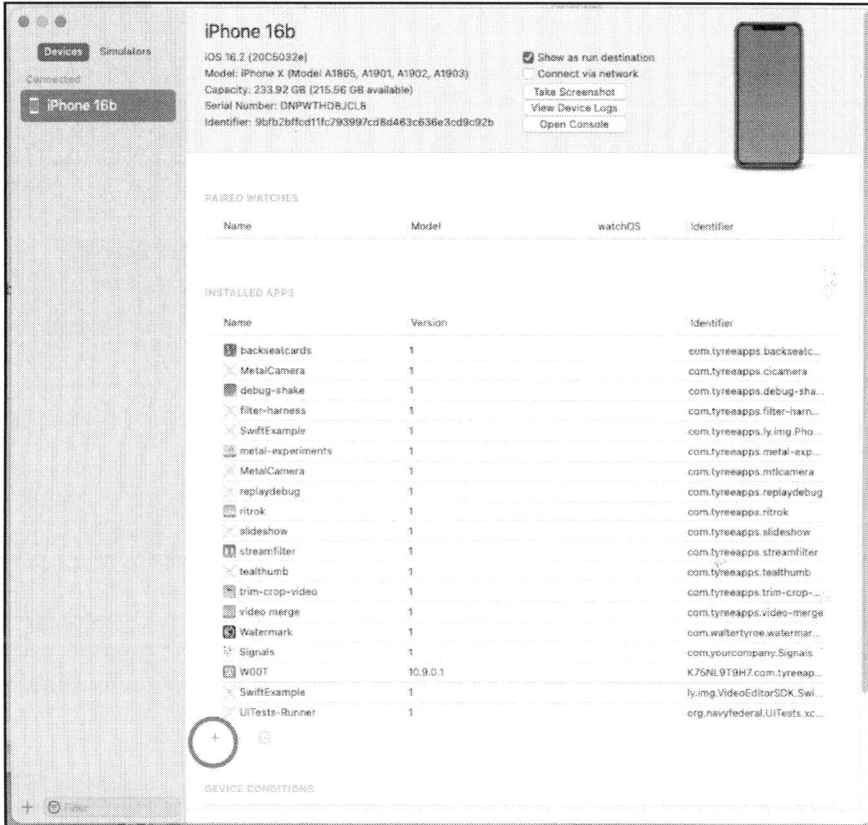

Did It Succeed?

Provided you have followed the steps *exactly*, you'll see a new app with the WordPress logo with the name "Woot" underneath it!

Even better, provided you signed your application with a developer provisioning profile, you'll have the `get-task-allow` entitlement, meaning you can debug this WordPress application!

Launch the newly installed WordPress application on your iOS device.

Fire up Xcode, select the **Debug** menu, select **Attach to Process** and search for the WordPress application. Then click the pause execution button to launch LLDB.

Key Points

- Use the PEM format for displaying certificate information in a human-readable way.

- Query a certificate using the `openssl` command line tool or using the GUI Keychain Utility on your Mac.

- Entitlements specify what permissions your app has. The `get-task-allow` entitlement is required if you want to attach with LLDB.

- Normally, Xcode handles the codesigning and provisioning profiles for you automatically, but you can go to the Developer portal to make your own.

- When working with `.xml` files the `xpath` utility queries for data while maintaining the structure.

Where to Go From Here?

This chapter has only scratched the surface of code signing. There is a lot more great content out there that focuses on other components to code signing.

If you want to truly know the in and outs of code signing, check out Jonathan Levin's *OS Internals Volume III Security & Insecurity*, which discusses code signing at an unprecedented level and gives you a look at everything, right down to the C structs.

Also check out this objc.io article (https://www.objc.io/issues/17-security/inside-code-signing/), which is one of the my favorite code signing articles out there from a developer standpoint.

Section IV: Custom LLDB Commands

You've learned the basic LLDB commands, the assembly that goes into code and the miscellaneous low-level concepts that make a program...well, a program.

It's time to put that knowledge together to create some very powerful and complex debugging scripts. As you will soon see, you're only limited by your skill and imagination — and finding the correct class (or header file) to do your debugging bidding.

LLDB ships with an integrated Python module that allows you to access most parts of the debugger through Python. This lets you leverage all the power of Python (and its modules) to help uncover whatever dark secrets vex you.

Chapter 20: Hello, Script Bridging

LLDB has several ways you can use to create your own customized commands. The first way is through the easy-to-use command `alias` you saw in Chapter 9, "Persisting & Customizing Commands". This command simply creates an alias for a static command. While easy to implement, it really only allowed you to execute commands with no input.

After that came command `regex`, which let you specify a regular expression to capture input then apply it to a command. You learned about this command in Chapter 10, "Regex Commands". This command works well when you want to feed input to an LLDB command, but it was inconvenient to execute multiline commands and supplying multiple, optional parameters could get really messy.

Next up in the tradeoff between convenience and complexity is LLDB's **script bridging**. With script bridging, you can do nearly anything you like. Script bridging is a **Python** interface LLDB uses to help extend the debugger to accomplish your wildest debugging dreams.

However, there's a cost to the script bridging interface. It has a steep learning curve, and the documentation, to put it professionally, sucks. Fortunately, you've got this book in your hands to help guide you through learning script bridging. Once you've a grasp on LLDB's Python module, you can do some very cool (and excitingly dangerous!) things.

Credit Where Credit's Due

Before we officially begin talking about script bridging, I want to bring up one Python script that has blown my mind. If it wasn't for this script, this book would not be in your hands.

```
/Applications/Xcode.app/Contents/SharedFrameworks/
LLDB.framework/Versions/A/Resources/Python/lldb/macosx/heap.py
```

This is *the* script that made me take a deep dive into learning LLDB. I've never had a mental butt-kicking as good as I did trying to initially understand what was happening in this code.

This script has it all: finding stack traces for `malloc`'d objects (`malloc_info -s`), getting all instances of a particular subclass of `NSObject` (`obj_refs -O`), finding all pointers to a particular reference in memory (`ptr_refs`), finding C strings in memory (`cstr_ref`).

You can load the contents of this script into any LLDB session, and use its functions, with the following LLDB command:

```
(lldb) command script import lldb.macosx.heap
```

Sadly, this script has fallen a bit out of functionality as the compiler has changed, while this code has not, rendering several of its components unusable.

When you're done reading this section, I would strongly encourage you to attempt to understand the contents of this script. You can learn *a lot* from it.

Ok, now back to our regularly scheduled, reading program...

Python 101

As mentioned, LLDB's script bridge is a Python interface to the debugger. This means you can load and execute Python scripts in LLDB. In those Python scripts, you include the `lldb` module to interface with the debugger to obtain information such as the arguments to a custom command.

Don't know Python? Don't fret. Python is one of the most friendly languages to learn. And just like the Swift Playgrounds everyone's losing their mind over, Python has an attractive REPL for learning.

Note: LLDB has completely transitioned from Python version 2 to Python 3. However, there are still lots of tutorials and blog posts out in the world that were written for Python 2. Since there are breaking changes between these different versions, pay careful attention to what version of Python you're using and what version someone is blogging about. At the time of writing, LLDB uses Python 3.9.6.

Let's figure out which version of Python LLDB is using. Open a Terminal window and type the following:

```
lldb
```

As expected, LLDB will start. From there, execute the following commands to find out which Python version is linked to LLDB:

```
(lldb) script print (sys.version)
```

The **script** command brings up the Python interpreter for LLDB. If you just typed in `script` without arguments, you'd be greeted with LLDB's Python REPL.

If LLDB's Python version is different than 3.x.x, freak out and complain loudly on the book's forum.

Note: Your system-installed Python version does not have to match 3.9.6 exactly; bug fix releases work fine also.

Now you know the Python version LLDB works with, ensure you have the correct version of Python symlinked to the `python` Terminal command. Open a new Terminal window and type the following:

```
python3 --version
```

If the Python version matches the one that LLDB has, then launch Python with no arguments in the Terminal:

```
python3
```

If you have a different version of Python symlinked (i.e. 3.X.Y), you need to launch Python with the correct version number. For example, in Terminal, type `python` and press Tab. Different version(s) of Python might pop up with the correct version number.

Enter the correct version number associated with the LLDB version of Python:

```
python3.9.6
```

Either way, ensure the LLDB version of Python matches the one you have in your Terminal:

```
>>> import sys
>>> print (sys.version)
```

Notice in the actual Python REPL there's no need to prefix any of the commands with the LLDB script command.

Playing Around in Python

If you are unfamiliar with Python, this section will help you get familiar with the language quickly. If you're already knowledgeable about Python, feel free to jump to the next section.

In your Terminal session, open a Python REPL by typing the following:

```
python3
```

Next, in the Python REPL, type the following:

```
>>> h = "hello world"
>>> h
```

You'll see the following output:

```
'hello world'
```

Python lets you assign variables without needing to declare the type beforehand. Unlike Swift, Python doesn't really have the notion of constants, so there's no need for a `var` or `let` declaration for a variable.

> **Note**: If you have a different version of Python, then some of the commands
> might have different syntax. You'll need to consult Google to figure out the
> correct equivalent command.

Going a step further, play around with the variable h and do some basic string
manipulation:

```
>>> h.split()
['hello', 'world']
```

This will give a Python **list**, which is somewhat like an array that can store different
types of objects.

If you need your Swift fix equivalent, then imagine a list is something similar to the
following Swift code:

```
var h: [Any] = []
```

You can verify this by looking up the Python's class type. In the Python REPL, press
the up arrow to bring up the previous command and append the .__class__ call to
the end like so:

```
>>> h.split(" ").__class__
<type 'list'>
```

Note there's two underscores preceding and following the word *class*.

What type of class is the h variable?

```
>>> h.__class__
<type 'str'>
```

That's good to know; a string is called str. You can get help on the str object by
typing the following:

```
>>> help (str)
```

This will dump all the info pertaining to str, which is too much to digest at the
moment.

Exit out of this documentation by typing the q character and narrow your search by looking only for the split function used previously:

```
>>> help (str.split)
```

You'll get some documentation output similar to the following:

```
Help on method_descriptor:

split(self, /, sep=None, maxsplit=-1)
    Return a list of the words in the string, using sep as the
delimiter string.

    sep
        The delimiter according which to split the string.
        None (the default value) means split according to any
whitespace,
        and discard empty strings from the result.
    maxsplit
        Maximum number of splits to do.
        -1 (the default value) means no limit.
```

Reading the above documentation, you can see the first optional argument expects a string, and an optional second argument to indicate the maximum upper limit to split the string.

What do you think will happen when you try to execute the following command? Try your best to figure it out before executing it.

```
>>> h.split(" ", 0)
```

Now to turn your attention towards functions. Python uses indentation to define scope, instead of the braces that many other languages use, including Swift and Objective-C. This is a nice feature of Python, since it forces developers to not be lazy slobs with their code indentation.

Declare a function in the REPL:

```
>>> def test(a):
...
```

You'll get an ellipsis as output, which indicates you have started creating a function. Type two spaces and then enter the following code. If you don't have a consistent indentation, the python function will produce an error.

```
...    print(a + " world!")
```

Press **Enter** again to exit out of the function. Now, test out your newly created `test` function:

```
>>> test("hello")
```

You'll get the expected `hello world!` printed out.

Now that you can "truthfully" put three years of Python experience on your resume, it's time to create an LLDB Python script.

Creating Your First LLDB Python Script

From here on out, you'll be creating all your LLDB Python scripts in the `~/lldb` directory. If you want to have them in a different directory, every time I say `~/lldb`, you'll need to invoke your "mental symlink" to whatever directory you've decided to use.

In Terminal, create the ~/lldb directory:

```
mkdir ~/lldb
```

In your favorite ASCII text editor, create a new file named **helloworld.py** in your newly created `~/lldb` directory. For this particular example, I'll use the my-editor-is-better-neutral-argument, nano.

> **Note**: If you've looked ahead to Appendix B "Python Environment Setup" and have started to or want to start using a more powerful Python IDE than nano, employ another "mental symlink" and start using it now. Even Apple has a symlink for nano that points to `pico` since both text editors are not installed on macOS systems anymore. Throughout this book, if you see any screenshots of Python code, it'll be from VS Code or vim since those are what I use.

```
nano ~/lldb/helloworld.py
```

Add the following code to the file:

```
def your_first_command(debugger, command, result,
  internal_dict):
    print ("hello world!")
```

Make sure you indent the `print ("hello world")` line (ideally with two spaces) or else it won't be included as part of the function!

For now, ignore the parameters passed into the function. Remember when you learned about your `hello_world.c` or `hello_world.java`, and the instructor (or the internet) said to just ignore the params in main for now? Yeah, same thing here. These params are the defined way LLDB interacts with your Python code. You'll explore them in upcoming chapters.

Save the file. If you're using nano, pressing **Control-O** will write to disk.

Create a new tab in Terminal and launch a new LLDB session:

```
lldb
```

This will launch a blank, unattached LLDB session.

In this new LLDB session, import the script you created:

```
(lldb) command script import ~/lldb/helloworld.py
```

If the script is imported successfully, there will be no output.

But how do you execute the command? The only thing the above command did was bring the `helloworld` (yes, named after the file) module's path in as a candidate to use for Python.

If you plan to use any of the code in `helloworld`, you'll need to import the module. This is a similar concept to Swift: you can link a Swift package by adding it to the Swift Package Manager list, but you can't actually use the code until you `import` it into a Swift file. Type the following into LLDB:

```
(lldb) script import helloworld
```

You can verify you've successfully imported the module by dumping all the methods in the `helloworld` python module:

```
(lldb) script dir(helloworld)
```

The `dir` function will dump the contents of the module. If you successfully imported the module, you'll see the following output:

```
['__builtins__', '__cached__', '__doc__', '__file__',
'__loader__', '__name__', '__package__', '__spec__',
'your_first_command']
```

Take note, the function you created earlier: `your_first_command` is listed in the output.

Although the above two commands weren't necessary to set up the command, it does show you how this script bridging works. You imported the `helloworld` module into the Python context of LLDB, but when you execute normal commands, you aren't executing in a Python context (although the command logic underneath could be using Python).

So how do you make your command available only through LLDB, and not through the Python context of LLDB?

Head back to LLDB and type the following:

```
(lldb) command script add -f helloworld.your_first_command yay
```

This adds a command to LLDB, which is implemented in the `helloworld` Python module with the function `your_first_command`. This scripted function is assigned to the LLDB command **yay**.

Execute the yay command now:

```
(lldb) yay
```

Provided everything worked, you'll get the expected `hello world!` output.

Setting Up Commands Efficiently

Once the high of creating a custom function in script bridging has worn off, you'll come to realize you don't want to type this stuff each time you start LLDB. You want those commands to be there ready for you as soon as LLDB starts.

Fortunately, LLDB has a lovely function named **__lldb_init_module**, which is a hook function called as soon as your module loads into LLDB.

This means you can stick your logic for creating the LLDB command in this function, eliminating the need to manually set up your LLDB function every time LLDB starts!

Open the `helloworld.py` class you created and add the following function below `your_first_command`'s definition:

```
def __lldb_init_module(debugger, internal_dict):
    debugger.HandleCommand('command script add -f
helloworld.your_first_command yay')
```

Here you're using a parameter passed into the function named debugger. With this object, an instance of SBDebugger, you're using a method available to it called HandleCommand. Calling debugger.HandleCommand is pretty much equivalent to typing something directly into LLDB.

For example, to get the command po "hello world" from the LLDB console into a script, the equivalent command would be debugger.HandleCommand('po "hello world"')

Remember the python help command you used earlier? You can get help documentation for this command by typing:

```
(lldb) script help(lldb.SBDebugger.HandleCommand)
```

At the time of writing, you'll get a rather disappointing amount of help documentation:

```
HandleCommand(self, command)
   HandleCommand(SBDebugger self, char const * command)
```

This is why there's such a steep learning curve to this stuff, and the reason not many people venture into learning about script bridging. That's why you picked up this book, right?

Save your **helloworld.py** file and open up your ~/.lldbinit file in your favorite editor.

You're now going to specify you want the helloworld module to load at startup every time LLDB loads up.

At the end of the file, add the following line to the end of you r ~/.lldbinit:

```
command script import ~/lldb/helloworld.py
```

Save and close the file.

Open Terminal and start up another tab with LLDB in it like so:

```
lldb
```

Since you specified to have the helloworld module imported into LLDB upon startup, and you also specified to create the yay function as soon as the helloworld python module loads through the __lldb_init_module module, the yay LLDB command will be available immediately to you.

Try it out now:

```
(lldb) yay
```

If everything went well you'll see the following output:

```
hello world!
```

Awesome! You now have a foundation for building some very complex scripts into LLDB. In the following chapters, you'll explore more of how to use this incredibly powerful tool.

For now, close all those Terminal tabs and give yourself a pat on the back.

Key Points

- MacOS and the embedded `lldb` use Python3, which is not Python 2. Be mindful of what version someone is referencing in blog posts and online tutorials.

- Run `lldb` and type `script print(sys.version)` to check which version of Python LLDB is using.

- In Terminal, use `python3 --version` to check which version of Python your system is using by default.

- Python uses whitespace instead of braces to denote different scopes in code.

- In the Python REPL (run `python3` in a terminal) type `help (<whatever>)` to view the online documentation for a keyword or object.

- This book will assume you're putting all of your scripts in a `~/lldb` folder on your system.

- In a `.py` file, create a `__lldb_init_module` function to load your commands into `lldb` sessions automatically.

Where to Go From Here?

If you don't feel comfortable with Python, now is the time to start brushing up on it. If you have past development experience, you'll find Python to be a fun and friendly language to learn. It's a great language for quickly building other tools to help with everyday programming tasks.

Chapter 21: Debugging Script Bridging

You've learned the basics of LLDB's Python script bridging. Now you're about to embark on the frustrating yet exhilarating world of making full LLDB Python scripts.

As you learn about the classes and methods in the Python lldb module, you're bound to make false assumptions or simply type incorrect code. *In short, you're going to screw up.* Depending on the error, sometimes these scripts fail silently, or they may blow up with an angry stderr.

You need a methodical way to figure out what went wrong in your LLDB script so you don't pull your hair out. In this chapter, you'll explore how to inspect your LLDB Python scripts using the Python pdb module, which is used for debugging Python scripts. In addition, you can execute your own "normal" Objective-C, Objective-C++, C, Swift, or even other languages code within **SBDebugger**'s, or **SBCommandReturnObject**'s, **HandleCommand** method.

In fact, there's alternative ways to execute non-Python code that you'll learn about in an upcoming chapter, but for now, you'll stick to **HandleCommand** and see how to manage a build time error, or fix a script that produces an incorrect result.

Although it might not seem like it at first, this is the **most important** chapter in the LLDB Python section, since it will teach you how to explore and debug methods while you're learning this new Python module. I would have (figuratively?) killed for a chapter like this when I was first learning the **Script Bridging** module.

Debugging Your Debugging Scripts With pdb

Included in the Python distribution on your system is a Python module named pdb you can use to set breakpoints in a Python script, just like you do with LLDB itself! In addition, pdb has other essential debugging features that let you step into, out of, and over code to inspect potential areas of interest. If you've decided to set up VS Code or vim with plugins, after finishing this chapter, be sure to explore how they interact with pdb as well. Any fancy IDE you use for Python will include some integration with pdb.

You're going to continue using the **helloworld.py** script in **~/lldb** from the previous chapter. If you haven't read that chapter yet, copy the **helloworld.py** from the **starter** directory into a directory named **lldb** inside your home directory.

Either way, you should now have a file at **~/lldb/helloworld.py**.

Open up **helloworld.py** and navigate to the your_first_command function, replacing it with the following:

```
def your_first_command(debugger, command, result,
internal_dict):
    breakpoint()
    print ("hello world")
```

Note: It's worth pointing out pdb will not work when you're debugging Python scripts in Xcode. The Xcode console window will hang once pdb is tracing a script, so you'll need to do all pdb Python script debugging outside of Xcode.

Save your changes and open a Terminal window and type the following to create a new LLDB session:

```
lldb
```

Next, execute the yay command (which is defined in helloworld.py, remember?) like so:

```
(lldb) yay woot
```

Execution will stop and you'll get output similar to the following:

```
> /Users/wtyree/lldb/helloworld.py(3)your_first_command()
-> print ("hello world")
(Pdb)
```

The LLDB script gave way to pdb. The Python debugger has stopped execution on the print line of code within helloworld.py inside the function your_first_command.

When creating an LLDB command using Python, there are specific parameters expected in the defining Python function. You'll now explore these parameters, namely **debugger**, **command**, and **result**. Since pdb stopped inside of the function, those parameters are currently in scope and are assigned values.

Explore the command argument first, by typing the following into your pdb session:

```
(Pdb) command
```

This dumps out the commands you supplied to your yay custom LLDB command. This always comes in the form of a str, even if you have multiple arguments or integers as input. Since there's no logic to handle any commands, the yay command silently ignores all input. If you typed in yay woot as indicated earlier, only woot would appear as the command.

Next up on the parameter exploration list is the result parameter. Type the following into pdb:

```
(Pdb) result
```

This will dump out something similar to the following:

```
<lldb.SBCommandReturnObject; proxy of <Swig Object of type
'lldb::SBCommandReturnObject *' at 0x110323060> >
```

This is an instance of SBCommandReturnObject, which is a class the lldb module uses to let you indicate if the execution of an LLDB command was successful. In addition, you can append messages to display when your command finishes.

Type the following into pdb:

```
(Pdb) result.AppendMessage("2nd hello world!")
```

This appends a message which LLDB will shown when this command finishes. In this case, once your command finishes executing, it will display 2nd hello world!. However, your script is currently frozen in time thanks to pdb.

As your LLDB scripts get more complicated, the SBCommandReturnObject will come into play, but for simple LLDB scripts, it's not really needed. You'll explore the SBCommandReturnObject command more later in this chapter.

Finally, onto the debugger parameter. Type the following into pdb:

```
(Pdb) debugger
```

This will dump out an object of class SBDebugger, similar to the following:

```
<lldb.SBDebugger; proxy of <Swig Object of type
'lldb::SBDebugger *' at 0x110067180> >
```

You explored this class briefly in the previous chapter to help create the LLDB yay command. You've already learned one of the most useful commands in SBDebugger: HandleCommand.

Resume execution in pdb. Like LLDB, it has logic to handle a c or continue to resume execution.

Type the following into pdb:

```
(Pdb) c
```

You'll get this output:

```
hello world!
2nd hello world!
```

pdb is great when you need to pause execution in a certain spot to figure out what's gone wrong. For example, you could have some complicated setup code, and pause in an area where the logic doesn't seem to be correct.

This is a much more attractive solution than constantly typing script in LLDB to execute one line of Python code at a time.

pdb's Post-Mortem Debugging

Now that you've a basic understanding of the process of debugging your scripts, it's time to throw you into the deep end with an actual LLDB script and see if you can fix it using pdb's post-mortem debugging features.

Depending on the type of error, pdb has an attractive option that lets you explore the problematic stack trace in the event the code you're running threw an exception. This type of debugging methodology will only work if Python threw an exception; this method will *not* work if you receive unexpected output but your code executed without errors.

However, if your code has error handling (and as your scripts get more complex, they really should), you can easily hunt down potential errors while building your scripts.

Find the **starter** folder of the resources for this chapter. Next, copy the findclass.py file over to your default ~/lldb directory. Remember, if you're stubborn and decided to go with a different directory location, you'll need to adjust accordingly.

Don't even look at what this code does yet. It's not going to finish executing as-is, and you'll use pdb to inspect it after you view the error.

Once the script has been copied to the correct directory, open a Terminal window and launch and attach LLDB to any program which contains Objective-C. You could choose a macOS application or something on the iOS Simulator, or maybe even a watchOS application.

For this example, I'll attach to the macOS Photos application, but you're strongly encouraged to attach to a different application. Hey, that's part of being an explorer!

> **Note**: You will need to disable SIP to attach to most processes on your Mac. You will be unable to attach to apps on the simulator that you didn't write. To attach to something you wrote on your iOS simulator, launch the app by tapping on its icon in the simulator, then use pgrep in terminal to search for the PID of the app. Now, attach using the PID. For example, launch the Signals app from section 1 and then type pgrep Signals into terminal to get the PID. Then type lldb -p <the pid> to attach. If you launched Signals using Xcode, then you cannot attach as Xcode will be attached.

Make sure the application is alive and running and attach LLDB to it:

```
lldb -n Photos
```

Once the process has attached, import the new script into LLDB:

```
(lldb) command script import ~/lldb/findclass.py
```

Provided you placed the script in the correct directory, you should get no output. The script will install quietly.

Figure out what this command does by looking at the documentation, since you haven't looked at the source code yet. Type the following into LLDB:

```
(lldb) help findclass
```

You'll get output similar to the following:

```
Syntax: findclass

The `findclass` command will dump all the Objective-C runtime
classes it knows about. Alternatively, if you supply an argument
for it, it will do a case-sensitive search looking only for the
classes that contain the input.

Usage: findclass  # All Classes
Usage: findclass UIViewController # Only classes that contain
UIViewController in name
```

Cool! Let's try this command. Try dumping out all classes the Objective-C runtime knows about.

```
(lldb) findclass
```

You'll get a rather cheeky error assertion similar to the following:

```
Traceback (most recent call last):
  File "/Users/wtyree/lldb/findclass.py", line 40, in findclass
    raise AssertionError("Uhoh... something went wrong, can you
figure it out? :]")
AssertionError: Uhoh... something went wrong, can you figure it
out? :]
```

It's clear the author of this script is horrible at providing decent information into what happened in the AssertionError. Fortunately, it raised an error! You can use pdb to inspect the stack trace at the time the error was thrown.

In LLDB, type the following:

```
(lldb) script import pdb
(lldb) findclass
(lldb) script pdb.pm()
```

This imports pdb into LLDB's Python context, runs findclass again, then asks pdb to perform a "post mortem".

LLDB will change to the pdb interface and jump to the line that threw the error. So, now the script is paused at the very beginning of line 40, just about to execute `raise AssertionError`

```
> /Users/<username>/lldb/findclass.py(71)findclass()
-> raise AssertionError("Uhoh... something went wrong, can you
figure it out? :]")
(Pdb)
```

From here, you can use pdb as your new BFF to help explore what's happening.

Speaking of what's happening, you haven't even looked at the source code yet! Let's change that.

Type the following into pdb:

```
(Pdb) l 32, 83
```

This will list the lines from 32 through to 83 of the `findclass.py` script.

You have the typical function signature which handles the majority of the logic in these commands:

```
def findclass(debugger, command, result, internal_dict):
```

Next up in interesting tidbits is a big long string named **codeString**, which starts its definition on line 49. It's a Python multi-line string, which starts with three quotes and finishes with three quotes on line 66. This string is where the meat of this command's logic lives.

In your pdb session, type the following:

```
(Pdb) codeString
```

You'll get some not-so-pretty output, since dumping a Python string includes all newlines.

```
'\n    @import Foundation;\n    int numClasses;\n    Class *
classes = NULL;\n    classes = NULL;\n    numClasses =
objc_getClassList(NULL, 0);\n    NSMutableString *returnString =
[NSMutableString string];\n    classes = (__unsafe_unretained
Class *)malloc(sizeof(Class) * numClasses);\n    numClasses =
objc_getClassList(classes, numClasses);\n\n    for (int i = 0; i
< numClasses; i++) {\n        Class c = classes[i];\n
[returnString appendFormat:@"%s,", class_getName(c)];\n    }\n
free(classes);\n    \n    returnString;\n    '
```

Let's try that again. Use pdb to print out a pretty version of the codeString variable.

```
(Pdb) print (codeString)
```

Much better!

```
@import Foundation;
int numClasses;
Class * classes = NULL;
classes = NULL;
numClasses = objc_getClassList(NULL, 0);
NSMutableString *returnString = [NSMutableString string];
classes = (__unsafe_unretained Class *)malloc(sizeof(Class) *
numClasses);
numClasses = objc_getClassList(classes, numClasses);

for (int i = 0; i < numClasses; i++) {
  Class c = classes[i];
  [returnString appendFormat:@"%s,", class_getName(c)];
}
free(classes);

returnString;
```

This codeString contains Objective-C code which uses the Objective-C runtime to get all the classes it knows about. The final line of this code, returnString, essentially lets you return the value of returnString back to the Python script. More on that shortly.

Scan for the next interesting part. On line 40, the debugger is currently at a raise call. This is also the line that provided the annoyingly vague message you received from LLDB.

```
68      res = lldb.SBCommandReturnObject()
69      debugger.GetCommandInterpreter().HandleCommand("po " ...
70      if res.GetError():
71 ->       raise AssertionError("Uhoh... something went wron...
72      elif not res.HasResult():
73          raise AssertionError("There's no result. Womp wom...
```

Note the -> on line 71. This indicates where pdb is currently paused.

But wait, res.GetError() looks interesting. Since everything is fair game to explore while pdb has the stack trace, why don't you explore this error to see if you can actually get some useful info out of this?

```
(Pdb) print (res.GetError())
```

There you go! Depending whether you decided to break on a macOS, iOS, watchOS, or tvOS app, you might get a slightly different count of error messages, but the idea is the same.

```
error: warning: got name from symbols: classes
error: 'objc_getClassList' has unknown return type; cast the
call to its declared return type
error: 'objc_getClassList' has unknown return type; cast the
call to its declared return type
error: 'class_getName' has unknown return type; cast the call to
its declared return type
```

The problem here is the code within codeString is causing LLDB some confusion. This sort of error is very common in LLDB. You often need to tell LLDB the return type of a function, because it doesn't know what it is. In this case, both objc_getClassList and class_getName have unknown return types.

A quick check of Apple's docs (https://developer.apple.com/documentation/objectivec/objective-c_runtime) tells us the two problematic methods in question have the following signatures:

```
int objc_getClassList(Class *buffer, int bufferCount);
const char * class_getName(Class cls);
```

All you need to do is cast the return type to the correct value in the codeString code.

Open up ~/lldb/findclass.py and find the following line:

```
numClasses = objc_getClassList(NULL, 0);
```

Replace it with the following:

```
numClasses = (int)objc_getClassList(NULL, 0);
```

This casts the return value from objc_getClassList to an int.

Next find the following:

```
numClasses = objc_getClassList(classes, numClasses);
```

Add the cast to int again, like the following:

```
numClasses = (int)objc_getClassList(classes, numClasses);
```

Finally, find this line:

```
    [returnString appendFormat:@"%s,", class_getName(c)];
```

Add the cast of the return value from class_getName to char *, like so:

```
    [returnString appendFormat:@"%s,", (char *)class_getName(c)];
```

Save your work and jump back to your LLDB Terminal window. You'll still be inside pdb, so press **Control-D** to exit. Next, type the following:

```
(lldb) command script import ~/lldb/findclass.py
```

This will reload the script into LLDB with the new changes in the source code. This is required if you make any changes to the source code and you want to test out the command again without having to restart LLDB.

> **Note**: When you reload, LLDB may complain error: cannot add command: user command exists and force replace not set however, it will still reload the script. A quick check of help command script import notes that "reloading is always allowed", so just be sure to pay attention when you're loading things, this feels like something that will change in future releases.

Try your luck again and dump all of the Objective-C classes available in your process.

```
(lldb) findclass
```

Boom! You'll get a slew of output containing all the Objective-C classes in your program. From your app, from Foundation, from CoreFoundation, and so on. Heh... there's more than you thought there would be, right?

Try limiting your query to something slightly more manageable. Search for all classes containing the word ViewController:

```
(lldb) findclass ViewController
```

Depending on the process you've attached to, you'll get a different amount of classes containing the name ViewController.

When developing commands using the Python script bridging, pdb is a superb tool to keep in your toolbox to help you understand what is happening. It works well for inspecting complicated sections and breaking on problematic areas in your Python script.

How to Handle Problems

As I alluded to in the introduction to this chapter, you're going to run into problems when building these scripts. Let's recap what options you have, depending on the type of problem you encounter when building out these scripts.

Typically, you should perform iterative development on a Python script, save, then reload your script while LLDB is attached to a process and the process is still running.

Python Build Errors

When reloading your script, you might encounter something like this:

```
(lldb) command script import ~/lldb/findclass.py
error: module importing failed: Traceback (most recent call last):
  File "<string>", line 1, in <module>
  File "/Users/wtyree/lldb/findclass.py", line 37
    res = lldb.SBCommandReturnObject()
IndentationError: unexpected indent
(lldb) ▮
```

This is an example of a build error that occurred when I was creating my script. This command will not successfully load since there are Python syntax errors in it. Avoiding these is one of the best reasons to explore a Python IDE instead of just using a text editor.

This is the most straightforward type of problem, because reloading the script will show me the error. I can tell that on line 37, I have unmatched indentation in the findclass Python script.

Python Runtime Errors or Unexpected Values

What if your Python script loads just fine, and you don't get any build errors to the console when reloading — but you receive unexpected output, or your script crashes and you need to further inspect what's happening?

Now, you can use the Python pdb module. When the code isn't crashing, but the output seems wrong, go to your Python script (in this case, **findclass.py**) and add the following line of code right before you expect the problem to occur:

```
breakpoint()
```

Jump over to Terminal (again, pdb will freeze Xcode, so Terminal is your only option for pdb) and attach to a process with LLDB, then try your command again.

From there, execution will eventually freeze and hit your pdb-triggered breakpoint, where you can inspect parameters and step through the flow of execution.

```
● ● ●                        wtyree — lldb — lldb — lldb — 79×23
> /Users/wtyree/lldb/findclass.py(40)findclass()
-> raise AssertionError("Uhoh... something went wrong, can you figure it out? :
]")
(Pdb) print (codeString)

    @import Foundation;
    int numClasses;
    Class * classes = NULL;
    classes = NULL;
    numClasses = (int)objc_getClassList(NULL, 0);
    NSMutableString *returnString = [NSMutableString string];
    classes = (__unsafe_unretained Class *)malloc(sizeof(Class) * numClasses);
    numClasses = (int)objc_getClassList(classes, numClasses);
```

When your code handles errors and raises exceptions, you can import pdb into your LLDB session, run the crashing command again and then use the pdb.pm() command to get back into the code where the exception occurs.

JIT Code Build Errors

Often, you're executing actual code inside the process and then return the value back to your Python script. Again, this will be referred to as *JIT code* throughout the remainder of the book.

Imagine the following: you're executing a long batch of JIT code, and when running the JIT code in a HandleCommand method from the LLDB Python module you get an error saying something is not working.

This is one of the more annoying aspects with working with these scripts, since the debugger won't give you line information along with the error. If you can't uniquely identify where the error could have originated, you'll need to systematically comment out areas of your code until HandleCommand produces no errors for the JIT code.

From there, you can hone in on any locations giving you problems, and fix them.

Key Points

- Add `import pdb; pdb.set_trace()` to set a breakpoint in your Python script.

- For Python scripts that handle errors and throw exceptions, the `script pdb.pm()` command can pause execution just before an exception is thrown.

- When inspecting variables with `pdb` use the `print(<the thing>)` to get nicely formatted output.

- When using `command script import` to reload a Python command script, LLDB might say it didn't realod the script, but it really did.

- Using an IDE that knows Python will help to avoid Python build errors before `command script import`.

Where to Go From Here?

You're now equipped to tackle the toughest debugging problems while making your own custom scripts!

There's a lot more you can do with pdb than what I described here. Check out pdbthe docs for (https://docs.python.org/3.9/library/pdb.html) and read up on the other cool features of pdb. Be sure to remember that the version of pdb must match the version of Python that LLDB is using.

While you're at it, now's the time to start exploring other Python modules to see what other cool features they have. Not only do you have the lldb Python module, but you also have the full power of Python to use when creating advanced debugging scripts.

Chapter 22: Script Bridging Classes & Hierarchy

You've learned the essentials of working with LLDB's Python module, as well as how to correct any errors using Python's pdb debugging module.

Now you'll explore the main players within the lldb Python module for a good overview of the essential classes.

You'll be building a more complex LLDB Python script as you learn about these classes. You'll create a regex breakpoint that only stops after the scope in which the breakpoint hit has finished executing. This is useful when exploring initialization and accessor-type methods, and you want to examine the object that's being returned after the function executes.

In this chapter, you'll learn how to create the functionality behind this script while learning about the major classes within the LLDB module. You'll continue on with this script in the next chapter by exploring how to add optional arguments to tweak the script based on your debugging needs.

The Essential Classes

Within the lldb module, there are several important classes:

- **lldb.SBDebugger**: The "bottleneck" class you'll use to access instances of other classes inside your custom debugging script.

  There will always be one reference to an instance of this class passed in as the debugger function parameter to your script. This class is responsible for handling input commands into LLDB, and can control where and how it displays the output.

- **lldb.SBTarget**: Responsible for the executable being debugged in memory, the debug files, and the physical file for the executable resident on disk.

  In a typical debugging session, you'll use the instance of SBDebugger to get the selected SBTarget. From there, you'll be able to access the majority of other classes through SBTarget.

- **lldb.SBProcess**: Handles memory access (reading/writing) as well as the multiple threads within the process.

- **lldb.SBThread**: Manages the stack frames (SBFrames) within that particular thread, and also manages control logic for stepping.

- **lldb.SBFrame**: Manages local variables (given through debugging information) as well as any registers frozen at that particular frame.

- **lldb.SBModule**: Represents a particular executable. You've learned about modules when exploring dynamic libraries; a module can include the main executable or any dynamically loaded code (like the Foundation framework).

  You can obtain a complete list of the modules loaded into your executable using the image list command.

- **lldb.SBFunction**: This represents a generic function — the code — that is loaded into memory. This class has a one-to-one relationship with the SBFrame class.

Got it? No? Don't worry about it! Once you see how these classes interact with each other, you'll have a better understanding of their place inside your program.

This diagram is a *simplified* version of how the major LLDB Python classes interact with each other.

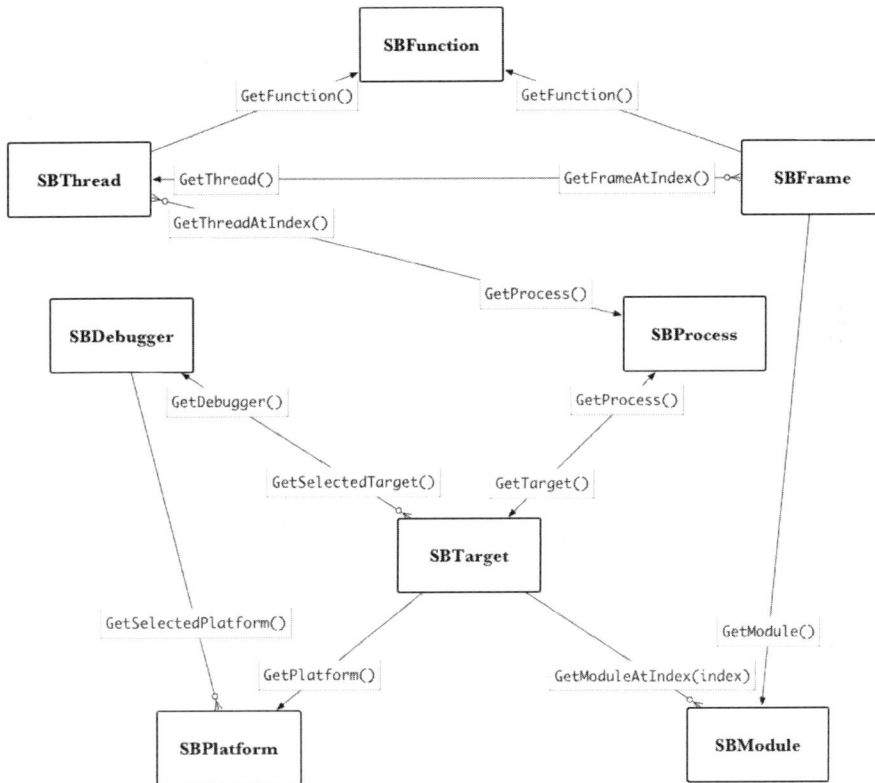

If there's no direct path from one class to another, you can still get to a class by accessing other variables, not shown in the diagram, that point to an instance (or all instances) of a class (many of which are not shown in the diagram).

That being said, the entry-point into the majority of these objects will be through an instance of SBDebugger, passed in as an instance variable called debugger in your scripts. From there, you'll likely go after the SBTarget through GetSelectedTarget() to access all the other instances.

Exploring the lldb Module Through... LLDB

Since you'll be incrementally building a reasonably complex script over the next two chapters, you'll need a way to reload your LLDB script without having to stop, rerun and attach to a process. You'll create an alias for reloading the ~/.lldbinit script while running LLDB.

Append the following to your ~/.lldbinit file:

```
command alias reload_script command source ~/.lldbinit
```

This adds a command called `reload_script` which reloads the ~/.lldbinit file. Now whenever you save your work, you can simply reload the updated contents without having to restart LLDB and the process it's attached to.

In addition, this is a useful command to ensure everything inside your ~/.lldbinit file is still valid. Typically, errors in your ~/.lldbinit will go unnoticed since LLDB doesn't have access to your stderr when it's starting up. However, reloading while LLDB is alive and active will dump any syntax errors in your scripts right to the LLDB console.

While you're building out this new script, you'll create a one-time-use burner project to explore these LLDB Python APIs. To mix things up, you'll create a **tvOS** project this time.

Open Xcode. Select **File ▸ New ▸ Project…** . Choose **tvOS\Single View Application**. Call this new project **Meh** (because I am out of creative names to use!). Make sure the language is set to **Swift**. Then save the project wherever you want.

Once the project has been created, open **ViewController.swift** and add a GUI breakpoint to the beginning of `viewDidLoad()`.

Build, run and wait for the breakpoint to be triggered. Jump over to the LLDB console.

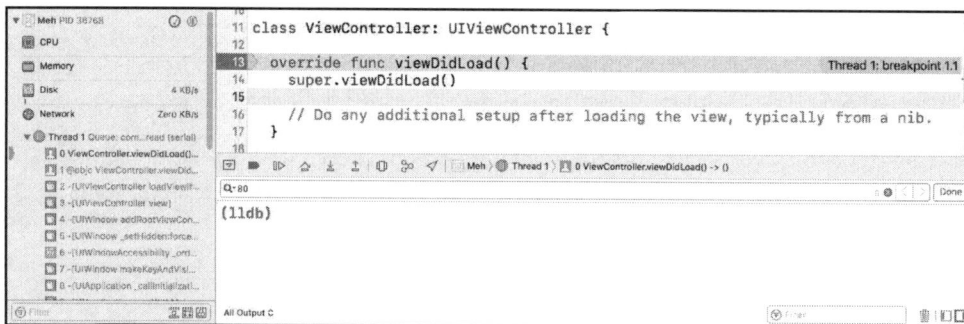

Next, type the following into LLDB:

```
(lldb) script lldb.debugger
```

You'll get output similar to the following:

```
<lldb.SBDebugger; proxy of <Swig Object of type
'lldb::SBDebugger *' at 0x113f2f990> >
```

LLDB has a few easily accessible global variables that map to some of the classes described above:

- `lldb.SBDebugger -> lldb.debugger`

- `lldb.SBTarget -> lldb.target`

- `lldb.SBProcess -> lldb.process`

- `lldb.SBThread -> lldb.thread`

- `lldb.SBFrame -> lldb.frame`

You've just explored the global variable `lldb.debugger`. Now it's time to explore the other variables.

Type the following into LLDB:

```
(lldb) script lldb.target
```

You'll get output similar to the following:

```
<lldb.SBTarget; proxy of <Swig Object of type 'lldb::SBTarget *'
at 0x1142daae0> >
```

This probably doesn't mean much to you at the moment because it's only displaying the instance of the class, and not the context of what it does, nor what it represents.

This is why the `print` command might be more useful when you're starting to explore these classes.

```
(lldb) script print (lldb.target)
```

This will give you some intelligible output to provide some context:

```
Meh
```

Using the `print` command is a useful trick when you want to get a summary of an instance, just as calling po on an object gives you an NSObject's `description` method in Objective-C. If you didn't use the `print` command, you'd have to hone in on properties and attributes of `SBTarget` to figure out the name of the target.

> **Note**: It's fine that you're playing with global Python variables in one-line
> scripts. However, it's important you don't use these global variables in your
> actual Python scripts since you can modify the state (i.e step out of a
> function), and these global variables will not update until your script has
> finished.
>
> The correct way to reference these instances is to start from SBDebugger,
> which is passed into your script function, and drill down to the appropriate
> variable from there.

Go through the remainder of the major global variables and print them out. Start
with the following:

```
(lldb) script print (lldb.process)
```

You'll get the following:

```
SBProcess: pid = 47294, state = stopped, threads = 7, executable
= Meh
```

This printed the process being run. As always, your data might differ (pid, state,
thread etc...).

Next, type the following into LLDB:

```
(lldb) script print (lldb.thread)
```

This time you'll get something similar to the following:

```
thread #1: tid = 0x13a921, 0x000000010fc69ab0
Meh`ViewController.viewDidLoad(self=0x00007fa8c5b015f0) -> () at
ViewController.swift:13, queue = 'com.apple.main-thread', stop
reason = breakpoint 1.1
```

This has printed out the thread that triggered the breakpoint.

Next, try the frame variable:

```
(lldb) script print (lldb.frame)
```

Finally, this one results in the following:

```
frame #0: 0x000000010fc69ab0
Meh`ViewController.viewDidLoad(self=0x00007fa8c5b015f0) -> () at
ViewController.swift:13
```

This will get you the specific frame where the debugger is paused. You could, of course, access other frames in other threads. These global variables are merely convenience getters for you. I would strongly recommend using these global LLDB variables when you're playing with and learning about these classes.

Check out llvm's Python reference (http://lldb.llvm.org/python_reference/index.html) to learn about which methods these classes implement.

Alternatively, you can use Python's help function to get the docstrings for a particular class.

For example, if you were in the Xcode debugging console, and you wanted info on the active SBTarget, you could do this:

```
(lldb) script help(lldb.target)
```

Alternatively, you could go after the actual class instead of the global variable:

```
(lldb) script help(lldb.SBTarget)
```

Don't be afraid to ask for help from the help function. I use it all the time when I'm figuring out my plan of attack through the lldb module.

Learning & Finding Documentation on Script Bridging Classes

Learning this stuff isn't easy. You're faced with the learning curve of the LLDB Python module, as well as learning Python along the way.

The best way to go about learning these foreign APIs is to start in easy, small steps. This means attaching to a process and using the **script** command to explore a class or API. Once you've mastered how to use a certain API, it's fair game to throw it into a custom Python script.

For example, if I stumbled across the SBTarget class and saw the global variable, lldb.target, I would jump to the LLVM documentation (https://lldb.llvm.org/ python_reference/lldb.SBTarget-class.html) and use the LLDB script command while exploring the online documentation.

```
(lldb) script lldb.target
<lldb.SBTarget; proxy of <Swig Object of type 'lldb::SBTarget *' at 0x106324120> >
(lldb) script lldb.target.GetTriple()
'arm64-apple-tvos16.1.0-simulator'
(lldb) b -[UIViewController viewDidLoad]
Breakpoint 2: where = UIKitCore`-[UIViewController viewDidLoad], address = 0x00000001b6ea5378
(lldb) script lldb.target.ResolveLoadAddress(0x00000001b6ea5378)
<lldb.SBAddress; proxy of <Swig Object of type 'lldb::SBAddress *' at 0x1063242a0> >
(lldb) script print(lldb.target.ResolveLoadAddress(0x00000001b6ea5378))
UIKitCore`-[UIViewController viewDidLoad]
(lldb) script print (lldb.target.GetNumBreakpoints())
2
(lldb) script print (lldb.target.DeleteAllBreakpoints())
True
(lldb) script print (lldb.target.GetNumBreakpoints())
0
(lldb) script lldb.target.module['UIKitCore']
<lldb.SBModule; proxy of <Swig Object of type 'lldb::SBModule *' at 0x1061be360> >
(lldb) script print (lldb.target.module['UIKitCore'])
(arm64) /Library/Developer/CoreSimulator/Volumes/tvOS_20K67/Library/Developer/CoreSimulator/Profiles/Runtimes/tvOS
   16.1.simruntime/Contents/Resources/RuntimeRoot/System/Library/PrivateFrameworks/UIKitCore.framework/UIKitCore
(lldb)
```

Easy Reading

I frequently find myself scouring the class documentation to see what the different classes can do for me with their APIs. However, doing that in the LLDB Terminal makes my eyes water. I typically jump to the online documentation because I am a sucker for basic Cascading Style Sheet(s) with more colors than just the background color and text color.

In fact, I do this *so* much, I often use this LLDB command to directly bring up any class I want to explore:

```
command regex gdocumentation 's/(.+)/script import os;
os.system("open https:" + unichr(47) + unichr(47) +
"lldb.llvm.org" + unichr(47) + "python_reference" + unichr(47) +
"lldb.%1-class.html")/'
```

Stick this command in your ~/.**lldbinit** file and then reload the ~/.**lldbinit**. Make sure the above command is only on one line or else this will not work.

This command is called **gdocumentation**; it takes a case-sensitive query and opens up the class of interest in your web browser. For example, if I installed this command into my ~/.**lldbinit** file, and I was attached to a process and wanted to explore the online help documentation for SBTarget, I would type the following into LLDB:

```
(lldb) gdocumentation SBTarget
```

This will direct my web browser to the online documentation of SBTarget. Neat!

Documentation for the More Serious

If you're one of those developers who really, really needs to master LLDB's Python module, or if you have plans to build a commercial product which interacts with LLDB, you'll need to take a more serious approach for digging through the lldb module APIs and documentation.

Since there's no search functionality available on the llvm Python reference (http:// lldb.llvm.org/python_reference/) (at the time of writing), you need a way to easily search all the classes for a particular query. A drastic but excellent suggestion is to copy the entire documentation (http://lldb.llvm.org/python_reference/) site for offline storage using a tool like HTTrack (http://www.httrack.com/). From there, you can search using Terminal commands.

For example, if I scraped the entire site into ~/websites/lldb on my computer and I wanted to search for all classes that had an API that pertained to SBProcess, I would type the following in Terminal:

```
mdfind SBProcess —onlyin ~/websites/lldb
```

It's not a bad idea to also go after the LLDB mailing lists (http://lists.llvm.org/ pipermail/lldb-dev/) and grab that website for offline use. There's are a *ton* of useful hints and explanations given by the authors of LLDB which are buried in the list's archives. However, the LLDB mailing list moved to a new forum site (https:// discourse.llvm.org) a little while back and that *does* have a nice search feature.

One final way to search for content is to use an often overlooked feature of Google to filter queries to a particular website using the **site:** keyword.

For example, if I wanted to search for all occurrences of SBTarget in LLDB's mailing archives, I could use the following two queries with Google:

```
SBTarget site:lists.llvm.org/pipermail/lldb—dev/
SBTarget site:discourse.llvm.org
```

Fortunately, the next couple of chapters will guide you through most of the important classes, so the above suggestions are only meant for the crazy ones out there.

Creating the BreakAfterRegex Command

It's time to create the command you were promised you'd build at the beginning of this chapter!

How would you design a command to stop immediately after a function, print out the return value, then continue? Take a bit of happy thinking time for yourself, and try to figure out how you'd go about creating this script.

I'm serious — stop reading until you've given this an honest attempt. I'll wait.

...

...

...

Good. What did you come up with?

When writing these types of scripts, it's always good practice to envision what you want to achieve, and work your way back from there.

You'll name your command script **BreakAfterRegex.py**. The steps the command needs to take are as follows:

- First, use LLDB to create a regex breakpoint.

- Next, add a breakpoint action to **step-out** of execution (from Chapter 6, "Thread, Frame & Stepping Around") until the current frame has finished executing.

- Finally, you'll use your knowledge of registers from Section II to print out the correct register that holds the return value.

Using your favorite text editor, create **BreakAfterRegex.py** in your **~/lldb** directory.

Once the file is created, open it and add the following:

```python
import lldb

def breakAfterRegex(debugger, command, result, internal_dict):
  print ("yay. basic script setup with input: {}".format(command))

def __lldb_init_module(debugger, internal_dict):
  debugger.HandleCommand('command script add -f BreakAfterRegex.breakAfterRegex bar')
```

You should know what this is doing by now — but in case you forgot, `__lldb_init_module` is a callback function called by LLDB after your script has finished loading into the Python address space.

From there, it references an `SBDebugger` instance passed in as `debugger` to execute the following line of code:

```
command script add -f BreakAfterRegex.breakAfterRegex bar
```

This adds a command named `bar` which is implemented by `breakAfterRegex` within the module `BreakAfterRegex` (named after the file, naturally). If you gave a silly command like `wootwoot` instead of `bar`, your LLDB command would be named that instead.

Open your `~/.lldbinit` file and append the following line:

```
command script import ~/lldb/BreakAfterRegex.py
```

Save the file. Open Xcode, which should still be paused on `viewDidLoad()`. In the LLDB console, reload the script using your newly created convenience command:

```
(lldb) reload_script
```

You'll get a variable amount of output, as LLDB will display all the scripts it's loading. This will reload the contents in your `lldbinit` file and make the `bar` command functional.

Let's try out the `bar` command. In LLDB, type the following:

```
(lldb) bar UIViewController test -a -b
```

The output in your new LLDB script will echo back the parameters you've supplied to it.

You've got the basic skeleton up and working. It's time to write the code to create a breakpoint based upon your input. You'll start with creating input designed solely for handling the regular expression.

Head back to BreakAfterRegex.py and find def breakAfterRegex(debugger, command, result, internal_dict):.

Remove the print statement and replace it with the following logic:

```
def breakAfterRegex(debugger, command, result, internal_dict):
  # 1
  target = debugger.GetSelectedTarget()
  breakpoint = target.BreakpointCreateByRegex(command)

  # 2
  if not breakpoint.IsValid() or breakpoint.num_locations == 0:
    result.AppendWarning(
      "Breakpoint isn't valid or hasn't found any hits.")
  else:
    result.AppendMessage("{}".format(breakpoint))

  # 3
  breakpoint.SetScriptCallbackFunction(
    "BreakAfterRegex.breakpointHandler")
```

Here's what you're doing:

1. Create a breakpoint using the regex input from the supplied parameter. The breakpoint object will be of type SBBreakpoint.

2. If breakpoint creation is unsuccessful, the script will warn you it couldn't find anything to break on. If successful, the breakpoint object is printed out.

3. Finally, the breakpoint is set up so the function breakpointHandler is called whenever the breakpoint hits.

What's an SBBreakpoint? Well, you can look it up through LLDB!

```
(lldb) script help(lldb.SBBreakpoint)
```

If perusing the output in the LLDB console makes your eyes water, a more convenient way to view the documentation can be found here:

https://lldb.llvm.org/python_reference/lldb.SBBreakpoint-class.html.

If you installed the gdocumentation command mentioned earlier, you can simply type the following instead:

```
(lldb) gdocumentation SBBreakpoint
```

Grabbing the first line of the help documentation indicates an SBBreakpoint class represents a logical breakpoint and its associated settings.

OK — back on the main road after that little sightseeing trip. Where were we? Oh right — you haven't created the handler function that will be called when the breakpoint is hit. You'll do that now.

Right below breakAfterRegex, add the following function:

```
def breakpointHandler(frame, bp_loc, dict):
    function_name = frame.GetFunctionName()
    print("stopped in: {}".format(function_name))
    return True
```

This function is called whenever any of the breakpoints you created using your new command are hit, and will then print out the function name. Notice the return of True at the end of the function. Returning True will result in your program stopping execution. Returning False, or even omitting a return statement will result in the program continuing to run after this method executes.

This is a subtle but important point. When creating callback functions for breakpoints (i.e. the breakpointHandler function you just created), you have a different method signature to implement. This consists of a SBFrame, SBBreakpointLocation, and a Python dictionary.

The SBFrame represents the frame you've stopped in. SBBreakpointLocation is an instance of one of your breakpoints found in SBBreakpoint. This makes sense, since you could have many hits for one breakpoint, especially if you try to break on a frequently implemented function, such as main, or if you use a well-matched regular expression.

Here's another diagram that showcases the simplified interaction of classes when you've stopped on a particular function:

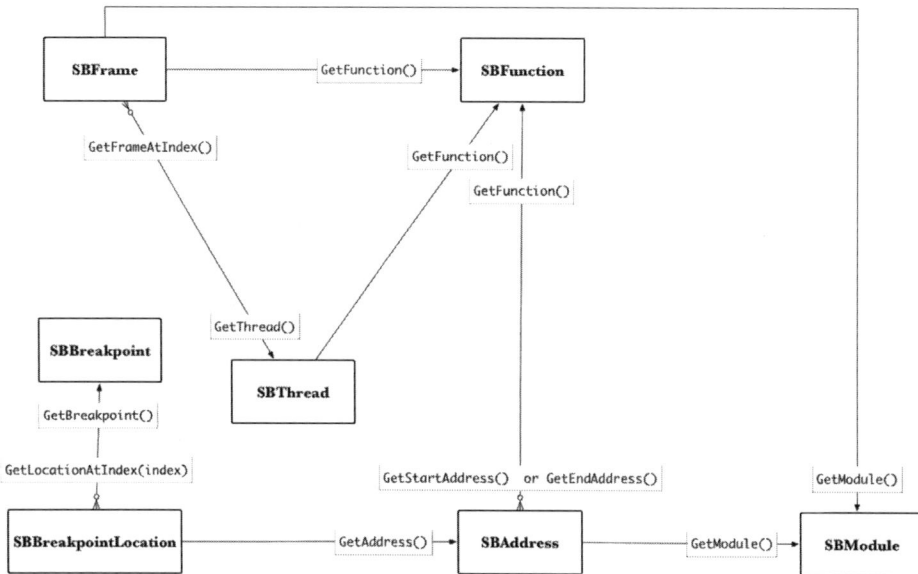

As you (might have?) noticed, SBFrame, and SBBreakpointLocation are your lifelines to the majority of important lldb classes while in your breakpoint callback function. Using the previous diagram, you can get to all the major class instances through SBFrame or through SBFrame's reference to SBModule.

Remember, you should never use lldb.frame or other global variables inside your scripts since they could hold a stale state while being executed in a script, so you must traverse the variables starting with the frame, or bc_loc to get to the instance of the class you want.

If you accidentally make a typo, or don't understand some code, simply insert a breakpoint in the script using the Python pdb module and work your way back from there. You learned about the pdb module in Chapter 21, "Debugging Script Bridging".

This script is starting to get complicated — looks like a good time to reload and test it out. Open the Xcode console window and reload your script:

```
(lldb) reload_script
```

Go through the motions of executing some commands again to test it out:

```
(lldb) bar
somereallylongmethodthatapplehopefullydidntwritesomewhere
```

You'll get output similar to the following:

```
warning: Breakpoint isn't valid or hasn't found any hits
```

OK, good. Time to try out an actual breakpoint. Let's go after a rather frequently executed method.

In the LLDB console type:

```
(lldb) bar NSObject.init\]
```

You'll see something similar to the following:

```
SBBreakpoint: id = 3, regex = 'NSObject.init\]', locations = 2
```

If you get about a million locations, look to see if auto-complete "helped" you and added an extra bracket so that you actually typed [NSObject.init\]. Thanks auto-complete.

Continue execution and use the Simulator remote to click around the tvOS Simulator to trigger the breakpoint. If you're having trouble tripping the breakpoint, one surefire way is to navigate to the simulator's home screen. From the Simulator, **Device ▸ Home** or press **Command-Shift-H**.

Cool. You've successfully added a command to create a regex breakpoint! That's pretty darn neat-o.

Right now, you've stopped on one of NSObject's init methods, which could be a class or an instance method. This is very likely a subclass of NSObject. You'll manually replicate the actions you're about to implement in the Python script using LLDB.

Using the LLDB console, finish executing this method:

```
(lldb) finish
```

Remember your register calling conventions? Since you're working on the tvOS Simulator and this architecture might be arm64 or x64, you'll want to use the **ARG1** register that LLDB maps to either x0 or rax. Print out the return value of NSObject's init in LLDB.

```
(lldb) po $arg1
```

Depending on where and how you were playing with the Simulator, you'll see a different object. I received the following output:

```
<_CFXNotificationNameWildcardObjectRegistration: 0x61000006e8c0>
```

Stepping out and printing is the exact logic you'll implement now in your custom script callback function.

Open **BreakAfterRegex.py** and revisit the **breakpointHandler** function. Modify it to look like the following:

```python
def breakpointHandler(frame, bp_loc, dict):
  # 1
  '''The function called when the regular
  expression breakpoint gets triggered
  '''

  # 2
  thread = frame.GetThread()
  process = thread.GetProcess()
  debugger = process.GetTarget().GetDebugger()

  # 3
  function_name = frame.GetFunctionName()

  # 4
  debugger.SetAsync(False)

  # 5
  thread.StepOut()

  # 6
```

```
    output = evaluateReturnedObject(debugger,
                                    thread,
                                    function_name)
  if output is not None:
    print(output)

  return False
```

B-B-B-B-B-Breakdown time!

1. Yep, if you're building a full-on Python command script, you've got to add some docstrings. You'll thank yourself later. Trust me.

2. You're climbing the hierarchical reference chain to grab the instance of SBDebugger and SBThread. Your starting point is through SBFrame.

3. This grabs the name of the parent function. Since you're about to step out of this current SBFrame, it's about to get invalidated, so grab any stack references you can before the stepping-out occurs.

4. SetAsync is an interesting function to use when tampering with control flow while scripting in a program. The debugger will run asynchronously while executing the program, so you need to tell it to synchronously wait until stepOut completes its execution before handing control back to the Python script.

   A good programmer will clean up the state to the async's previous value, but that becomes a little complicated, as you could run into threading issues when this callback function triggers if multiple breakpoints were to hit this callback function. This is not a noticeable setting change when you're debugging, so it's fine to leave it off.

5. You then step out of the method. After this line executes, you'll no longer be in the frame you previously stopped in.

6. You're calling a soon-to-be implemented method **evaluateReturnedObject** that takes the appropriate information and generates an output message. This message will contain the frame you've stopped in, the return object, and the frame the breakpoint stepped out to.

You're all done with that Python function! Now you need to implement evaluateReturnedObject. Add it below the previous function you just wrote:

```python
def evaluateReturnedObject(debugger, thread, function_name):
    '''Grabs the reference from the return register
    and returns a string from the evaluated value.
    TODO ObjC only
    '''

    # 1
    res = lldb.SBCommandReturnObject()

    # 2
    interpreter = debugger.GetCommandInterpreter()
    target = debugger.GetSelectedTarget()
    frame = thread.GetSelectedFrame()
    parent_function_name = frame.GetFunctionName()

    # 3
    expression = 'expression -lobjc -O -- $arg1'


    # 4
    interpreter.HandleCommand(expression, res)

    # 5
    if res.HasResult():
        # 6
        output = '{}\nbreakpoint: '\
            '{}\nobject: {}\nstopped: {}'.format(
                '*' * 80,
                function_name,
                res.GetOutput().replace('\n', ''),
                parent_function_name)
        return output
    else:
        # 7
        return None
```

Here's what that does:

1. You first instantiate a new **SBCommandReturnObject**. You've seen this class already in your primary functions as the `result` parameter. However, you're creating your own here because you'll use this instance to evaluate and modify an expression. A typical `po "something"` will produce output, including two newlines, straight to the console. You need to grab this output before it goes to the console and remove those newlines... because you're fancy like that. In Chapter 24, "Script Bridging With SBValue & Memory", you'll explore a cleaner alternative to evaluating code and obtaining output, but for now you'll make do with your existing knowledge of the SBCommandReturnObject class.

2. You grab a few variables for use later on.

3. Here you create the expression to be executed that prints out the return value using the virtual register that LLDB creates.

    This is required because you can't know if this script is running on a watchOS, iOS, tvOS, or macOS device, so you'll need to let LLDB decide which register. Remember, you also need to use the Objective-C context, since Swift hides the registers from you.

4. Finally, you execute the expression through the debugger's command interpreter, **SBCommandInterpreter**. This class interprets your commands but allows you to control where the output goes, instead of immediately piping it to stderr or stdout.

5. Once HandleCommand has executed, the output of the expression should now reside in the SBCommandReturnObject instance. However, it's good practice to ensure the return object actually has any output to give to you.

6. If everything worked correctly, you format the old, stepped-out function along with the object and currently stopped function into a string and return that.

7. However, if there was no input to print from the SBCommandReturnObject, you return None.

You've done it! Save your work, jump back to Xcode and reload the script with your trusty reload_script command in the LLDB command line.

Next, before you get started with the full-blown command, remove all previous breakpoints like so:

```
(lldb) br del
About to delete all breakpoints, do you want to do that?: [Y/n]
```

```
Y
All breakpoints removed. (1 breakpoint)
```

It's time to take this beauty for a spin!

Type the following into LLDB:

```
(lldb) bar NSObject.init\]
```

This time your script will execute your completed command's script when it hits the breakpoint.

Do whatever you need to do through the tvOS Simulator to trigger the init breakpoint; closing the application will work by pressing **Command-Shift-H**, as will bringing up the Apple TV Remote (found in the **Window** menu) and tapping on the remote.

Once hit, you'll get some beautiful output which showcases the method you've stopped on (in this case –[NSObject init]), the object that is being created, and the calling method as well.

Since you've created a breakpoint on a frequently-called method, you'll soon hit the same breakpoint again.

This is a fun tool to have at your disposal. You could, for instance, create a well-crafted regex breakpoint to trigger each time an NSURL is created within any application... owned by you or not. For example, you could try:

```
(lldb) bar NSURL(\(\w+\))?\ init
```

The "weird" syntax is needed because a lot of the initialization methods for NSURL are in categories. Alternatively, you could use this script on a problematic getter method of a Core Data object that is returning unusual values.

Key Points

- Use `lldb.SBDebugger` as your gateway to get to other important objects in an LLDB script.

- You can use the `GetSelectedTarget()` method on `lldb.SBDebugger` to get the `lldb.SBTarget` which is the code being executed and debugged.

- The `lldb.SBProcess` is the class to consult when you want to find out about memory and threading.

- Stack frames and stepping logic comes from the `lldb.SBThread` class.

- The `lldb.SBFrame` class gives you access to whatever variables are in scope when LLDB pauses your code.

- The `lldb.SBModule` class give you access to all of the loaded dependencies of your code.

- Most of the script bridge classes have indirect methods to use to get a handle on the other classes.

- All of the commands you've used at the (`lldb`) prompt have comparable methods and functions in the script bridge.

- Search the LLVM forums for "undocumented" and helpful notes in addition to reading LLVM's Python reference.

- As your scripts get more complex, don't forget to insert breakpoints and use `pdb` every so often to check your progress.

Where to Go From Here?

You've begun your quest to create Python LLDB scripts of real-world complexity. In the next chapter, you'll take this script even further and add some cool options to customize this script.

But for now, have fun and play around with this `bar` script! Attach LLDB to some applications running in the simulator and play around with the command. Try the already mentioned `NSURL` initialization, or `NSURLRequest` initialization, breakpoints.

Once you get bored of that, see what objects are using Core Data by inspecting the return value of `-[NSManagedObject valueForKey:]` or check out all the items being created from a nib or storyboard by breaking on an `initWithCoder:` method.

Chapter 23: Script Bridging With Options & Arguments

When you're creating a custom debugging command, you'll often want to slightly tweak functionality based upon options or arguments supplied to your command. A custom LLDB command that can do a job only one way is a boring one-trick pony.

In this chapter, you'll explore how to pass optional parameters (a.k.a. options) as well as arguments (parameters which are *expected*) to your custom command to alter functionality or logic in your custom LLDB scripts.

You'll continue working with the **bar**, "break-after-regex", command you created in the previous chapter. In this chapter, you'll finish up the bar command by adding logic to handle options in your script.

By the end of this chapter, the bar command will have logic to handle the following optional parameters:

- **Non-regular expression search**: Using the **-n** or **--non_regex** option will result in the bar command using a non-regular expression breakpoint search instead. This option will *not* take any additional parameters.

- **Filter by module**: Using the **-m** or **--module** option will only search for breakpoints in that particular module. This option will expect an additional parameter which specifies the name of the module.

This will be a dense but fun chapter. Make sure you've got a good supply of caffeine!

Setting Up

If you've gone through the previous chapter and your `bar` command is working, then you can continue using that script and ignore this part. Otherwise, head on over to the **starter** folder in this chapter's resources, and copy the **BreakAfterRegex.py** file into your **~/lldb** folder. Make sure your **~/.lldbinit** file has the following line which you should have from the previous chapter:

```
command script import ~/lldb/BreakAfterRegex.py
```

If you've any doubts if this command loaded successfully into LLDB, simply fire up a new LLDB instance in Terminal:

```
lldb
```

Then check for the help docstring of the `bar` command:

```
(lldb) help bar
```

```
● ● ●                        wtyree — lldb — lldb — lldb — 80×24
Last login: Mon Apr 10 13:00:51 on ttys002
→  ~ lldb
(lldb) help bar
For more information run 'help bar'  Expects 'raw' input (see 'help raw-input'.)

Syntax: bar
(lldb)
```

If you get an error, it's not successfully loaded. However, even if it is loaded, you don't get some very useful help. You'll fix that now. Remember earlier in the book, you added –h and –H flag to add some help string. Another way to add help text is using a **docstring**. Add this in **BreakAfterRegex.py** right after the line that reads `def breakAfterRegex(debugger, command, result, internal_dict):` but before the first line of code:

```
'''Creates a regular expression breakpoint and adds it.
   Once the breakpoint is hit, control will step out of the
current
   function and print the return value. Useful for stopping on
   getter/accessor/initialization methods
   '''
```

Now, save your work and restart `lldb` and run `help bar` again. You should see your nice, more robust help text now.

The RWDevCon Project

For this chapter, you'll use an app called **RWDevcon**.

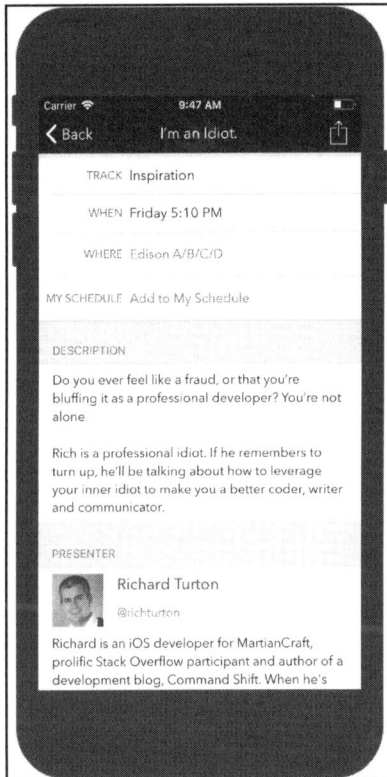

This app was the companion app for the RWDevCon conference (https://www.rwdevcon.com/) a few years ago.

For this project, I've forked from commit 84167c68 which can be found in the **starter** folder. However, you can get a more up-to-date, though still somewhat ancient, version on GitHub (https://github.com/kodecocodes/RWDevCon-App).

Navigate to the **starter** folder then open, build, then run this application. Take a look around to get acquainted with the project.

There's no need to explore any of the source code. With the aid of the bar command, you'll be able to explore different items of interest with smart breakpoint queries.

But before we can do that, let's talk about how to make this bar command much more powerful.

The optparse Python Module

The lovely thing about LLDB Python scripts is you have all the power of Python — and its modules — at your disposal.

There are three notable modules that ship with Python that are worth looking into when parsing options and arguments: **getopt**, **optparse**, and **argparse**.

getopt is kind of low level and optparse is on its way out since it's been deprecated after Python 2.7. Unfortunately argparse is mostly designed to work with Python's sys.argv — which is not available to your Python LLDB command scripts directly. This means optparse will be your go-to option. Facebook's Chisel, Apple's own custom LLDB scripts, and I all use this module. So, it's kinda the de-facto standard for parsing arguments. ;]

The optparse module will let you define an instance of type **OptionParser**, a class responsible for parsing all your arguments. For this class to work, you need to declare what arguments and options your command supports. This makes sense because optional parameters may or may not take additional values for that particular option.

Take a brief look at an example. Consider the following:

```
some_command woot -b 34 -a "hello world"
```

The command is named some_command. But what are the arguments and options being passed into this command?

If you didn't give any context to the parser, then this statement is ambiguous. The parser doesn't know whether or not the –b or –a option should take in parameters for the option. For example, the parser could think this command is passed three arguments: ['woot', '34', 'hello world'], and two options –b, –a with no parameters. However, if the parser expected –b and –a to take parameters, the parser would give you the argument of ['woot'], '34' for the –b option and 'hello world' for –a.

Let's dive into optparse some more, and see how we can use it to handle cases like this.

Adding Options Without Params

With the knowledge you need to educate your parser with what arguments are expected, it's time to add your first option which will alter the functionality of the bar command to apply the SBBreakpoint without using a regular expression, but instead use a normal expression.

This argument will be backed by a Python boolean value, so no parameters are needed for this option. The existence (or lack thereof) of this option is all the information you need to determine the boolean value. If the argument exists, then it'll be True. Otherwise, False.

It's worth noting some script authors will engineer an option that will encourage a boolean option which explicitly requires a parameter for the Boolean value and default to either True or False if the option is not supplied.

For example, the following command takes an option, **-f** with no parameters:

```
some_command -f
```

This would then turn into:

```
some_command -f true
```

That's not really my style. But you might want to consider this design decision if you're building scripts for a wider audience, since it gives the user more explicit intentions.

OK, enough chit-chat. Let's get to implementing this parser thing.

Open up **BreakAfterRegex.py** and add the following import statements at the top of the file either after or before the import lldb line:

```
import optparse
import shlex
```

The **optparse** module was just covered previously, it contains the OptionParser class to parse any extra input given to your command.

The **shlex** module has a nice little Python function that conveniently splits up the arguments supplied to your command on your behalf while keeping string arguments intact. It acts in the same way as a shell does, like bash or zsh.

For example, consider the following Python code:

```
import shlex
command = '"hello world" "2nd parameter" 34'
shlex.split(command)
```

This will produce the following output:

```
['hello world', '2nd parameter', '34']
```

This returns a Python list of parsed Python strs.

If you had split this by spaces, then you would have "hello and world" as the first two items in the list. This is clearly not what was intended. This shows the power of shlex.

But before you go using this split method, you'll need to create the parser itself. Head to the very bottom of **BreakAfterRegex.py** and add the following method:

```
def generateOptionParser():
    '''Gets the return register as a string for lldb
    based upon the hardware
    '''
    usage = "usage: %prog [options] breakpoint_query\n" +\
            "Use 'bar -h' for option desc"
    # 1
    parser = optparse.OptionParser(usage=usage, prog='bar')
    # 2
    parser.add_option("-n", "--non_regex",
                      # 3
                      action="store_true",
                      # 4
                      default=False,
                      # 5
                      dest="non_regex",
                      # 6
                      help="Use a non-regex breakpoint instead")
    # 7
    return parser
```

Let's break this down, parameter by parameter:

1. You're creating the `OptionParser` instance and supplying it a **usage** param and a **prog** param. The usage will get displayed if you screw up and give the parser an argument it doesn't know how to handle. The `prog` option is used to address the name of the program. I always incorporate it because it resolves a weird little issue which lets you run the –h or ––help option to get all the supported options for a custom command. If the `prog` arg is not in there, the –h command will not work correctly. It's one of life's little mysteries. :]

2. This line (followed by the next four lines of non-commented code) add the ––**non_regex** or –**n** parameter to the `parser`.

3. The **action** param describes what action should be done when this param is supplied. `"store_true"` informs the parser to store the Python Boolean `True` when this option is supplied.

4. The **default** param indicates that the initial value will be `False`. If this option is not given, this will be the value.

5. The **dest** parameter will determine the name, **non_regex**, that you're giving to the property when the `OptionParser` parses your input.

As you'll see shortly, the `parse_args` method produces a Python tuple containing a list of options (called `options`) and a list of arguments (called `args`). The `options` variable will now contain the `non_regex` property.

6. **help** will give you help documentation. You can get all the parameters and their info with the ––help option. For example, when this is correctly set up in the `bar` command, all you have to do is type `bar –h` to see a list of all the options and what they do.

7. Once you've created the `OptionParser` and added the –n option, you're returning the instance of the `OptionParser`.

You've just created a method that will generate this `OptionParser` instance you need to start parsing those arguments. Now it's time to use this thing.

Jump back to the beginning of the breakAfterRegex function. Remove the following two lines:

```
target = debugger.GetSelectedTarget()
breakpoint = target.BreakpointCreateByRegex(command)
```

Then, in their place, add the following code:

```
# 1
command = command.replace('\\', '\\\\')
# 2
command_args = shlex.split(command, posix=False)

# 3
parser = generateOptionParser()

# 4
try:
  # 5
  (options, args) = parser.parse_args(command_args)
except:
  result.SetError(parser.usage)
  return

target = debugger.GetSelectedTarget()

# 6
clean_command = shlex.split(args[0])[0]

# 7
if options.non_regex:
  breakpoint = target.BreakpointCreateByName(
                    clean_command)
else:
  breakpoint = target.BreakpointCreateByRegex(
                    clean_command)

# The rest remains unchanged
```

Make sure you have your indentation correct! This should be indented by two spaces, or whatever your single-tab width of choice is, as it's all part of the function.

Here's what that code does:

1. When parsing your input to the `OptionParser`, it will interpret slashes as escaping characters. For example, "\'" is interpreted as just "'". This means you'll need to escape any backslash characters in your commands.

2. As you learned in a previous chapter, the `command` parameter passed into your custom LLDB scripts is a Python `str`, which contains all input that is passed into your argument. You'll pass this variable into the `shlex.split` method to obtain a Python `list` of Python `str`s. In addition, there's that `posix=False` which helps combat any input which contains special characters like a dash; otherwise, `OptionParser` will incorrectly assume that's an option being passed in. This is important because Objective-C has dashes in instance methods, so you don't want the dash to be incorrectly interpreted as an option!

3. Using the newly created `generateOptionParser` function, you create a parser to handle the command's input.

4. Parsing input can be error-prone. Python's usual approach to error handling is throwing exceptions. It's no surprise that `optparse` throws if it finds an error. If you don't catch exceptions in your scripts, LLDB will go down, which will also tank the process! Therefore, the parsing is contained in a try-except block to prevent LLDB from dying due to bad input.

5. The `OptionParser` class has a **parse_args** method. You're passing in your `command_args` variable to this method, and will receive a tuple in return. This tuple consists of two values: **options**, which consists of all option arguments, which is only the `non_regex` option right now. The other half of the tuple contains all of the **args** which consists of any other input parsed by the parser.

6. You're taking the first captured argument (the breakpoint query) and assigning it to a variable called **clean_command**. Remember that `posix=False` mentioned in bullet 2? That logic will maintain the quotes around your captured argument which preserves your exact syntax. If you didn't have that `posix=False`, you could just use `args[0]`, but then you'd forfeit a lot of power in your regex by not being able to use the escape backslash character in your regex query.

7. You're putting your first option to use! You're checking the truthiness of `options.non_regex`. If `True`, you'll execute the `BreakpointCreateByName` method in `SBTarget` to implement a non-regular expression breakpoint. If the `non_regex` is `False`, then your script will use a regex search. Again, all you need to do is add the `-n` to your input for the `bar` command to make the `non_regex` `True`.

Testing Out Your First Option

Enough code. Time to test this script out.

Instead of using that **reload_script** command you've used in the previous chapters, try an alternative tactic that you might appreciate to reload the script.

Jump to Xcode and create a new symbolic breakpoint.

Make sure the **Breakpoint Navigator** tab is selected, then hunt down that lonely + icon in the lower left corner. Then select **Symbolic breakpoint....** Alternatively for you cool kids, press *Command-Control-**

In the **Symbol** section type **getenv**.

Add **two actions**. The first action adds the following command:

```
br dis 1
```

Click the + icon to add a second action. In this action, add your bar command:

```
bar -n "-[NSUserDefaults(NSUserDefaults) objectForKey:]"
```

Finally select **Automatically continue after evaluating actions**.

When all is said and done, your symbolic breakpoint should look like the following:

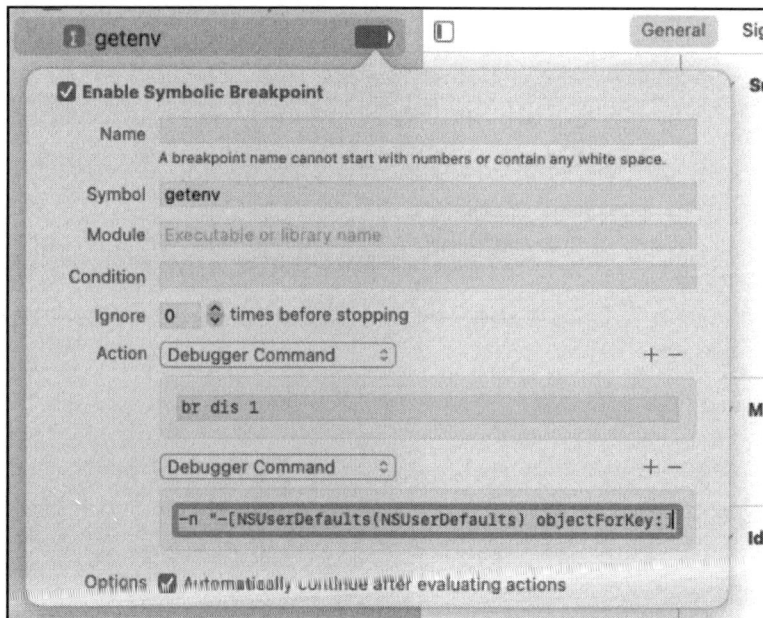

Can you figure out what you've just done? You've created a symbolic breakpoint on the getenv C function. If I want to setup breakpoints or run some scripts before "my" code starts executing, or before reverse engineering an app, this is a good go-to to hook any logic for custom commands you want in LLDB.

I'm not a fan of setting breakpoints like this in main, since a lot of executables contain the function main, and the primary executable's main symbol might be stripped in a production build of an executable. We know that getenv will get hit for sure and will get hit before my code starts running.

What about those actions? The first action says to get rid of that getenv breakpoint. You're not deleting it; you're just disabling it. This is ideal since getenv gets called a fair bit and you need to get rid of this breakpoint once you've setup your LLDB logic. The use of **1** is mentioned because this breakpoint is the first breakpoint created for this session, which disables this symbolic breakpoint after it has run once.

After that, you're creating a non regular expression breakpoint on NSUSerDefaults's objectForKey: method. We expect this method to return an id or nil, so let's see what this RWDevCon app is reading (or writing) to our NSUserDefaults.

Build and run the application.

If you haven't taken a deep dive into the app, you'll likely get a lot of nil values. This means that this method is definitely getting read by some code in this app. Keep clicking the resume button in Xcode or type c or continue into the (lldb) console until you finally get to the main view for the app.

Tap on any one of the workshops to bring up the detail view controller. Keep resuming the app until the detail view appears.

Before you continue, clear the LLDB window by pressing **Command-K**.

From there, tap **Add to my Schedule** while keeping an eye on the console output.

Resume the app a few more times until you can see there's an object that gets added to the NSUserDefaults that matches the When time.

Adding Options With Params

You've learned how to add an option that expects no arguments. You'll now add another option that expects a parameter. This next option will be the **--module** option to specify which module you want to constrain your regular expression query to.

This is very similar to breakpoint set's -s or --shlib option where it expects the name of the module immediately after the option. You explored this back in Chapter 4, "Stopping in Code."

In the **BreakAfterRegex.py** script jump back down to the generateOptionParser function and add the following code right before return parser:

```
    # 1
    parser.add_option("-m", "--module",
                      # 2
                      action="store",
                      # 3
                      default=None,
                      # 4
                      dest="module",
                      help="Filter a breakpoint by only searching
within a specified Module")
```

1. You're adding a new option –m or ––module to the OptionParser instance.

2. In the previous option, the action was "store_true"; this time it is "store". This means this option expects a parameter.

3. This parameter's default value is None.

4. The name of this property will be **module**.

Jump back to the **breakAfterRegex** function and scan for the following lines:

```
if options.non_regex:
    breakpoint = target.BreakpointCreateByName(clean_command)
else:
    breakpoint = target.BreakpointCreateByRegex(clean_command)
```

Add **options.module** as the second parameter to both of these functions.

```
if options.non_regex:
    breakpoint = target.BreakpointCreateByName(clean_command,
options.module)
else:
    breakpoint = target.BreakpointCreateByRegex(clean_command,
options.module)
```

So how does this work? Let's print out the method signature right now for **BreakpointCreateByRegex**. Type the following in LLDB:

```
(lldb) script help (lldb.SBTarget.BreakpointCreateByRegex)
```

This will dump the small amount of documentation for this function. Although there is no help documentation for this method, it does give you a list of its method signatures.

```
(lldb) script help (lldb.SBTarget.BreakpointCreateByRegex)
Help on method BreakpointCreateByRegex in module lldb:

BreakpointCreateByRegex(self, *args) unbound lldb.SBTarget method
    BreakpointCreateByRegex(self, str symbol_name_regex, str module_name = None) ->
SBBreakpoint
    BreakpointCreateByRegex(self, str symbol_name_regex) -> SBBreakpoint
    BreakpointCreateByRegex(self, str symbol_name_regex, LanguageType symbol_language,
        SBFileSpecList module_list, SBFileSpecList comp_unit_list) -> SBBreakpoint

(lldb) |
```

The following signature is worth discussing:

```
BreakpointCreateByRegex(SBTarget self, str symbol_name_regex,
str module_name=None) -> SBBreakpoint
```

Take note of the final parameter: module_name=None. The fact it's an optional parameter means if you don't supply a parameter, the module_name will take the value as None. This means when the OptionParser instance parses the options, you can supply options.module into the BreakpointCreateByRegex method regardless, since the default value of options.module will be None, which is the same as not applying an extra argument.

Time to test this out. Save your work in your script. Jump over to Xcode and modify that getenv Symbolic breakpoint. Replace the second action with the following line of code:

```
bar @objc.*.init —m RWDevCon
```

Make sure that 'C' in 'Con' is capitalized! Also, remember that first action br dis 1? It's disabling the breakpoint every time, so don't forget to check the box in the top left corner to "Enable Symbolic Breakpoint". There aren't any references to −NSUserDefaults(NSUserDefaults) objectForKey:] in the RWDevCon module, so we'll need to experiment with a different breakpoint.

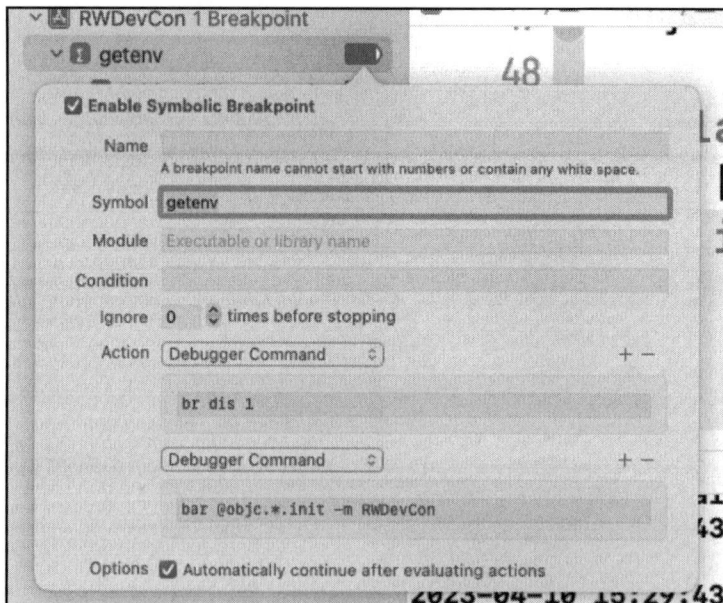

This will create a regex breakpoint on all Objective-C objects that are subclassed by a Swift object and stick a breakpoint on their initializer. You are filtering this breakpoint query to only search for breakpoints inside the **RWDevCon** module.

Run the application and check out all the Objective-C objects that are subclassed by Swift objects.

Take a quick look at the output. Keep resuming the app as it works through all of the classes before displaying the main view. You'll get a lot of __ObjC.NSEntityDescription hits. That must mean there's some CoreData logic that's written in Swift, right?

Right!

Keep resuming the app as it starts loading the Session objects from the CoreData store. Notice that the last frame in the stack trace that is Swift is pretty far down the list, 22 in the screenshot. Now pick out any of the Session objects that you like.

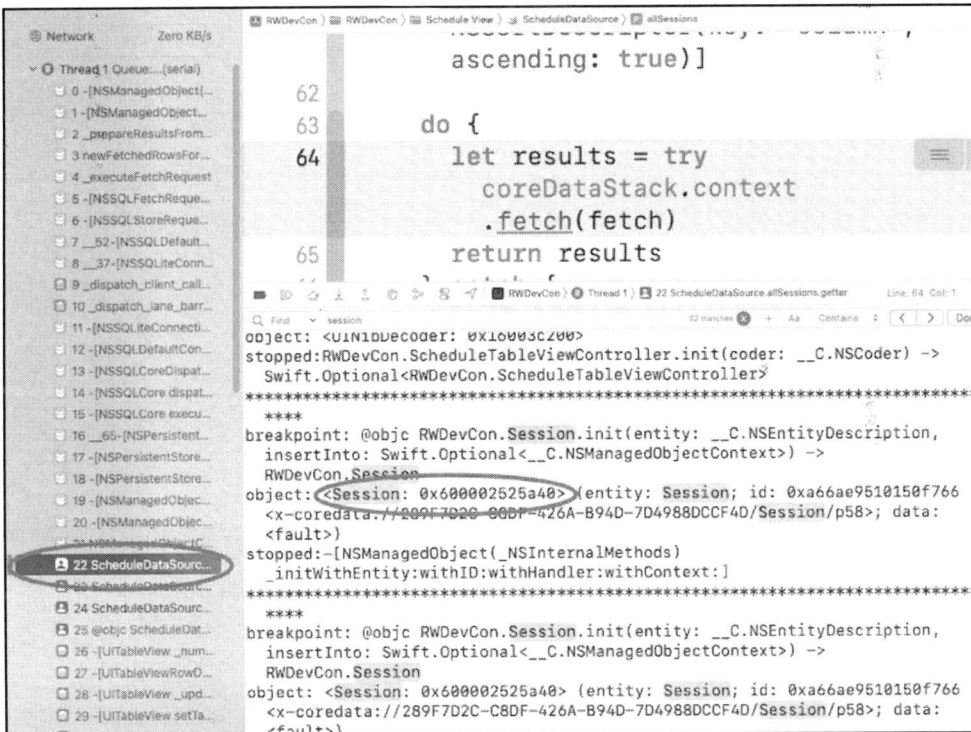

Copy the address into your clipboard.

Before you paste in your address to a command, let's dump all the methods implemented by this Session class. Since it's an Objective-C subclass, it's fair game to all those introspection commands you've made earlier.

In LLDB type the following:

```
(lldb) methods Session
```

If you didn't create the `methods` command in an earlier chapter, recall it's just using the private `_shortMethodDescription` introspection helper method. You can type out the whole thing:

```
(lldb) expression -lobjc -O -- [Session _shortMethodDescription]
```

This will dump all the methods the **Session** class implements that the Objective-C runtime knows about. Note that I said *Objective-C runtime*. There still could be Swift methods that this class implements that the Objective-C runtime doesn't even know about if the class inherits from NSObject!

You can of course execute any of these methods on your valid Session instance by replacing "Session" with the memory address you copied earlier.

```
        @property (nonatomic, retain) NSOrderedSet* presenters;   (@dynamic
          presenters;)
        @property (nonatomic, copy) NSString* tweetBody;   (@dynamic tweetBody;)
  Instance Methods:
    - (id) initWithEntity:(id)arg1 insertIntoManagedObjectContext:(id)arg2;
      (0x10060d49c)
(NSManagedObject ...)

(lldb) po [0x600002525a40 sessionDescription]
Thoughtful design of the boundaries between your apps subsystems is the
  foundation of a stable codebase. In this workshop, we cover how to create
  a well designed boundary between subsystems, dependency injection, use
  case driven development, creating injectable subsystems, and using state
  management to result in a clean architecture for your apps.

(lldb)
All Output ¢                                           🔍 Filter              🗑 ⬜ ⬜
```

This is just your regular reminder that beneath the shiny SwiftUI and Swift code is still a whole lot of Objective-C code and objects.

Key Points

- Placing some help at the beginning of a Python `def` within `'''` quotes will be treated as the function's documentation. This documentation is shown when you run `help <my_function>`.

- The `optparse` module is deprecated in Python, but is still widely used with the `lldb` modules. Watch for an official switch to `argparse`, but it hasn't happened quite yet.

- The `shlex` lexer offers `.split` and `.join` commands you can use to manipulate arguments passed to your function, treating them in a way you'd expect as a shell user. For example when passing strings with spaces in them you can wrap in quotes.

- The `.add_option` command of a parser allows you to supply default values and help text for that option.

- Placing a symbolic breakpoint in `getenv` or `main` is a common technique to set up `lldb` commands and breakpoints every time your code runs. You could also use it to create an `.lldbinit` type of file for a specific project.

Where to Go From Here?

That was pretty intense, but you've learned how to incorporate options into your own Python scripts.

In the very unlikely chance you still have energy after reading this chapter, you should implement some sort of backtrace option for the `bar` command. There are many times, when debugging, where I wish I'd known the stack trace of an interesting object!

However, adding options like this and using `.HandleCommand` to execute code becomes tedious quickly. In the next chapter you'll see how to use `SBValue` to interact with the objects in your code.

Chapter 24: Script Bridging With SBValue & Memory

So far, when evaluating JIT code (i.e. Objective-C, Swift, C, etc. code that's executed through your Python script), you've used a small set of APIs to evaluate the code.

For example, you've used SBDebugger and SBCommandReturnObject's **HandleCommand** method to evaluate code. SBDebugger's HandleCommand goes straight to stderr, while you have a little more control over where the SBCommandReturnObject result ends up. Once evaluated, you had to manually parse the return output for anything of interest. This manual searching of the output from the JIT code is a bit unsightly and hinders you making anything usefully complex. Nobody likes stringly typed things!

So, it's time to learn about another class in the lldb Python module, **SBValue**, and how it can simplify the parsing of JIT code output. Open up the Xcode project named **Allocator** in the **starter** folder for this chapter. This is a simple application that dynamically generates classes based upon input from a text field.

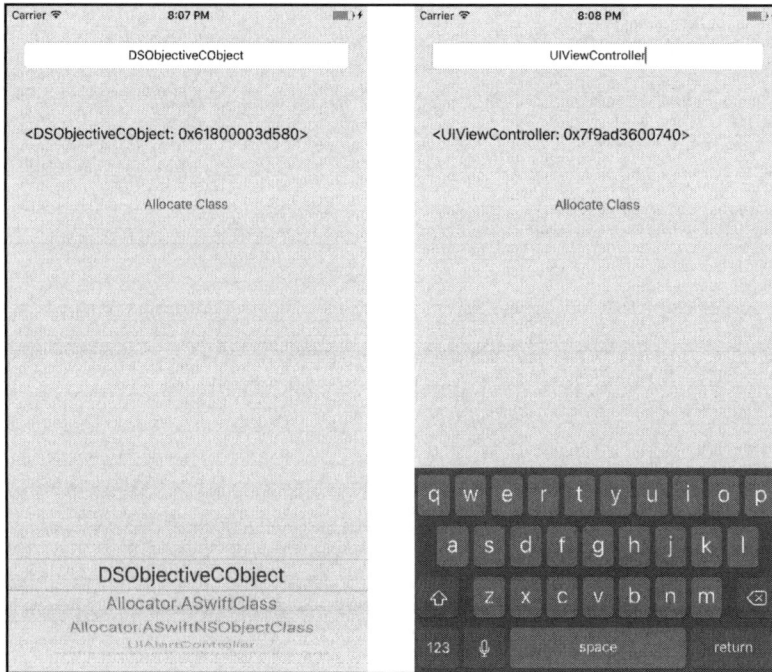

This is accomplished by taking the string from the text field and using it as an input to the NSClassFromString function. If a valid class is returned, it's initialized using the plain old init method. Otherwise, it generates an error.

Build and run the application. You'll make zero modifications to this project, yet you'll explore object layouts in memory through SBValue, as well as manually with pointers through LLDB.

A Detour Down Memory Layout Lane

To truly appreciate the power of the SBValue class, you're going to explore the memory layout of three unique objects within the Allocator application. You'll start with an Objective-C class, then explore a Swift class with no superclass, then finally explore a Swift class that inherits from NSObject.

All three of these classes have three properties with the following order:

- A UIColor called **eyeColor**.

- A language specific string (String/NSString) called **firstName**.

- A language specific string (String/NSString) called **lastName**.

Each instance of these classes is initialized with the same values. They are:

- eyeColor will be UIColor.brown or [UIColor brownColor] depending on language.

- firstName will be "Derek" or @"Derek" depending on language.

- lastName will be "Selander" or @"Selander" depending on language.

Objective-C Memory Layout

You'll explore the Objective-C class first, as it's the foundation for how these objects are laid out in memory. Jump over to the **DSObjectiveCObject.h** and take a look at it. Here it is for your reference:

```
@interface DSObjectiveCObject : NSObject

@property (nonatomic, strong) UIColor *eyeColor;
@property (nonatomic, strong) NSString *firstName;
@property (nonatomic, strong) NSString *lastName;

@end
```

As mentioned earlier, there are three properties: eyeColor, firstName, and lastName in that order.

Jump over to the implementation file **DSObjectiveCObject.m** and give it a gander to understand what's happening when this Objective-C object is initialized:

```
@implementation DSObjectiveCObject

- (instancetype)init
{
  self = [super init];
  if (self) {
    self.eyeColor = [UIColor brownColor];
    self.firstName = @"Derek";
    self.lastName = @"Selander";
  }
  return self;
}
@end
```

Nothing too crazy. The properties will be initialized to the values just described above.

When this compiles, this Objective-C class actually looks like a C struct. The compiler creates a struct similar to the following pseudocode:

```
struct DSObjectiveCObject {
  Class isa;
  UIColor *eyeColor;
  NSString *firstName
  NSString *lastName
}
```

Take note of the Class isa variable as the first parameter. This is the magic behind an Objective-C class being considered an Objective-C class. This isa value is always the first value in an object instance's memory layout, and is a pointer to the class the object is an instance of. After that, the properties are added to this struct in the order they appear in your source code.

Let's see this in action through LLDB. Perform the following steps:

1. Make sure the **DSObjectiveCObject** is selected in the UIPickerView.

2. Tap on the **Allocate Class** button.

3. Once the reference address appears in the console, copy that address to your clipboard.

4. Pause execution and bring up the LLDB console window.

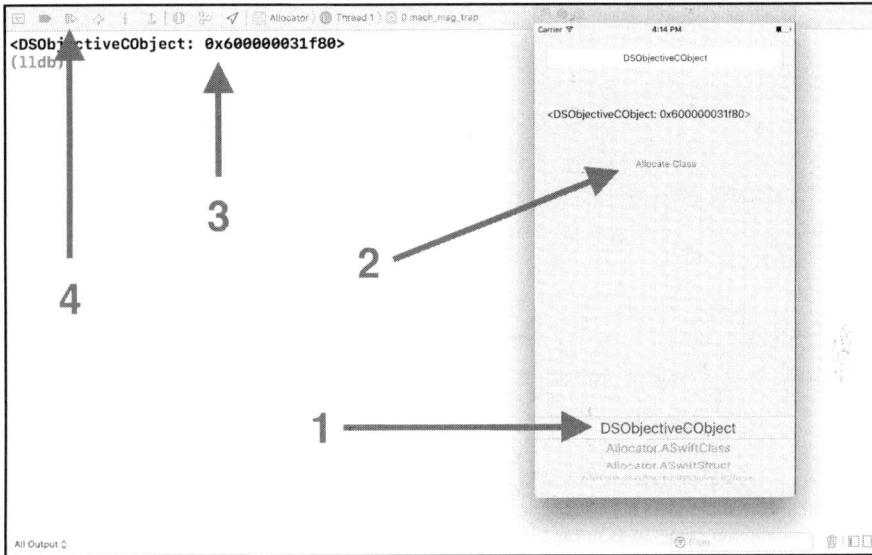

An instance of the DSObjectiveCObject has been created. You'll now use LLDB to spelunk into offsets of this object's contents.

Copy the memory address from the console output and make sure po'ing it will give you a valid reference (e.g. you're not stopped on a Swift stack frame when printing out this address).

In my case, I got the pointer 0x600000031f80. As always, yours will be different. Print out the address through LLDB:

```
(lldb) po 0x600000031f80
```

You should get output similar to the following:

```
<DSObjectiveCObject: 0x600000031f80>
```

Since this can be treated as a C struct, you'll start spelunking into offsets of this pointer's contents.

In the LLDB console, type the following (replacing the pointer with yours):

```
(lldb) po object_getClass(0x600000031f80)
```

This will give you the value of the **isa** class, therefore the type of the object. You cannot reference the isa pointer directly, because it doesn't exist as a normal pointer. Instead you have to go through the object_getClass function to obtain the isa pointer.

In about 2012 or so, when Apple started really moving to 64-bit as the future, someone noticed a whole bunch of space in **isa** pointer that would never be used. So, in the name of optimization, it got repurposed. Now metadata about the instance gets encoded in the formerly unused bits. You can look at the header for objc-object.h to see how they are being used. Things like retain count, whether the object is currently being deallocated, does it have associated objects and more are encoded in the bits. All of this is a long way to say: use object_getClass instead of isa when you want to see the class of an object.

You should see this output:

```
DSObjectiveCObject
```

That's the class object's description, as expected.

Let's look at another way of viewing this memory. Use the **x** command (aka examine, a port from GDBs popularity with this command) to jump to the starting pointer, then po it. Enter the following:

```
(lldb) x/gt 0x600000031f80
```

This command says the following:

- Examine the memory (x)

- Print out the size of a **giant** word, (64 bits, or 8 bytes) (g)

- Finally, format it in binary (t).

If, hypothetically, you only wanted to view the first byte at this location in binary instead, you could type x/bt 0x600000031f80 instead. This would be interpreted as examine (x), a byte (b) in binary (t). The examine command is definitely one of those nice commands to keep in your toolkit when exploring memory.

You'll see the following output (or at least, similar output, as the values will be different for you):

```
0x600000031f80:
0b0000000010000000000000000000000010000010010111011110011111010100
01
```

This gives you output that tells you the value at memory address 0x600000031f80 which is all of that isa metadata. You could cross reference it with the objc-object header to decode everything, but that's an exercise left for you.

Let's jump a little further into the eyeColor property. In the LLDB console:

```
(lldb) po *(id *)(0x600000031f80 + 0x8)
```

This says "start at 0x600000031f80 (or equivalent), go up 8 bytes and get the contents pointed at by this pointer." You'll get the following output:

```
UIExtendedSRGBColorSpace 0.6 0.4 0.2 1
```

How did I get to the number 8? Try this out in LLDB:

```
(lldb) po sizeof(Class)
```

The isa variable is of type Class. So by knowing how big a Class is, you know how much space that takes up in the struct, and therefore you know the offset of eyeColor.

> **Note**: When working with 64-bit architectures (x64 or ARM64), all pointers will be 8 bytes. In addition, the Class class itself is a pointer to a C struct not defined in the headers. This means in 64-bit architecture, all you need to do to move between different pointers is to jump by 8 bytes!
>
> There are types which are different sizes in bytes, such as int, short, bool and others, and the compiler may pad that memory to fit into a predefined size. However, there's no need to worry about that for now, since this DSObjectiveCObject class only contains pointers to NSObject subclasses, along with the metadata held in the isa variable.

Keep on going. Increment the offset by another 8 bytes in LLDB:

```
(lldb) po *(id *)(0x600000031f80 + 0x10)
```

You're adding another 8 to get 0x10 in hexadecimal (or 16 in decimal). You'll get @"Derek", which is the contents of the firstName property. Increment by yet another 8 bytes to get the lastName property:

```
(lldb) po *(id *)(0x600000031f80 + 0x18)
```

You'll get @"Selander". Cool, right? Let's visually revisit what you just did to hammer this home:

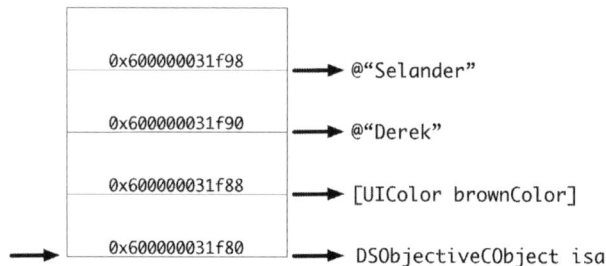

You started at a base address that pointed to the instance of DSObjectiveCObject. For this particular example, this starting address is at 0x600000031f80. You started by dereferencing this pointer, which gave you the isa metadata, then you jumped by offsets of 8 bytes to the next Objective-C property, dereferenced the pointer at that offset, cast it to type id and spat it out to the console.

Spelunking memory is a fun and instructional way to see what's happening behind the scenes. This lets you appreciate the SBValue class even more. But you're not at the point of talking about the SBValue class, as you still have two more classes to explore. The first is a Swift class with no superclass, and the second is a Swift class which inherits from NSObject. You'll explore the non-superclass Swift object first.

Swift Memory Layout With no Superclass

Note: It's worth mentioning right up front: the Swift is still evolving. Though Swift achieved ABI stability in version 5 and module stability in version 5.1, things are still changing and evolving as Swift begins to support other CPUs and operating systems. So, if you find that something has changed, be sure to check the forums as we will all be adapting.

Time to explore a Swift class with no superclass! In the Allocator project, jump to **ASwiftClass.swift** and take a look at what's there.

```swift
class ASwiftClass {
    let eyeColor = UIColor.brown
    let firstName = "Derek"
    let lastName = "Selander"

    required init() { }
}
```

Here, you have the Swift equivalent for DSObjectiveCObject with the obvious "Swifty" changes.

Again, you can imagine this Swift class as a C struct with some interesting differences from its Objective-C counterpart. Check out the following pseudocode:

```
struct ASwiftClass {
  Class isa;

  // Simplified, see "InlineRefCounts"
  // in https://github.com/apple/swift
  uintptr_t refCounts;

  UIColor *eyeColor;

  // Simplified, see "_StringGuts"
  // in https://github.com/apple/swift
  struct _StringObject {
    uintptr_t _countAndFlagBits; // packed bits for string type
    uintptr_t _object;           // raw data
  } firstName;

  struct _StringObject {
    uintptr_t _object;    // packed bits for string type
    uintptr_t rawBits;    // raw data
  } lastName;
}
```

Pretty interesting right? You still have that isa variable as the first parameter.

After the isa variable, there's an eight byte variable reserved for reference counting and alignment called **refCounts**. This differs to your typical Objective-C object which doesn't contain this varible at this offset.

Next, you have the normal UIColor, but now this ASwiftClass struct goes completely off the rails.

A Swift String is a very interesting "object". In fact, a String is a struct within the ASwiftClass struct. You can think of String as sort of a facade design pattern that hides different types of String types based upon if they are hardcoded, Cocoa, use ASCII, etc. To make it even more interesting, the types and layout will differ if the string being stored is longer or shorter than 16 bytes or compiled for 32-bit or 64-bit platforms.

For 64-bit platforms, the memory layout of a Swift String comprises 16 bytes with the structural layout depending on the type of String. To help you think it through, here is an excellent ASCII art diagram to demonstrate the layout of a "small" Swift string.

This documentation is taken from the https://github.com/apple/swift/blob/master/stdlib/public/core/StringObject.swift.

On 64-bit platforms, small strings have the following per-byte layout. When stored in memory (little-endian), their first character ('a') is in the lowest address and their top-nibble and count is in the highest address.

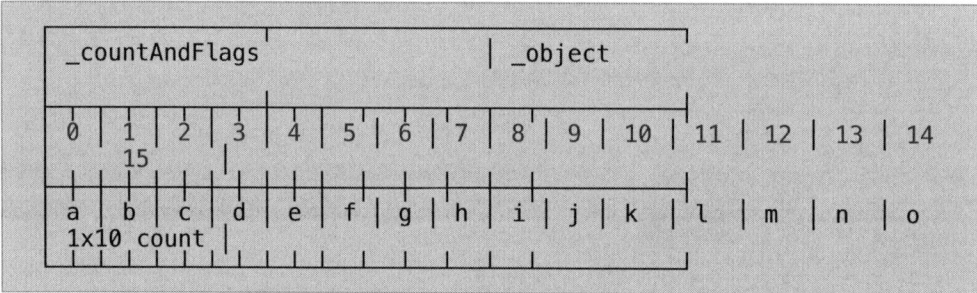

```
 _countAndFlags              | _object

| 0 | 1 | 2 | 3 | 4 | 5 | 6 | 7 | 8 | 9 | 10 | 11 | 12 | 13 | 14
      15
| a | b | c | d | e | f | g | h | i | j | k | l | m | n | o
1x10 count
```

From the documentation, you can see that if a regular string will fit in a 16 byte spot, it gets stored directly and the last byte is the length count. However, if it becomes one byte longer, or is Unicode or somehow "special" it magically gets stored differently. Again from the `StringObject` documentation:

All non-small forms share the same structure for the other half of the bits(i.e. non-object bits) as a word containing code unit count and various performance flags. The top 16 bits are nonessential flags; these aren't critical for correct operation, but they may provide additional guarantees that allow more efficient operation or more reliable detection of runtime errors. The lower 48 bits contain the code unit count (aka endIndex).

b63	b62	b61	b60	b59	b58:48	b47:0
ASCII	NFC	native	tail	UTF8	reserved	count

So, for a larger strings, or a non-ASCII or plain-C string, the string itself is stored somewhere else and the 16 bytes just contain some metadata and the pointer to the "real" string.

The layout of the `String` struct makes the assembly calling convention rather interesting. If you pass a `String` to a function, it will actually pass in two parameters (and use two registers) instead of a pointer to a struct containing the two parameters (in one register). Don't believe me? Check it out yourself when you're done with this chapter!

Back to LLDB and jumping through an object. For this next part, you'll use the graphical tools Xcode provides to sift through the memory. Remember from before, that many of the debug tools Xcode provides are just graphical wrappers around LLDB. Start by placing a GUI breakpoint in **ViewController.swift** right after the Swift class gets created:

```
else if let clsSwift = cls as? ASwiftClass.Type {
    let object = clsSwift.init()
```

You're going to inspect the `object`, so make sure the GUI breakpoint is after this code, but before the end of this scope.

With the breakpoint set, ensure that the app is running. You'll do the exact same thing with the `ASwiftClass` that you did with `DSObjectiveCObject`. Use the developer/designer "approved" `UIPickerView` and select **Allocator.SwiftClass**. Remember, to correctly reference a Swift class (i.e. in `NSClassFromString` and friends), you need the module name prepended to the classname with a period separating the two.

Tap the **Allocate Class** button and wait for your breakpoint to hit. Now, arrange your Xcode window panes to you can see the variables view and have at least a little bit of space below the stack trace in the **Debug navigator**. Next, open the details of the `object` variable. Your screen should look something like the picture:

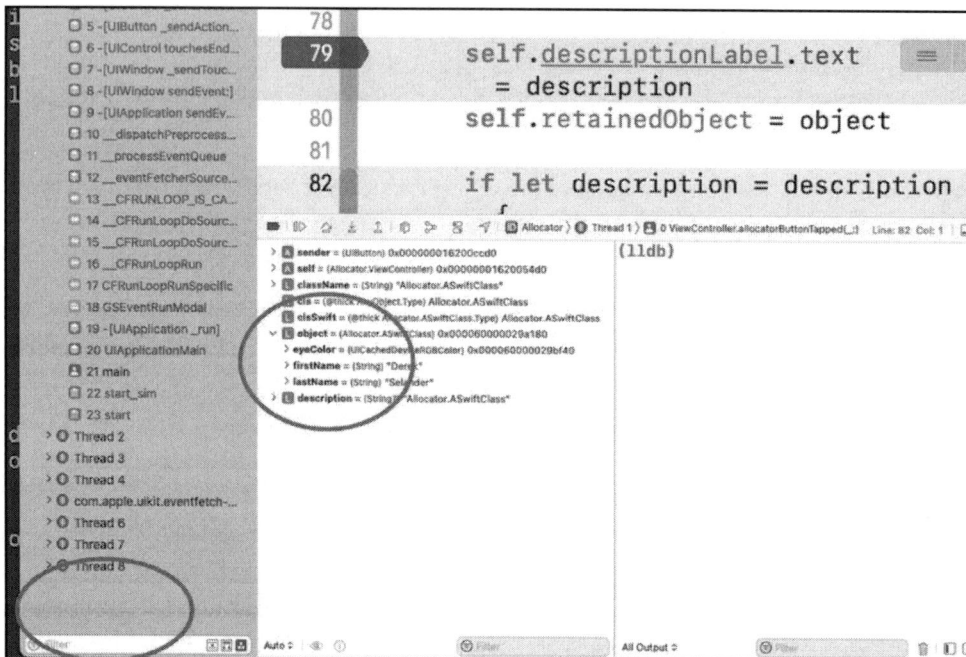

The hex number on the `object` line is its memory address. Right-click on the memory address to bring up the context menu and select **View memory of "object"**. Now, you'll see the actual memory. At this point, I usually resize my Xcode window so that the memory display wraps at a reasonable place and the addresses in the gray column make sense.

You'll get something similar to the following:

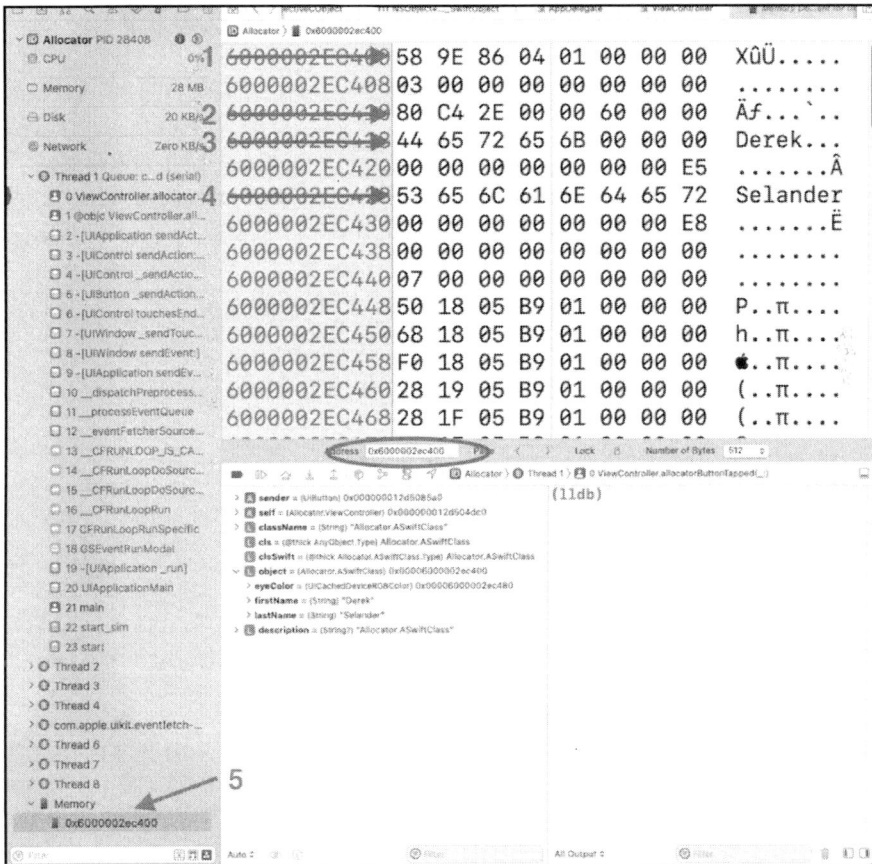

Here you can see the Xcode window is resized to show 8 bytes per row and you can see:

1. The memory address of the object itself

2. The memory for the `eyeColor` property

3. The memory for `firstName`

4. The memory for `lastName`

5. A running list of all of the memory locations you visit, so you can quickly jump back to them.

Recall from before that in the first part of the class, where the **isa** variable lives, Apple now puts metadata. One of the things you can see is the retain count byte.

Using the location of your `object` type this into the lldb console:

```
exp -l objc -O -- [0x6000002ec400 retain]
```

Because you used a GUI breakpoint in Swift code, you're in a Swift context, so you have to jump to the Objective-C context. For fun, use the up arrow and execute the command a few more times. Now right-click on the `object` variable and **View memory of "object"** to refresh the memory map. If you've resized Xcode to show 8 bytes per row, you should see the retain count in the middle of the second row. Now execute a few `release` commands and make it go down:

```
exp -l objc -O -- [0x6000002ec400 release]
```

After a few `release` commands, **View memory of "object"** again and it will have changed. Wheeee! :]

The memory for `eyeColor` is interesting. The `eyeColor` value should be at offset `0x10`. This would be at `0x6000002ec410` in this example. However notice that in the variable view in the screenshot, the `eyeColor` object is at `0x00006000002ec480`. Looking at the memory map at the `0x10` offset (i.e. `0x6000002ec410`) you can see that is what is actually stored at the `0x10` offset is the memory address of the "real" data where the `UIColor` is. This is because `UIColor` is a class and Swift is using a pointer to reference the object.

Looking back at the variable view, notice that `firstName` and `lastName` don't get memory addresses. However, you can see them offset by `0x18` and `0x28` from the base. Because they are both shorter than 16 bytes, they get stored inline and the last nibble is the length. The string "Derek" has a count of 5 and "Selander" has a count of 8. In the variables view click the to display details of `firstName`, you'll see the `_guts` and then another `_object` and then the `_countAndFlagBits` and `_object`. The `_countAndFlagBits` and the `_object` are the two 8 byte pieces of the string struct.

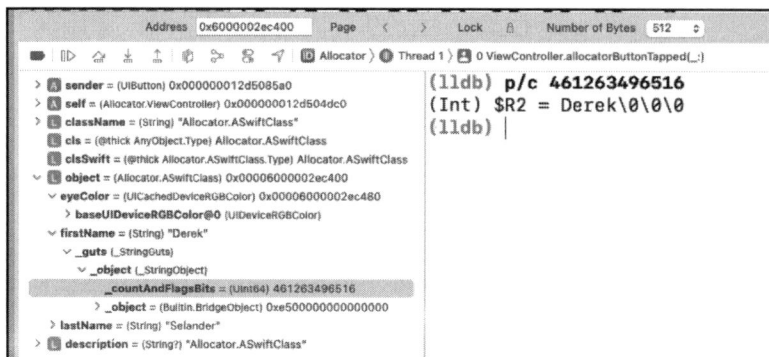

In fact, you can use the type formatting from way back in Chapter 5, "Expression", to prove that the UInt64 for _coundAndFlagBits is the original string.

Swift Memory Layout With NSObject Superclass

Final one. You know the drill, so we'll speed this one up a bit and skip the actual debugging session.

Check out the sourcecode for **ASwiftNSObjectClass.swift**:

```
class ASwiftNSObjectClass: NSObject {
    let eyeColor = UIColor.brown
    let firstName = "Derek"
    let lastName = "Selander"

    required override init() { }
}
```

It's the same thing as the ASwiftClass, except it inherits from NSObject instead of from nothing.

So is there any difference in the generated C struct pseudocode?

```
struct ASwiftNSObjectClass {
    Class isa;
    UIColor *eyeColor;

    struct _StringCore {
        uintptr_t _object;
        uintptr_t rawBits;
    } firstName;

    struct _StringCore {
        uintptr_t _object;
        uintptr_t rawBits;
    } lastName;
}
```

Almost! The only difference is that the ASwiftNSObjectClass instance is missing the refCounts variable at offset 0x8, the rest of the layout in memory will be the same.

Let's skip the debugging session and just talk about what will happen when you try **retain**'ing an instance of this class: the **refCounts** variable will *not* be modified. This makes sense because Objective-C has its own implementation of retain/release that's different from the Swift implementation.

You can finally look at the **SBValue** class I've been itching to describe to you! Hopefully, this exercise shows you why using an abstraction like SBValue in your code instead of trying to go directly to the data is going to be curcial in more complex LLDB scripts.

SBValue

Yay! Time to talk about this awesome class.

SBValue is responsible for interpreting the parsed expressions from your JIT code. Think of SBValue as a representation that lets you explore the members within your object, just as you did above, but without all that ugly dereferencing. Within the SBValue instance, you can easily access all members of your struct... er, I mean, your Objective-C or Swift classes.

Within the SBTarget and SBFrame class, there's a method named **EvaluateExpression**, which will take your expression as a Python str and return an SBValue instance. In addition, there's an optional second parameter that lets you specify how you want your code to be parsed. You'll start without the optional second parameter, and explore it later.

Jump back into the LLDB console and make sure the Allocator project is still running. If it's paused, resume it. The GUI breakpoint from before put you in a Swift context, you want an ObjectiveC context, so you want to pause the Allocator project using the **pause program execution** button of Xcode. Make sure the LLDB console is up (i.e. the program is paused), clear the console and type the following:

```
(lldb) po [DSObjectiveCObject new]
```

You'll get something similar to the following:

```
<DSObjectiveCObject: 0x61800002eec0>
```

This ensures you can create a valid instance of a DSObjectiveCObject.

This code works, so you can apply it to the EvaluateExpression method of either the global SBTarget or SBFrame instance:

```
(lldb) script lldb.frame.EvaluateExpression('[DSObjectiveCObject
new]')
```

You'll get the usual cryptic output with the class but no context to describe what this does:

```
<lldb.SBValue; proxy of <Swig Object of type 'lldb::SBValue *'
at 0x10ac78b10> >
```

You've got to use print to get context for these classes:

```
(lldb) script print
(lldb.target.EvaluateExpression('[DSObjectiveCObject new]'))
```

You'll get your happy debugDescription you've become accustomed to.

```
(DSObjectiveCObject *) $2 = 0x0000618000034280
```

> **Note**: If you mistype something, you'll still get an instance of SBValue, so make sure it's printed out the item you expect it should. For example, if you mistyped the JIT code, you might get something like ** = <could not resolve type>** from the SBValue.
>
> You can verify the SBValue succeeded by checking the **SBError** instance within your SBValue. If your SBvalue was named sbval, you could do sbval.GetError().Success(), or more simply sbval.error.success.print as a quick way to see if it worked or not.

Modify this command so you're assigning it to the variable **a** inside the Python context:

```
(lldb) script a =
lldb.target.EvaluateExpression('[DSObjectiveCObject new]')
```

Now apply the Python print function to the a variable:

```
(lldb) script print (a)
```

Again, you'll get something similar to the following:

```
(DSObjectiveCObject *) $3 = 0x0000608000033260
```

Great! You have a SBValue instance stored at a and are already knowledgeable about the memory layout of the DSObjectiveCObject. You know a is holding a SBValue that is a pointer to the DSObjectiveCObject class.

You can grab the description of the DSObjectiveCObject class by using the GetDescription(), or more simply description property of SBValue.

Type the following:

```
(lldb) script print (a.description)
```

You'll see something similar to the following:

```
<DSObjectiveCObject: 0x608000033260>
```

You can also get the value property, which returns a Python String containing the address of this instance:

```
(lldb) script print (a.value)
```

Just the value this time:

```
0x0000608000033260
```

Copy the output of a.value and ensure po'ing this pointer gives you the original, correct reference:

```
(lldb) po 0x0000608000033260
```

Yup:

```
<DSObjectiveCObject: 0x608000033260>
```

If you want the address expressed in a Python number instead of a Python str, you can use the signed or unsigned property:

```
(lldb) script print (a.signed)
```

Like this:

```
106102872289888
```

Formatting the number to hexadecimal will produce the pointer to this instance of DSObjectiveCObject:

```
(lldb) p/x 106102872289888
```

And you're back to where you were before:

```
(long) $5 = 0x0000608000033260
```

Exploring Properties Through SBValue Offsets

What about those properties stuffed inside that DSObjectiveCObject instance? Let's explore those!

Use the **GetNumChildren** method available to SBValue to get its child count:

```
(lldb) script print (a.GetNumChildren())
```

You'll get 4 (or potentially 3 depending on the version of LLDB/run conditions which hides an instance's isa variable).

You can think of children as just an array. There's a special API to traverse the children in a class called **GetChildAtIndex**, so you can explore children 0-3 in LLDB.

Child 0:

```
(lldb) script print (a.GetChildAtIndex(0))
(NSObject) NSObject = {
  isa = DSObjectiveCObject
}
```

Child 1:

```
(lldb) script print (a.GetChildAtIndex(1))
(UICachedDeviceRGBColor *) _eyeColor = 0x0000608000070e00
```

Child 2:

```
(lldb) script print (a.GetChildAtIndex(2))
(__NSCFConstantString *) _firstName = 0x000000010db83368
@"Derek"
```

Child 3:

```
(lldb) script print (a.GetChildAtIndex(3))
(__NSCFConstantString *) _lastName = 0x000000010db83388
@"Selander"
```

Each of these will return a SBValue in itself, so you can explore that object even further if you desired. Take the firstName property for example, type the following to get just the description:

```
(lldb) script print (a.GetChildAtIndex(2).description)
Derek
```

It's important to remember the Python variable a is a pointer to an object. Type the following:

```
(lldb) script (a.size)
8
```

This will print out a value saying a is 8 bytes long. But you want to get to the actual content! Fortunately, the SBValue has a **deref** property that returns another SBValue. Explore the output with the size property:

```
(lldb) script a.deref.size
```

This returns the value **32** since it makes up the isa, eyeColor, firstName, and lastName, each of them being 8 bytes long themselves as they are all pointers.

Here's another way to look at what the deref property is doing. Explore the SBType class (you can look that one up yourself) of the SBValue.

```
(lldb) script print (a.type.name)
```

You'll get this:

```
DSObjectiveCObject *
```

Now do the same thing through the **deref** property:

```
(lldb) script print (a.deref.type.name)
```

You'll now get the normal class:

```
DSObjectiveCObject
```

Viewing Raw Data Through SBValue

You can even dump the raw data out with the **data** property in SBValue! This is represented by a class named **SBData**, which is yet another class you can check out on your own.

Print out the data of the pointer to DSObjectiveCObject:

```
(lldb) script print (a.data)
```

This will print out the physical bytes that make up the object. Again, this is the pointer to DSObjectiveCObject, not the object itself.

```
60 32 03 00 80 60 00 00
```

Remember, each byte can be represented as two digits in hexadecimal.

Do you remember covering the **little-endian** formatting in Chapter 12, "Assembly & Memory," and how the raw data is reversed?

Compare this with the **value** property of SBValue.

```
(lldb) script print (a.value)
```

Which will give you the expected 0x0000608000033260:

```
(lldb) script print a.data
60 32 03 00 80 60 00 00
(lldb) script print a.value
0x0000608000033260
(lldb)
```

Notice how the values have been flipped. For example, the final two hex digits of my pointer are the first grouping (aka byte) in the raw data. In my case, the raw data contains 0x60 as the first value, while the pointer contains 0x60 as the final value.

Use the **deref** property to grab *all* the bytes that make up this DSObjectiveCObject.

```
(lldb) script print (a.deref.data)
f0 54 b8 0d 01 00 00 00 00 0e 07 00 80 60 00
00  .T...........`..
68 33 b8 0d 01 00 00 00 88 33 b8 0d 01 00 00 00
h3.......3......
```

This is yet another way to visualize what is happening. You were jumping 8 bytes each time when you were spelunking in memory with that cute po *(id*) (`0x0000608000033260` + `multiple_of_8`) command.

SBExpressionOptions

As mentioned when discussing the `EvaluateExpression` API, there's an optional second parameter that will take an instance of type **SBExpressionOptions**. You can use this command to pass in specific options for the JIT execution.

In LLDB, clear the screen, start fresh and type the following:

```
(lldb) script options = lldb.SBExpressionOptions()
```

You'll get no output upon success. Next, type:

```
(lldb) script options.SetLanguage(lldb.eLanguageTypeSwift)
```

SBExpressionOptions has a method named **SetLanguage** (when in doubt, use **gdocumentation SBExpressionOptions**), which takes an LLDB module enum of type **lldb::LanguageType**. The LLDB authors have a convention for sticking an "e" before an enum, the enum name, then the unique value.

This sets the options to evaluate the code as Swift instead of whatever the default is, based on the language type of `SBFrame`.

Now tell the `options` variable to interpret the JIT code as a of type ID (i.e. po, instead of p):

```
(lldb) script options.SetCoerceResultToId()
```

SetCoerceResultToId takes an optional Boolean, which determines if it should be interpreted as an `id` or not. By default, this is set to `True`.

To recap what you did here: you set the options to parse this expression using the Python API instead of the options passed to us through the expression command.

For example, `SBExpressionOptions` you've declared so far is pretty much equivalent to the following options in the `expression` command:

```
expression -lswift -O -- your_expression_here
```

Next, create an instance of the `ASwiftClass` method only using the `expression` command. If this works, you'll try out the same expression in the `EvaluateExpression` command. In LLDB type the following:

```
(lldb) e -lswift -O -- ASwiftClass()
```

You'll get an ugly little error for output...

```
error: <EXPR>:3:1: error: use of unresolved identifier
'ASwiftClass'
ASwiftClass()
^~~~~~~~~~~
```

Oh yeah, — you need to import the **Allocator** module to make Swift play nicely in the debugger.

In LLDB:

```
(lldb) e -lswift -- import Allocator
```

> **Note**: This is a problem many LLDB users complain about: LLDB can't properly evaluate code that should be able to execute. Adding this import logic will modify LLDB's Swift **expression prefix**, which is basically a set of header files that a referenced right before you JIT code is evaluated.
>
> LLDB can't see the class `ASwiftClass` in the JIT code when you're stopped in the non-Swift debugging context. This means you need to append the headers to the expression prefix that belongs to the Allocator module.
>
> There's a great explanation from Jim Ingham, one of the LLDB authors, about this very problem an an answer to this StackOverflow Question (http:// stackoverflow.com/questions/19339493/why-cant-lldb-evaluate-this-expression).

Execute the previous command again. Up arrow twice then Enter:

```
(lldb) e -lswift -O -- ASwiftClass()
```

You'll get a reference to an instance of the `ASwiftClass()`.

Now that you know this works, use the **EvaluateExpression** method with the options parameter as the second parameter this time and assign the output to the variable **b**, like so:

```
(lldb) script b =
lldb.target.EvaluateExpression('ASwiftClass()', options)
```

If everything went well, you'll get a reference to a SBValue in the b Python variable.

> **Note**: It's worth pointing out some properties of SBValue will not play nicely with Swift. For example, dereferencing a Swift object with SBValue's deref or address_of property will not work properly. You can coerce this pointer to an Objective-C reference by casting the pointer as a SwiftObject, and everything will then work fine. Like I said, they make you work for it when you're trying to go after pointers in Swift!

Referencing Variables by Name With SBValue

Referencing child SBValues via **GetChildAtIndex** from SBValue is a rather ho-hum way to navigate to an object in memory. What if the author of this class added a property before eyeColor that totally screwed up your offset logic when traversing this SBValue?

Fortunately, SBValue has yet *another* method that lets you reference instance variables by name instead of by offset: **GetValueForExpressionPath**.

Jump back to LLDB and type the following:

```
(lldb) script print (b.GetValueForExpressionPath('.firstName'))
```

You can keep drilling down into the child's own struct if you wish:

How did I obtain the name of child SBValues? If you had no clue of the name for the child SBValue, all you have to do is get to the child using the **GetIndexOfChild** API, then use the **name** property on that SBValue child.

For example, if I didn't know the name of the `UIColor` property found in the **b** SBValue, I could do the following:

```
(lldb) script print (b)
(Allocator.ASwiftClass) $R1 = 0x000060000145f640 {
  eyeColor = 0x0000600001459880 {
    ObjectiveC.NSObject = {}
  }
  firstName = "Derek"
  lastName = "Selander"
}
(lldb) script print (b.GetChildAtIndex(0))
(UICachedDeviceRGBColor) eyeColor = 0x0000600001459880 {
  baseUIDeviceRGBColor@0 = {
    baseUIColor@0 = {
      baseNSObject@0 = {
        isa = UICachedDeviceRGBColor
      }
      _systemColorName = 0x000060000015b840 "brownColor"
      _cachedStyleString = 0x0000000000000000
    }
    redComponent = 0.59999999999999998
    greenComponent = 0.40000000000000002
    blueComponent = 0.20000000000000001
    alphaComponent = 1
  }
}
(lldb) script print (b.GetChildAtIndex(0).name)
eyeColor
(lldb) script print (b.GetValueForExpressionPath('.eyeColor'))
(UIColor) eyeColor = 0x0000600001459880 {
  ObjectiveC.NSObject = {}
}
(lldb) script print
  (b.GetValueForExpressionPath('.eyeColor').description)
UIExtendedSRGBColorSpace 0.6 0.4 0.2 1

(lldb)
```

lldb.value

One final cool thing you can do is create a Python reference that contains the SBValue's properties as the Python object's properties (wait... what?). Think of this as an object through which you can reference variables using Python properties instead of Strings.

Back in the console, instantiate a new **value** object from your **b** SBValue:

```
(lldb) script c = lldb.value(b)
```

This will create the special LLDB Python object of type `value`. Now you can reference its instance variables just like you would a normal object!

Type the following into LLDB:

```
(lldb) script print (c.firstName)
```

You can also cast the child object back into a SBValue so you can query it or apply it to a for loop, like so:

```
(lldb) script print (c.firstName.sbvalue.signed)
```

Again, if you don't know the name of a child SBValue, use the GetChildAtIndex API to get the child and get its name from the name property.

> **Note**: Although the lldb.value class is awesome, this comes at a cost. It's rather expensive to create and access properties through this type of class. If you are parsing a huge NSArray (or Array<Any>, for you Swifties), using this class will definitely slow you down. Play around with it and find the sweet spot between speed and convenience.

Key Points

- The **isa** variable's unused bits are being repurposed for other things, so use object_getClass to find out what kind of object you're exploring.

- Use the x command in lldb or the **View Memory** debug workflow to see the actual bytes for an object.

- Class objects in Swift and Objective-C offset properties by 0x8 or 0x10 depending on the type. Pointers are always of size 0x8.

- Depending on its properties, a Swift String may be stored in the class directly, or somewhere else in memory. This can change at runtime as the string changes.

- Swift classes that do not inherit from NSObject keep their own retain count.

- SBValue abstracts different data into something with a common interface.

- Use GetNumChildren() to explore the properties of the object SBValue represents.

- Use the .data property of SBValue to get back to the raw bytes of an object.

- Use SBExpressionOptions to set options that impact the EvalutateExpression command.

- The lldb.value() creates a special Python object to help you avoid having to stringly type properties.

Where to Go From Here?

Holy cow... how dense was that chapter!? Fortunately you have come full circle. You can use the options provided by your custom command to dynamically generate your JIT script code. From the return value of your JIT code, you can write scripts that have custom logic based upon the return `SBValue` that is parsed through the `EvaluateExpression` APIs.

This can unlock some amazing scripts for you. In any process to which you can attach LLDB, you can run your own custom code and handle your own custom return values within your Python script. There's no need to deal with signing issues or loading of frameworks or anything like that.

The remaining chapters in this section will focus on the composition of some creative scripts and how they can make your debugging (or reverse engineering) life much simpler. Theory time is over. It's time for some fun!

Chapter 25: SB Examples, Improved Lookup

For the rest of the chapters in this section, you'll focus on Python scripts.

As alluded to earlier, the image lookup -rn command is on its way out. Time to make a prettier script to display content.

Here's what you get right now with the image lookup -rn command:

When you finish this chapter, you'll have a new script named **lookup** which queries in a *much* cleaner way.

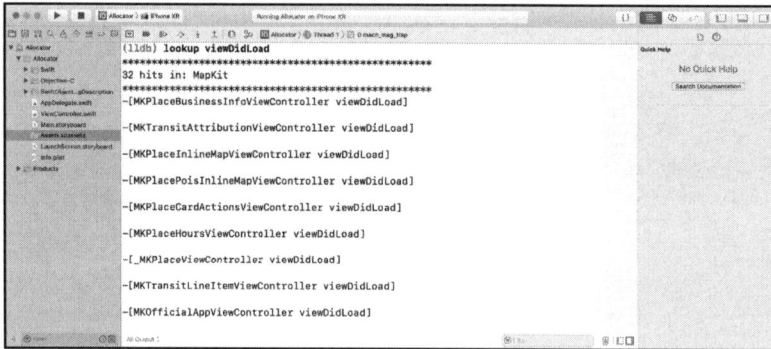

In addition, you'll add a couple of parameters to the lookup command to add some bells and whistles for your new searches.

Automating Script Creation

Included in the **starter** directory of this project are two Python scripts that will make your life easier when creating LLDB script content. They are as follows:

- **generate_new_script.py**: This creates new skeletons script with whatever name you provide it and stick it into the same directory generate_new_script resides in.

- **lldbinit.py**: This script will enumerate all scripts (files that end with .py) located within the same directory as itself and try to load them into LLDB. In addition, if there are any files with a txt extension, LLDB will try to load those files' contents through command import.

Take both of these files found in the **starter** folder of this chapter and stick them into your **~/lldb/** directory.

Once the files are in their correct locations, jump over to your ~/**.lldbinit** file and add following line of code:

```
command script import ~/lldb/lldbinit.py
```

This will load the **lldbinit.py** file which will enumerate all .py files and .txt files found in the same directory and load them into LLDB. This means from here on out, simply adding a script file into the ~/lldb directory will load it automatically once LLDB starts.

Creating the Lookup Command

With your new tools properly set up, open up a Terminal window. Launch a new instance of LLDB:

```
lldb
```

As expected, you'll be greeted by the LLDB prompt. If you've been following along and adding things to your .lldbinit you should see the error: cannot add command errors as it tries to load things twice. Remember that the scripts *are* getting loaded. If you decide to keep this lldbinit.py you'll want to clean up your .lldbinit at some point.

Make sure there are no build errors in any of your existing LLDB scripts:

```
(lldb) reload_script
```

If your output is free of *actual* errors, it's time to try out your new command **__generate_script**.

In LLDB, type:

```
(lldb) __generate_script lookup
```

If everything went as expected, you'll get output similar to the following:

```
Opening "/Users/derekselander/lldb/lookup.py"...
```

In addition, a Finder window will pop up showing you the location of the file. It's pretty crazy what you can do with these Python scripts, right?

Hold onto the Finder window for a second — don't close it. Head back to the LLDB Terminal window and apply the **reload_script** command.

Since the lookup.py script was created in the same directory as the lldbinit.py file and you have just reloaded the contents of ~/.lldbinit, you'll now have a working skeleton of the lookup.py file. Give the command a go.

```
(lldb) lookup
```

You'll get the following output:

```
Hello! The lookup command is working!
```

Now you can create and use custom commands in as little as two LLDB commands.

Yeah, you could do all the setup in one command, but I like having control over when my scripts reload.

lldbinit Directory Structure Suggestions

The way I've structured my own lldbinit files might be insightful to some. This is not a required section, but more of a suggestion on how to organize all of your custom scripts and content for LLDB.

I tend to keep my ~/.lldbinit as light as possible and use a script like lldbinit.py to load all my contents from a particular directory. Facebook's Chisel (https://github.com/facebook/chisel) does the same thing with the **fblldb.py** file. Check it out if you're interested.

I keep that directory under source control in case I need to transfer logic to a different computer, or in case I completely screw something up. For example, my actual ~/.lldbinit file (when not working on this book) only contains the following items:

```
command script import /Users/derekselander/lldb_repo/
lldb_commands/lldbinit.py
command script import /Users/derekselander/chisel/chisel/
fblldb.py
```

The lldb_repo is a public git repository at https://github.com/DerekSelander/lldb which contains some LLDB scripts designed for reverse engineering. There is a fork of that repo and some additional scripts in the **materials** download for this book. Check out Appendix C "Helpful Python Scripts" for more information.

I also have Facebook's Chisel on source control, so whenever those developers push a new, interesting release, I'll just pull the latest from their repo on GitHub. I'll have everything I need the next time I run LLDB, or reload my scripts through reload_script.

Inside my lldb_commands directory, I have all my Python scripts as well as two text files. One text file is named **cmds.txt** and holds all my command regex's and command alias's. I also have another file named **settings.txt**, which I use to augment any LLDB settings.

For example, the only content I have in my `settings.txt` file at the moment is:

```
settings set target.skip-prologue false
settings set target.x86-disassembly-flavor intel
```

You may already have added settings to your ~/.`lldbinit` file earlier in this book, but I prefer this implementation to separate out my custom LLDB commands to my LLDB settings so I don't get lost when `grep`'ing my ~/.`lldbinit` file.

However, for this book, I chose to keep each chapter content independent for each script installation. This means you've manually added content to your ~/.`lldbinit` file so you know what's happening. You should revisit this new structure implementation when (if?) you finish this book, as there are several benefits to this suggested layout. The benefits are as follows:

1. Calling `reload_script` only displays the commands ~/.`lldbinit` is loading; it will not display the sub-scripts being loaded. For example this will echo back the `lldbinit.py` being loaded, but not echo out the content `lldbinit.py` itself loads.

    This makes it easier to create scripts because I often use `reload_script` as a way to check for any error messages as I'm working on my latest script. The less output there is from executing `reload_script`, the less output there is to review when checking for errors in the console.

2. As noted, having as little content as possible in ~/.`lldbinit` lets you easily transfer content between computers, especially if that content is under source control.

3. Finally, it's much easier to add new scripts with this implementation. Just stick them in the same directory as the `lldbinit.py` file and they will be loaded next time. The alternative is to manually add the path to your script to the ~/.`lldbinit` file, which can get annoying if you do this frequently.

That's my two cents on the subject. You'll use this implementation strategy for the remaining scripts in this section as you only have to add scripts to your ~/`lldb` directory for them to get loaded into LLDB... which is rather nice, right?

Back to the `lookup` command!

Implementing the Lookup Command

As you saw briefly in the Chapter 7 "Image", the foundation behind this `lookup` command is rather simple. But, with the default `image lookup`, specifying filters and reading the output are difficult. You'll focus on enhancing how **FindGlobalFunctions** works.

You'll continue working with the **Allocator** Xcode project, found in the **starter** folder for this chapter.

Open the project, and build and run. You'll use this project to test out your new `lookup` command queries as the script progresses throughout the chapter.

Once running, pause the application and bring up LLDB.

The first step is to determine what inputs you'll need to gather for `FindGlobalFunctions`. Type the following into LLDB:

```
(lldb) script help(lldb.SBTarget.FindGlobalFunctions)
```

You'll get the following output showing the method signature:

```
FindGlobalFunctions(self, *args) unbound lldb.SBTarget method
    FindGlobalFunctions(self, str name, uint32_t max_matches,
MatchType matchtype) -> SBSymbolContextList
```

Since it's a Python class, you can ignore that first **self** parameter. The `str` parameter named **name** will be your lookup query. **max_matches** will dictate the maximum number of hits you want. If you specify the number 0, it will return all available matches. The **matchType** parameter is a lldb Python enum on which you can perform different types of searches, such as regex or non-regex.

Since regex searching really is the only way to go, you'll use the LLDB enum value **lldb.eMatchTypeRegex**.

The other enum values can be found at the LLVM reference for eMatchTypeRegex (https://lldb.llvm.org/python_reference/_lldb%27-module.html#eMatchTypeRegex).

Time to implement this in the **lookup.py** script. Open up **~/lldb/lookup.py** in your favorite text editor. Find the following code at the end of **handle_command**:

```
# Uncomment if you are expecting at least one argument
# clean_command = shlex.split(args[0])[0]
result.AppendMessage('Hello! The lookup command is working!')
```

Delete the above code, and replace it with the following, making sure you preserve the indentation:

```
# 1
clean_command = shlex.split(args[0])[0]
# 2
target = debugger.GetSelectedTarget()

# 3
contextlist = target.FindGlobalFunctions(clean_command, 0,
lldb.eMatchTypeRegex)
# 4
result.AppendMessage(str(contextlist))
```

Here's what this does:

1. Obtains a cleaned version of the command that was passed to the script, using the same magic as you saw earlier.

2. Uses SBDebugger to get the current instance of SBTarget.

3. Uses the FindGlobalFunctions API with clean_command. You're supplying 0, for no upper limit on number of results and giving it the eMatchTypeRegex match type to use a regular expression search.

4. You're turning the contextlist into a Python str and then appending it to the SBCommandReturnObject.

Back in Xcode, reload the contents through the LLDB console:

```
(lldb) reload_script
```

Give the lookup command a go. Remember that DSObjectiveCObject class you spelunked in the previous chapter? Dump everything pertaining to that through LLDB:

```
lookup DSObjectiveCObject
```

You'll get output that actually looks worse than **image lookup -rn DSObjectiveCObject**:

```
(lldb) lookup DSObjectiveCObject
        Module: file = "/Users/derekselander/Library/Developer/Xcode/
DerivedData/Allocator-czsgsdzfgtmanrdjnydkbzdmhifw/Build/Products/Debug-
iphonesimulator/Allocator.app/Allocator", arch = "x86_64"
CompileUnit: id = {0x00000000}, file = "/Users/derekselander/iOS/dbg/s4-
custom-lldb-commands/22.  Ex 1, Improved Lookup/projects/final/Allocator/
Allocator/DSObjectiveCObject.m", language = "objective-c"
    Function: id = {0x100000268}, name = "-[DSObjectiveCObject
setLastName:]", range = [0x0000000100001c00-0x0000000100001c37)
    FuncType: id = {0x100000268}, decl = DSObjectiveCObject.h:33,
compiler_type = "void (NSString *)"
      Symbol: id = {0x0000001e}, range =
[0x0000000100001c00-0x0000000100001c40), name="-[DSObjectiveCObject
setLastName:]"
        Module: file = "/Users/derekselander/Library/Developer/Xcode/
DerivedData/Allocator-czsgsdzfgtmanrdjnydkbzdmhifw/Build/Products/Debug-
iphonesimulator/Allocator.app/Allocator", arch = "x86_64"
CompileUnit: id = {0x00000000}, file = "/Users/derekselander/iOS/dbg/s4-
custom-lldb-commands/22.  Ex 1, Improved Lookup/projects/final/Allocator/
Allocator/DSObjectiveCObject.m", language = "objective-c"
    Function: id = {0x1000002a6}, name = "-
```

Use LLDB's **script** command to figure out which APIs to explore further:

```
(lldb) script k =
lldb.target.FindGlobalFunctions('DSObjectiveCObject', 0,
lldb.eMatchTypeRegex)
```

This will replicate what you've done in the lookup.py script and assign the output of FindGlobalFunctiona, an instance of SBSymbolContextList, to the value k. I am a fan of short variables names when exploring API names — if you haven't noticed.

Explore the documentation of SBSymbolContextList:

```
(lldb) gdocumentation SBSymbolContextList
```

Or find the documentation at llvm.org if you didn't implement the gdocumentation script earlier.

While you're at it, dump all the all the methods implemented by SBSymbolContextList. In LLDB:

```
(lldb) script dir(lldb.SBSymbolContextList)
```

This will dump out all the methods SBSymbolContextList implements or overrides. There's a lot there. But focus on the **__iter__** and the **__getitem__**.

```
(lldb) script dir(lldb.SBSymbolContextList)
['Append', 'Clear', 'GetContextAtIndex', 'GetDescription', 'GetSize',
'IsValid', '__class__', '__del__', '__delattr__', '__dict__', '__doc__',
'__format__', '__getattr__', '__getattribute__', '__getitem__', '__hash__',
'__init__', '__iter__', '__len__', '__module__', '__new__', '__nonzero__',
'__reduce__', '__reduce_ex__', '__repr__', '__setattr__', '__sizeof__',
'__str__', '__subclasshook__', '__swig_destroy__', '__swig_getmethods__',
'__swig_setmethods__', '__weakref__', 'blocks', 'compile_units', 'functions',
'get_block_array', 'get_compile_unit_array', 'get_function_array',
'get_line_entry_array', 'get_module_array', 'get_symbol_array',
'line_entries', 'modules', 'symbols']
(lldb)
```

This is good news for your script, since this means SBSymbolContextList is **iterable** as well as **indexable**. A second ago, you just assigned an instance of SBSymbolContextList to a variable named k through LLDB.

In the LLDB console, use indexing to explore the first item in the k object.

```
(lldb) script k[0]
```

This is equivalent to, though much less typing than: script k.__getitem__(0). You'll get something similar to the following:

```
<lldb.SBSymbolContext; proxy of <Swig Object of type
'lldb::SBSymbolContext *' at 0x113a83780> >
```

Good to know! The SBSymbolContextList holds an "array" of SBSymbolContext.

Use the print command to get the context of this SBSymbolContext:

```
(lldb) script print (k[0])
```

Your output could differ, but I got the SBSymbolContext which represents – [DSObjectiveCObject setLastName:], like so:

```
Module: file = "/Users/wtyree/Library/Developer/Xcode/
DerivedData/Allocator-adwweurwxijqutezmvmbahiztsjd/Build/
Products/Debug-iphonesimulator/Allocator.app/Allocator", arch =
"arm64"

CompileUnit: id = {0x00000000}, file = "/Users/wtyree/Repos/dbg-
materials/26-sb-examples-improved-lookup/projects/starter/
Allocator/Allocator/DSObjectiveCObject.m", language = "<not
loaded>"
   Function: id = {0x100000258}, name = "-[DSObjectiveCObject
setLastName:]", range = [0x0000000100003b0c-0x0000000100003b40)
```

```
   FuncType: id = {0x100000258}, byte-size = 0, decl =
DSObjectiveCObject.h:36, compiler_type = "void (NSString *)"
   Symbol: id = {0x00000112}, range =
[0x0000000100003b0c-0x0000000100003b40), name="-
[DSObjectiveCObject setLastName:]"
```

You'll use properties and/or getter methods from the SBSymbolContext to grab the name of this function.

The easiest way to do this is to grab the **SBSymbol** from the SBSymbolContext through the **symbol** property. From there the SBSymbol contains a **name** property, which returns your happy Python string.

Make sure this works in your LLDB console:

```
(lldb) script print (k[0].symbol.name)
```

In my case, I received the following:

```
-[DSObjectiveCObject setLastName:]
```

This is enough information to work with in building out your script. You'll start with the SBSymbolContextList, iterate through the items and print out the name of each function you find.

Head back over to your **lookup.py** script and modify the contents in the **handle_command** function. Find the following lines:

```
contextlist = target.FindGlobalFunctions(clean_command, 0,
lldb.eMatchTypeRegex)

result.AppendMessage(str(contextlist))
```

Replace them with the following (indenting correctly!):

```
contextlist = target.FindGlobalFunctions(clean_command, 0,
lldb.eMatchTypeRegex)

output = ''
for context in contextlist:
    output += context.symbol.name + '\n\n'

result.AppendMessage(output)
```

You're now iterating all SBSymbolContext's within the returned SBSymbolContextList, hunting down the name of the function and separating it by two newlines.

Jump back to Xcode, and reload your script:

```
(lldb) reload_script
```

Then give your updated lookup command a test in LLDB:

```
(lldb) lookup DSObjectiveCObject
```

You'll get much prettier output than before:

```
-[DSObjectiveCObject setLastName:]

-[DSObjectiveCObject .cxx_destruct]

-[DSObjectiveCObject setFirstName:]

-[DSObjectiveCObject eyeColor]

-[DSObjectiveCObject init]

-[DSObjectiveCObject lastName]

-[DSObjectiveCObject setEyeColor:]

-[DSObjectiveCObject firstName]
```

This is nicer, but it would be even better if you could see where these functions reside in the process. You'll group all functions to a particular module (an **SBModule**) when they're being printed out separated by a header with the module name and number of hits for the module.

Head on back to the **lookup.py** file. You'll now create two new functions.

You'll name the first function: **generateFunctionDictionary**, which will take your SBBreakpointContextList and generate a Python Dictionary of lists. This dict will contain keys for each module. For the value in the dict, you'll have a Python list for each SBSymbolContext that gets hit.

The second function will be: **generateOutput**, which will parse this dictionary you've created along with the options you've received from the OptionParser instance. This method will return a String to be printed back to the console.

Start by implementing the **generateModuleDictionary** function right below the handle_command function in your **lookup.py** script:

```
def generateModuleDictionary(contextlist):
    mdict = {}
    for context in contextlist:
        # 1
        key = context.module.file.fullpath
        # 2
        if not key in mdict:
            mdict[key] = []

        # 3
        mdict[key].append(context)
    return mdict
```

Here's what's going on:

1. You're using the context which is of type SBSymbolContext, to get an SBModule (**module**), then the SBFileSpec (**file**), then the Python string of the **fullPath** and assigning it to a variable named **key**. It's important to grab the fullPath (instead of, say, SBFileSpec's **basename** property, since there could be multiple modules with the same basename).

2. This mdict variable is going to hold a list of all symbols found, split by module. The key in this dictionary will be the module name, and the value will be an array of symbols found in that module. On this line, you're checking if the dictionary already contains a list for this module. If not, add a blank list for this module key.

3. You're adding the SBSymbolContext instance to the appropriate list for this module. You can safely assume that for every key in the mdict variable, there will be at least one or more SBSymbolContext instances.

> **Note**: A much easier way of getting a unique key would be to just use the **__str__()** method SBModule has (and pretty much every class in the LLDB Python module). This is the function that gets called when you call Python's **print** on one of these objects. However, you wouldn't be learning about all these classes, properties and methods in the process if you just relied on the __str__() method. :]

Right below the `generateModuleDictionary` function, implement the
generateOutput function:

```
def generateOutput(mdict, options, target):
    # 1
    output = ''
    separator = '*' * 60 + '\n'
    # 2
    for key in mdict:
        # 3
        count = len(mdict[key])
        firstItem = mdict[key][0]
        # 4
        moduleName = firstItem.module.file.basename
        output += '{0}{1} hits in {2}\n{0}'.format(separator,
                                                   count,
                                                   moduleName)

        # 5
        for context in mdict[key]:
            query = ''
            query += context.symbol.name
            query += '\n\n'
            output += query
    return output
```

Here's what this does:

1. The **output** variable will be the return string containing all the content
    eventually passed to your `SBCommandReturnObject`.

2. Enumerate all the keys found in the `mdict` dictionary.

3. This will grab the count for the array and the very first item in the list. You'll use
    this information to query the module name later.

4. You're grabbing the module name to use in the header output for each section.

5. This will iterate all the `SBSymbolContext` items in the Python `list` and add the
    names to the `output` variable.

One final tweak before you can test this out.

Augment the code in the **handle_command** function so it utilizes the two new
methods you've just created. Find the following code:

```
output = ''
for context in contextlist:
    output += context.symbol.name + '\n\n'
```

And replace it with the following:

```
mdict = generateModuleDictionary(contextlist)
output = generateOutput(mdict, options, target)
```

You know what to do. Go to Xcode; reload contents in LLDB.

```
(lldb) reload_script
```

Check out your new and improved lookup command:

```
(lldb) lookup DSObjectiveCObject
```

You'll get something similar to the following:

```
*****************************************************************
8 hits in Allocator
*****************************************************************
-[DSObjectiveCObject setLastName:]

-[DSObjectiveCObject .cxx_destruct]

-[DSObjectiveCObject setFirstName:]

-[DSObjectiveCObject eyeColor]

-[DSObjectiveCObject init]

-[DSObjectiveCObject lastName]

-[DSObjectiveCObject setEyeColor:]

-[DSObjectiveCObject firstName]
```

Cool. Go after all Objective-C methods that begin with **initWith**, and only contain two parameters.

```
(lldb) lookup initWith([A-Za-z0-9_]+\:){2}\]
```

You'll get hits from both public and private modules, all loaded into the Allocator process.

Note: When writing this chapter, using \w or [[:word:]] wasn't working for some reason, so the equivalent [A-Za-z0-9_] it is then. The LLVM documentation suggests it support POSIX ERE syntax, so maybe it's a bug.

Adding Options to Lookup

You'll keep the options nice and simple and implement only two options that don't require any extra parameters.

You'll implement these options:

- Add load addresses to each query. This is ideal if you want to know where the actual function is in memory.

- Provide a module summary only. Don't produce function names, only list the count of hits per module.

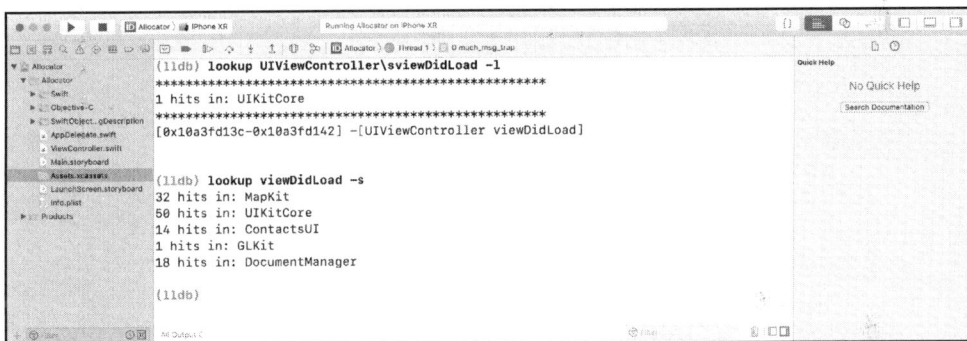

The __generate_script command added some placeholders for the **generateOptionParser** method found at the bottom of the **lookup.py** file. In the **generateOptionParser** function, change the function so it contains the following code:

```python
def generateOptionParser():
    usage = "usage: %prog [options] code_to_query"
    parser = optparse.OptionParser(usage=usage, prog="lookup")

    parser.add_option("-l", "--load_address",
            action="store_true",
            default=False,
            dest="load_address",
            help="Show the load addresses for a particular hit")

    parser.add_option("-s", "--module_summary",
            action="store_true",
            default=False,
            dest="module_summary",
            help="Only show the amount of queries in the module")
    return parser
```

There's no need to take a deep dive in this code since you learned about this in an earlier chapter. You're creating two supported options, **-l**, or **--load_address** and **-s**, or **--module_summary**.

You'll implement the load address option first. In the **generateOutput** function, navigate to the for-loop iterating over the SBSymbolContext, which starts with the for context in mdict[key]: line of code.

Make that for-loop look like this:

```
for context in mdict[key]:
    query = ''

    # 1
    if options.load_address:
        # 2
        start = context.symbol.addr.GetLoadAddress(target)
        end = context.symbol.end_addr.GetLoadAddress(target)
        # 3
        startHex = '0x' + format(start, '012x')
        endHex = '0x' + format(end, '012x')
        query += '[{}-{}]\n'.format(startHex, endHex)

    query += context.symbol.name
    query += '\n\n'
    output += query
```

Here's what that does:

1. You're adding the conditional to see if the load_address option is set. If so, this will add content to the output.

2. This traverses the SBSymbolContext to the SBSymbol (**symbol** property) to the SBAddress (**addr** or **end_addr**) and gets a Python long through the **GetLoadAddress** method. There's actually a load_addr available to SBAddress, but I've found it to be a bit buggy at times, so I usually use the GetLoadAddress API instead. This method expects the SBTarget as an input parameter.

3. After you have the start and end addresses expressed in Python long's, format them to look pretty and consistent using the Python **format** function. This pads the number with zeros if needed, notes it should be 12 digits long, and formats it in hexadecimal.

Save your work and revisit Xcode and the LLDB console. Reload.

```
(lldb) reload_script
```

Give your new option a go:

```
(lldb) lookup -l DSObjectiveCObject
```

You'll get output similar to the truncated output:

```
**************************************************************
8 hits in Allocator
**************************************************************
[0x0001099d2c00-0x0001099d2c40]
-[DSObjectiveCObject setLastName:]

[0x0001099d2c40-0x0001099d2cae]
-[DSObjectiveCObject .cxx_destruct]
```

Put a breakpoint at an address from this list to confirm it matches with the function. Do it like so, replacing the address with one from your list:

```
(lldb) b 0x0001099d2c00
Breakpoint 3: where = Allocator`-[DSObjectiveCObject
setLastName:] at DSObjectiveCObject.h:33, address =
0x00000001099d2c00
```

Great job! One more option to implement and then you're done!

Revisit the **generateOutput** function for the final time. Find the following line:

```
moduleName = firstItem.module.file.basename
```

Add the following code right after that line:

```
if options.module_summary:
    output += '{} hits in {}\n'.format(count, moduleName)
    continue
```

This simply adds the number of hits in each module and skips adding the actual symbols.

That's it. No more code. Save, then head back to Xcode to reload your script:

```
(lldb) reload_script
```

Give your **module_summary** option a go:

```
(lldb) lookup -s viewWillAppear
```

You'll get something similar to this:

```
2 hits in Allocator
1 hits in DocumentManager
54 hits in UIKitCore
6 hits in ShareSheet
5 hits in PrintKitUI
1 hits in GLKit
8 hits in MapKit
```

That's it! You're done! You've made a pretty powerful script from scratch. You'll use this script to search for code in future chapters. The summary option is a great tool to have when you're casting a wide search and then want to narrow it down further.

Key Points

- Give some thought to organizing your `.lldbinit` and loading scripts now, while you've only got a few.

- Experiment with commands in the `lldb` console before attempting to write scripts so you can experiment and iterate faster.

- There's often more than one API in LLDB's Script Bridge module that will return the same information. Always be on the lookout for alternatives.

- You can add options to your `generateOptionParser` that don't yet do anything. Then add code for each option one-by-one so you can code and test each one separately.

Where to Go From Here?

There are many more options you could add to this `lookup` command. You could make a **–S** or **–Swift_only** query by going after SBSymbolContext's SBFunction (through the **function** property) to access the **GetLanguage()** API. While you're at it, you should also add a **–m** or **––module** option to filter content to a certain module. Also, don't forget to add some general help text.

If you want to see what else is possible, check out my implementation of lookup in the `lookup.py` materials for Appendix C "Helpful Python Scripts".

Enjoy adding those options!

Chapter 26: SB Examples, Resymbolicating a Stripped ObjC Binary

This will be a novel example of what you can do with some knowledge of the Objective-C runtime mixed in with knowledge of the lldb Python module.

When LLDB comes up against a stripped executable (an executable devoid of DWARF debugging information), LLDB won't have the symbol information to give you a proper stack trace.

Instead, LLDB generates a **synthetic** name for any method it recognizes as a method, but doesn't know what to call it.

Here's an example of a synthetic method created by LLDB on a fun-to-explore process...

```
___lldb_unnamed_symbol906$$SpringBoard
```

One strategy to reverse engineer the name of this method is to create a breakpoint on it and explore the registers right at the start of the method.

Using your assembly knowledge of the Objective-C runtime, you know the **RSI** register (x64) or the **X1** register (ARM64) will contain the Objective-C Selector that holds the name of method. In addition, you also have the **RDI** (x64) or **X0** (ARM64) register which holds the reference to the instance (or class). Remember that you can use **arg1** and **arg2** as aliases for these registers, so you don't have to worry about chip architecture.

However, as soon as you leave the function prologue, you have no guarantee that either of these registers will contain the values of interest, as they will likely be overwritten. What if a stripped method of interest calls another function? The registers you care about are now lost, as they're set for the parameters for this new function. You need a way to resymbolicate a stack trace without having to rely upon these registers.

In this chapter, you'll build an LLDB script that will resymbolicate stripped Objective-C functions in a stack trace.

```
(lldb) bt
* thread #1, queue = 'com.apple.main-thread', stop reason = breakpoint 1.1
    frame #1: 0x0000000105fec4fc ShadesOfRay`___lldb_unnamed_symbol13$$ShadesOfRay + 924
    frame #3: 0x0000000105febd5f ShadesOfRay`___lldb_unnamed_symbol1$$ShadesOfRay + 79
    frame #5: 0x0000000107a9f5c7 UIKit`-[UIBarButtonItem(UIInternal) _sendAction:withEvent:] + 149
    frame #6: 0x0000000107664d22 UIKit`-[UIApplication sendAction:to:from:forEvent:] + 83
    frame #7: 0x000000001077e925c UIKit`-[UIControl sendAction:to:forEvent:] + 67
    frame #8: 0x00000001077e9577 UIKit`-[UIControl _sendActionsForEvents:withEvent:] + 450
    frame #9: 0x00000001077e96eb UIKit`-[UIControl _sendActionsForEvents:withEvent:] + 822
    frame #10: 0x00000001077e84b2 UIKit`-[UIControl touchesEnded:withEvent:] + 618
```

When you called **bt** for this process, LLDB didn't have the function names for the highlighted methods. You will build a new command named **sbt** that will look for stripped functions and try to resymbolicate them using the Objective-C runtime. By the end of the chapter, your sbt command will produce this for the same stack trace:

```
(lldb) sbt
frame #1: 0x105fec4fc ShadesOfRay`-[RayView initWithFrame:] + 924
frame #3: 0x105febd5f ShadesOfRay`-[ViewController generateRayViewTapped:] + 79
frame #5: 0x107a9f5c7 UIKit`-[UIBarButtonItem(UIInternal) _sendAction:withEvent:] + 149
frame #6: 0x107664d22 UIKit`-[UIApplication sendAction:to:from:forEvent:] + 83
frame #7: 0x1077e925c UIKit`-[UIControl sendAction:to:forEvent:] + 67
frame #8: 0x1077e9577 UIKit`-[UIControl _sendActionsForEvents:withEvent:] + 450
frame #9: 0x1077e96eb UIKit`-[UIControl _sendActionsForEvents:withEvent:] + 822
frame #10: 0x1077e84b2 UIKit`-[UIControl touchesEnded:withEvent:] + 618
```

Those once stripped-out Objective-C function calls are now resymbolicated. As with any of these scripts, you can run this new sbt script on any Objective-C executable provided LLDB can attach to it.

So How Are You Doing This, Exactly?

Let's first discuss how one can go about resymbolicating Objective-C code in a stripped binary with the Objective-C runtime.

The Objective-C runtime can list all classes from a particular image (an image being the main executable, a dynamic library, an NSBundle, etc.) provided you have the full path to the image. This can be accomplished through the **objc_copyClassNamesForImage** API.

From there, you can get a list of all classes returned by objc_copyClassNamesForImage where you can dump all class and instance methods for a particular class using the **class_copyMethodList** API.

Therefore, you can grab all the method addresses and compare them to the addresses of the stack trace. If the stack trace's function can't generate a default function name (such as if the SBSymbol is synthetically generated by LLDB), then you can assume LLDB has no debug info for this address.

Using the lldb Python module, you can get the starting address for a particular function — even when a function's execution is partially complete. This is accomplished using SBValue's reference to an SBAddress. From there, you can compare the addresses of all the Objective-C methods you've obtained to the starting address of the synthetic SBSymbol. If two addresses match, then you can swap out the stripped (synthetic) method name and replace it with the function name that was obtained with the Objective-C runtime.

Don't worry: You'll explore this systematically using LLDB's **script** command before you go building the Python script.

50 Shades of Ray

Included in the starter directory is an application called **50 Shades of Ray**. A well-chosen name (in my humble opinion) for a project that showcases the many faces of Ray Wenderlich. There's gentle Ray, there's superhero Ray, there's confused Ray, there's even goat BFF Ray!

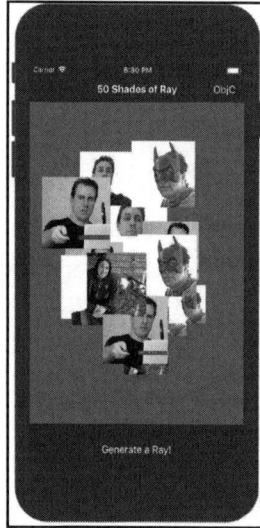

Tapping the UIButton at the bottom generates a random picture of Ray in a UIView of random size.

Wow, that will make *billions* on the App Store!

Open the **50 Shades of Ray** project and build and run the app. In the Xcode project, there are two schemes. Make sure you select the **50 Shades of Ray** scheme and not the **Stripped** scheme. You'll use that scheme later.

Once you've gotten your enjoyment out of generating random pictures of Ray, click on the **ObjC** UIBarButtonItem in the upper right hand corner.

This UIBarButtonItem is tied to an IBAction that prints out all the methods implemented by the main executable and displays them to stderr in your console. In fact, you can see the name of the method that triggered the console output within the console output!

Scan the console for the method -**[ViewController dumpObjCMethodsTapped:]**. It's this method that dumped all the Objective-C methods in the main executable.

Preceding the function is a number (in my case, 4449531728), which holds the starting address for this Objective-C method.

Don't believe me? Pause execution and type the following into LLDB:

```
(lldb) image lookup -a 4449531728
```

You address will be different. This is hunting down the location of the address **4449531728** in memory and seeing where it relates in reference to your project.

```
Address: 50 Shades of Ray[0x00000001000017e0] (50 Shades of
Ray.__TEXT.__text + 624)
Summary: 50 Shades of Ray`-[ViewController
dumpObjCMethodsTapped:] at ViewController.m:36
```

Groovy. This is telling you the location in memory 4449531728 is what was loaded from –**[ViewController dumpObjCMethodsTapped:]**. Now look at the code in this method.

Head on in to **ViewController.m** and hunt for the **dumpObjCMethodsTapped:**

The exact details don't need to be covered too closely, but it's worth pointing out the following:

- All the Objective-C classes implemented in the main executable are enumerated through **objc_copyClassNamesForImage**.

- For each class, there's logic to grab all the class and instance methods.

- In order to grab the class methods for a particular Objective-C Class, you must get the **meta class**. No, that term was not made up by some hipster developer in tight jeans, plaid shirt & beard. The meta class is the class responsible for the static methods of a particular class. For example, all methods that begin with + are implemented by the meta Class and not the Class.

- All the methods are aggregated into a NSMutableDictionary, where the key for each of these methods is the location in memory where the function resides.

Using Script to Guide Your Way

Time to use the **script** LLDB command to explore the lldb module APIs and build a quick POC to see how you're going to tackle finding the starting address of a function in memory.

In the LLDB console, set a breakpoint on **NSLog**:

```
(lldb) b NSLog
```

You'll get multiple SBBreakpointLocation hits. That's fine. Now continue running the application.

Tap on the **ObjC** UIBarButtonItem in the upper right corner of the Simulator.

Execution will stop right before the app writes to stderr.

Using the global variable **lldb.frame**, dig into what APIs are available to you to grab the starting address of the NSLog function.

Start with the global variable and build from there.

```
(lldb) script print (lldb.frame)
```

You'll get the __str__() representation of the SBFrame. Nothing new.

```
frame #0: 0x000000010b472390 Foundation`NSLog
```

If you decided to use **gdocumentation** to search documentation for SBFrame (from Chapter 22, "Script Bridging Classes & Hierarchy," you'll see SBFrame has a few potential candidates for getting the start address of a function.

pc looks interesting to grab the RIP regster (x64) or the PC (ARM64), but that will only work at the start of a function. You need to grab the starting address from any offset inside the SBFrame.

Unfortunately, there are no APIs you can use in the SBFrame to get the starting address from any instruction offset within the function. You'll need to turn your attention to other classes referenced by the SBFrame to get what you need.

Grab the **SBSymbol** reference for the SBFrame:

```
(lldb) script print (lldb.frame.symbol)
```

The SBSymbol is responsible for the implementation offset address of NSLog. That is, the SBSymbol will tell you where this function is implemented in a module; it doesn't hold the actual address of where the NSLog was loaded into memory.

However, you can use the SBAddress property along with the **GetLoadAddress** API of SBAddress to find where the start location of NSLog is in your current process.

```
(lldb) script print
(lldb.frame.symbol.addr.GetLoadAddress(lldb.target))
```

You'll get a number in decimal. I got **4484178832**. Convert it to hex using LLDB and compare the output to the start address of NSLog:

```
(lldb) p/x 4484178832
```

I got **0x000000010b472390** as my hexadecimal representation.

Compare your output with the starting address of NSLog to see if they match.

```
    1     Foundation`NSLog:
    2  -> 0x180ba86b8 <+0>:   sub    sp, sp, #0x20      ≡  Thre
    3     0x180ba86bc <+4>:   stp    x29, x30, [sp, #0x10]
    4     0x180ba86c0 <+8>:   add    x29, sp, #0x10
    5     0x180ba86c4 <+12>:  adrp   x8, 237823
    6     0x180ba86c8 <+16>:  ldr    x8, [x8, #0xd80]
    7     0x180ba86cc <+20>:  ldr    x8, [x8]
    8     0x180ba86d0 <+24>:  str    x8, [sp, #0x8]
    9     0x180ba86d4 <+28>:  add    x8, x29, #0x10
   10     0x180ba86d8 <+32>:  str    x8, [sp]
   11     0x180ba86dc <+36>:  add    x1, x29, #0x10
⏸ ⏭ ⏴ ⏶ ⏷ ⏺ ⏹ ⏩ 🖼 50 Shades of Ray ⏵ Thread 1 ⏺ 0 NSLog
  File "<input>", line 1
    print lldb.frame
          ^
SyntaxError: Missing parentheses in call to 'print'. Did you mean print(lldb.frame)?
(lldb) script print (lldb.frame)
frame #0: 0x0000000180ba86b8 Foundation`NSLog
(lldb) script print (lldb.frame.symbol)
id = {0x0001a2cb}, range = [0x00000000004986b8-0x0000000000498710), name="NSLog"
(lldb) script print (lldb.frame.symbol.addr.GetLoadAddress(lldb.target)
(lldb) )
error: ')' is not a valid command.
(lldb) script print (lldb.frame.symbol.addr.GetLoadAddress(lldb.target))
6454675128
(lldb) p/x 6454675128
(long) $0 = 0x0000000180ba86b8
(lldb)
```

Woot! A match! That's your path to resymbolication redemption.

lldb.value With NSDictionary

Since you're already here, you can explore one more thing. How are you going to parse this NSDictionary with all these addresses?

You'll copy the code, *almost* verbatim, that generates all the methods and apply it to an **EvaluateExpression** API to get an SBValue.

You should still be paused at the beginning of NSLog. Jump to the calling frame, -**[ViewController dumpObjCMethodsTapped:]**.

```
(lldb) f 1
```

This will get to the previous frame, dumpObjCMethodsTapped:. You now have access to all variables within this method, including the **retdict** that's responsible for dumping out all the methods implemented within the main executable.

Grab the SBValue interpretation of the **retdict** reference.

```
(lldb) script print (lldb.frame.FindVariable('retdict'))
```

This will print the SBValue for retdict:

```
(__NSDictionaryM *) retdict = 0x000060800024ce10 10 key/value
pairs
```

Since this an NSDictionary, you actually want to dereference this value so you can enumerate it.

```
(lldb) script print (lldb.frame.FindVariable('retdict').deref)
```

You'll get some more relevant output (which is truncated):

```
(__NSDictionaryM) *retdict = {
  [0] = {
    key = 0x000060800002bb80 @"4411948768"
    value = 0x000060800024c660 @"-[AppDelegate window]"
  }
  [1] = {
    key = 0x000060800002c1e0 @"4411948592"
    value = 0x000060800024dd10 @"-[ViewController toolBar]"
  }
  [2] = {
    key = 0x000060800002bc00 @"4411948800"
    value = 0x000060800024c7e0 @"-[AppDelegate setWindow:]"
  }
  [3] = {
```

```
        key = 0x000060800002bba0 @"4411948864"
        value = 0x000060800004afe0 @"-[AppDelegate .cxx_destruct]"
    }
```

It's this you want to start with, since this prints out all the values for the keys.

Make a **lldb.value** out of this SBValue and assign it to a variable **a**.

```
(lldb) script a =
lldb.value(lldb.frame.FindVariable('retdict').deref)
```

This is one of those times where I would prefer to work with an lldb.value over an SBValue. From here, you can easily explore the values within this NSDictionary.

Print the first value within this lldb.value NSDictionary.

```
(lldb) script (print a[0])
```

From there, you can have either the key or value that you can print out.

Print out the key first:

```
(lldb) script print (a[0].key)
```

You'll get something similar to the following:

```
(__NSCFString *) key = 0x000060800002bb80 @"4411948768"
```

Print the value:

```
(lldb) script print (a[0].value)
```

This will print something similar to the following:

```
(__NSCFString *) value = 0x000060800024c660 @"-[AppDelegate
window]"
```

```
(lldb) script print a[0]
(__lldb_autogen_nspair) [0] = {
  key = 0x000060800002bb80
  value = 0x000060800024c660
}
(lldb) script print a[0].key
(__NSCFString *) key = 0x000060800002bb80 @"4411948768"
(lldb) script print a[0].value
(__NSCFString *) value = 0x000060800024c660 @"-[AppDelegate window]"
(lldb) |
```

If you only want the return value without the referencing address, you'll need to cast this lldb.value back into a SBValue then grab the description.

```
(lldb) script print (a[0].value.sbvalue.description)
```

This will get you the desired **–[AppDelegate window]** for output. Note you may have a different method.

If you wanted to dump all keys in this lldb.value a instance, you can use Python List comprehensions to dump all the keys out.

```
(lldb) script print ('\n'.join([x.key.sbvalue.description for x
in a]))
```

You'll get output similar to the following:

```
4411948768
4411948592
4411948800
4411948864
4411948656
4411948720
4411949072
4411946944
4411946352
4411946976
```

Same approach for values:

```
(lldb) script print ('\n'.join([x.value.sbvalue.description for
x in a]))
```

You now know how to parse this NSDictionary if, hypothetically, it were to be placed in some JIT code...

The plan is to copy the code from the dumpObjCMethodsTapped: into the Python script, and have it execute as JIT code. From there, you'll use the same procedure to parse it out from the NSDictionary.

You've done a lot of exploring in the console. Xcode does save the console for a little while in `DerivedData`, but that's not a safe long term location. In Xcode, you can go to the **Reports Navigator** and click one of the **Run** items to see the lldb console output for that session.

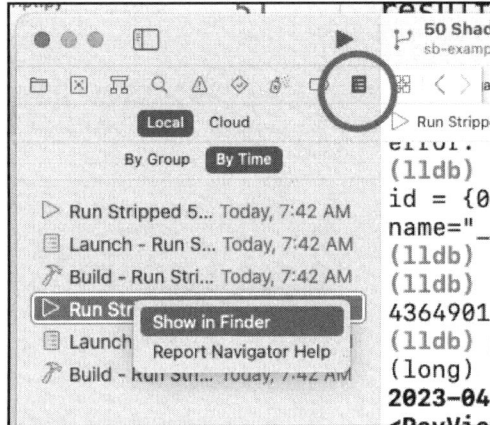

Then you can right-click to bring up the context menu and **Show in Finder** to reveal the actual logs. Copy the `.xcresult` file somewhere safe.

You can open it in Xcode at anytime to review your notes.

Sounds good? Get your gameplan ready and head on in to the next section!

The "Stripped" 50 Shades of Ray

Yeah, that title got your attention, didn't it?

Within the Xcode schemes of the 50 Shades of Ray executable, there is a scheme named **Stripped 50 Shades of Ray**.

Stop the execution of the current process by pressing **Command-.** or whatever method you prefer, and select the **Stripped 50 Shades of Ray** Xcode scheme.

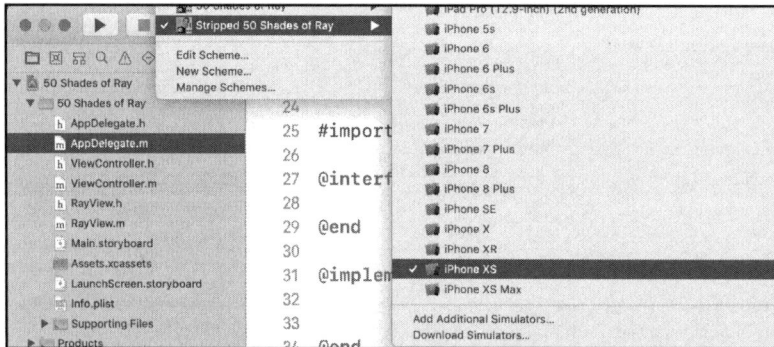

This scheme builds a debug executable, but removes the debugging information that you have become accustomed to in your day-to-day development cycles.

Build and run the executable. Included within this project is a **shared symbolic breakpoint**. Enable this breakpoint.

There's no need to modify this symbolic breakpoint, but it's worth noting what this breakpoint does.

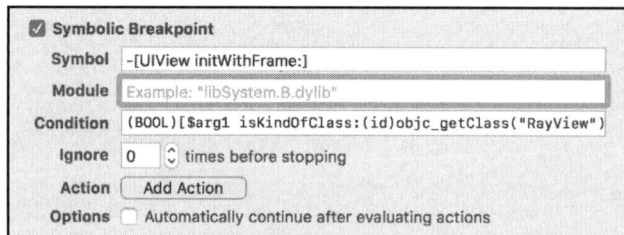

This breakpoint will stop on **–[UIView initWithFrame:]** and has a condition to only stop if the UIView is of type **RayView**, a subclass of UIView. This RayView is responsible for displaying the lovely images of Ray Wenderlich within the application.

Tap the **Generate a Ray!** button. Execution will stop on **–[UIView initWithFrame:]** method.

Take a look at the stack trace.

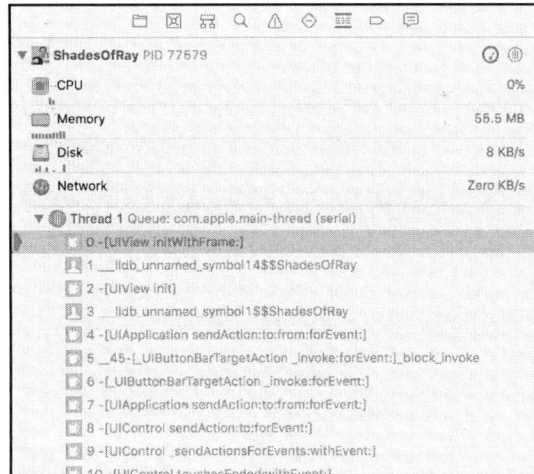

There's something interesting about stack frame 1 & 3: There's no debug information in there. LLDB has defaulted to generating a synthetic function name for those methods. Depending on your hardware, you may see things in a slightly different order, but there should be two stripped frames near the top of the backtrace.

Confirm this in LLDB.

In LLDB, make sure you are in the starting `initWithFrame:`. If you're in a different frame, or you just want to be certain you're in the right place, type `f 0` in the `lldb` console.

Use **script** to see if frame zero is synthetic or not:

```
(lldb) script lldb.frame.symbol.synthetic
```

You'll get `False`. Makes sense, because you know this is `initWithFrame:`. Jump to one of the synthetic frames:

```
(lldb) f 1
```

Execute the previous `script` logic:

```
(lldb) script lldb.frame.symbol.synthetic
```

You'll get `True` this time.

This is enough research to get you going with the Python script.

Building sbt.py

Included within the **starter** folder is a Python script named **sbt.py**.

Stick this script into your **~/lldb** directory. Provided you've installed the **lldbinit.py** script, this will load all the Python files into the LLDB directory.

If you didn't follow along in Chapter 25, "SB Examples, Improved Lookup", you can manually install the sbt.py by modifying your ~/.lldbinit file.

Once you've placed the sbt.py file into the **~/lldb directory**, reload your commands in ~/.**lldbinit** using the **reload_script** you created in Chapter 22 "Script Bridging Classes & Hierarchy".

Check and see if LLDB correctly recognizes the sbt command:

```
(lldb) help sbt
```

You'll get some help text if LLDB recognizes the command. This will be the starting point for the sbt command.

With the symbolic breakpoint still active and program stopped, give the script a run by typing sbt in the lldb console.

You should see the same stack trace as before with some stripped frames because you haven't yet added logic to resymbolicate the symbols.

It's time to make a few modifications to fix that.

Implementing the Code

The JIT code is already set up. All you need to do is call it, then compare the return NSDictionary against any synthetic SBValues.

Find **processStackTraceStringFromAddresses** and search for these comments:

```
# New content start 1
# New content end 1
```

Add some new code here that calls the JIT code to generate a list of potential methods in a NSDictionary:

```
# New content start 1
methods = target.EvaluateExpression(script,
                                    generateOptions())
methodsVal = lldb.value(methods.deref)
# New content end 1
```

You've called the code that returns the NSDictionary representation and assigned it to the SBValue instance variable **methods**.

You can cast the **SBValue** into a **lldb.value** (technically it's just a **value**, but you might get confused if I don't have the module in there) and assign it to the variable **methodsVal**.

Now for the final part of Python code. All you need to do is determine if a SBFrame's SBSymbol is synthetic or not and perform the appropriate logic.

Search the following commented out code further down in processStackTraceStringFromAddresses:

```
# New content start 2
name = symbol.name
# New content end 2
```

Change this to look like the following:

```
# New content start 2
if symbol.synthetic: # 1
    children = methodsVal.sbvalue.GetNumChildren() # 2
    name = symbol.name + r' ... unresolved womp womp' # 3

    loadAddr = symbol.addr.GetLoadAddress(target) # 4

    for i in range(children):
        key = long(methodsVal[i].key.sbvalue.description) # 5
        if key == loadAddr:
            name = methodsVal[i].value.sbvalue.description # 6
            break
else:
    name = symbol.name # 7

# New content end 2

offset_str = ''
```

Breaking this down, you have the following:

1. You're enumerating the frames, which occur outside the scope of this code block. For each symbol, a check is performed to see if the symbol is synthetic or not. If it is, compare the memory address to the NSDictionary of addresses that were gathered.

2. This grabs the number of children in the lldb.value and checks to see if there's a match from the Objective-C list of classes.

3. Either way, a valid reference to the name variable needs to be produced for the display of the stack trace. You're opting to say you know this is a synthetic function, but fail to resolve it if your upcoming logic fails to produce a result.

4. This gets the address in memory to the synthetic function in question.

5. The key value given by the lldb.value is internally made up from an NSNumber, so you need to grab the **description** of this method and cast it into a number. Confusingly, it's assigned to a Python variable named key as well.

6. If the key variable is equal to the loadAddr, then you have a match. Assign the name variable to the description of the variable in the NSDictionary.

That should be it. Save your work and reload your LLDB contents using reload_script and give it a go.

Provided you are still in the Stripped 50 Shades of Ray scheme and are paused in the symbolic breakpoint that stops only in UIView's initWithFrame: (with the special condition), run the **sbt** command in the debugger to see if the originally unavailable frames have symbols.

```
(lldb) sbt
frame #0 : 0x11466a130 UIKitCore`-[UIView initWithFrame:]
frame #1 : 0x1042b1d78 ShadesOfRay`-[RayView initWithFrame:] +
556
frame #2 : 0x1042b12f8 ShadesOfRay`-[ViewController
generateRayViewTapped:] + 72
frame #3 : 0x1141fb6c8 UIKitCore`-[UIApplication
sendAction:to:from:forEvent:] + 96
```

Beautiful.

Key Points

- Using the `EvaluateExpression` command with `SBTarget` allows you to execute Swift or Objective-C from your Python script in the context of the running application.

- The Objective-C runtime has access to *all* of the methods in an application whether the symbols are stripped or not.

- When planning an LLDB script, use the interactive console to experiment with ideas.

- Console logs are stored in `DerivedData`, if you want to keep them for reference, you need to move them somewhere safe.

Where to Go From Here?

Congratulations! You've used the Objective-C runtime to successful resymbolicate a stripped binary! It's crazy what you can do with the proper application of Objective-C.

There are still a few holes in this script. This script doesn't play nice with Objective-C blocks. However, a careful study of how blocks are implemented as well as exploring the lldb Python module *might* reveal a way to indicate Objective-C block functions that have been stripped away.

In addition, this script will not work with an iOS executable in release mode. LLDB will not find the functions for a synthetic `SBSymbol` to reference the start address. This means that you would have to manually search upwards in the ARM64 assembly until you stumbled across an assembly instruction that looked like the start of a function (can you guess which instruction(s) to look for?).

If those script extensions don't interest you, try your luck with figuring out how to resymbolicate a Swift executable. The challenge definitely goes up by an order of magnitude, but it's still within the realm of possibility to do with LLDB. Have fun!

Chapter 27: SB Examples, Malloc Logging

For the final chapter in this section, you'll go through the same steps I myself took to understand how the **MallocStackLogging** environment variable is used to get the stack trace when an object is created.

From there, you'll create a custom LLDB command which gives you the stack trace of when an object was allocated or deallocated in memory — even after the stack trace is long gone from the debugger.

Knowing the stack trace of where an object was created in your program is not only useful for reverse engineering, but also has great use cases in your typical day-to-day debugging. When a process crashes, it's incredibly helpful to know the history of that memory and any allocation or deallocation events that occurred before your process went off the deep end.

This is another example of a script using stack-related logic, but this chapter will focus on the complete cycle of how to explore, learn, then implement a rather powerful custom command.

Setting Up the Scripts

You have a couple of scripts to use (and implement!) for this chapter. Let's go through each one of them and how you'll use them:

- **msl.py**: This is the command (which is an abbreviation for `MallocStackLogging`) script you'll be working on in this chapter. This has a basic skeleton of the logic.

- **lookup.py**: Wait — you already made this command, right? Yes, but I'll give you my own version of the `lookup` command that adds a couple of additional options at the price of uglier code. You'll use one of the options to filter your searches to specific modules within a process.

- **sbt.py**: This command takes a backtrace with unsymbolicated symbols, and symbolicate it. You made this in the previous chapter, and you'll need it at the very end of this chapter. And in case you didn't work through the previous chapter, it's included in this chapter's resources for you to install.

> **Note**: These scripts are also in Appendix C "Helpful Python Scripts" Check it out for some other novel ideas for LLDB scripts. It's important to note that a lot of scripts in Appendix C have dependencies on other files, so if you try to use only one script then it might not compile until the full set of files are included.

Now for the usual setup. Take all the Python files found in the **starter** directory for this chapter and copy them into your ~/lldb directory. I am assuming you have the lldbinit.py file already set up, found in Chapter 25, "SB Examples, Improved Lookup."

Launch an LLDB session in Terminal and go through all the `help` commands to make sure each script has loaded successfully:

```
(lldb) help msl
(lldb) help lookup
(lldb) help sbt
```

MallocStackLogging Explained

In case you're unfamiliar with the `MallocStackLogging` environment variable, when the `MallocStackLogging` environment variable is set to `true`, it'll monitor and record allocations and deallocations of memory on the heap. Pretty neat!

Included within the **starter** directory is the **50 Shades of Ray** Xcode project from the last chapter with some additional logic for this chapter. Open the project.

Before you run it, you'll need to modify the scheme for your purposes. Select the **50 Shades of Ray** scheme (make sure there's no "Stripped" in the name), then press **Command-Shift-<** to edit the scheme.

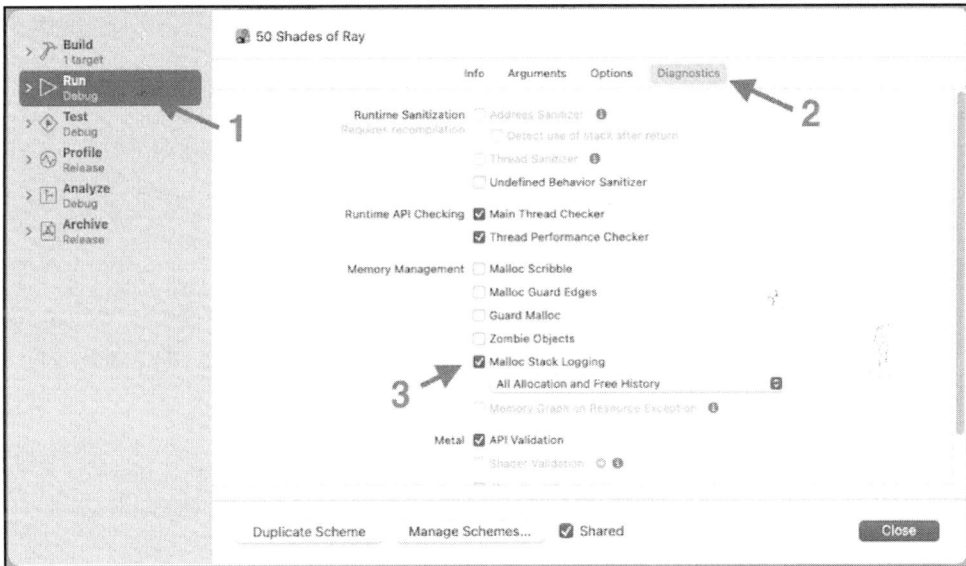

1. Select **Run**.

2. Select **Diagnostics**.

3. Select **Malloc Stack Logging**, then **All Allocation and Free History**.

Once you've enabled this environment variable, build the **50 Shades of Ray** program and run it.

If the `MallocStackLogging` environment variable is enabled, you'll see some output from the LLDB console similar to the following:

```
ShadesOfRay(12911,0x104e663c0) malloc: stack logs being written
into /tmp/stack-logs.12911.10d42a000.ShadesOfRay.gjehFY.index

ShadesOfRay(12911,0x104e663c0) malloc: recording malloc and VM
allocation stacks to disk using standard recorder

ShadesOfRay(12911,0x104e663c0) malloc: process 12673 no longer
exists, stack logs deleted from /tmp/stack-
logs.12673.11b51d000.ShadesOfRay.GVo3li.index
```

Don't worry about the details of the output; simply look for the presence of output like this as it indicates the `MallocStackLogging` is working properly.

While the app is running, click the **Generate a Ray** button at the bottom.

Once a new Ray is created (that is, you see an instance of Ray Wenderlich's amazingly innovative & handsome face pop up in the Simulator), perform the following steps:

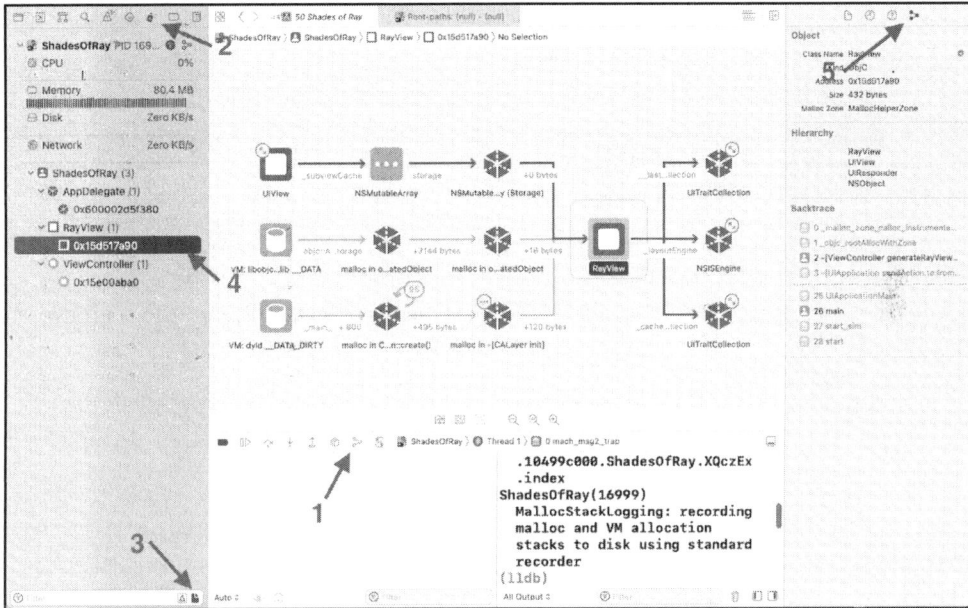

1. Select the **Debug Memory Graph** located at the top of the LLDB console in Xcode.

2. Select the **Show the Debug navigator** in the left panel.

3. At the bottom of the left panel select the **Show only content from workspace**.

4. Select the memory address that references the **RayView**.

5. In the right panel of Xcode, make sure the **Show the Memory Inspector** is selected.

Once you've jumped through all those hoops, you'll have the exact stack trace of where this RayView instance was created through the **Backtrace** section on the right side of the Xcode window. How cool is that?! The authors of Xcode (and its *many* modules) have made our lives a bit easier with these memory debugging features!

Plan of Attack

You've seen it's possible to grab a stack trace for an instantiated object, but you're going to do one better than Apple.

Your command will be able to turn on the `MallocStackLogging` functionality at will through LLDB, which means you won't have to rely on an environment variable. This has the additional benefit that you won't need to restart your process in case you forget to turn it on during a debug session.

So how are you going to figure out how this `MallocStackLogging` feature works?

When I am absolutely clueless as to where to begin when exploring built-in code, I follow the rather loose process below and alter queries, depending on the scenario or the output:

- I look for chokepoints where I can safely assume some logic of interest will be executed. If I know I can replicate something of interest, I'll force that action to occur while monitoring it.

- When monitoring the code of interest, I'll use various tools like LLDB or DTrace (which you'll learn about in the next section) to find the module holding the code of interest. Again, a module is a dynamic library, framework, `NSBundle`, or something of that sort.

- Once I find the module of interest, I'll dump all the code from the module, then filter for what I need using various custom scripts like **lookup.py**.

- If I find a particular function that looks relevant to my interests, I'll first try a web search for it. I'll often find some incredibly useful hints on Apple's open-source code site (https://opensource.apple.com/) that reveal how I can use what I've found.

- Searching through Apple's open-source URLs, I'll grab as much context as I can about the code of interest. Sometimes there's code in the C/C++ source file that will give me an idea of how to formulate the parameters into the function, or perhaps I'll get a description of the code or its purpose in the header file.

- If there's no documentation to be gained from a web search, I'll set breakpoints on the code of interest and see if I can trigger that function naturally. Once hit, I'll explore both the stack frames and registers to see what kind of parameters are being passed in, as well as the context.

You're going to follow these same steps to see where the code for `MallocStackLogging` resides, explore the module responsible for handling stack tracing logic, then explore any interesting code of interest within that module.

Let's get cracking!

Hunting for a Starting Point

As you just saw, Xcode provides a special backtrace for any object that gets allocated when `MallocStackLogging` is enabled. Go ahead and build and run the app and then tap on `Generate a Ray!` a few times to create some instances of `RayView`. Now use the **Debug Memory Graph** a few times to stop the app. Now inspect some of the `RayView` instances to look for patterns.

One thing you might notice is that *ALL* of the malloc stack traces in the Memory inspector have in frame 0 something like this:

```
_malloc_zone_calloc_instrumented_or_legacy
```

In the LLDB console, use the `lookup` command to see if you can find that anywhere:

```
(lldb) lookup _malloc_zone_calloc_instrumented_or_legacy
```

From the output, you can see that there is a `.dylib` that holds that symbol:

```
*********************************************************
1 hits in: libsystem_malloc.dylib
*********************************************************
_malloc_zone_calloc_instrumented_or_legacy
```

> **Note**: your stack trace might show **_malloc_zone_calloc** and not the **_malloc_zone_calloc_instrumented_or_legacy** in frame 0.

The module name, **libsystem_malloc.dylib** fits the bill for something implementing malloc stack logging related logic. Is this it? Maybe. Worth checking out? Totally!

Take a deeper dive into this module and see what it has to offer you.

Using `lookup` command, explore all the methods implemented by the **libsystem_malloc.dylib** module that you can execute within your process.

```
(lldb) lookup . —m libsystem_malloc.dylib
```

In iOS 16.0, I get 593 hits. I *could* gloss through all these methods, but I am getting increasingly lazy as a debugger person. Let's just hunt for everything that pertains to the word "log" (for logging) and see what we get. Type the following in LLDB:

```
(lldb) lookup [lL]og —m libsystem_malloc.dylib
```

I get 26 hits from using a case insensitive search for the word `log` inside the `libsystem_malloc.dylib` module.

This hit count is bearable enough to weed through. Another way you could have filtered down the 593 hits would be to use the **Filter** in the bottom right of the LLDB console in Xcode. Just remember to clear the filter when you're done, or you'll go crazy wondering why all of your lldb commands aren't producing output.

Do any of those functions look interesting? Hell yeah! Here are some of the following functions that look interesting to me:

```
__mach_stack_logging_get_frames

__mach_stack_logging_get_frames_for_stackid

turn_off_stack_logging

turn_on_stack_logging

_malloc_register_stack_logger
```

Of these, the **turn_on_stack_logging** and the **__mach_stack_logging_get_frames** look like they're worth checking out.

You've found the module of interest, as well as some functions worth further exploration. Time to jump out on the Internet and see what's out there.

Googling JIT Function Candidates

Google for any code pertaining to **turn_on_stack_logging**. Take a look at this search query:

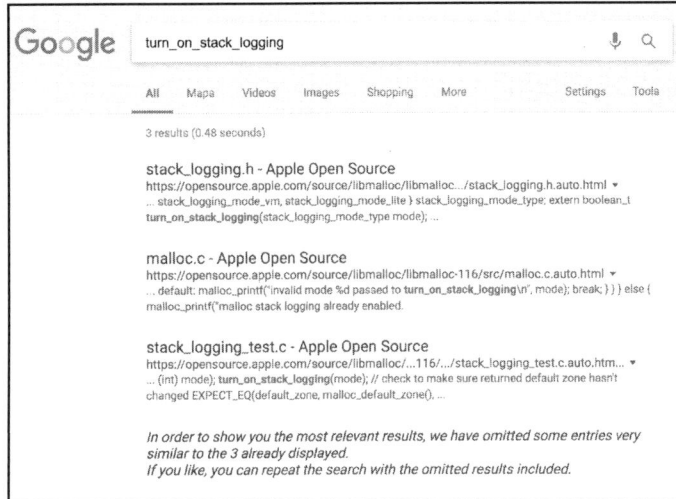

At the time I wrote this, I got three hits from Google (well, it was actually eight hits with "exclude similar searches" off, but that's not the point).

These functions are not well-known and are not typically discussed in any circle outside of Apple. In fact, I am rather confident the majority of iOS application developers in Apple don't know about them either, because when would they use them for writing apps?

This stuff belongs to the low-level C developers of Apple, whom we totally take for granted.

From the Google search, check out the following code from the libmalloc (https://opensource.apple.com/source/libmalloc/libmalloc-116/private/stack_logging.h.auto.html) header file at Apple's open-source site:

```
typedef enum {
    stack_logging_mode_none = 0,
    stack_logging_mode_all,
    stack_logging_mode_malloc,
    stack_logging_mode_vm,
    stack_logging_mode_lite
} stack_logging_mode_type;

extern boolean_t turn_on_stack_logging(stack_logging_mode_type
mode);
```

This is some **really good** information to work with. The `turn_on_stack_logging` function expects one parameter of type `int` (C enum). The enum **stack_logging_mode_type** tells you if you want the **stack_logging_mode_all** option, it will be at value 1.

You'll run an experiment by turning off the stack logging environment variable, execute the above function via LLDB, and see if Xcode is recording stack traces for any malloc'd object after you've called `turn_on_stack_logging`.

Before you do that, you'll first explore the other function, `__mach_stack_logging_get_frames`.

Exploring __mach_stack_logging_get_frames

Fortunately, for your exploration efforts, `__mach_stack_logging_get_frames` can also be found in the same header file. This function signature looks like the following:

```
extern kern_return_t __mach_stack_logging_get_frames(
                              task_t task,
                      mach_vm_address_t address,
           mach_vm_address_t *stack_frames_buffer,
                      uint32_t max_stack_frames,
                              uint32_t *count);
    /* Gets the last allocation record (malloc, realloc, or
free) about address */
```

This is a good starting point, but what if there are parameters you're not 100% sure how to obtain? For example, what's `task_t task` all about? This is basically a parameter that specifies the process you want this function to act on. But what if you didn't know that?

Using Google and searching for any implementation files that contain `__mach_stack_logging_get_frames` can be a big help when you're uncertain about things like this.

After a casual Googling, the heap_find.cpp URL provides insight to the first parameter that's expected within this function.

This file contains the following code:

```
task_t task = mach_task_self();
/* Omitted code.... */
    stack_entry->address = addr;
    stack_entry->type_flags = stack_logging_type_alloc;
    stack_entry->argument = 0;
```

```
      stack_entry->num_frames = 0;
      stack_entry->frames[0] = 0;

      err = __mach_stack_logging_get_frames(task,
                        (mach_vm_address_t)addr,
                          stack_entry->frames,
                                MAX_FRAMES,
                    &stack_entry->num_frames);

    if (err == 0 && stack_entry->num_frames > 0) {
      // Terminate the frames with zero if there is room
      if (stack_entry->num_frames < MAX_FRAMES)
        stack_entry->frames[stack_entry->num_frames] = 0;
    } else {
      g_malloc_stack_history.clear();
    }
  }
}
```

The task_t parameter has an easy way to get the task representing the current process through the mach_task_self function located in **libsystem_kernel.dylib**. You can confirm this yourself with the lookup LLDB command.

Testing the Functions

To prevent you from getting bored to tears, I've already implemented the logic for the __mach_stack_logging_get_frames inside the app.

Hopefully, you still have the application running. If not, get the app running with MallocStackLogging still enabled.

It's always a good idea to build your proof-of-concept JIT code in Xcode first, and once it's working, then (and only then!) transfer it to your LLDB script. You're gonna hate your life if you try to write your POC JIT script code straight in LLDB first. Trust me.

In Xcode, navigate to the **stack_logger.cpp** file. __mach_stack_logging_get_frames was written in C++, so you'll need to use C++ code to execute it.

The only function in this file is trace_address:

```
void trace_address(mach_vm_address_t addr) {

  typedef struct LLDBStackAddress {
    mach_vm_address_t *addresses;
```

```
    uint32_t count = 0;
  } LLDBStackAddress;    // 1

  LLDBStackAddress stackaddress; // 2
  __unused mach_vm_address_t address = (mach_vm_address_t)addr;
  __unused task_t task = mach_task_self_;   // 3

  stackaddress.addresses = (mach_vm_address_t *)calloc(100,
                       sizeof(mach_vm_address_t)); // 4

  __mach_stack_logging_get_frames(task,
                      address,
              stackaddress.addresses,
                      100,
              &stackaddress.count); // 5

  // 6
  for (int i = 0; i < stackaddress.count; i++) {

    printf("[%d] %llu\n", i, stackaddress.addresses[i]);
  }

  free(stackaddress.addresses); // 7
}
```

Breakdown time!

1. As you know, LLDB only lets you return one object to be evaluated. But, as a creative string-theory version of yourself, can create C structs that contain any types you want to be returned.

2. Declare an instance of said struct for use within the function.

3. Remember mach_task_self that was referenced earlier? The global variable mach_task_self_ is the value returned when calling mach_task_self.

4. Since you're in a lower level, you don't have ARC to help you allocate items on the heap. You're allocating 100 mach_vm_address_t's, which is more than enough to handle any stack trace.

5. The __mach_stack_logging_get_frames then executes. The addresses array of the LLDBStackAddress struct will be populated with the addresses if there's any stack trace information available.

6. Print out all the addresses that it found

7. Finally, free the mach_vm_address_t objects you created.

Time to give it a whirl!

LLDB Testing

Make sure the app is running, then tap the **Generate a Ray!** button a few times. Click the **Debug Memory Graph** button again to pause the app and bring up the graph.

I have three wondrously magical Ray Wenderlich faces on my simulator, so I get the following output:

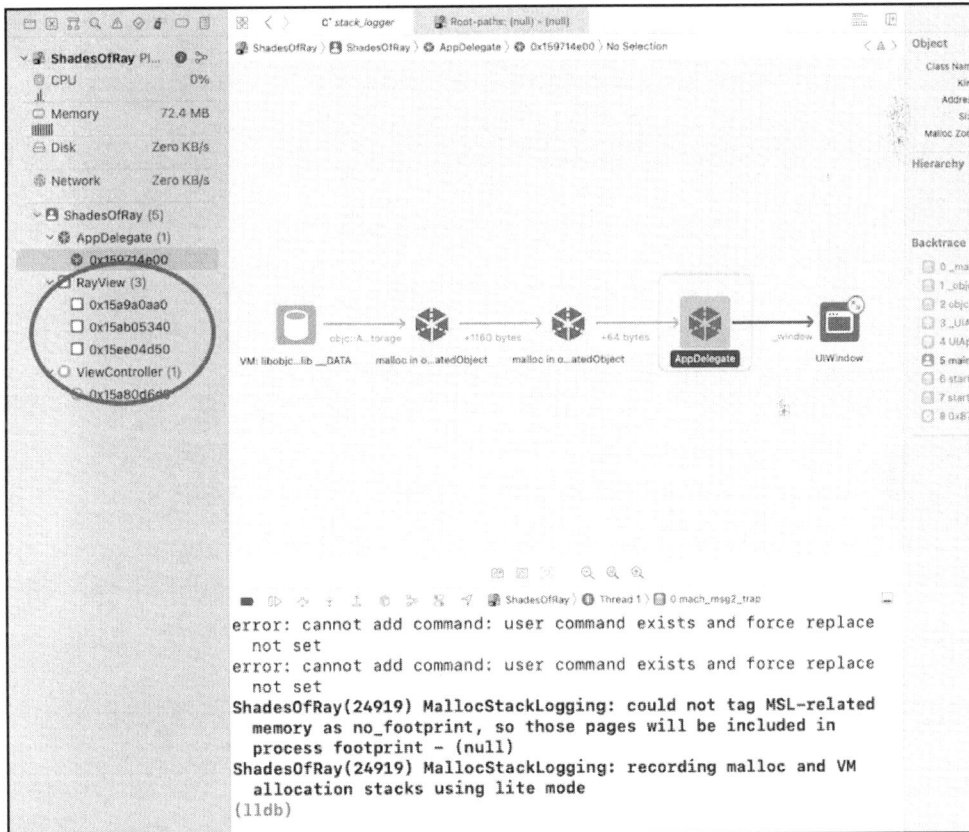

Grab any one of those addresses and execute the logic in the trace_address function:

```
(lldb) po trace_address(0x152d047c0)
```

You'll get output that looks like the following truncated snippet:

```
[0] 4362273848
[1] 4346078816
[2] 4340224704
[3] 4711642824
[4] 4701717412
[5] 4701577380
[6] 4701577128
[7] 4711642824
[8] 4705047740
[9] 4705048576
...
```

Note: if you didn't get any output, ensure that you've set the **Malloc Stack Logging** to **All Allocations and Free History**.

These are the actual addresses of the code where this object is created. Verify the first address is code in memory using image lookup:

```
(lldb) image lookup -a 4362273848
```

You'll get the details about that function:

```
Address: libsystem_malloc.dylib[0x000000000000f485]
(libsystem_malloc.dylib.__TEXT.__text + 56217)
Summary: libsystem_malloc.dylib`calloc + 30
```

There's more than one way to skin a memory address. Now use SBAddress to get the information out of this address:

```
(lldb) script print lldb.SBAddress(4454012240, lldb.target)
```

You'll get stack frame 0 in a slightly different format, like so:

```
libsystem_malloc.dylib`_malloc_zone_calloc_instrumented_or_legac
y + 220
```

Knowing different ways to get the same data can come in handy when you're writing scripts and are in different contexts with different objects available.

Navigating a C Array With lldb.value

You'll again use the **lldb.value** class to parse the return value of this C struct which was generated inline while executing this function.

Set a GUI breakpoint at the end of the trace_address function.

```
11
12  void trace_address(mach_vm_address_t addr) {
13
14    typedef struct LLDBStackAddress {
15      mach_vm_address_t *addresses;
16      uint32_t count = 0;
17    } LLDBStackAddress;
18
19    LLDBStackAddress stackaddress;
20    mach_vm_address_t address = (mach_vm_address_t)addr;
21    task_t task = mach_task_self_;
22    stackaddress.addresses = (mach_vm_address_t *)calloc(100, sizeof(mach_vm_address_t));
23    __mach_stack_logging_get_frames(task, address, stackaddress.addresses, 100, &stackaddress.count);
24
25    for (int i = 0; i < stackaddress.count; i++) {
26
27      printf("[%d] %llu\n", i, stackaddress.addresses[i]);
28    }
29
30    free(stackaddress.addresses);
31  }
32
```

Use LLDB to execute the same function, but honor breakpoints, and remember to replace the address with one of your RayView instances:

```
(lldb) e -lobjc++ -O -i0 -- trace_address(0x00007fa838414330)
```

Execution will stop on the final line of trace_address. You know the drill. Grab the reference to the C struct LLDBStackAddress, stackaddress.

```
(lldb) script print (lldb.frame.FindVariable('stackaddress'))
```

If successful, you'll get the synthetic format of the stackaddress variable:

```
(LLDBStackAddress) stackaddress = {
  addresses = 0x00007fa838515cd0
  count = 30
}
```

Cast this struct into a lldb.value and call the reference **a**:

```
(lldb) script a =
lldb.value(lldb.frame.FindVariable('stackaddress'))
```

Ensure a is valid:

```
(lldb) script print (a)
```

You can now easily reference the variables you declared in the LLDBStackAddress struct inside the lldb.value. Type the following into LLDB:

```
(lldb) script print (a.count)
```

You'll get the stack frame count:

```
(uint32_t) count = 30
```

What about the addresses array inside the LLDBStackAddress struct?

```
(lldb) script print (a.addresses[0])
```

That's the memory address of the first frame. What about that generateRayViewTapped: method found in frame 2?

```
(lldb) script print (a.addresses[2])
```

You'll get something similar to:

```
(mach_vm_address_t) [2] = 4454012240
```

Do you see how this tool is coming together? From finding chokepoints of items of interest, to exploring code in modules, to researching tidbits of useful information in Apple's open-source site (https://opensource.apple.com/), to implementing proof of concepts in Xcode before jumping to LLDB Python code, there's a lot of power under the hood.

Don't slow down — it's *command implementin'* time!

Turning Numbers Into Stack Frames

Included within the **starter** directory for this chapter is the **msl.py** script for malloc script logging. You've already installed this msl.py script earlier in the "Setting up the scripts" section.

Unfortunately, this script doesn't do much at the moment, as it doesn't produce any output. Time to change that.

Open up ~/lldb/msl.py in your favorite editor. Find **handle_command** and add the following code to it:

```
command_args = shlex.split(command)
```

```
parser = generateOptionParser()
try:
    (options, args) = parser.parse_args(command_args)
except:
    result.SetError(parser.usage)
    return

cleanCommand = args[0]
process = debugger.GetSelectedTarget().GetProcess()
frame = process.GetSelectedThread().GetSelectedFrame()
target = debugger.GetSelectedTarget()
```

All this logic shouldn't be new to you, as it's the "preamble" required to start up the command. The only thing of interest is you opted to omit the posix=False argument that's sometimes used in the shlex.split(command). There's no need to provide this parameter, since this command won't be handling any weird backslash or dash characters. This means the parsing of the output from the options and args variables is much cleaner as well.

Now that you have the basic script going, add the following (meat of this script) right below the code you just wrote:

```
# 1
script = generateScript(cleanCommand, options)

# 2
sbval = frame.EvaluateExpression(script, generateOptions())

# 3
if sbval.error.fail:
    result.AppendMessage(str(sbval.error))
    return

val = lldb.value(sbval)
addresses = []

# 4
for i in range(val.count.sbvalue.unsigned):
    address = val.addresses[i].sbvalue.unsigned
    sbaddr = target.ResolveLoadAddress(address)
    loadAddr = sbaddr.GetLoadAddress(target)
    addresses.append(loadAddr)

# 5
retString = processStackTraceStringFromAddresses(
                                    addresses,
                                        target)

# 6
freeExpr = 'free('+str(val.addresses.sbvalue.unsigned)+')'
```

```
frame.EvaluateExpression(freeExpr, generateOptions())
result.AppendMessage(retString)
```

Here are the items of interest:

1. Use the generateScript function I supplied, which returns a string containing roughly the same code as in the trace_address function.

2. Execute the code. You know this will return an SBValue.

3. Do a sanity check to see if the EvaluateExpression fails. If it does, dump out the error and exit early.

4. This for-loop enumerates the memory addresses in the val object, which are the output of the script code, and pulls them out into the addresses list.

5. Now that the addresses are pulled out into a list, you pass that list to a predefined function for processing. This returns the stack trace string you'll spit out.

6. Finally, you manually free memory, as you're a good memory citizen and always clean up after yourself. Most of these scripts you've written leak memory, but now that you're getting more advanced with this stuff, it's time to do the right thing and free any allocated memory.

Jump back to the Xcode LLDB console and reload your stuff:

```
(lldb) reload_script
```

Provided you have no errors, grab a reference to a RayView from the memory graph. Once you have a reference to a RayView, run your newly created msl command on it, like so:

```
(lldb) msl 0x00007fa838414330
```

You'll get your expected output just like in Xcode!

```
frame #0 : 0x11197d485 libsystem_malloc.dylib`calloc + 30
frame #1 : 0x10d3cbba1 libobjc.A.dylib`class_createInstance + 85
frame #2 : 0x10d3d5de4 libobjc.A.dylib`_objc_rootAlloc + 42
frame #3 : 0x10cde7550 ShadesOfRay`-[ViewController
generateRayViewTapped:] + 64
frame #4 : 0x10e512d22 UIKit`-[UIApplication
sendAction:to:from:forEvent:] + 83
```

Congratulations! You've created a script that gives you the stack trace for an object.

Now it's time to level up and give this script some cool options!

Stack Trace From a Swift Object

OK — I know you want me to talk about Swift code. You'll cover a Swift example as well.

Included in the 50 Shades of Ray app is a Swift module, ingeniously named **SomeSwiftModule**. Within this module is a class named SomeSwiftCode with a static variable to get your singleton quota going.

The code in **SomeSwiftCode.swift** is about as simple as you can get:

```
public final class SomeSwiftCode {
   private init() {}
   static let shared = SomeSwiftCode()
}
```

You'll use LLDB to call this singleton and examine the stack trace where this function was created.

First off, you have to import your Swift modules! Enter the following into LLDB:

```
(lldb) e -lswift -O -- import SomeSwiftModule
```

You'll get no result if the above was successful.

In LLDB, access the singleton, like so:

```
(lldb) e -lswift -O -- SomeSwiftCode.shared
```

You'll get the address to this object:

```
<SomeSwiftCode: 0x600000033640>
```

Now you'll pass this address in to the msl command. Use the msl command on this address:

```
(lldb) msl 0x600000033640
```

You'll get your expected stack trace.

Let's jump to one final topic I want to discuss briefly: how to build these scripts so you "Don't Repeat Yourself" when creating functionality in your LLDB scripts.

DRY Python Code

Stop the app! In the schemes, select the **Stripped 50 Shades of Ray** Xcode scheme.

Ensure the MallocStackLogging environment variable is unchecked in the Stripped 50 Shades of Ray scheme.

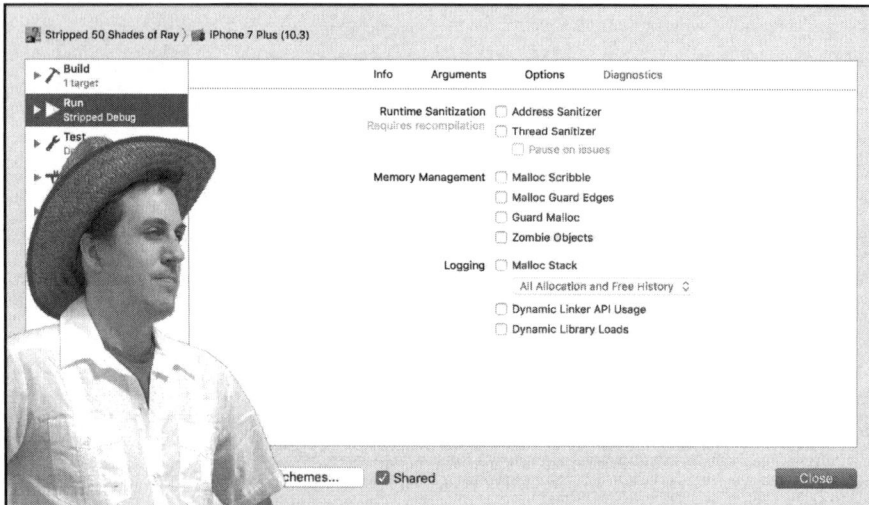

Good. Ray approves.

Time to try out the turn_on_stack_logging function. Build and run the application.

As you found out in the previous chapter, the "Stripped 50 Shades of Ray" scheme strips the main executable's contents so there's no debugging information available. Remember that factoid when you use the msl command.

Once the application is up and running, tap the **Generate a Ray!** button to create a new instance of the RayView. Since the MallocStackLogging isn't enabled, let's see what happens...

Open the **Debug Memory Graph** again and find one of the RayView instances. Notice in the **Memory inspector** that there isn't a backtrace.

See if the msl command works on this address:

```
(lldb) msl 0x1268051d0
```

Nothing. That makes sense though, because the environment variable was not supplied to the process. Time to circle back and call `turn_on_stack_logging` to see what it does. Type the following in LLDB:

```
(lldb) po turn_on_stack_logging(1)
```

You'll get some output similar to the kind you get when you supply your process with the `MallocStackLogging` environment variable:

```
(lldb) search RayView -b
RayView * [0x00007f8250e030c0]
(lldb) msl 0x00007f8250e030c0

(lldb) po turn_on_stack_logging(1)
ShadesOfRay(24537,0x1147d43c0) malloc: stack logs being written into /tmp/stack-logs.
24537.11ea53000.ShadesOfRay.g0Y5EW.index
ShadesOfRay(24537,0x1147d43c0) malloc: recording malloc and VM allocation stacks to disk using
standard recorder
0x0000000000000001

(lldb)
```

Resume execution and create another instance of `RayView` by tapping the bottom button.

Once you've done that, back to the **Debug Memory Graph** view and inspect all of your `RayView` instances. Any of them you created since turning on logging should now have a backtrace.

Copy this new address and apply the `msl` command to it.

```
(lldb) msl 0x00007f8250f0a170
```

This will give you the stack trace!

```
(lldb) po turn_on_stack_logging(1)
ShadesOfRay(24537,0x1147d43c0) malloc: stack logs being written into /tmp/stack-logs.
24537.11ea53000.ShadesOfRay.g0Y5EW.index
ShadesOfRay(24537,0x1147d43c0) malloc: recording malloc and VM allocation stacks to disk us
standard recorder
0x0000000000000001

(lldb) continue
Process 24537 resuming
(lldb) search RayView -b
RayView * [0x00007f8250e030c0]
RayView * [0x00007f8250f0a170]
(lldb) msl 0x00007f8250f0a170
frame #0 : 0x11465c485 libsystem_malloc.dylib`calloc + 30
frame #1 : 0x110194ba1 libobjc.A.dylib`class_createInstance + 85
frame #2 : 0x11019ede4 libobjc.A.dylib`_objc_rootAlloc + 42
frame #3 : 0x10fbb3570 ShadesOfRay`___lldb_unnamed_symbol4$$ShadesOfRay + 64
frame #4 : 0x1112dbd22 UIKit`-[UIApplication sendAction:to:from:forEvent:] + 83
frame #5 : 0x1117165c7 UIKit`-[UIBarButtonItem(UIInternal) _sendAction:withEvent:] + 149
frame #6 : 0x1112dbd22 UIKit`-[UIApplication sendAction:to:from:forEvent:] + 83
```

This is awesome! You can enable malloc logging at will to monitor any allocation or deallocation events without having to restart your process.

Wait wait wait. Hold on a second... there's a symbol that's stripped.

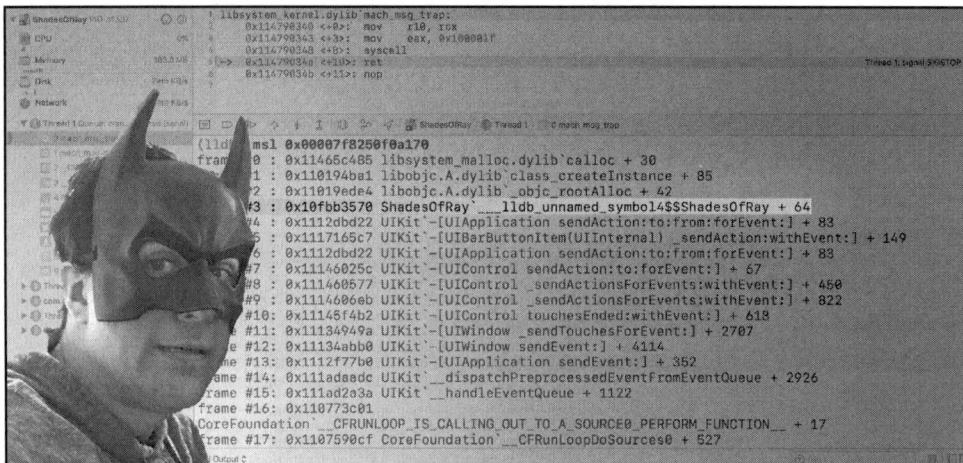

Ray don't like no stripped functions.

If you recall in the previous chapter, you created the sbt command which symbolicated a stack trace. In the sbt.py script, you created the processStackTraceStringFromAddresses function which took a list of numbers (representing memory addresses for code) and the SBTarget. This function then returned a potentially symbolicated string for the stack trace.

You've already done the hard work to write this function, so why not include this work in the msl.py script to optionally execute it?

Jump to the very top of the msl.py function and add the following import statement:

```
import sbt
```

In the handle_command function in **msl.py**, hunt for the following code:

```
retString = sbt.processStackTraceStringFromAddresses(
                                          addresses,
                                          target)
```

Replace that code with the following:

```
if options.resymbolicate:
    retString = sbt.processStackTraceStringFromAddresses(
                                        addresses,
                                        target)
else:
    retString = processStackTraceStringFromAddresses(
                                        addresses,
                                        target)
```

You're conditionally checking for the options.resymbolicate option (which I've already set up for you). If True, then call the logic in the sbt module to see if it can generate a string of resymbolicated functions.

Since you wrote that function to be generic and handle a list of Python numbers, you can easily pass this information from your msl script.

Before you test this out, there's one final component to implement. You need to make a convenience command to enable the turn_on_stack_logging.

Jump up to the **__lldb_init_module** function (still in msl.py) and add the following line of code:

```
debugger.HandleCommand('command alias enable_logging expression
-lobjc -O -- extern void turn_on_stack_logging(int);
turn_on_stack_logging(1);')
```

This declares a convenience command to turn on malloc stack logging by calling the method in libsystem_malloc.dylib. Wait what? Remember that the .dylib is always loaded as part of the runtime, and unlike some languages you know, you don't have to carefully import and define everything in order to use it, just call the function. If something, *anything* matches the signature, the code runs.

Woot! Done! Jump back to Xcode and reload your script:

```
(lldb) reload_script
```

Use the --resymbolicate option on the previous RayView to see the stack in its fully symbolicated form.

```
(lldb) msl 0x00007f8250f0a170 -r
```

```
(lldb) msl 0x00007f8250f0a170 -r
frame #0 : 0x11465c485 libsystem_malloc.dylib`calloc + 30
frame #1 : 0x1       ba1 libob  .A  lib    ss_createI    nce + 85
frame #2 : 0x11   9ede4 libobjc.A.dylib  objc_ro  lloc + 42
frame #3 : 0x10fbb3570 ShadesOfRay`-[ViewController generateRayViewTapped:] + 64
frame #4    0x1112dbd22 UIKit`-[   licati n s   tion:to:from: orEve t  + 83
frame #5    0x111 165c7 U  it`-[U  rButtonItem(  intern   _sendAction   hEvent:] + 149
frame #6 : 0x1112dbd22 UIKit`-[UIApplication sendAction:to:from:forEvent:] + 83
frame #7 : 0x1146025c UIKit`-[UIControl sendAction:to:forEvent:] + 67
frame #8 : 0x111460577 UIKit`-[UIControl _sendActionsForEvents:withEvent:] + 450
frame #9 : 0x1114606eb UIKit`-[UIControl _sendActionsForEvents:withEvent:] + 822
frame #10: 0x11145f4b2 UIKit`-[UIControl touchesEnded:withEvent:] + 618
frame #11: 0x11134949a UIKit`-[UIWindow _sendTouchesForEvent:] + 2707
frame #12: 0x11134abb0 UIKit`-[UIWindow sendEvent:] + 4114
frame #13: 0x1112f77b0 UIKit`-[UIApplication sendEvent:] + 352
frame #14: 0x111adaadc UIKit`__dispatchPreprocessedEventFromEventQueue + 2926
frame #15: 0x111ad2a3a UIKit`__handleEventQueue + 1122
frame #16: 0x110773c01
CoreFoundation`__CFRUNLOOP_IS_CALLING_OUT_TO_A_SOURCE0_PERFORM_FUNCTION__ + 17
frame #17: 0x1107590cf CoreFoundation`__CFRunLoopDoSources0 + 527
```

I am literally crying with happiness in the face of this wholly beautiful stack trace. Snif.

Key Points

- Some Xcode functionalities are just wrappers around LLDB so enhancing them is a good way to practice creating scripts.

- **Malloc Stack Logging** will log when objects are allocated and deallocated.

- **Malloc Stack Logging** has an **All Allocation and Free History** and an **All Allocation** option. The **Free History** option records more data.

- Use `image lookup -rn` or our custom `lookup` to search for any interesting symbol names you find as a first step in exploring.

- Search `https://opensource.apple.com` to find header files that often have useful notes and documentation you won't find anywhere else.

- Write and test code in Xcode for any functions you later want to bring into a Python script as JIT-ed code. The tools for debugging JIT-ed code within your scripts are effectively nonexistent.

- Python scripts can import Python scripts. As you write code, always look for ways to refactor so that you can reuse your best work in multiple places.

Where to Go From Here?

Hopefully, this full circle of idea, research & implementation has proven useful and even inspired you to create your own scripts. There's a lot of power hidden quietly away in the many frameworks that already exist on your `[i|mac|tv|watch]OS` device.

All you need to do is find these hidden gems and exploit them for some crazy commercial debugging tools, or even to use in reverse engineering to better understand what's happening.

Here's a list of directories you should explore on your actual iOS device:

- `/Developer/`
- `/usr/lib/`
- `/System/Library/PrivateFrameworks/`

Go forth, my little debuggers, and build something that completely blows my mind!

Section V: DTrace

What? Youve never heard of DTrace?! It is AWESOME! DTrace is a tool that lets you explore code in dynamic & static ways.

http://dtrace.org/guide/preface.html

You can create DTrace probes to be compiled into your code (static), or you can inspect any code that is already compiled and running (dynamic). DTrace is a versatile tool: it can be a profiler, an analyzer, a debugger or anything you want.

I often will use DTrace to cast a wide-reaching net over code I want to explore, when I have no clue where I should start.

Chapter 28: Hello, DTrace

Omagerd! It's **DTrace** time! DTrace is one of the coolest tools you've (likely?) never heard about. With DTrace, you can hook into a function or a group of functions using what's called a **probe**. From there, you can perform custom actions to query information out of a specific process, or even system wide on your computer (and monitor multiple users)!

If you've ever used the Instruments application it might surprise you that a lot of the power underneath it is powered by DTrace.

In this chapter, you'll explore a very small section of what DTrace is capable of doing by tracing Objective-C code in already compiled applications. Using DTrace to observe iOS frameworks (like UIKit) can give you an incredible insight into how the authors designed their code.

The Bad News

Let's get the bad news out of the way first, because after that it's all exciting and cool things from there. There are several things you need to know about DTrace:

- **You need to disable Rootless for DTrace to work**. Do you remember decades ago in Chapter 1 where I mentioned you need to disable Rootless for certain functionality to work? In addition to letting LLDB attach to any process on your macOS, DTrace will not correctly function if **System Integrity Protection** is enabled. If you skipped Chapter 1, go back and disable Rootless now. Otherwise, you'll need to sit on the sidelines for the remainder of this section.

- **DTrace is not implemented for iOS devices**. Although the Instruments application uses DTrace under the hood for a fair amount of things, it can not run custom DTrace scripts on your iOS device. This means you can only run a limited set of predefined functionality on your iOS device. However, you can still run whatever DTrace scripts you want on the Simulator (or any other application on your macOS) regardless if you're the owner of the code or not.

- **DTrace has a steep learning curve**. DTrace expects you know what you're doing and what you're querying. The documentation assumes you know the underlying terminology for the DTrace components. You'll learn about the fundamental concepts in this chapter but there is quite literally a whole book on this topic which explores the many aspects of DTrace that are out of the scope of what I'll teach you.

In fact, it's worth noting right up front, if DTrace interests you, get visit Brendan Gregg's site (http://www.brendangregg.com/dtracebook/index.html) and maybe read his book. It focuses on a wider range of topics that might not pertain to your Apple debugging/reverse engineering strategies, but it does teach you how to use DTrace.

Now that I've got that off my chest with the bad stuff, it's time to have some fun.

Jumping Right In

I am not going to start you off with boring terminology. Ain't nobody got time for that. Instead, you'll first get your hands dirty, then figure out what you're doing later.

Launch your favorite **iPhone Simulator**. Once alive, create a new **Terminal** window. Type the following into Terminal:

```
sudo dtrace -n 'objc$target:UIViewController::entry' -p `pgrep
SpringBoard`
```

No, this will not secretly destroy your computer, you need that sudo in there because DTrace is incredibly powerful and can query information about other users on your computer. This means you need to be root to use it.

This DTrace command takes in two options, the **name** option (**-n**) and the PID (**-p**), both of which will be discussed later. Make sure to surround your query in single quotes or else it will not work. Take note of the backtics instead of single quotes that surround pgrep SpringBoard.

If you typed out everything correctly, you'll get output in the Terminal window similar to the following:

```
dtrace: description 'objc$target:UIViewController::entry'
matched 718 probes
```

Navigate around the simulator while keeping an eye on the Terminal window.

This will dump out every hit (aka **probe**) that contains the Objective-C class name "UIViewController". Since you left the **function** field blank (don't worry - terminology descriptions are coming in the next section), it matches every single Objective-C method so long as the class is a UIViewController.

Once you get bored of looking at what pops up, kill the Terminal DTrace script with the **Ctrl + C** combination.

Back in your Terminal, enter the following:

```
sudo dtrace -n 'objc$target:UIViewController:-
viewWillAppear?:entry { ustack(); }' -p `pgrep SpringBoard`
```

There's a couple of subtle changes this time:

• The query -viewWillAppear? has been added to the **function** location. Again, you'll cover terminology later. For now, all you need to know is instead of matching every function for any class that contains the string "UIViewController", this new DTrace script will only match -**[UIViewController viewWillAppear:]**. The question mark stands for a wildcard character in DTrace, which will resolve to the ':' in the viewWillAppear: method.

- Finally, you are adding brackets with a function called **ustack()**. This logic will be called every time –[UIViewController viewWillAppear:] gets hit. The ustack() is one of DTrace's built-in functions that dumps the userland stack trace (aka SpringBoard for this case) when this method gets hit.

- Keep an eye on that single quote which moved from the end of entry part to the end of the squiggly bracket.

If you typed in everything correctly, you'll get:

```
dtrace: description 'objc$target:UIViewController:-
viewWillAppear?:entry ' matched 1 probe
```

Navigate around SpringBoard. Swipe up, swipe down, tap on the **Edit** button by scrolling to the far left, whatever you need to do to trigger a UIViewController's viewWillAppear:.

When UIViewController's viewWillAppear: gets hit, the stack trace will be printed out in the Terminal.

Take note of some stack traces that don't have the actual function name, but just a module and address.

```
 2 304571         -viewWillAppear::entry
        UIKit`-[UIViewController viewWillAppear:]
        UIKit`-[UIViewController _setViewAppearState:isAnimating:]+0x1bf
        UIKit`__52-[UIViewController _setViewAppearState:isAnimating:]_block_invoke+0xc3
        CoreFoundation`__53-[__NSArrayI enumerateObjectsWithOptions:usingBlock:]_block_invoke+0x4d
        CoreFoundation`-[__NSArrayI enumerateObjectsWithOptions:usingBlock:]+0xcf
        UIKit`-[UIViewController _setViewAppearState:isAnimating:]+0x4cf
        UIKit`-[UIViewController __viewWillAppear:]+0x93
        SpringBoard`0x00000001072bdc12+0x52d
        SpringBoard`0x0000000127fe2e6b+0x2c
        SpringBoard`0x00000001072be7f7+0x37
        SpringBoard`0x00000001072be846+0x6d
        SpringBoard`0x00000001072bcd00+0xd3
        SpringBoard`0x00000001072bcba3+0xff
        UIKit`-[UIGestureRecognizerTarget _sendActionWithGestureRecognizer:]+0x39
        UIKit`_UIGestureRecognizerSendTargetActions+0x14d
        UIKit`_UIGestureRecognizerSendActions+0xe1
```

This is telling us we don't have debugging information or an indirect symbol table to reference the name of this function.

Once you get bored of exploring the stack trace of all the viewWillAppear:'s in the SpringBoard process, kill the DTrace script again.

Now... Do you remember the whole spiel about **objc_msgSend** with registers and how the first parameter will be the instance (or class) of an Objective-C class?

For example, when objc_msgSend executes, the function signature will look like:

```
objc_msgSend(self_or_class, SEL, ...);
```

You can grab that first parameter (aka the instance of the UIViewController) in DTrace with the **arg0** parameter. Unfortunately, you can only get the reference to the pointer - you can't run any Objective-C code, like [arg0 title].

Add the following line of code right before the ustack() function in your DTrace command:

```
printf("\nUIViewcontroller is: 0x%p\n", arg0);
```

Your DTrace one-liner will now look like the following:

```
sudo dtrace -n 'objc$target:UIViewController:-
viewWillAppear?:entry { printf("\nUIViewcontroller is: 0x%p\n",
arg0); ustack(); }' -p `pgrep SpringBoard`
```

Right before printing out the stack trace, you're printing the reference to the UIViewController that is calling **viewWillAppear:**.

If you were to copy the address of this pointer spat out by DTrace and attached LLDB to SpringBoard, you will find that it points to a valid UIViewController (provided it hasn't been dealloc'd yet).

> **Note**: It's easy to get the pointer from arg0, but getting any other information (i.e. the class name) is a tricky process.
>
> You can't execute any Objective-C/Swift code in the DTrace script that belongs to the userland process (e.g. SpringBoard). All you can do is traverse memory with the references you have.

Let's do one more DTrace example.

Kill any DTrace scripts and create a script which aggregates all the unique classes that are being executed as you explore SpringBoard:

```
sudo dtrace -n 'objc$target:::entry { @[probemod] = count() }' 
-p `pgrep SpringBoard`
```

Navigate around SpringBoard again. You're not going to get any output yet, but as soon as you terminate this script with **Ctrl + C**, you'll get an aggregated list of all the times a method for a particular class was executed. This is called **Aggregations** and you'll learn about this later.

As you can see from my output, SpringBoard had **417171** method calls implemented by NSObject that were hit during my run of the above DTrace one-liner.

```
UIWindow                                               66141
 __NSDictionaryM                                       60339
 __NSSetM                                              60408
NSArray                                                62976
OS_object                                              66802
UIWindowScene                                          73264
 __NSMallocBlock__                                     84882
UIView(UIKitManual)                                    89393
_UIFocusMapSnapshot                                    94242
 __NSStackBlock__                                     110119
 __NSCFNumber                                         126589
 __NSCFConstantString                                 151803
CALayer                                               205919
 __NSCFString                                         241941
 __NSArrayM                                           271903
UIView                                                293942
NSObject                                              417171
virtualadmin@Virtuals-Virtual-Machine /Applications % 
```

It's important to differentiate the fact that these were *very* likely instances of classes which were subclasses of NSObject calling methods implemented by NSObject (i.e. the subclass of the NSObject didn't override any of these methods).

For example, calling -[UIViewController class] would count as a hit towards the total methods executed by NSObject because UIViewController doesn't override the Objective-C method, class, nor does UIViewController's parent class, UIResponder.

DTrace Terminology

Now that you've gotten your hands dirty on some quick DTrace one-liners, it's time to learn about the terminology so you actually know what's going on in these scripts.

Let's revisit a DTrace **probe**. You can think of a probe as a query. These probes are events that DTrace can monitor either in a specific process or globally across across your computer.

Consider the following DTrace one-liner:

```
dtrace -n 'objc$target:NSObject:-description:entry / arg0 = 0 /
{ @[probemod] = count(): }' -p `pgrep SpringBoard`
```

This example will monitor `NSObject`'s implementation of the `description` method in the process named `SpringBoard`. In addition, this says as soon as the `description` method begins, execute logic to aggregate the amount of times this method is called.

This DTrace one-liner can be further broken down into the following terminology:

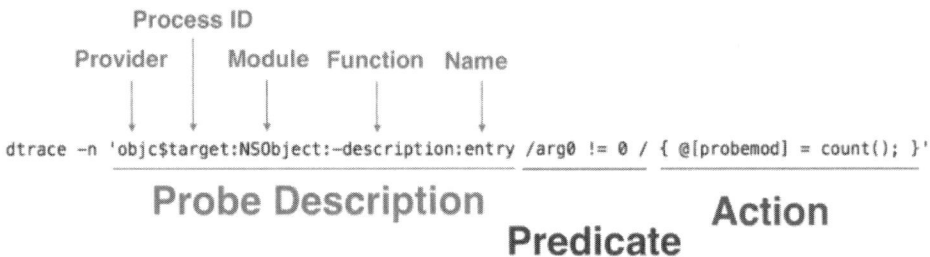

- **Probe Description**: Encapsulates a group of items that specify 0 or more probes. This consists of a **provider**, **module**, **function**, and **name**, each separated by colons. Omitting any of these items between the colons will cause the probe description to include all matches. You can use the * or ? operators for pattern matching. The ? operator will act as a wildcard for a single character, while the * will match anything.

- **Provider**: Think of the provider as a grouping of code or common functionality. For this particular chapter, you'll primarily use the **objc** provider to trace into Objective-C method calls. The `objc` provider groups all of the Objective-C code. You'll explore other providers later.

> **Note**: The **$target** keyword is a special keyword which will match whatever PID you supply DTrace. Certain `providers` (like `objc`) expect you to supply this.
>
> Think of $target as a placeholder for the actual PID, which monitors Objective-C in a specific process. If you do reference the `$target` placeholder, you must specify the target PID through the –p or –c option flags in your DTrace command.
>
> Typically this is done either by –p `PID` if you knew the exact PID, or more likely –p `` `pgrep NameOFProcess` ``. The `pgrep` Terminal command will look for the PID whose process name is `NameOFProcess` then return the PID, which then gets applied to the `$target` variable.

- **Module**: In the `objc` provider, the **module** section is where you specify the class name you wish to observe. Using the `objc` provider is a little unique in this sense, because typically the module is used to reference a library in which the code is coming from. In fact, in some providers, there's no module at all! However, the authors of the `objc` provider chose to use the module to reference the Objective-C classname. For this particular example, the module is `NSObject`.

- **Function**: The part of the probe description that can specify the function name you wish to observe. For this example, the function is -**description**. The authors of the `objc` provider used the + or - to determine if the Objective-C function is a class or instance method (as you'd expect!). If you changed the function to `+description`, it would query for any probes with `+[NSObject description]` instead.

- **Name**: This typically specifies the location of the probe within a function. Typically, there's the **entry** and **return** names which correspond to a function's entry and exit. In addition, within the `objc` provider, you can also specify any assembly instruction offset to create a probe at! For this particular example, the name is `entry`, or the start of the function.

- **Predicate**: An optional expression to evaluate if the `action` is a candidate for execution. Think of the predicate as the condition in a if-statement. The action section will only execute if the predicate evaluates to true. If you omit the predicate section, then the action block will execute every time for a given probe. For this particular example, the predicate is the `/ arg0 != 0 /`, meaning the content following the predicate will only get evaluated if `arg0` is not `nil`.

- **Action**: The action to perform if the probe matches the probe description and the predicate evaluates to true. This could be as simple as printing something to the console, or performing more advanced functions. For this example, the action is the `@[probemod] = count();` code.

When all of these components are combined, this will form a DTrace **clause**. This consists of the probe description, the optional predicate and optional action.

Put simply, a DTrace clause is constructed like this:

```
provider:module:function:name / predicate / { action }
```

DTrace "one-liners" can comprise multiple clauses which can monitor different items with the probe description, check for different conditions in the predicate and execute different logic with different actions.

So, with the example:

```
dtrace -n 'objc$target:NSView:-init*:entry' -p `pgrep -x Xcode`
```

You have a probe description of `objc$target:NSView:-init*:entry`, which includes `NSView` as the module, `-init*` as the function, and `entry` as the name with no predicate and no action. DTrace produces a default output for tracing (which you can silence with the **-q** option). This default output only displays the `function` and `name`. For example, if you were tracing `-[NSObject init]` without silencing the default DTrace action, your DTrace output would look like the following:

```
dtrace: description 'objc$target:NSObject:-init:entry' matched 1
probe
CPU     ID                      FUNCTION:NAME
  2 512130                      -init:entry
  2 512130                      -init:entry
  2 512130                      -init:entry
  2 512130                      -init:entry
```

From the output, the `-[NSObject init]` got hit 4 times while the process was being traced. You can tell DTrace to use a different formatted output by combining the –q option with one of the `print` functions to display alternative formatting for output.

What does that **-n** argument mean again? The –n argument specifies the DTrace **name** which can come in the form `provider:module:function:name`, `module:function:name` or `function:name`. In addition, the name option can take an optional probe `clause`, which is why you surround all your one-liner script content in single quotes to pass to the –n argument.

Got it? No? You'll repeat the above terminology steps with a useful DTrace option to emphasize what you've learned.

Learning While Listing Probes

Included in the DTrace command options is a nice little option, **-l**, which will list all the probes you've matched against in your probe description. When you have the **-l** option, DTrace will only list the probes and not execute any actions, regardless of whether you supply them or not.

This makes the –l option a nice tool to learn what will and *will not* work.

You will look at a probe description one more time while building up a DTrace script and systematically limiting its scope. Consider the following, Do NOT execute this:

```
sudo dtrace -ln 'objc$target:::' -p `pgrep -x Finder`
```

This will create a probe description on every Objective-C every class, method, and assembly instruction within the **Finder** application. This is a *very bad* idea for a DTrace script and will likely not run on your computer because of the hit count you'll get.

> **Note**: I've supplied the –x option to pgrep because I could get multiple PIDs for a pgrep query, which will screw up the placeholder, $target. The –x option says only give me the PID(s) that match **exactly** for the name, Finder. If there are multiple instances of a process. You can get the oldest one or newest one in pgrep with the –o or –n option. If this sounds confusing, play around with the pgrep command in Terminal without DTrace to understand how it works.

Don't execute the above script because it will take too long. However, execute the rest of these scripts so you understand what's happening.

Let's filter this down a bit. In Terminal, type the following:

```
sudo dtrace -ln 'objc$target:NSView::' -p `pgrep -x Finder`
```

Press enter, then enter your password.

This will list a probe on every single method implemented by NSView for all of its methods and every assembly instruction within each of those methods. Still a horrible idea, but at least this one will actually print out after a second.

How many probes is this? You can get that answer by piping your output to the **wc** command:

```
sudo dtrace -ln 'objc$target:NSView::' -p `pgrep -x Finder` | wc
-l
```

On my macOS machine in 13.3 (at the time of writing), I get 1423 Objective-C DTrace probes for any code pertaining to NSView within the Finder process. Wow! That's a lot fewer than a few years ago, maybe this whole migration to SwiftUI thing is going well.

Filter the probe description down some more:

```
sudo dtrace -ln 'objc$target:NSView:-initWithFrame?:' -p `pgrep
-x Finder`
```

This will filter the probe description down to every assembly instruction that's executed within -[NSView initWithFrame:] in addition to the **entry** and **return** probes. Notice the use of a ? instead of a colon to specify the Objective-C selector (which takes a parameter). If a colon was used, then DTrace will incorrectly parse the input thinking the function part was complete and have moved onto specifying the name within the DTrace probe. There's also the – at the beginning of the function description to indicate this is an instance Objective-C method.

Now execute a probe that will monitor the beginning of the -[NSView initWithFrame:] method and no other parts.

```
sudo dtrace -ln 'objc$target:NSView:-initWithFrame?:entry' -p
`pgrep -x Finder`
```

This will say to only set a probe to the beginning of -[NSView initWithFrame:] and no other parts in this Objective-C method.

Using the –l option is a nice way to learn the scope of your probes before you shoot off making your DTrace actions. I would recommend you make heavy use of the –l option when you're starting to learn DTrace.

A Script That Makes DTrace Scripts

When working with DTrace, not only do you get to deal with an exceptionally steep learning curve, you also get to deal with some cryptic errors if you get a build time or runtime DTrace error (yeah, it's on the same level of cryptic as some of those Swift compiler errors).

To help mitigate these build issues as you learn DTrace, I've created a lovely little script called **tobjectivec.py** (trace Objective-C), which is an LLDB Python script that will generate a custom DTrace script for you so long as you ask it nicely.

> **Note**: Oh yeah, now is a good time to mention you can create DTrace scripts as well as DTrace one-liners. As the complexity in your DTrace logic rises, it becomes a better idea to use a script. For simple DTrace queries, stick with the one-liners.

You'll find the **tobjectivec.py** script located within the starter directory for this chapter. I am assuming you went through Chapter 25, "SB Examples, Improved Lookup" and have installed the **lldbinit.py** script and have stuck it in your ~/lldb folder. Provided you did this, all you have to do is copy & paste the tobjectivec.py script into your ~/lldb directory and it will be launched next time LLDB starts up.

If you haven't done this yet, go back to Chapter 25 and follow the instructions for installing the lldbinit.py file. Alternatively, if you're extremely stubborn, I suppose you can install this tobjectivec.py manually by augmenting your ~/.lldbinit file.

Exploring DTrace Through tobjectivec.py

Time to take a whirlwind tour of this script while exploring DTrace on Objective-C code.

Included in the starter folder is the recycled project **Allocator**. Open that project up, build, run, then pause in the debugger.

Once you've got the Allocator project paused, bring up the LLDB console and type the following:

```
(lldb) tobjectivec -g
```

Typically, the `tobjectivec` script generates a script in the **/tmp/** directory of your computer. However, this **-g** option says that you're debugging your script so it displays the output to LLDB instead of creating a file in /tmp/. With the –g (or –– debug) option, your current script displays to the console.

This dry run of the `tobjectivec.py` with no extra parameters produces this output:

```
#!/usr/sbin/dtrace -s   /* 1 */

#pragma D option quiet   /* 2 */

dtrace:::BEGIN { printf("Starting... use Ctrl + c to stop\n"); }
/* 3 */
dtrace:::END   { printf("Ending...\n"  ); }
/* 4 */

/* Script content below */

objc$target:::entry /* 5 */
{
    printf("0x%016p %c[%s %s]\n", arg0, probefunc[0], probemod,
(string)&probefunc[1]); /* 6 */
}
```

Let's break this down:

1. When executing a DTrace script, the first line needs to be **#!/usr/sbin/dtrace -s** or else the script might not run properly.

2. This line says to not list the probe count nor perform the default DTrace action when a probe fires. Instead, you'll give DTrace your own custom action.

3. This is one third of the DTrace clauses within this script. There are probes for DTrace that monitor for certain DTrace events... like when a DTrace script is about to start. This says, as soon as DTrace starts, print out the "Starting... use Ctrl + c to stop" string.

4. Here's another DTrace clause that prints out "Ending..." as soon as the DTrace script finishes.

5. This is the DTrace probe description of interest. This says to trace *all* the Objective-C code found in whatever process ID you supply to this script.

6. The action part of this clause prints out the instance of the Objective-C probe that was triggered, followed by Objective-C styled output. In here, you can see **probefunc** and **probemod** being utilized which will be a char* representation of the function and module. DTrace has several builtin variables that you can use, probefunc & probemod being two of them. You also have **probeprov** and **probename** at your disposal. Remember the module will represent the class name while the function will represent the Objective-C method. This takes a combination of the probemod & probefunc and displays it in the pretty Objective-C syntax you're accustomed to.

Now you've got an idea of this script, remove the –g option so you're no longer using the debug option. Type in LLDB:

```
(lldb) tobjectivec
```

You'll get different output this time:

```
Copied script to clipboard... paste in Terminal
```

Your clipboard's contents have been modified. Jump over to your Terminal, then paste in the contents of your clipboard. Here's mine, but yours will of course be different:

```
sudo /tmp/lldb_dtrace_profile_objc.d  -p 95129  2>/dev/null
```

The content you originally saw is now in **/tmp/lldb_dtrace_profile_objc.d**. If you are at all paranoid about what this script does, I recommend you cat it first to ensure you know what it's doing.

The script provides the process identifier that LLDB is attached to (so you don't have to type pgrep Allocator).

Once you get your password prompt, enter your password to get those root privs:

```
$ sudo /tmp/lldb_dtrace_profile_objc.d  -p 95129  2>/dev/null
Password:
Starting... use Ctrl + c to stop
```

Wait until the DTrace script indicates to you that it's starting.

With both Xcode and Terminal visible, type a simple po [NSObject class] in the console. Check out the slew of Objective-C messages that appear for just this method.

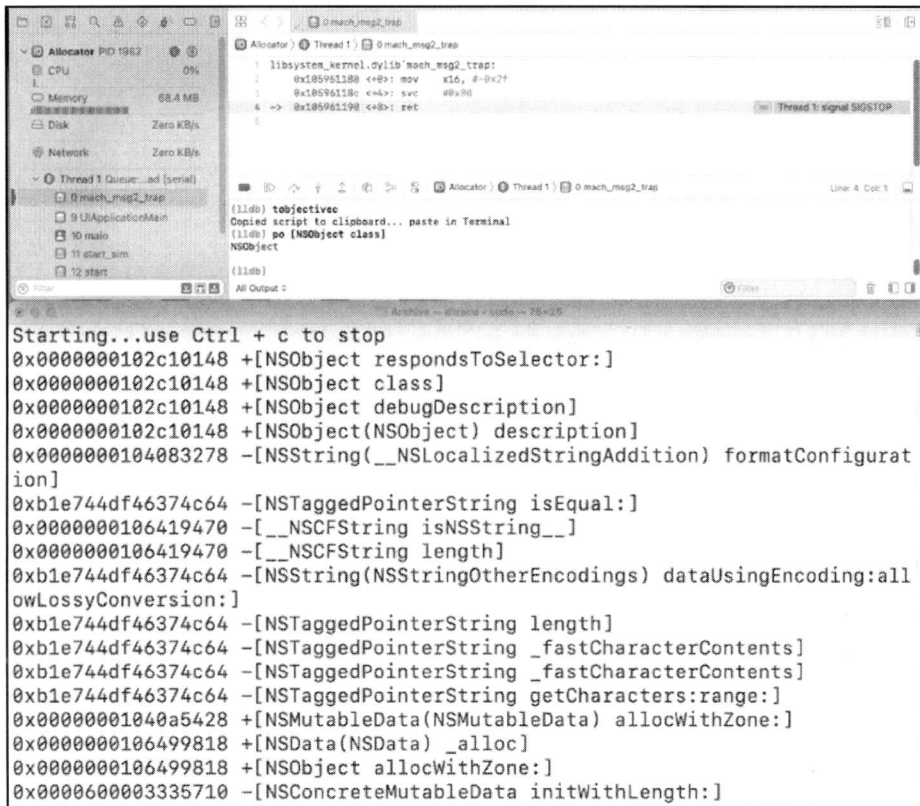

This will prepare you for what's about to come. Resume execution using LLDB:

```
(lldb) continue
```

Navigate around the Allocator app (tap on views, bring down the in-call status bar in the Simulator with **Command-Y**) iOS Simulator while keeping an eye on the DTrace Terminal window.

Scary, right?

This is too much stuff to be useful for anything beyond showing off. Filter some of the noise by adding content to the module specifier.

Back in Xcode, pause execution of the Allocator process and bring up LLDB.

Generate a new script that only focuses on Objective-C classes that have the phrase StatusBar in their name. Type the following in LLDB:

```
(lldb) tobjectivec -m *StatusBar* -g
```

This will do a dry run and give you the following truncated output:

```
objc$target:*StatusBar*::entry
{
    printf("0x%016p %c[%s %s]\n",
      arg0, probefunc[0], probemod, (string)&probefunc[1]);
}
```

Notice how the module portion of the probe has changed. The * can be thought of as .* that you know and love in your regular expressions. This means you're querying for probes that contain the case sensitive word StatusBar for any Objective-C classes when the probe enters the start of the function.

In LLDB, remove the −g option so this script will get copied to your clipboard, then re-execute the command.

```
(lldb) tobjectivec -m *StatusBar*
```

Jump over to your Terminal window. Kill the previous DTrace instance by pressing **Control-C**, then paste in your new script.

```
sudo /tmp/lldb_dtrace_profile_objc.d  -p 2646  2>/dev/null
```

Resume execution back in Xcode.

Jump to the Simulator and toggle the in-call status bar by pressing **Command-Y** or rotate the Simulator by pressing **Command-←** or **Command-→** while keeping an eye on the DTrace Terminal window.

You'll get a slew of output again.

You can use DTrace to cast a wide net on code with minimal performance hits and quickly drill down when you need to.

Tracing Debugging Commands

I often find it insightful to know what's happening behind the scenes when I'm executing simple debugging commands and the code that's going on behind them to make it work for me.

Observe how many Objective-C method calls it takes to make a simple Objective-C NSString.

Back in LLDB, type the following:

```
(lldb) tobjectivec
```

Paste the contents in the Terminal window, but do not resume execution in LLDB. Instead, just type the following:

```
(lldb) po @"hi this is a long string to avoid tagged pointers"
```

As soon as you press enter, check out the DTrace Terminal window and see what gets spat out. You'll get something similar to the following:

```
virtualadmin@Virtuals-Virtual-Machine Archive %  sudo /tmp/lldb_dtrace_prof
ile_objc.d  -p 11038

Starting...use Ctrl + c to stop
0x00006000026d8820 -[NSObject debugDescription]
0x00006000026d8820 -[NSString description]
0x00006000026d8820 -[__NSCFString isEqual:]
0x00006000026d8820 -[NSString(NSStringOtherEncodings) dataUsingEncoding:all
owLossyConversion:]
0x00006000026d8820 -[__NSCFString length]
0x0000000104085428 +[NSMutableData(NSMutableData) allocWithZone:]
0x00000001063bd818 +[NSData(NSData) _alloc]
0x00000001063bd818 +[NSObject allocWithZone:]
0x0000600000b16250 -[NSConcreteMutableData initWithLength:]
0x0000600000b16250 -[NSConcreteMutableData setLength:]
0x0000600000b16250 -[NSConcreteMutableData mutableBytes]
0x0000600000b16250 -[NSConcreteMutableData setLength:]
0x0000600000b16250 -[NSConcreteMutableData length]
0x0000600000b16250 -[NSConcreteMutableData bytes]
0x0000600000b16250 -[NSConcreteMutableData length]
0x0000600000b16250 -[NSConcreteMutableData length]
0x0000600000b16250 -[NSConcreteMutableData dealloc]
0x0000600000b16250 -[NSConcreteMutableData _freeBytes]
0x0000600000b16250 -[NSObject dealloc]
```

We just printed out a simple NSString and look how many Objective-C calls this took!

Here's one for all you Swift "purists" out there.

Clear the Terminal screen by pressing **Command-K**, make sure the DTrace Terminal script is still running. Head back to LLDB and type the following:

```
(lldb) expression -l swift -O -- class b { }; let a = b()
```

You are using the Swift debugging context to create a pure Swift class then instantiating it. Observe the Objective-C method calls when this class is created.

DTrace will dump out:

```
0x000000010336eb08 +[_TtCs12_SwiftObject initialize]
0x000000010336eb08 +[_TtCs12_SwiftObject class]
0x000000010589c9e8 +[_TtCs12_SwiftObject initialize]
0x000000010589c9e8 -[_TtCs12_SwiftObject self]
```

If you were to copy any of these addresses DTrace just presented and then po that, you'd be greeted with an onslaught of Objective-C method calls for this pure Swift class.

A "pure" Swift class ain't as pure as you thought, right?

Tracing an Object

You can use DTrace to trace method calls for a particular reference.

Stop the previous DTrace script by pressing **Control-C**.

While the application is paused, use LLDB to get the reference to the UIApplication. Make sure you are in an Objective-C stack frame.

```
(lldb) po UIApp
```

You'll get something like:

```
<UIApplication: 0x7fa774600f90>
```

Copy the reference and use this to build a predicate which only stops when this reference is arg0 — remember, objc_msgSend's param is an instance of a Class or the Class itself.

```
(lldb) tobjectivec -g -p 'arg0 == 0x7fa774600f90'
```

You'll get the dry run output of your script printed to the console similar to this truncated output:

```
/* Script content below */

objc$target:::entry / arg0 == 0x7fa774600f90 /
{
    printf("0x%016p %c[%s %s]\n", arg0, probefunc[0], probemod,
(string)&probefunc[1]);
}
```

Looks good! Execute the command again without the –g option:

```
(lldb) tobjectivec -p 'arg0 == 0x7fa774600f90'
```

Resume execution in LLDB, then paste your script into Terminal.

Trigger the home button by pressing **Command-Shift-H** or the status bar using **Command-Y** in the Simulator.

This is dumping every Objective-C method call on the [UIApplication sharedApplication] instance.

Oh, is that too much output to look at? Then aggregate the content!

Back in Xcode, pause execution and in LLDB:

```
(lldb) tobjectivec -g -p 'arg0 == 0x7fa774600f90' -a
'@[probefunc] = count()'
```

This will produce the following script, truncated:

```
/* Script content below */

objc$target:::entry / arg0 == 0x7fa774600f90 /
{
    @[probefunc] = count()
}
```

You know the drill. Rerun the above tobjectivec command without the –g option, then paste your clipboard contents into Terminal and resume execution in LLDB.

No content will be displayed in Terminal yet. But DTrace is quietly aggregating every method that is being sent to the UIApplication instance.

Move around in the Simulator to get a healthy count of methods being sent to the
UIApplication. As soon as you kill this script by pressing **Control-C**, DTrace will
dump out the total count of all the Objective-C methods that were applied to the
UIApplication instance.

Other DTrace Ideas

Here's some other ideas for you to try out on your own time:

Trace all the initialization methods for all objects:

```
(lldb) tobjectivec -f ?init*
```

Monitor inter-process communication related logic (i.e. Webviews, keyboards, etc):

```
(lldb) tobjectivec -m NSXPC*
```

Print the UIControl subclass which is handling your starting touch event on your
iOS device:

```
(lldb) tobjectivec -m UIControl -f -touchesBegan?withEvent?
```

Key Points

- Using DTrace requires disabling `System Integrity Protection` and `sudo`.

- DTrace can run as a one line command or with a script for more complex procedures.

- Use the `-l` switch when testing out DTrace commands to keep from crashing your system.

- When working with DTrace, always think about filtering results so you aren't overwhelmed with output.

- DTrace doesn't work on an iOS device, but does work on the Simulator.

Where to Go From Here?

This is only the tip of the DTrace iceberg. There's a **lot** more that is possible with DTrace.

I would recommend you check out the following URLs as they are a great resource for learning DTrace.

- https://www.bignerdranch.com/blog/hooked-on-dtrace-part-1/

- https://www.objc.io/issues/19-debugging/dtrace/

In the next chapter, you'll take a deeper dive into whats possible with DTrace and explore profiling Swift code.

Chapter 29: Intermediate DTrace

This chapter will act as a grab-bag of more DTrace fundamentals, destructive actions (yay!), as well as how to use DTrace with Swift. I'll get you excited first before going into theory. I'll start with how to use DTrace with Swift then go into the sleep-inducing concepts that will make your eyes water. Nah, trust me, this will be fun!

In this chapter, you'll learn additional ways DTrace can profile code, as well as how to augment existing code without laying a finger on the actual executable itself. Magic!

Getting Started

We're not done picking on Ray Wenderlich. Included in this chapter is yet another movie-title inspired project with Ray's name spliced into it.

Open up the **Finding Ray** application in the **starter** directory for this chapter. No need to do anything special for setup. Build and run the project on the iPhone simulator.

The majority of this project is written in Swift, though many Swift subclasses inherit from NSObject as they need to be visually displayed (if it's an on-screen component, it must inherit from UIView, which inherits from NSObject, meaning Objective-C)

DTrace is agnostic to whatever Swift code inherits from whatever class as it's all the same to DTrace. You can still profile Objective-C code subclassed by a Swift object so long as it inherits from NSObject using the objc$target provider. The downside to this approach is if there are any new methods implemented or any overridden methods implemented by the Swift class, you'll not see them in any Objective-C probes.

DTrace & Swift in Theory

Let's talk about how one can use DTrace to profile Swift code. There are some pros along with some cons that should be taken into consideration.

First, the happy news: Swift works well with DTrace modules! This means it's very easy to filter out Swift code based on the particular module it's implemented in. The module (aka the probemod) will likely be the name of your target in Xcode which contains the Swift code (unless you've changed the target name in Xcode's build settings).

This means you can filter the following Swift code implemented in the SomeTarget module like so:

```
pid$target:SomeTarget::entry
```

This will set a probe on the start of every single function implemented inside the SomeTarget module. Since the pid$target goes after all the non-Objective-C code, this probe will pick C & C++ code as well, but as you'll see in a second, that's easy to filter out with a well-designed query.

Now for the bad news. Since the information about the module is taken up, the Swift classname and function name all go into the DTrace `function` section (aka `probefunc`) for a Swift method. This means you need to be a little more creative with your DTrace querying.

So without further ado, let's look at a quick example of a Swift DTrace probe.

Imagine you have a subclass of `UIViewController` named **ViewController** which only overrides `viewDidLoad`. Like so:

```
class ViewController: UIViewController {
  override func viewDidLoad() {
    super.viewDidLoad()
  }
}
```

If you want to create a breakpoint on this function, the fullname to this breakpoint would be the following:

```
SomeTarget.ViewController.viewDidLoad() -> ()
```

No surprise there; you've beaten that concept to death in Section 1. If you wanted to search for every `viewDidLoad` implemented by Swift in the `SomeTarget` target (catchy name, right?), you could create a DTrace probe description that looks like the following:

```
pid$target:SomeTarget:*viewDidLoad*:entry
```

This effectively says, "As long as `SomeTarget` and `viewDidLoad` are in the function section, gimme the probe."

Time to try this theory out in the **Finding Ray** application.

DTrace & Swift in Practice

If the **Finding Ray** application is not already running, spark it up! iPhone Simulator. You know what's up.

Create a fresh window in `Terminal` and type the following:

```
sudo dtrace -n 'pid$target:Finding?Ray::entry' -p `pgrep
"Finding Ray"`
```

I chose an Xcode project name that has a space on purpose. Take note of what you need to do to resolve spaces in an Xcode target when using a DTrace script. The `probemod` section uses a `?` as a placeholder wildcard character for the space. In addition, you need to surround your query when `pgrep`'ing for the process name, otherwise it won't work.

After you've finished typing your password, you'll get ~240 probe `entry` hits for all the non-Objective-C functions inside the **Finding Ray** module.

Click on Ray and drag him around in the Simulator while keeping an eye on all the methods that are getting hit in the `Terminal`.

```
virtualadmin@Virtuals-Virtual-Machine Archive % sudo dtrace -n 'pid$target:Finding?Ray::
entry' -p `pgrep "Finding Ray"`
Password:
dtrace: description 'pid$target:Finding?Ray::entry' matched 262 probes
CPU     ID                    FUNCTION:NAME
  6 252637 @objc QuickTouchPanGestureRecognizer.touchesBegan(_:with:):entry
  6 252635 type metadata accessor for UITouch:entry
  6 252636 lazy protocol witness table accessor for type UITouch and conformance NSObjec
t:entry
  6 252635 type metadata accessor for UITouch:entry
  6 252634 QuickTouchPanGestureRecognizer.touchesBegan(_:with:):entry
  6 252642 @objc QuickTouchPanGestureRecognizer.gestureRecognizerShouldBegin(_:):entry
  6 252641 QuickTouchPanGestureRecognizer.gestureRecognizerShouldBegin(_:):entry
  6 252635 type metadata accessor for UITouch:entry
  6 252636 lazy protocol witness table accessor for type UITouch and conformance NSObjec
t:entry
  6 252613 type metadata accessor for QuickTouchPanGestureRecognizer:entry
  6 252633 @objc QuickTouchPanGestureRecognizer.shouldRequireFailure(of:):entry
  6 252632 QuickTouchPanGestureRecognizer.shouldRequireFailure(of:):entry
  6 252633 @objc QuickTouchPanGestureRecognizer.shouldRequireFailure(of:):entry
  6 252632 QuickTouchPanGestureRecognizer.shouldRequireFailure(of:):entry
  8 252629 @objc QuickTouchPanGestureRecognizer.canPrevent(_:):entry
  8 252628 QuickTouchPanGestureRecognizer.canPrevent(_:):entry
  8 252616 @objc QuickTouchPanGestureRecognizer.delaysTouchesBegan.getter:entry
```

There's still a bit too much noise. You only want the Swift functions to *only* be displayed. No need to see the probe ID nor the CPU columns.

Kill the DTrace script and replace it with the following:

```
sudo dtrace -qn 'pid$target:Finding?Ray::entry { printf("%s\n",
probefunc); } ' -p `pgrep "Finding Ray"`
```

It's subtle, but you've added the -q (or --quiet) option. This will tell DTrace to not display the number of probes you've found, nor to display its default output when a probe gets hit. Fortunately, you've also added a `printf` statement to spit out the `probefunc` manually instead.

Wait for DTrace to start up, then drag again.

Much prettier. Unfortunately, you're still getting some methods the Swift compiler generated that I didn't write. You don't want to see any code the Swift compiler has created; you only want to see code I wrote in the Swift classes.

Kill the previous DTrace script and augment this probe description to *only* contain code that you've implemented, and not that of the Swift compiler:

```
sudo dtrace -qn 'pid$target:Finding?Ray::entry { printf("%s\n",
probefunc); } ' -p `pgrep "Finding Ray"` | grep -E "^[^@].*\."
```

Jump over to the Simulator and drag Ray around. Notice the difference?

```
QuickTouchPanGestureRecognizer.touchesBegan(_:with:)
QuickTouchPanGestureRecognizer.gestureRecognizerShouldBegin(_:)
QuickTouchPanGestureRecognizer.shouldRequireFailure(of:)
QuickTouchPanGestureRecognizer.shouldRequireFailure(of:)
QuickTouchPanGestureRecognizer.canPrevent(_:)
QuickTouchPanGestureRecognizer.delaysTouchesBegan.getter
QuickTouchPanGestureRecognizer.delaysTouchesBegan.getter
ViewController.handleGesture(panGesture:)
ViewController.dynamicAnimator.getter
ViewController.snapBehavior.getter
ViewController.containerView.getter
MotionView.animate(isSelected:)
```

This is piping the output to grep which is using a regular expression query to say return anything that doesn't contain a "@" and contains a period in the output. This essentially is saying don't return any @objc bridging methods and a period is guaranteed in any Swift code you write thanks to module namespacing.

One final addition. Augment the script to remove the grep filtering, and instead trace all Swift function entries and exits in the "Finding Ray" module, and use DTrace's **flowindent** option.

The flowindent option will properly indent function entries and returns.

```
sudo dtrace -qFn 'pid$target:Finding?Ray::*r* { printf("%s\n",
probefunc); } ' -p `pgrep "Finding Ray"`
```

There are a couple of items to note on this one. You've added the -F option for flowindent. Check out the name section in the probe description, *r*. What does this do?

From a DTrace standpoint, most functions in a process have entry, return and function offsets for every assembly instruction. These offsets are given in hexadecimal. This says "give me any name that contains the letter 'r'."

This returns both the `entry` & `return` in the probe description `name`, but omits any function offsets since assembly only goes as high as `f`. Clever, eh?

With both the `enter` & `return` probes of each Swift function enabled, you can clearly see what functions are being executed and where they're being executed from.

Wait for DTrace to start, then drag Ray Wenderlich's face around. You'll get pretty output that looks like this:

```
virtualadmin@Virtuals-Virtual-Machine ~ % sudo dtrace -qFn 'pid$target:Finding?Ray::*r* { printf("%s\n", probefunc); } ' -p '
pgrep "Finding Ray"'
Password:
CPU FUNCTION
  4   -> @objc QuickTouchPanGestureRecognizer.touchesBegan(_:with:) @objc QuickTouchPanGestureRecognizer.touchesBegan(_:with:)
  4     -> type metadata accessor for UITouch  type metadata accessor for UITouch
  4     <- type metadata accessor for UITouch  type metadata accessor for UITouch
  4     -> lazy protocol witness table accessor for type UITouch and conformance NSObject lazy protocol witness table accessor
for type UITouch and conformance NSObject
  4     <- lazy protocol witness table accessor for type UITouch and conformance NSObject lazy protocol witness table accessor
for type UITouch and conformance NSObject
  4     -> QuickTouchPanGestureRecognizer.touchesBegan(_:with:) QuickTouchPanGestureRecognizer.touchesBegan(_:with:)
  4     -> @objc QuickTouchPanGestureRecognizer.gestureRecognizerShouldBegin(_:) @objc QuickTouchPanGestureRecognizer.gestur
eRecognizerShouldBegin(_:)
  4       -> QuickTouchPanGestureRecognizer.gestureRecognizerShouldBegin(_:) QuickTouchPanGestureRecognizer.gestureRecognize
rShouldBegin(_:)
  4       <- QuickTouchPanGestureRecognizer.gestureRecognizerShouldBegin(_:) QuickTouchPanGestureRecognizer.gestureRecognize
rShouldBegin(_:)
  4     <- @objc QuickTouchPanGestureRecognizer.gestureRecognizerShouldBegin(_:) @objc QuickTouchPanGestureRecognizer.gestur
eRecognizerShouldBegin(_:)
  4     -> type metadata accessor for UITouch type metadata accessor for UITouch
  4     <- type metadata accessor for UITouch type metadata accessor for UITouch
  4     -> lazy protocol witness table accessor for type UITouch and conformance NSObject lazy protocol witness table access
or for type UITouch and conformance NSObject
  4     <- lazy protocol witness table accessor for type UITouch and conformance NSObject lazy protocol witness table access
or for type UITouch and conformance NSObject
  4     -> type metadata accessor for QuickTouchPanGestureRecognizer type metadata accessor for QuickTouchPanGestureRecogniz
er
  4     <- type metadata accessor for QuickTouchPanGestureRecognizer type metadata accessor for QuickTouchPanGestureRecogniz
```

Hehehe… thought you would get a kick out of that one!

DTrace Variables & Control Flow

You'll jump into a bit of theory now, which you'll need for the remainder of this section.

DTrace has several ways to create and reference variables in your script. All of them have their own pros and cons as they battle between speed and convenience of use in DTrace.

Scalar Variables

The first way to create a variable is to use a **scalar variable**. These are simple variables that can take items of fixed size. You don't need to declare the type of scalar variables, or any variables for that matter in your DTrace scripts.

I tend to lean towards using a scalar variable in DTrace scripts to represent a Boolean value, which is due to the limited conditional logic with DTrace — you only have predicates and ternary operators to really branch your logic.

For example, here is a practical example with a scalar variable:

```
#!/usr/sbin/dtrace -s
#pragma D option quiet

dtrace:::BEGIN
{
    isSet = 0;
    object = 0;
}
objc$target:NSObject:-init:return / isSet == 0 /
{
    object = arg1;
    isSet = 1;
}
objc$target:::entry / isSet && object == arg0 /
{
    printf("0x%p %c[%s %s]\n",
        arg0, probefunc[0], probemod, (string)&probefunc[1]);
}
```

This script declares two scalar variables: the **isSet** scalar variable will check and see if the **object** scalar variable has been set. If not, the script will set the the next object to the object variable. This script will trace all Objective-C method calls that are being used on the object variable.

Clause-Local Variables

Another type are **clause-local** variables. These are denoted by the word **this->** used right before the variable name and can take any type of value, including char*'s. Clause-local variables can survive across the *same* probe. If you you try to reference them on a different probe, it won't work.

For example, consider the following:

```
pid$target::objc_msgSend:entry
{
    this->object = arg0;
}

pid$target::objc_msgSend:entry / this->object != 0 / {
    /* Do some logic here */
}
```

```
obc$target:::entry {
    this->f = this->object; /* Won't work since different probe */
}
```

I tend to stick with clause-local variables as much as I can since they're quite fast and I don't have to manually free them like I do with the next type of variable...

Thread-Local Variables

Thread-local variables offer the most flexibility at the price of speed. Additionally, you have to manually release them, otherwise you'll leak memory. Thread-local variables can be used by preceding the variable name with **self->**.

The nice thing about thread-local variables is they can be used in different probes, like so:

```
objc$target:NSObject:init:entry {
    self->a = arg0;
}

objc$target::-dealloc:entry / arg0 == self->a / {
    self->a = 0;
}
```

This will assign self->a to whatever object is being initialized. When this object is released, you'll need to manually release it as well by setting a to 0.

With variables in DTrace out of the way, let's talk about how you can use variables to execute conditional logic.

DTrace Conditions

DTrace has extremely limited conditional logic built in. There's no such thing as the if/else-statement in DTrace! This is a conscious decision, because a DTrace script is designed to be fast.

However, it does present a problem for you when you want to conditionally perform logic based upon a particular probe, or information contained within that probe.

To get around this limitation, there are two notable methods you can use to perform conditional logic.

The first workaround is to use a **ternary operator**.

Consider the following contrived Objective-C logic:

```
int b = 10;
int a = 0;

if (b == 10) {
    a = 5;
} else {
    a = 6;
}
```

This can be rewritten in DTrace to use a ternary operator:

```
b = 10;
a = 0;
a = b == 10 ? 5 : 6
```

Here's another example of conditional logic with no else-statement:

```
int b = 10;
int a = 0;
if (b == 10) {
    a++;
}
```

In DTrace form, this would look like:

```
b = 10;
a = 0;
a = b == 10 ? a + 1 : a
```

The other solution to this is to use multiple DTrace clauses along with a predicate. The first DTrace clause sets up the information needed by the second clause to see if it should perform the action in the predicate.

I know you probably forgot all the terminology for these DTrace components so let's also look at an example for this.

For example, let's say you wanted to trace every call in between the start and stop of a function. Typically, I would recommend just setting a DTrace script to catch everything and then use LLDB to execute the command. But what if you wanted to do this solely in DTrace?

For this particular example, you want to trace all Objective-C method calls being executed by `-[UIViewController initWithNibName:bundle:]` with the following DTrace script:

```
#!/usr/sbin/dtrace -s
#pragma D option quiet

dtrace:::BEGIN
{
   tracing = 0;
}

objc$target:UIViewController:-initWithNibName?bundle?:entry {
   tracing = 1;
}

objc$target:::entry / tracing / {
   printf("%s\n", probefunc);
}

objc$target:UIViewController:-initWithNibName?bundle?:return {
   tracing = 0;
}
```

As soon as the `initWithNibName:bundle:` is entered, the `tracing` variable is set. From there on out, every single Objective-C method is displayed until `initWithNibName:bundle:` returns.

Not being able to use loops and conditions can appear annoying at first when writing DTrace scripts, but think of not relying on the common programming idioms you've become accustomed to as a nice brain teaser.

Time for another big discussion: inspecting process memory in your DTrace scripts.

Inspecting Process Memory

It may come as surprise, but the DTrace scripts you've been writing are actually executed in the kernel itself. This is why they're so fast and also why you don't need to change any code in an already compiled program to perform dynamic tracing. The kernel has direct access!

DTrace has probes all over your computer. There are probes in the kernel, there's probes in userland, there's even probes to describe the crossing between the kernel and userland (and vice versa) using the **fbt** provider.

Here's a visualization showing a *very very* small percentage of the DTrace probes on your computer.

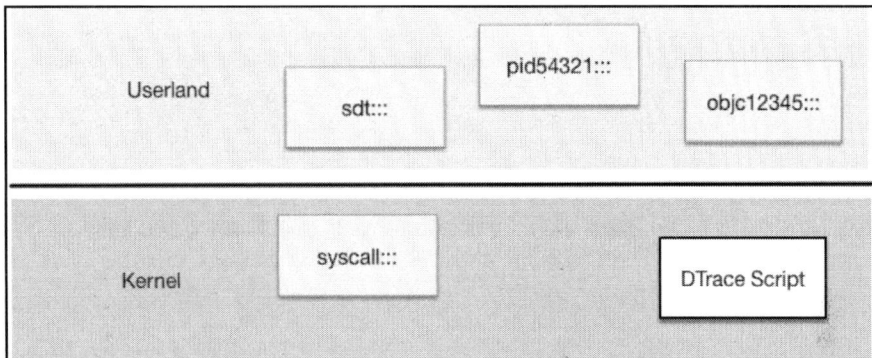

Narrow down your focus to just two probes of the thousands by exploring the **open** system call and the **open_nocancel** system call. Both of these functions are implemented in the kernel and are responsible for any type of file openings for reading, writing, or both.

The system open has the following function signature:

```
int open(const char *path, int oflag, ...);
```

Internally, open will sometimes call the open_nocancel, which has the following function signature:

```
int open_nocancel(const char *path, int flags, mode_t mode);
```

Both of these functions contain a char* as the first parameter. You've already grabbed parameters from functions before in DTrace probes using arg0 and arg1. What you haven't done yet is dereference those pointers to look at their data. Just as in the previous chapters with SBValue, you can spelunk in memory with DTrace and even get the string representation of this first parameter in the open system calls.

There's one gotcha though. A DTrace script executes in the kernel. The argX parameters are given to you, but these are pointers to the value in the address space of the program. However, DTrace runs in the kernel. So you need to manually copy whatever data you're reading into the kernel's memory space.

This is done through the **copyin** and **copyinstr** functions. copyin will take an address with the amount of bytes you want to read, while the copyinstr expects to copy a char* representation. In the case of the open family of system calls, you could read the first parameter as a string with the following DTrace clause:

```
sudo dtrace -n 'syscall::open:entry { printf("%s",
copyinstr(arg0)); }'
```

For example, if a process whose PID was 12345 was attempting to open "/Applications/SomeApp.app/", DTrace could read this first parameter using copyinstr(arg0).

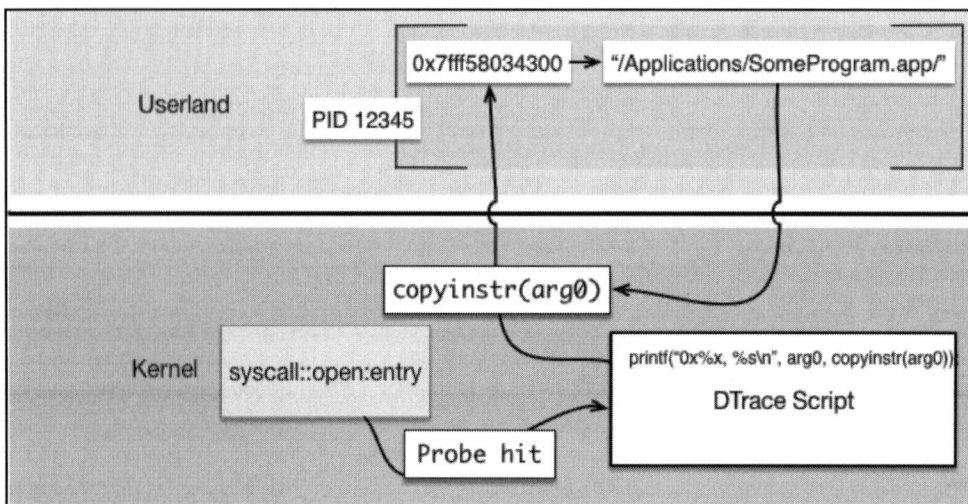

For this particular example, DTrace will read in arg0, which for this example equals 0x7fff58034300. With the copyinstr function, the 0x7fff58034300 memory address will be dereferenced to grab the char* representation for the pathname, "/Applications/SomeApp.app/".

Playing With Open Syscalls

With the knowledge you need to inspect process memory, create a DTrace script that monitors the open family of system calls. In Terminal, type the following:

```
sudo dtrace -qn 'syscall::open*:entry { printf("%s opened %s\n",
execname, copyinstr(arg0)); ustack(); }'
```

This will print the contents of open (or open_nocancel) along with the program that called the open* system call with the userland stack trace that was responsible for the call. There sure are a lot of calls, even when your computer isn't doing anything.

Isn't DTrace awesome!?

Augment your open family of system calls to only focus on the **Finding Ray** process.

```
sudo dtrace -qn 'syscall::open*:entry / execname == "Finding
Ray" / { printf("%s opened %s\n", execname, copyinstr(arg0));
ustack(); }'
```

Note: The actions you perform with DTrace can sometimes produce errors to stderr in Terminal. Depending on the error, you can get around this by creating checks for appropriate input with a DTrace predicate, or you can filter your probe description query with less probes. An alternative to this is to ignore all errors produced by DTrace by adding 2>/dev/null in your DTrace one-liner. This effectively tells your DTrace one-liner to pipe any stderr content, 2 is the standard error file descriptor, to be ignored. I often use this solution to cast a wide net on probes that can be error-prone, but ignore any errors that my tracing produces.

Rebuild and launch the application.

Stack traces will now only be displayed on any open* system call being called from the **Finding Ray** application. Play around with the app in the Simulator a bit and see if you can make it output something!

Filtering Open Syscalls by Paths

Inside the **Finding Ray** project, I remember I used the image named Ray.png for something, but I can't remember where. Good thing I have DTrace along with grep to hunt down the location of where Ray.png is being opened.

Kill your current DTrace script and modify the script so it pipes stderr straight to hell. While you're doing that, append a grep query to it so it looks like:

```
sudo dtrace -qn 'syscall::open*:entry / execname == "Finding
Ray" / { printf("%s opened %s\n", execname, copyinstr(arg0));
ustack(); }' 2>/dev/null | grep Ray.png -A40
```

This pipes all stderr to nowhere, stdout to grep and searches for any references to the Ray.png image. If there's a hit, print out the next 40 lines of the DTrace output.

> **Note**: There's actually a pretty awesome DTrace script called **opensnoop** found in /usr/bin/ on your computer which has many options for monitoring the open family of system calls and is wayyyyyyyy easier to use than writing these scripts. But you wouldn't learn anything if I just gave you the easy way out, right? Check out this script on your own time, with a good ol' man opensnoop. You won't be disappointed in what it can do.

There's a more elegant way to do this without relying on piping (well, more elegant in *my* opinion). You can use the predicate section of the DTrace clause to search the userland char* input for the Ray.png string.

You'll use the **strstr** DTrace function to do this check. This function takes two strings and returns a pointer to the first occurrence of the second string in the first string. If it can't find an occurrence, it will return NULL. This means you can check if this function equals NULL in the predicate to search for a path which contains Ray.png!

Augment your increasingly ugly — er, *complex* DTrace script to look like the following:

```
sudo dtrace -qn 'syscall::open*:entry / execname == "Finding
Ray" && strstr(copyinstr(arg0), "Ray.png") != NULL /
{ printf("%s opened %s\n", execname, copyinstr(arg0)); ustack();
}' 2>/dev/null
```

Build and rerun the application.

You threw out the grep piping and replaced it with a conditional check in the predicate for anything containing the name Ray.png that's opened in the **Finding Ray** process.

In addition, you've easily pinpointed the stack trace responsible for opening the Ray.png image.

DTrace & Destructive Actions

Note: What I am about to show you is very dangerous.

Let me repeat that: This next bit is very dangerous.

If you screw up a command you could lose some of your beloved images. Follow along only at your own risk!

In fact, to be safe, please close any applications that pertain to using photos (i.e. Photos, PhotoShop, etc). Neither I, nor the publisher are legally responsible for anything that could happen on your computer.

You have been warned!

Heh... I bet that above legal section made you nervous.

You'll use DTrace to perform a **destructive action**. That is, normally DTrace will only monitor your computer, but now you'll actually alter logic in your program.

You'll monitor the open family of system calls that are executed by the **Finding Ray** app. If one of the open system calls contain the phrase .png in its first parameter (aka the parameter of type char* to the path it's opening), you'll replace that argument with a different PNG image.

This can all be accomplished with the **copyout** and **copyoutstr** DTrace commands. You'll use the copyoutstr explicitly for this example. You'll notice these name are similar to copyin and copyinstr. The in and out in this context refer to the direction in which you're copying data, either into where DTrace can read it, or out to where the process can read it.

In the **projects** directory, there's a standalone image named **troll.png**. Create a new window in Finder with ⌘ + **N**, then navigate to your home directory by pressing ⌘ + **Shift** + **H**. Drop **troll.png** into this directory (feel free to remove it when this chapter is done). There's a method to this madness — just bear with me!

Why did you need to do this? You're about to write to memory in an existing program. There's only a finite amount of space that is already allocated for this string in the program's memory.

This will likely be some long string because you're in the iPhone Simulator and your process (mostly) reads images found in its own sandbox.

Do you remember searching for **Ray.png**? Here's that full path on my computer. Yours will obviously be different.

```
/Users/virtualadmin/Library/Developer/CoreSimulator/Devices/
97F8BE2C-4547-470C-955F-3654A8347C41/data/Containers/Bundle/
Application/102BDE66-79CB-453C-BA71-4062B2BC5297/Finding
Ray.app/Ray.png
```

The plan of attack is to use DTrace with a shorter path to an image, which will result in something like this in the program's memory:

```
/Users/virtualadmin/troll.png\0veloper/CoreSimulator/Devices/
97F8BE2C-4547-470C-955F-3654A8347C41/data/Containers/Bundle/
Application/102BDE66-79CB-453C-BA71-4062B2BC5297/Finding
Ray.app/Ray.png
```

You see that \0 in there? That's the NULL terminator for char*. So essentially this string is really just:

```
/Users/virtualadmin/troll.png
```

Because that's how NULL terminated strings work!

Getting Your Path Length

When writing data out, you'll need to figure out how many chars your fullpath is to the troll.png. I know the length of mine, but unfortunately, I don't know your name nor the name of your computer's home directory.

Type the following in Terminal:

```
echo ~/troll.png
```

This will be dump the fullpath to the troll.png image. Hold onto this for a second as you'll paste this into your script. Also figure out how many characters this is in Terminal:

```
echo ~/troll.png | wc -m
```

In my case, /Users/virtualadmin/troll.png is 30 char's. But here's the gotcha: *You need to account for the null terminator.* This means the total length I need to insert my new string needs to be an existing char * of length 31 or greater.

The arg0 in open* is pointing to something in memory. If you were to write in this location with something longer than this string, then this could corrupt memory and kill the program. Obviously, you don't want this, so what you'll do is stick **troll.png** in a directory that has a shorter character count.

You'll also perform checks via the DTrace predicate to ensure you have enough room as well. C'mon, you're a thorough and diligent programmer, right?

Type the following in Terminal, replacing /Users/virtualadmin and 31 with your values:

```
sudo dtrace -wn 'syscall::open*:entry / execname == "Finding
Ray" && arg0 > 0xfffffffe && strstr(copyinstr(arg0), ".png") !=
NULL && strlen(copyinstr(arg0)) >= 32 / { this->a = "/Users/
virtualadmin/troll.png"; copyoutstr(this->a, arg0, 31); }'
```

Rebuild and run **Finding Ray** while this new DTrace script is active.

Provided you've executed everything correctly, each time the **Finding Ray** process tries to open a file that contains the phrase ".png", you'll return troll.png instead.

Other Destructive Actions

In addition to `copyoutstr` and `copyout`, DTrace has some other destructive actions worth noting:

- **stop(void)**: This will freeze the currently running *userland* process (given by the **pid** built-in argument). This is ideal if you want to stop execution of a userland program, attach LLDB to it and explore it further.

- **raise(int signal)**: This will raise a signal to the process responsible for a probe.

- **system(string program, ...)**: This lets you execute a command just as if you were in `Terminal`. This has the added benefit of letting you access all the DTrace built-in variables, such as `execname` and `probemod`, to use in a `printf`-style formatting.

I encourage you to explore these destructive actions (especially the `stop()` action) on your own time. That being said, be careful with that `system` function. You can do a lot of damage really easily if used incorrectly.

Key Points

- Because Swift sits on top of C and Objective-C for now, DTrace can easily trace Swift applications.

- Use the –q flag with DTrace to limit some of the output.

- Filter output through `grep` to limit the volume of output even further.

- The –F switch will indent function entries and returns.

- Scalar variables have limited scope but don't slow execution.

- Use `this->` when working with **clause-local** variables which can live in different places across a single probe.

- Use `self->` to designate **thread-local** variables which live the longest, remember to release them though or you'll leak memory.

- DTrace uses ternary operators to address the lack of proper conditional branching.

- DTrace probes can read from and write to memory addresses, potentially causing destruction.

Where to Go From Here?

There are many powerful DTrace scripts on your macOS machine. You can hunt for them using the man -k dtrace, then systematically man'ing what each script does. In addition, you can learn a lot by studying the code in them. Remember, these are *scripts*, not compiled executables, so source-code is fair game.

Also, be very careful with destructive actions. That being said, you can put Ray Wenderlich *everywhere on your computer*:

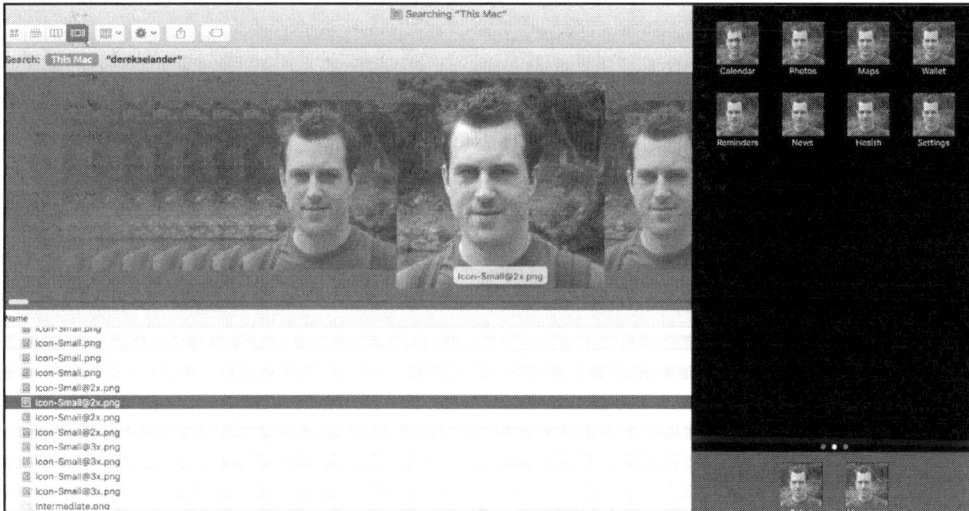

Isn't that what you've always wanted?

In all seriousness, you can do some pretty crazy stuff to your computer and gain a lot of insight using DTrace.

Conclusion

Wow! You made it all the way to this conclusion! You either must have jumped straight to this page or you're way more masochistic than I could have anticipated.

If you have any questions or comments about the projects or concepts in this book, or have any stories to tell from your own debugging adventures, please stop by our forums at https://forums.kodeco.com.

From here, you have a few paths to explore depending on what you found most interesting in this book.

- If exploring code in Python to make better debugging scripts interests you, then you might want to see what other modules exist in Python 3 (or the equivalent Python version LLDB has) to see how far down the rabbit hole you can go. You can find the list of modules in Python 3 here: https://docs.python.org/3/py-modindex.html or hunt down one of the many books on Amazon about Python.

- If reverse engineering Apple internals interests you, I would strongly recommend you check out **Jonathan Levin**'s work on anything related to Apple, namely his updated books like **MacOS and iOS Internals, Volume III: Security & Insecurity** or **MacOS and iOS Internals, Volume I: User Mode** at http://www.newosxbook.com/.

- Also check out @snakeninny (https://twitter.com/snakeninny)'s free book, https://github.com/iosre/iOSAppReverseEngineering/

- If more generic reverse engineering/hacking interests you, then you might be interested in **Hacking: The Art of Exploitation, 2nd Edition** by **Jon Erickson** at https://www.nostarch.com/hacking2.htm.

- If you want the equivalent of an LLDB newsletter, I would recommend to (nicely!) stalk **Jim Ingham**'s activity on Stack Overflow https://stackoverflow.com/users/2465073/jim-ingham. He works on LLDB at Apple, and combing through his responses on StackOverflow will give you a tremendous amount of insight into LLDB. In addition, check out the LLDB archives https://lists.llvm.org/pipermail/lldb-dev/. There's a lot to dig through, but you can find some incredibly useful hidden gems from the LLDB authors.

- If DTrace interested you, check out https://www.brendangregg.com/dtracebook/index.html. This book will cover a much wider range of how to use DTrace than what I've discussed.

And finally... *Thank you* for purchasing this book. Your continued support is what makes the books, tutorials, videos and other things we do at **Kodeco** possible. We truly appreciate it!

– Walter, Darren, Matt and Emily

The *Advanced Apple Debugging & Reverse Engineering* team

Appendices

Appendix A: LLDB Cheat Sheet

A cheat sheet for commands and ideas on how to use LLDB.

Getting Help

```
(lldb) help
```

List all commands and aliases.

```
(lldb) help po
```

Get help documentation for po (expression) command.

```
(lldb) help break set
```

Get help documentation for breakpoint set.

```
(lldb) apropos step-in
```

Search through help documentation containing step-in.

Finding Code

```
(lldb) image lookup -rn UIAlertController
```

Look up all code containing `UIAlertController` that's compiled or loaded into an executable.

```
(lldb) image lookup -rn (?i)hosturl
```

Case insensitive search for any code that contains "hosturl".

```
(lldb) image lookup -rn 'UIViewController\ set\w+:\]'
```

Look up all setter property methods `UIViewController` implements or overrides.

```
(lldb) image lookup -rn . Security
```

Look up all code located within the `Security` module.

```
(lldb) image lookup -a 0x10518a720
```

Look up code based upon address `0x10518a720`.

```
(lldb) image lookup -s mmap
```

Look up code for the symbol named `mmap`.

Breakpoints

```
(lldb) b viewDidLoad
```

Creates a breakpoint on all methods named `viewDidLoad` for both Swift and Objective-C.

```
(lldb) b setAlpha:
```

Creates a breakpoint on either the `setAlpha:` Objective-C method or the setter of the Objective-C `alpha` property.

```
(lldb) b -[CustomViewControllerSubclass viewDidLoad]
```

Creates a breakpoint on the Objective-C method [CustomViewControllerSubclass viewDidLoad].

```
(lldb) rbreak CustomViewControllerSubclass.viewDidLoad
```

Creates a regex breakpoint to match either an Objective-C or Swift class CustomViewControllerSubclass which contains viewDidLoad. Could be Objective-C -[CustomViewControllerSubclass viewDidLoad] or could be Swift ModuleName.CustomViewControllerSubclass.viewDidLoad () -> ().

```
(lldb) breakpoint delete
```

Deletes all breakpoints.

```
(lldb) breakpoint delete 2
```

Deletes breakpoint ID 2.

```
(lldb) breakpoint list
```

List all breakpoints and their IDs.

```
(lldb) rbreak viewDid
```

Creates a regex breakpoint on .*viewDid.*.

```
(lldb) rbreak viewDid -s SwiftRadio
```

Creates a breakpoint on .*viewDid.*, but restricts the breakpoint(s) to the SwiftRadio module.

```
(lldb) rbreak viewDid(Appear|Disappear) -s SwiftHN
```

Creates a breakpoint on viewDidAppear or viewDidDisappear inside the SwiftHN module.

```
(lldb) rb "\-\[UIViewController\ set" -s UIKit
```

Creates a breakpoint on any Objective-C style breakpoints containing -[UIViewController set within the UIKit module.

```
(lldb) rb . -s SwiftHN -o 1
```

Create a breakpoint on every function in the `SwiftHN` module, but remove all breakpoints once the breakpoint is hit.

```
(lldb) rb . -f ViewController.m
```

Create a breakpoint on every function found in `ViewController.m`.

Expressions

```
(lldb) po "hello, debugger"
```

Prints `"hello, debugger"` regardless of the debugging context.

```
(lldb) expression -lobjc -O -- [UIApplication sharedApplication]
```

Print the shared `UIApplication` instance in an Objective-C context.

```
(lldb) expression -lswift -O -- UIApplication.shared
```

Print the shared `UIApplication` instance in a Swift context.

```
(lldb) b getenv
(lldb) expression -i0 -- getenv("HOME")
```

Creates a breakpoint on `getenv`, executes the `getenv` function, and stops at the beginning of the `getenv` function.

```
(lldb) expression -u0 -O -- [UIApplication test]
```

Don't let LLDB unwind the stack if you're executing a method that will cause the program to crash.

```
(lldb) expression -p -- NSString *globalString = [NSString
stringWithUTF8String: "Hello, Debugger"];
(lldb) po globalString
Hello, Debugger
```

Declares a global `NSString*` called `globalString`.

```
(lldb) expression -g -O -lobjc -- [NSObject new]
```

Debug the debugger that's parsing the [NSObject new] Objective-C expression.

Stepping

```
(lldb) thread return false
```

Return early from code with false.

```
(lldb) thread step-in
(lldb) s
```

Step in.

```
(lldb) thread step-over
(lldb) n
```

Step over.

```
(lldb) thread step-out
(lldb) finish
```

Step out of a function.

```
(lldb) thread step-inst
(lldb) ni
```

Step in if about to execute a function. Step an assembly instruction otherwise.

GDB Formatting

```
(lldb) p/x 128
```

Print value in hexadecimal.

```
(lldb) p/d 128
```

Print value in decimal.

```
(lldb) p/t 128
```

Print value in binary.

```
(lldb) p/a 128
```

Print value as address.

```
(lldb) x/gx 0x000000010fff6c40
```

Get the value pointed at by `0x000000010fff6c40` and display in 8 bytes.

```
(lldb) x/wx 0x000000010fff6c40
```

Get the value pointed at by `0x000000010fff6c40` and display in 4 bytes.

Memory

```
(lldb) memory read 0x000000010fff6c40
```

Read memory at address `0x000000010fff6c40`.

```
(lldb) po id $d = [NSData dataWithContentsOfFile:@"..."]
(lldb) mem read `(uintptr_t)[$d bytes]` `(uintptr_t)[$d bytes] +
(uintptr_t)[$d length]` -r -b -o /tmp/file
```

Grab an instance of a remote file and write it to `/tmp/file` on your computer.

Registers and Assembly

```
(lldb) register read -a
```

Display all registers on the system.

```
(lldb) register read rdi rsi
```

Read the RSI and the RDI register in x64 assembly.

```
(lldb) register read x0 x1
```

Read the X0 and the X1 register in arm64 assembly.

```
(lldb) register read arg1 arg2
```

Read the registers associated with the first two arguments passed to a function.

```
(lldb) register write rsi 0x0
```

Set the RSI register to 0x0 in x64 assembly.

```
(lldb) register write x2 0x0
```

Set the X2 register to 0x0 in arm64 assembly.

```
(lldb) register write arg2 0x42
```

Set the generic second register to 0x42.

```
(lldb) register write rflags `$rflags ^ 64`
```

Toggle the zero flag in x64 assembly (augment if condition logic).

```
(lldb) register write rflags `$rflags | 64`
```

Set the zero flag (set to 1) in x64 assembly (augment if condition logic).

```
(lldb) register write rflags `$rflags & ~64`
```

Clear the zero flag (set to 0) in x64 assembly (augment if condition logic).

```
(lldb) disassemble
```

Display assembly for function in which you're currently stopped.

```
(lldb) disassemble -p
```

Disassemble around current location; useful if in the middle of a function.

```
(lldb) disassemble -b
```

Disassemble function while showing opcodes; useful for learning what is responsible for what.

```
(lldb) disassemble -n '-[UIViewController setTitle:]'
```

Disassemble the Objective-C -[UIViewController setTitle:] method.

```
(lldb) disassemble -a 0x000000010b8d972d
```

Disassemble the function that contains the address 0x000000010b8d972d.

Modules

```
(lldb) image list
```

List all modules loaded into the executable's process space.

```
(lldb) image list -b
```

Get the names of all the modules loaded into the executable's process space.

```
(lldb) process load /Path/To/Module.framework/Module
```

Load the module located at path into the executable's process space.

Appendix B: Python Environment Setup

If you're actively looking for a Python editor for the Python-related chapters, here are some recommendations.

Getting Python

MacOS no longer ships with Python installed. However, if you open a terminal window and attempt to launch Python, the system will offer to download and install Apple's preferred version along with the other command line developer tools. In Terminal, type python3, and your computer will either launch the interactive Python shell or present a dialog like the one below:

```
virtualadministrator@Virtuals-Virtual-Machine ~ % python3
xcode-select: note: no developer tools were found at '/Applications/Xcode.app',
requesting install. Choose an option in the dialog to download the command line
developer tools.
virtualadministrator@Virtuals-Virtual-Machine ~ %
```

The "python3" command requires the command line developer tools. Would you like to install the tools now?

Choose Install to download and install the command line developer tools now.

Cancel   Install

If, for some reason, you like to rm random things in Terminal and you need to reinstall Python, you can download Python from the official download page (https://www.python.org/downloads/) or using the homebrew package manager. Make sure to download the version of Python that matches the version packaged with LLDB. If you're not sure which version to get, you can get the LLDB Python version through Terminal:

```
% lldb
(lldb) script import sys; print(sys.version)
```

You'll see something like this:

```
3.9.6 (default, Mar 10 2023, 20:16:38)
[Clang 14.0.3 (clang-1403.0.22.14.1)]
```

This is from Xcode version 14.3. Your output may vary if you have a newer Xcode installed. You can ignore the Clang version there, as that's not relevant. What's relevant is the 3.9.6.

Don't worry about the final part of the version number. As long as you have some version of Python 3, you'll be fine. There are many breaking changes between versions 2 and 3.

Python Text Editors

The official Python website maintains a list of Python editors (https://wiki.python.org/moin/PythonEditors). According to my daughter, who's studying CS at university (Hi, Kitty!), the cool Python developers who want a free editor use either **Visual Studio Code** (VS Code) or **Vim**.

For the small, quick Python scripts you'll write in this book and for an experience that approximates Xcode, I'd recommend using Microsoft's **Visual Studio Code**. VS Code is a general-purpose editor that's become pretty popular recently for Python and also with developers who write Swift on Linux. You can download it from the VS Code (https://code.visualstudio.com) website.

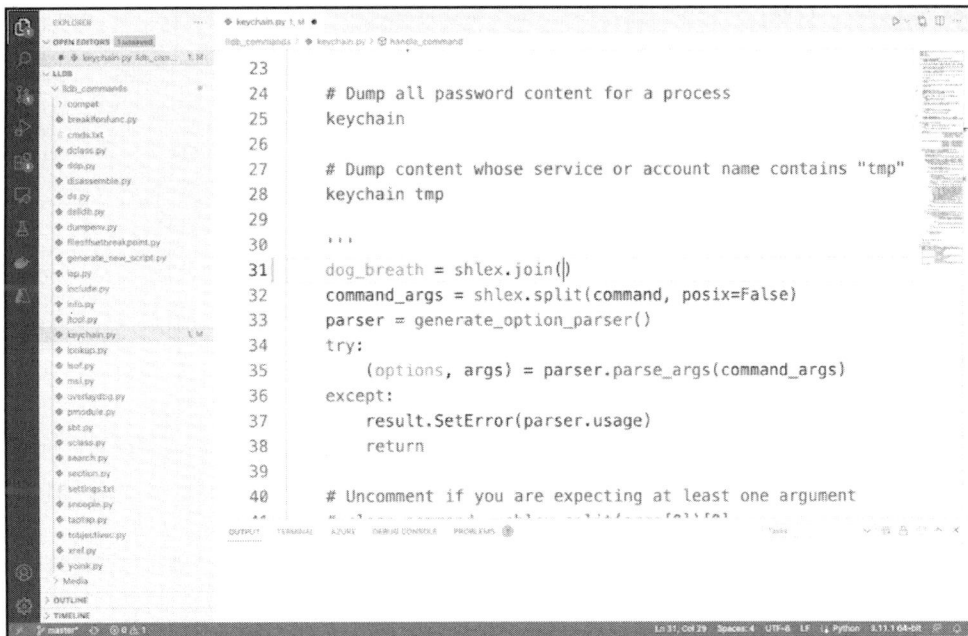

Above, is a screenshot of the VS Code editor, editing a python file in this case `keychain.py`.

All the LLDB Python scripts in this book have been edited and tested in VS Code.

You'll want to add a Python support extension to make developing and debugging LLDB Python scripts easier. Fortunately, Microsoft maintains an official extension to provide code completion, linting, debugging and more for Python code.

To add extensions to VS Code, press ⌘-**Shift-X** to switch to the **Extensions** view, and then type "python" in the search box. You'll see quite a few choices, but find the one from **Microsoft**, and select it. Then click **Install**.

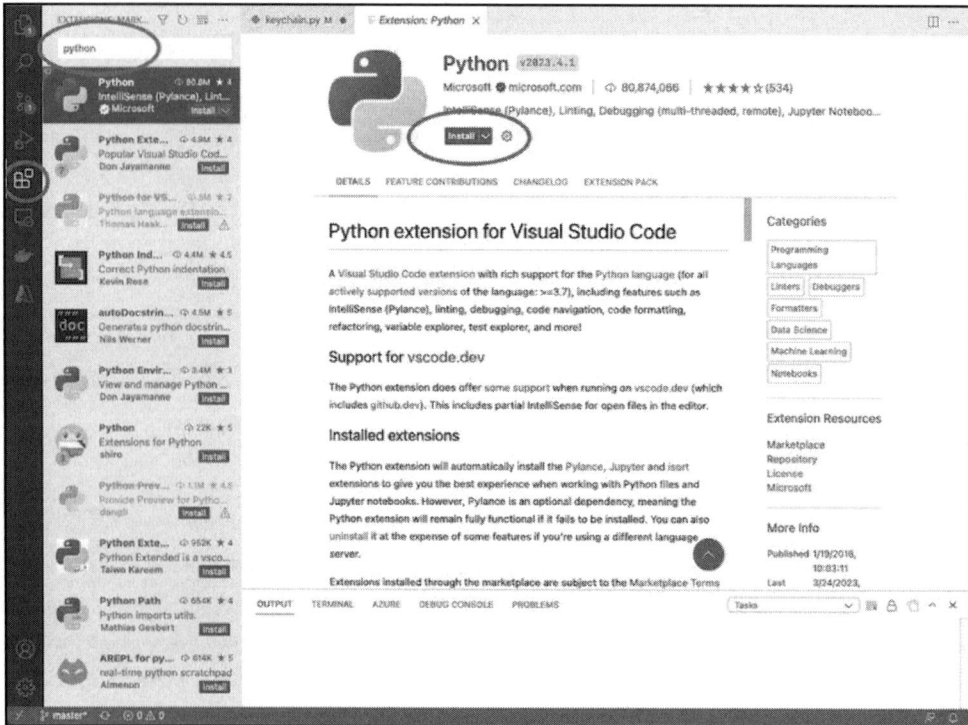

Another popular option is to use Vim. Even if you decide to use VS Code or some other editor, I highly recommend getting at least a working knowledge of Vim. It's installed by default on many *nix systems, including macOS. Though it doesn't come installed by default, it's usually very easy to install. So, when you're coding away from home, you can be sure it's available. This can be really important if you're on a remote web server somewhere or sitting on the floor of a cold data center in the middle of the night as you try to get the company's systems back online.

As with VS Code, extensions are available that make working with Python code easier. Unlike VS Code, which was released in 2015 and is guided by Microsoft, Vim and its predecessor, vi, have been around since the original Star Wars trilogy was first released in theaters. There are lots of package managers and Python extensions — in Vim, they're called **plugins** — available. Do a web search for "python vim ide", and you'll find a number of excellent tutorials and resources to get you going.

Working With the LLDB Python Module

When working with Python, you'll often import modules to execute code or classes within that module. When working with LLDB's Python module, you'll sometimes come across an `import lldb` somewhere in the script, usually right at the top.

By default, Xcode will launch a version of Python that's bundled within Xcode. When Xcode launches this bundled version of Python, the path to the `lldb` module's location is set up automatically. However, in your normal Python development, you won't have access to this module if you were to execute your script through VS Code or Vim. As a result, you'll need to modify your **PYTHONPATH** environment variable to include the appropriate directory where the LLDB Python module lives.

If you're not familiar with updating your Terminal environment, open a Terminal window and find which shell you're using. It will be shown in the title bar of the terminal window and is probably `zsh` or `bash`. If you don't see either of those in the title bar, type this command:

```
% echo $0
```

Terminal will respond with the name of your current shell. Now, in your home directory, use the `touch` command for a file named `.bash_profile` if you use `bash`, or `.zshrc` if you have `zsh`. This will create the file if it doesn't already exist.

```
% touch ~/.bash_profile
```

Or:

```
% touch ~/.zshrc
```

Open the file you just created in your favorite text editor, and add the following line of code:

```
export PYTHONPATH="/Applications/Xcode.app/Contents/
SharedFrameworks/LLDB.framework/Resources/Python:$PYTHONPATH"
```

Note: This assumes your Xcode is located at `/Applications/Xcode.app`. If it isn't, because you particularly like being different, then you'll need to change the path. Just type `xcode-select -p` in Terminal to find the correct path to your Xcode.

Save and close the file. Now, restart Terminal so it loads your changes. Confirm everything works by typing:

```
% echo $PYTHONPATH
```

Terminal should show the path you just added. You'll now be able to access the `lldb` module from any Python session on your computer.

Doing this gives you the advantage of checking for syntax errors in VS Code (or equivalent) during debugging time — instead of finding a syntax error when your script is loaded into LLDB.

Appendix C: Helpful Code Snippets

The original author of this book, Derek Selander, created a great repo of Python scripts and other utilities. You can explore the current version of Derek's repo (https://github.com/DerekSelander) and see all the interesting things he's working on now.

The materials for this appendix contain a fork of Derek's LLDB repo. This repo contains some of the utilities mentioned in the book that deserve a home outside their chapters. They're useful tools that you're welcome to explore and use as you wish.

As Apple evolves and updates its software, these tools will break, and we'll work to fix them or find workarounds. Check out the online forums for this book to ask questions or report that something no longer works.

Printed in Great Britain
by Amazon

35669997R10317